Hope Blooms in a Garden of Faith

by Suzy Q Winn

The contents of this work, including, but not limited to, the accuracy of events, people, and places depicted; opinions expressed; permission to use previously published materials included; and any advice given or actions advocated are solely the responsibility of the author, who assumes all liability for said work and indemnifies the publisher against any claims stemming from publication of the work.

All Rights Reserved
Copyright © 2022 by Suzy Q Winn

No part of this book may be reproduced or transmitted, downloaded, distributed, reverse engineered, or stored in or introduced into any information storage and retrieval system, in any form or by any means, including photocopying and recording, whether electronic or mechanical, now known or hereinafter invented without permission in writing from the publisher.

Dorrance Publishing Co
585 Alpha Drive
Suite 103
Pittsburgh, PA 15238
Visit our website at *www.dorrancebookstore.com*

ISBN: 978-1-6853-7513-3
eISBN: 978-1-6853-7525-6

1
Blessings

"Why me?" This is such a common thought and response when I share my story with others. I see the emotions cross their face as they process my story. However, when they hear my positive takeaway, they're not sure what to think or how to respond. Most responses have always been "I'm so sorry!" as if they had something to do with it. There's nothing to be sorry about, it happens. Everyone is different and as I progress through therapy for mental health, major depressive disorder, and PTSD, I've had to begin opening myself, in greater detail.

I recall more details of trauma that I've repressed. The deeper I delve into therapy; the more memories start to surface. It's hard, and frankly it sucks, but I know on the other side of these mountains is healing. I've learned ways to manage and cope with stress and trauma, but some trauma occurred before I had the mental capacity to understand and incorporate coping mechanisms. As you read, I hope you can find healing, hope and maybe inspiration, to begin your journey of healing.

I didn't expect the things that happened to me. Does anyone? I realized I needed to find the blessing and lesson or be filled with anger, hate, disgust and who knows what else. What kind of mom would that attitude make me? What would have happened to my children? The stigmas, trauma and negativity had to stop with me, I had to be the change I wanted to be and see.

Stop and think about how many times you've heard "Why me?" How many times have you thought or said it yourself? What was it in response or reaction to? Was the person saying it in reference to their own life situation or was it their reaction to something you shared or were going through, and was it an empathetic response?

As a child, I angered my parents and other adults by questioning them. A few switches to the backside, rulers to the knuckles, getting grounded, etc., taught me not to question everyone. While I learned questioning angered them, it was a bit longer before I understood they didn't have the answers. I'm not sure how old I was or where I was, when I heard someone ask, "Why me?" for the first time, but through the years, I've heard it with frequency.

At some point, most of us have asked the same question. Why is it that in times of trouble, frustration, sickness, injury and even death, do we first question God, or someone else? Yet, when great things happen and life is going well, we don't stop and ask, "Why me?"

My thoughts on "Why me?" through everything I've endured as I've matured over time, I now ask, "Why NOT me?"

Was I lacking? Was I not good enough, pretty enough, smart enough? Recognizing and accepting these thoughts were controlled by me, I needed to find a way to live my life without worrying or caring about what others thought. Clint Eastwood says it best, "Opinions are like assholes, everyone has one and they all stink"- Dirty Harry - *The Dead Pool.*

There's a story about a broken vessel; how most people viewed the vessel as broken, cracked, scarred, and how it would never be the same. God showed how that vessel, put back together with cracks, could finally let the light from within shine through. This analogy/metaphor had a profound impact on me.

My purpose was to find a way to let my light shine, from within, regardless of my cracks, scars, broken or missing pieces there may be from the outside looking in.

That's when it dawned on me to ask, "Why NOT me?" Why should I be exempt from the ugly we are all capable of and often victim of? What would make me, or anyone, special or different that these things couldn't or wouldn't happen to them? Why NOT me? Wouldn't my pain, struggle and growth have the ability to help, encourage or inspire someone else? MY story, MY testimony, my ups, downs, trials, and tribulations, were they for naught if I don't share how it strengthened my faith, and in return how my faith strengthened me? Why NOT me, to have the courage to face things head on, move forward, and conquer the trauma?

After decades, I found my voice. Not only did I find my voice, but some courage to share bits of my story. Now that I have found my voice and a dose of courage, perhaps sharing it will be my destiny or legacy. This book, while a cumulation of my life, has taken me several years to write, and has led me down multiple paths.

For years, people told me I needed to write a book. For whatever reason, I couldn't put thoughts into words until I knew the name for the book. I remember the night I thought of the name. During a typical night of insomnia, when my mind wouldn't shut off, I just laid in bed so as not to wake my husband. Then, I sat upright in bed, as if a light had exploded with the name, "Why me...." I jumped out of bed to write it down because I didn't want to forget it. My husband woke and asked what I was doing. Unfortunately, he was used to my insomnia and night owl life. I told him I had to write the name of my book down, but my notebook was in the living room.

After telling him to go back to sleep, I shut the door, then grabbed my notebook and a pen. After I wrote down the name of the book, the words started to swarm. Grabbing my laptop, I began to type. Over the course of writing the book, the underlying theme was about hope, therefore, the name change.

The outline formed itself. The words started building on each other. Despite being able to type approximately 100 words per minute, I was having a hard time keeping up with all the words. It was as if my brain was vomiting. When my husband got up for work at 6:00 A.M., I realized I also had to go to work.

At work, I couldn't concentrate, was extra fidgety and wired. My supervisor, Sgt. Towns, asked what was going on because he could see I was about to burst. I relayed I finally had a name for my book, and I had been up all night writing. I was excited. He was aware it was a big deal as we had talked about me writing a book for a while and figuring out a name was a mental block.

By 11:00 A.M., we had taught a couple of classes and were finished teaching for the day. Although the workday was not over, he told me to go home and work on my book. A few days went by with me working on the book, then life, work, volunteering, children, medical concerns, and other distractions derailed my efforts. Years later, I finally started working on it again. After several days of work, we had to fly out of state. While I was gone, I started having medical issues, one being blurred and double vision.

Several tests later and I tried a pair of glasses. They didn't help. Three months later, I began to write again. I made good inroads, then let distractions take over. In all reality, I was stalling the process because I knew there were going to be hard parts to write about.

Nine months of therapy and delving into PTSD later, I had to get my story out, for my healing. There was so much bottled up inside me. Once we started peeling back the layers, the memories started flowing like lava, scorching my synapses, and cooling into molten rock. The memories hit fast. I was not prepared for the onslaught. Tears ran down my face without realizing it at times. I cried often...quietly, violently, with loved ones and alone. There were mornings I woke with tearstains on my face and a drenched pillow.

I set a goal date to finish this book. I don't want the trauma to win. If one part of my story resonates with someone, then my purpose was twofold, my healing and possibly another's. Access to technology and social media platforms, designed for sharing, actually removes the caring. There's a disconnect in society and being real with one another.

By sharing my story, I'm reconnecting with myself, and others. Meaningless conversations, or "chitchat," are difficult for me when someone feels the need to fill the silence. I'm good with silence and I love being alone, but I know socialization is a part of living. So, I want to socialize in meaningful ways, not just "Man, did you see how hot it is outside this week" or "Hey, did you see (insert whatever here) on (insert social or news platform here)?"

Through my story I want to connect with others, and hear their stories, triumphs, setbacks, hopes and dreams. Real, raw, and honest. Feeling and sharing emotions. Currently, this book is a way for me to do that and my goal date will help to get me there faster. If procrastination runs your life, be aware that "someday" is nowhere on the calendar.

"Someday" never comes! Set a realistic and obtainable goal, complete little tasks that help you reach your overall goal, so it doesn't feel overwhelming. It's hard to break the procrastination habit. Instead of "busy" work, try productive work. I took "busy" out of my schedule and inserted "productive." It's productive to heal, create, imagine, and plan. However, until action is taken, then it's just procrastination. I thought and talked about writing a book, but until I started typing, it was nothing more than an unrealized dream...inaction.

Practice taking action. Little steps at a time if you're a procrastinator like me. Small steps every day will become a habit and replace the inaction. The reward is greater than the thought of a reward.

For years, I've had an infatuation with pens, crayons and paper, journals, notebooks, coloring books, anything I could write on. Ironically, I hated writing in class, for penmanship or "cursive" writing practice. I also hated having to write anything for homework, notes, and anything that had to do with school. I would go home and write all kinds of things as long as it wasn't for school.

Some of my closest friends, peers that I worked with, and family have witnessed firsthand my infatuation. I worked in an office with 4 guys and our office was the "hub," so we had many visitors. Sometimes coworkers and visitors would use one of my pens, to take notes, jot something down, or to peruse my "collection."

There were many instances where I hunted a person down, to get my pen back, especially if it was one of my "good" pens, the kind that writes smoothly and glides over the paper, doesn't smear or smudge and is comfortable to hold. Yes, I have pen issues! I also love notebooks, journals, and looseleaf paper. I have pen and paper issues!!!

The first time I got a diary, I must have been 10 or 11. It was a small diary, with a little lock and key, a green grass color, with a square gold trim. It was a bit bigger than my hand, but still provided enough room to write. As I held it, I felt there was so much I was going to share inside that diary. I sniffed it, lovingly ran my hands and fingers over the pages, feeling the crispness of the paper, letting the pages flutter open and through my fingers, as if it was caressing and coaxing my most inner thoughts out of me.

I didn't know why I felt this way, I hadn't even hit puberty, let alone understanding what puberty meant, so what did I really have to write about? I knew I had words, thoughts, stories, imagination, and all kinds of questions inside me that needed to come out. I loved the feel of the pen gliding over the pages as letters formed and became words. Words became sentences and then paragraphs, holding emotions, thoughts, and imaginings.

Soon, I realized the diary was entirely too small to hold my daily musings, trials, and tribulations, so I found a notebook that would do. As I got older, I heard the word "journal" and realized that's what I had been doing for years. It was such a soul-cleansing activity for me, and I've continued to journal as a release. Some of the things you will read are from these journals which captured emotions my memory alone wouldn't be able to recreate.

Reading and being surrounded by books is something I cherish. I love a great story. My infatuation with pens, literally hundreds, maybe thousands, had a reason behind it. I had more than questions inside me, I had a story, many. All the stories are mine. What I lived through, fought through. These stories carry my blood, sweat, tears and even laughter. This is my DNA. Who I am, who I've always been, even when I was that smalltown farm girl, struggling to find my way.

In my late 20s, I first shared my story. A story I had no idea was inside me. I never thought it was something others would want to hear. It wasn't because I lacked confidence or had low self-esteem, I just didn't feel what I had been through could help someone else by sharing it.

People find their way into our lives. Several helped me see what others saw, courage, bravery, inspiration, faith, strength, and hope.

Let me start at the beginning....

I was born in the 1970s, to a teen mother and father. They married while still in high school, the marriage and I were both born from the product of unprotected sex. In the 70s and society's eye, I had one strike against me prior to being born. This was a time before so much technology that most of us now enjoy daily: microwaves, cell phones, computers, *MTV.* If you must look up *MTV,* I will break it down: *Music Television.*

I assumed my conception was in the backseat of a car. I later learned my dad was staying at my mom's parents' house, allegedly "sleeping on the couch" when I was conceived.

At age 47, I realized I wanted to know more about how my parents met. Were they coming from a school event, a special occasion, did they date, how long, were they fighting hormones and confusing emotions? Previously, I was never concerned with these details because my parents separated and divorced before I was 10. To ask my mom anything was a battle, and it was an unspoken rule not bring up my father as there were a lot of heated emotions, anger, and likely guilt, not that I understood that as a child.

After calling my dad for further research and asking questions I'd never thought to ask before, he filled me in on their history. He shared humor, love, heartache, and the importance of not giving up, perseverance, and a strong work ethic. I witnessed my father's perseverance and strong work ethic from a young age, not realizing how much they would become a part of who and what I was.

My parents met in high school; a small K-12 school. My mom was in 9th grade, my dad was in 10th, when he went into a study hall and my mom caught his eye. I've seen pictures and my mom was a beautiful young lady with long, thick, dark hair, clear olive complexion and dark brown eyes. They said hi to each other and the next day, my dad sat closer to her, and they talked some more. Another guy told my dad not to talk to her because she was his girlfriend, so my dad asked my mom if that was true. After she said no, they started dating. My dad saw my mom a few times over the summer, enjoying each other's company at the drive-in.

When they went back to school, their relationship became serious, they met each other's parents and my dad said he knew he wanted to be with her. The next summer they were seeing each other a lot and when they started their junior and senior years, my dad started spending nights at my mom's parents' house. He was allowed to sleep on the couch and over time was persuaded to sneak into my mom's bedroom.

Needless to say, this was about the time I entered the picture. Though I would exist in my mother's womb for the next 9 months, my life had begun.

In January, my mom knew she was pregnant and told my dad. My dad said, "Okay, let's get married." Both sets of parents were told and no one had a problem with it. On February 25, 1972, my parents were married in a little church, in the town where they both attended school. It turned out to be the same church where I had a couple classes in the 2nd or 3rd grade. I've seen a few wedding photos; it is visually discernable my mom is pregnant. There was me, "photo-bombing" the wedding photos as my mother's wombmate.

I share my parents' history because sometimes, it helps to know where you came from, good, bad, or ugly. Their history didn't change who or what I am.

2
Farm Raised

My dad grew up on a dairy farm, milking cows, baling hay, and mucking stalls, as the oldest boy of 8 children. My mother grew up in a small village near my dad, cooking, cleaning, and learning how to survive off the land; what nature provided by fishing and hunting, while helping care for younger siblings. After my parents married, they moved to the dairy farm and lived with my dad's parents.

My mother had spent her junior year of high school pregnant, became a wife, lived with her in-laws, then over the summer, became a mom, giving birth to a healthy and beautiful baby girl. Me, it was me! My father found out he was going to be a father during his senior year of high school, became a husband, graduated high school, began working to support his new family and became a dad.

While my mom began her senior year of high school and my dad worked, I stayed at the farm. As the cold started and after enjoying a few months of being newlyweds then parents; "surprise," you're pregnant again. The winters are very, very cold, in western NY.

My mom graduated high school and a couple months later gave birth to my little sister, KJ, 360 days after giving birth to me. Not even a full year later and I was a big sister. We are known as Irish twins. I can't imagine the emotions, stress, uncertainty, and hormones my parents experienced as they began their life in a home already bustling with my father's 4 younger brothers still living at home.

My mom comes from a large Italian and German family, she was used to loud, but all families differ in their cultures, norms, and patience. While my father's siblings were mainly boys, five boys and two girls, my mother's siblings were mainly sisters, six girls and one boy. My mom's dad was a veteran of WWII and a master carpenter, while her mother worked at a local factory. I don't remember much about my grandmother, she died of lung cancer when I was about 5. Most of my memories are from pictures, a few hazy memories of family gatherings, but mostly I remember a very stern and hard woman, who smoked, a lot. I don't remember hugs or warm fuzzy feelings.

The last time I saw her, we had gone to the hospital to see her, one of the first times I visited someone in a hospital, it felt sterile and uninviting. I remember the hushed conversation around me. I'm not sure how long she was in the hospital before she passed, but I remember the funeral. I didn't understand what a funeral was, I just knew I felt heavy with emotions from the people around me. There were lots of tears and crying, but no one was paying attention to the kids.

When I peeked into the casket I saw a woman, my grandma. Her hair and makeup were done. She looked more peaceful than I ever remembered seeing her and she looked like she was sleeping. I was 5, I didn't understand death or grief, but she was in the casket, and she looked like she might have been a nice person.

Here my mother, barely out of her teen years, a wife and mother of two, loses her mother to cancer, a new and scary word in that decade. Most marriages and relationships are hard enough with 2 people, that have their life figured out. This marriage began with my conception, and before the first wedding anniversary, they were pregnant with my sister, then a few years later, my mother lost her mom to cancer. As I child, I didn't understand my mother's hardships. I grew up tangled with emotions from an extremely complicated relationship with my mom.

I've worked through many emotions, recently realizing how much they tie into my mindset, and spirit. I've taken the time trying to heal mentally and emotionally, but as time went on, I realized my spirit was out of balance. I'm not sure if it's bruised, scarred, bloody or just tired, but it's not broken.

When people talked about caring for yourself spiritually, I believed it meant having a relationship with a higher power, a strong faith, but it's so much more than that. My words may not give justice to what I mean, so I'm going to attempt to paint a picture. I will attempt to capture the emotions and work through healing my spirit. As I put my story to paper, I hope it inspires or helps someone else heal too.

After my sister, KJ, was born, while living at my grandparents', there was lots of noise, people and we were surrounded by boys. If you needed or wanted anything, you learned to be louder than the crowd to get the attention needed. I'm still loud and when people talk of using your "inside voice," I'm not sure what that is. I don't think it's in my DNA.

My dad is the oldest of the boys and my youngest uncle is about 2 ½ years older than me. KJ and I grew up being tossed around like footballs, understanding a hard day's work of physical labor from running and working a dairy farm. A day on the farm begins incredibly early, feeding, milking, cleaning the barn, the milk truck picking up the milk, breakfast, and showers, then school and jobs. My mom helped on the farm and my grandma and grandpa both had other jobs, after the chores were done. Some of my earliest memories are of the dairy farm, being in the barn, watching my grandma and mom milk the cows, one by one, by hand, every day.

My grandpa drove a school bus, worked at the school as a custodian and during the winters, drove the snowplow. My grandma also drove a school bus and took care of most of the farm while raising the boys. At this time, my 2 aunts and one uncle were out of the house, most of them married and the younger 4 boys were still in school.

My dad continued working and saving his money then bought an acre of land, just a couple miles from the farm. When he wasn't working, he cleared the land and continued saving to buy a single-wide trailer. He was working for the town, driving truck, running equipment, the scraper and bulldozer. After he bought the trailer and moved us into it, he started working on building the house. The land was on top of a hill, surrounded by open land, overlooking farms, towns, and friends. It was windy and cold during the winters.

The trailer was a pink salmon color on the outside, had a small living room at the front, a small kitchen and bathroom. When the water line froze, my mom had to heat water in a large pot on the kitchen stove for baths.

One night, my mom was filling the tub with hot water heated on the stove. I was getting ready to take a bath, it was dark outside, and it had been snowing. I was cold down to my bones as I got undressed to take my bath. I thought the sooner I got undressed, and in the water, the quicker I would warm up. My father had told me to wait for the water to cool down, but I didn't listen.

I don't recall if I screamed, but my dad heard me and knew exactly what had happened. I remember the searing heat as I stuck my foot in the water, going to my grandparents' to drop my sister off before riding to the hospital. I sat in the front seat, between my parents, as my dad drove to the hospital. It was dark and cold outside, but I was warmly bundled in my big coat. The inside of the car had a greenish blue light from the radio and my foot was throbbing as it sat on the middle hump of the floorboard. The floorboard had a textured, rubbery feel. I sensed the pent-up emotions radiating from my dad as he drove quickly, but carefully because of the snow and road conditions.

My dad has always been a big, strong guy. He was a wrestler in high school and went to state championships. He could lift and throw bales of hay like they were nothing. When he hugged me, his arms were hard and solid, but he never crushed me. He was not a man of many words, but when he was with his brothers and family, he was loud and laughed often. His voice was deep and when he raised it, it was booming, but I never feared him, for his size or his voice.

As we drove to the hospital, I felt safe because he was driving and I was sitting next to him, so I was confused as to why he felt tense. It was quiet in the car, except for background noise from the radio.

At the hospital, the cold air hit my face as my dad carried me inside. We went from the dark to bright white light and someone tending to my foot. They wrapped my foot in thick, white gauze. It looked like I had a boot on.

When we returned to my grandparents' house, it was lighter outside and my dad said I had to stay off my foot, no wrestling or rough-housing, and I had to keep the white gauze bandage clean. I remember the pain, the throbbing, feeling like my heart was beating in my foot and with each heartbeat, it hurt more. KJ sat next to my, trying to comfort me with her presence, as she never said much.

KJ and I spent most of our time together. We looked nothing alike; where I came into the world a hefty and loud 9 pounds, 5 ounces, she came in much smaller and quieter. Our nicknames were Moose, because I was so big, and Mouse, because she was so little. In pictures of the 2 of us, I look like a giant next to her, and we weren't even a year apart. She was always quiet and when in public or around family, she tended to hide behind me or hang onto my coat. She was never frail or weak, but I felt an overwhelming sense it was my job to take care of her and protect her.

Although we fought and wrestled, gave each other black eyes and bruises, we were a team against others if they hurt us.

My dad worked on the house in his free time. It was a huge house. It took a couple years to complete enough of the foundation and basement, for my dad to pull the trailer into the middle. This gave us more room because we could use the kitchen and the shower in the basement, as he continued building around the trailer. It took some time before he finished the house enough to take the trailer out and for us to move into the house.

With KJ and I having birthdates so close, we always had 1 party to celebrate our birthdays. After I turned 5, I began my first year of school. I rode the bus to/from school and KJ would be waiting for me when I came home. She was normally on the huge front porch, looking sad, until she saw me. During the winters, if she wasn't bundled up and outside, she was standing at the sliding glass door that opened to the front porch.

Sometimes, I had to get off the school bus with my uncles, at my grandparents'. We lived in a very rural area where K-12 all went to the same school and rode the same bus. Our bus driver knew my grandparents and our family. He was the pastor at a local church and there were times he told me I was getting off the bus at my grandparents' because my mom wasn't home.

My mom didn't work a job and was normally home during the day. She bowled with her sisters, and we spent many hours at the bowling alley on her bowling nights and during the summer. The bowling alley was next to the American Legion where my mother's father and brother-in-law went sometimes. KJ and I liked hanging out there. If it was daylight, KJ and I were running around outside, in the big parking lot, climbing trees, exploring where we could. The one place we weren't allowed to go near was the river, especially the falls.

I was born right after the historic "Flood of '72," when Hurricane Agnes, downgraded from a hurricane, was pulled to the southern tier area of western NY, known as the Allegany Basin, from a cold front that moved in from Canada. The cold front caused Agnes to stall, and it rained for 5 days. The rains caused massive flooding, wiping out Corning, Elmira, parts of Wellsville, Belmont, and Olean. The hospital where I was born, 2 months after the rains started falling/flooding the southern tier, suffered damage. Part of the 1-million-dollar wing of the hospital was damaged from the flood waters washing away the foundation, bridges, houses, cars and more.

The house that my mom grew up in, the house where I was conceived, sat on the Genesee River, near the falls. The Genesee River crested 24 feet, 17 feet above normal, by 4 A.M., Friday, June 23, 1972. The house wasn't washed away at that point but was severely damaged. The bridge that we liked running to so we could watch the falls, at one point had water mere inches from the bottom side of it, hence one of the reasons we were always told to stay away from the river.

When we were home, my sister and I would ride our tricycles, I had a huge one, all around our property. If there was snow on the ground, then we rode on the front porch, through the sliding glass doors, into the kitchen/dining room area, down the hall past the bathroom, into the big open room at the back of the house. There was a small area next to the staircase going upstairs that we would ride into and see how close we could get to the stairs while going under them, without hitting our heads. The we headed back down the hall, through the kitchen and out the door. This is when I learned to drift on turns.

We also had a swing set. My dad hung a wooden swing near the driveway so we could swing while he worked on his "big" truck. It was a 1949 Autocar, an old truck with no motor. This is where KJ and I learned how to turn a wrench, what the inside of a truck looked and smelled like, while learning a little grease never hurt anyone.

There were logs in the back of the house, and we were told to stay off, but every now and then we had to play king of the mountain and climbed them. My not listening began early.

One day I climbed them, and my sister wouldn't, so I stood at the top, beating my chest, yelling, "I am king of the mountain!" It must have been fall or spring because it wasn't extremely cold, but I had my big jacket on. I felt like I had conquered something huge. The sun felt warm on my face as I looked up, then something moved, and the logs started moving and rolling. My sister's eyes were huge. I lost my balance and started rolling with the logs.

The weight of the logs as they rolled over me felt heavy and the bark was rough, but it didn't hurt.

Once my dad knew I was okay, I could walk, no blood or broken bones, he yelled at me for playing on the logs. My sister kept looking at me with her huge brown eyes, like they were going to pop out of her head. What was she trying to process? What did I process at the age of 5 or 6 from the experience? Looking back on that event, I recognize the danger I had been in.

My dad was gone a lot driving truck for his own trucking company. As KJ and I got older, we didn't get off the bus at my grandparents' when our mother wasn't home. When we realized our mom wasn't home, we would get something out of the fridge and sit under the big picnic table in the dining room and eat. Most of the time, it was cottage cheese that had been processed at the local dairy that picked up milk from my grandparents' farm. This is when we found that cottage cheese mixed with ketchup was delicious. We normally weren't home alone for long, but long enough to eat cottage cheese and then get yelled at for ruining our dinner.

If our mom bowled on a school night, she didn't take us with her. A cousin or one of our dad's brothers would babysit us. Our cousin wanted us to sit still and be quiet, she hated noise and we were used to being able to make lots of noise and running free like the wild children we were. She tried blocking us with obstacles, to keep us from riding through the house and even locked us out of the house a couple times but we knew where to sneak in.

On one occasion, we had another relative babysitting. KJ and I were in our shared bedroom, and we were told it was time for bed. We argued because it was still light outside. We lost the argument and went to bed.

As I was lying in bed, I felt his weight pressing on me and the feel of his hot breath on my face. His sweaty hands started "petting" me. He put his hands inside my panties. I tried holding my legs closed, as if I had to go pee really bad. His hands were stronger than my legs. I don't know if he said anything because in my head it was loud, like being in a wind tunnel. At some point he raised above me, with his body between my open legs and I felt an object pushing against the area where I peed from. He didn't look at me and I felt I was ripping in half. I turned my head and saw my sister lying on her bed, both of us had tears falling, neither of us made a sound.

I don't know how long it lasted but when his weight was removed from me, I thought I had peed the bed because it was wet. I couldn't move, my body felt boneless and the loudness in my head had become an empty and hollow sound. My right arm was outstretched then as I saw him fix his pants and leave the room, my fingers touched my sisters. Neither of us knew what happened that day or the times that followed, but I felt dirty. I could never get the water hot enough or use enough soap to wash myself.

Each time was like an out-of-body experience. Looking at this person on top of me, not understanding what was happening.

When my parents were home together, there was a lot of arguing or my baby sister was crying. My new sister, SE, was born when I was five. KJ and I became closer, finding new hiding places when people came to visit or when someone was babysitting us.

We had forts in the house that only we could get in/out of, hiding places in the trees, under the porch, even in the huge ditch, inside the drainage pipe. We found if we stayed out of eyesight, we were left alone.

Nights were filled with nightmares; I was in the ditch and a large snake would wrap itself around me, squeezing until I couldn't breathe. I would wake up gasping for breath, sometimes a sheet was wrapped around me, and the nightmare stayed with me, for years. When I was older, I understood the trauma was manifesting itself in my dreams. This would later turn into issues with claustrophobia. I never liked snakes and to this day, I feel the pressure of the snake in my dreams, squeezing the life out of me.

My dad worked hard from the time he was in high school and went to a Vocational/Technical school for Diesel Mechanics. Years later, I would go to the same Vo/Tech center. During my dad's training, his teacher and mentor wound up becoming a lifelong friend. My dad continued to drive the plow for the town. In 1975, prior to my younger sisters being born, his mentor reached out and asked if my dad wanted to work with a company that was building the freeway. My dad worked for them for 2 months, then was laid off from working in the parts/supplies room. My dad went to work for another man that was pulling oil wells, clearing right of ways for Quaker State to come in and drill. My dad continued working in the mornings and went to work with another company, where he worked for a year.

In 1976, my dad bought his first dump truck, which he proudly named "Old Sal," and went to work for a local company. He started his own trucking company, working for the local company and expanding his business into Rushford and Jamestown as he continued work on the house. He worked long hours, providing for his growing family.

Due to the location of our house, on the hill, we were one of the highest points in the area and had a CB radio that reached further than most CBs. My dad could talk to my mom from the time he left our house, until he pulled into the parking lot where he worked, about an hour away. CB radios were the most common form of communication then. Most households had a base station, and most vehicles had a portable in it. Essentially, these were better than the technology of cell phones and you could have a "group chat" without needing anyone's number, you just joined in the conversation. However, the limitation was range. Someone a three-hour drive away would not be in range to join the chat.

If you've never used a CB (citizens band) radio, there's a few things you should know. First, channel 19 is for emergencies, letting people know of travel conditions, accidents, and where the "smokies" were hiding. Second, you needed a "handle." You did not use real names. My dad was Mountain Goat or "Goat," which many people still refer to him as. My mom was Mountain Laurel and normally manned the base station which was located on top of the refrigerator and had a big microphone. Mt. Goat and Mt. Laurel became the contacts for many people that needed to get an emergency message to a loved one, in a hurry.

Many times, someone reached out to my parents, to relay a message, share information, and get ahold of people. They kept a log of people's call signs, the areas they normally travelled and over time had their own network of approximately 2000 people. Most of the people in the network they had never met, while others became friends with friendships that lasted through kids, marriages, divorces, job changes, and even out-of-state moves. I know many of them by their "handle" only, but I also know I could get in contact with them today with just their handle.

Over the years, my parents met another driver over the CB, who went by the name "Woodburner." A friendship developed and our families began having dinners together. They would play cards for hours while the kids played and ultimately fell asleep. Woodburner had 2 kids close to my age. When company came over, the adults sat at the huge picnic table in the kitchen that served as our dining table and the kids sat at a smaller table.

Even though Woodburner's kids were close in age, we didn't have much in common. They were quiet while we were loud and rowdy. Sometimes we would play games in the back room which had been turned into more of a playroom. We would set the plastic pins up and bowl or we learned to play card games which would normally turn into a wrestling match between me and my sister. In hindsight, I think it was the only way we could work out our aggression for not being able to defend ourselves or protect each other from being physically and sexually victimized.

One evening when Woodburner's family was at our house, someone had made pudding for dessert. Whether I was already sick or became sick after eating a good portion of the pudding, I began vomiting. It was the color of the green pudding. The oldest, a boy, laughed especially when the pudding came out of my nose. Pudding- and custard-filled desserts have since been avoided as the texture triggers that memory.

Eventually, my dad hired Woodburner to drive one of his trucks and the families grew closer. My parents met many others through the CB, neighbors of family members, on job sites and those friends would also become like family.

Our family kept expanding. Soon, I had another baby sister, KM. KJ and I shared a bedroom on the other side of my parents' room, next to the attic and the staircase. Our room was huge and would become part of our self-made adventure course, to hide from our sisters' crying.

Once you came up the stairs, the walls were enclosed, on both sides and you stepped onto the landing. There was a time when it was just 2x4s where we could sit and listen to adult conversation or the TV when we were supposed to be in bed. If you went straight, you walked into my baby sister's room, if you turned to the right, you walked into my parents' room and if you did a U-turn to the right or left (technically a closet space), around the stairwell, you walked into mine and my sister's room.

We had 2 twin beds, against the far wall, with a little walkway between our beds. At the end of our beds, against opposite walls, was a dresser for each of us. If you continued straight through our room, you entered the attic, which had a sloping roof, and the chimney went up through.

The chimney was surrounded by concrete block and during the winter was a great place to snuggle next to because it was warm. If you walked through our room and before the attic entrance, turned right, there was a huge closet, behind the back of the staircase. You could continue through and turn right, to a little walkway/hallway which would bring you back to the staircase landing. That ceiling sloped too, so it was a great place to hide, especially when we had a babysitter and visitors.

KJ and I loved the freedom we had. We had so much area to explore and spent most of our time outdoors. If we were in the house, we were building something out of boxes, blankets, scrap wood and furniture. We didn't have many toys, but we always seemed to have a mess that needed to be cleaned up.

My parents had 4 daughters, ranging from newborn to 6. SE and KM were a year and half apart with 4 years between KJ and SE.

My mom was always creative and artistic, learning to feed and clothe a family of 6 on a limited budget. Many people might judge our homemade clothes, kitchen haircuts, hand-me-down shoes and clothes, as poor, country folk, but I learned to look at my childhood as a blessing. My parents decided to bring me into this world, even with 30 hours of labor. I had a warm place to stay, clothes and shoes to wear, hair that covered my head, even when the cowlick in my bangs stood straight up in the front.

As we grew older, the fighting between my parents grew louder. Friday nights when my dad was home, we would lay on the floor to watch *The Dukes of Hazard*, *The Incredible Hulk*, or some other show. My dad would wrestle with us, letting our baby sisters crawl all over him while he tickled us. There was lots of laughter with us, but I don't remember my mom laughing much during this time.

We had family and friends of our parents that would stop by, sometimes for dinner, sometimes for coffee, sometimes to help work on a project in the house or to help my dad fix his truck. When he was working on something, he would tell us to come help him. Most Saturday and Sunday mornings, my sister and I could be found inside my dad's truck, with him teaching us about the tools, parts, showing us which wrench was used for what. Even when he wasn't home, we were normally in or around the truck, to feel the closeness because it felt safe.

In 1977, my dad and "Woodburner" were working in Jamestown together. In 1978 they started hauling coal. On April 3rd, 1979, our lives would change. My dad and another driver were hauling coal during a snowstorm with icy conditions. As they came down a big hill, with a fully loaded semi-tractor and trailer, a vehicle stopped in front of my dad, in the middle of the road. Due to the icy road conditions and lack of indication the car was going to slow down or stop, my dad was unable to stop the truck and ran the car over. The driver was killed instantly, and my dad's truck started on fire. My dad and his passenger sustained burns after struggling to get out of the truck.

My dad tried calling our house to let my mom know what had happened and that he needed a ride, but there was no answer. He called his mom and dad next to learn we were at their house because mom was "out." His mother picked him up. Later that evening, my dad found my mom was with "Woodburner" and that night had been their first "intimate interaction."

My parents tried working things out, but by August of '79, my dad moved out. He couldn't stay focused at work, worrying about what was going on at home. After my dad moved out, "Woodburner" moved in. I had just started 3rd grade and I wasn't sure what was happening, other than my mom was having sleepovers.

In December, my mom moved my sisters and I into Woodburner's house with her. That Christmas would be the last holiday spent together as a "family" with both of my parents. It was also the last holiday we spent in the house my dad built, where so many childhood memories were made.

There was much going on during that time, with Christmas, moving, getting registered for a new school, I didn't have time to process what happened. Everything felt foreign. Living in a place that wasn't mine, I felt like a visitor. I found comfort outside, running around, exploring, climbing trees, playing in the dirt and mud.

I met the neighbors across the street, and the ones down the dirt road. The neighbors across the street had a daughter a year older than me. We had the same first name and clicked.

They lived in an old farmhouse, and someone had died in the house, which became part of our interest and exploration into spirits and ghosts.

The doors were all old and creaked when they opened/closed. The house was a huge, two-story house with a full finished basement. The stairs were in the middle of the house, with a door that separated the upstairs sleeping area from the main living area. There was a screened-in porch on the front of the house, which faced the street and our house. The porch was winterized so you could sit out there during winter and summer, but it wasn't used much. There were a couple of old wood rockers out there and indoor/outdoor carpet was on the floor. Most of our time was spent in the living room, playing games, learning, and talking about ghosts, sharing real stories that we turned into ghost stories. When the rest of the family was home, we would go to her room so we could whisper and share without being overheard.

Soon I was introduced to the "Ouija" board, which is branded by a well-known boardgame company, but I disagree that it should be for kids. The Ouija is also known as a spirit board or talking board. It's a flat board marked with the letters of the alphabet, the numbers 0-9, the words "yes," "no" and some have "hello" and goodbye," which is what this one had, along with various symbols and graphics. There is a "planchette" which is a small heart-shaped piece of wood or plastic, as a movable indicator to spell out messages. In the middle of the planchette on the games sold in department stores, there is a clear window to see where it lands as it spells the message.

This game was introduced as a "parlor game" in the 1800s and became more popular when mediums started using it as a way of communicating with the dead. Of course, we went through the standard questions, what were our names, where did we live, go to school, etc. I was skeptical it was real and felt someone was helping the planchette move around, until...

There were many random occurrences that began when we started using the board, asking questions, and digging into the history of the house. I didn't know my stepdad's family had lived there prior and had family that died there. As we asked questions about the previous owners and history, we asked if anyone had died in the house. The planchette moved to "yes." We asked how many people died and the genders. Soon we heard a door slam shut to one of the bedrooms, but we were the only ones in the house at the time.

After our hearts calmed down a bit, we went to see which room it was and to see if a window had been left open or if there was a breeze that caused it to shut. There was no breeze, no open window, and no one else in the house. The only animals they owned were goats and pigs outside and a snapping turtle in the basement.

We all went downstairs to make sure no one else was in the house. The house was set up that the main rooms were all situated around the stairs. Once you came down the stairs, you entered the informal dining room, which had a small room off that, where the brother slept, and the door to go down to the basement. Going to the right was the kitchen, which had the main door and mud room off it. As you continued through the kitchen, alongside the staircase, as it rose, you came into the formal dining room, which had the main bathroom off it. Leaving the dining room, you entered the living room/sitting room, which had the screened porch door, next to the entry to go back into the informal dining room.

After checking the informal dining room, her brothers' room, the kitchen, dining room, bathroom, we entered the living room where a light had been left on. There was a rocking chair next to the light which was rocking gently as if someone was sitting in it, rocking. The hair on my neck began to stand up, my heart raced faster, and my "hackles" began to rise. We all stopped moving and just stood watching the chair.

There was no TV, radio, or any noise other than our breathing as we stood there, clutching each other's hands, when we heard a creaking noise coming from the porch area. The rocking chair on the porch was a heavy wooden chair and it was also moving. I'm fairly sure we all needed to check our pants by this time, but instead, as youth does, we slowly moved towards the informal dining room because we had to check the basement.

This basement was clean, bright, and open so we could see every area about halfway down the stairs. The only thing we saw was the turtle and heard the hum of the freezer and extra refrigerator. We came back upstairs and decided to each go into a different room, so we could see the room, but stay in the doorway so we could still see each other and to see if anyone was moving or hiding as we went from room to room. There was no one.

Once our heart rates slowed and we felt calmer, we started joking about what we had seen and heard. None of us were ready to go back upstairs though and we had to go back home.

After we got home, we were whispering about what we'd seen and heard. My stepdad overheard some of the whispers, of course, our whispers sounded more like inside voices to normal people. He asked if we had been at the neighbors when we saw and heard the different things we were talking about. We told him that we had, which is when he told us about his family living there for years and that his parents or grandparents (this was 40-plus years prior) had both died there, in their rocking chairs. He told us that they both went peacefully in their sleep, in their favorite places, but this did nothing to relieve our minds knowing it wasn't just our imaginations.

The Ouija board and "seances" became our weekend routine when we weren't with my dad. A few years later, the neighbors moved, and I got a Ouija board as a gift. It became a regular pastime when my stepsister and brother were at the house. One of those days, KJ, our stepsister, and I were in one of the bedrooms, playing with the board. We were sitting on the bed, closest to the window, when we asked a few questions. None of us knew what my stepdad's middle name was, we only knew that it started with an L.

After asking the Ouija board, it spelled out a name that none of us were familiar with. I went downstairs and asked my mom if his middle name was what the board had spelled out. She stopped what she was doing and asked how we had found out. I started to get yelled at for going through his things and I told her we asked the Ouija board. She told me not to use his middle name because he didn't like it. After I said okay, I ran back up the stairs and told my sisters what happened.

Our house was an old farmhouse, probably 100 years old when we moved in. There were 2 stories, 4 bedrooms upstairs, with an attic above. The stairs were steep, and the steps were narrow, half your foot didn't even fit on the step. The dining room was at the bottom of the stairs, with a pantry off that and inside the pantry was the entrance to the cellar. The kitchen and living room were on opposite sides of the dining room. The main entrance and porch were located off the kitchen along with a store/laundry room and a bathroom. The living room also had an entrance and bigger porch and there was another room connected to the living room. More about that room later.

My stepbrother was sitting on the other bed in the room while we were playing with the Ouija. After I told my sisters the middle name was right, we started talking about spirits being in the house. My stepbrother yelled, "That's such bullshit!" and walked out of the room. There was a narrow hallway from the room to the stairs that passed by 2 bedrooms before you turned at the landing to go down the stairs.

We kept talking in the room when we heard something fall. We didn't think much of it until we heard my stepbrother yell, "Who pushed me? Who the hell pushed me down the stairs?" We all came running out of the bedroom, the 2 youngest girls ran out of the playroom, the room located off the living room, and my mom came from the laundry room to see what happened. My stepbrother was sitting on the floor of the dining room at the bottom of the stairs when we asked what happened.

He told us as he was going to take the 1st step down the stairs from the landing, he felt a pressure, like a hand, in the middle of his back, push him hard enough to make him lose his footing and fall. He kept saying, "I know it was one of you, I know it was." My mom asked if he was okay and which one of us pushed him. We kept saying we were all in the bedroom when he left, and he would have seen us if we'd left the room. We were told we needed to put the game away and get downstairs until someone admitted they did it.

None of us wanted anything more to do with the Ouija. I packed it up and put it in the attic because my sisters and I knew we did not cause the fall and we weren't prepared to deal with any more "incidents" or paranormal activity. I never touched a Ouija again. My brother never admitted he knew none of us could have pushed him, but he also didn't want to believe in ghosts or spirits either. Now he is a high school science teacher.

We stuck to more traditional boardgames after this and time outside of the house. None of us liked going in the cellar. It was a traditional cellar, with clay floor and walls, carved out of the ground, to keep food cold and to store canned goods for the winter. The stairs were wood and creaked, with the back open. Once in the cellar, there was an open space behind the stairs, the light string was at the top of the stairs and the light hung from the middle of the cellar ceiling so if the bulb was blown, you were in the dark. When at the bottom of the stairs, there were shelves on the walls, lined with canned goods and there was a heavy wooden door that led to the outside stairs which would bring you up by the main entrance porch/door.

We didn't use that door often because it was heavy and hard to open, especially during the winter when the outside cellar stairs filled with snow. The younger sisters hated the cellar, so I was the one that usually went down, as quickly as possible, to retrieve whatever canned good was requested by my mother. KJ would normally stand at the top of the stairs holding the door open because she knew I hated feeling closed in and to make sure I was okay.

The pantry held most of the dry goods to feed a family of 6 or 8 when my stepbrother and sister visited. This is also where we kept the boardgames, puzzles, and other miscellaneous items. In the laundry room, there was a large deep freezer. This mainly stored the meat obtained from hunting or the beef and pork that had been butchered. The laundry room wasn't as creepy as the cellar, but it was not a comfort either. It was big room with a huge door on the back side that led outdoors to the back lawn. The door was original to the house and was the entrance/exit to go to/from the outhouse before indoor plumbing.

The outhouse area got filled in and became an outdoor fire pit because it was far enough away from the house and garage. It had a concrete pad in front that had been the step into the outhouse. This is where we learned about S'mores and roasting hotdogs over the fire on a stick. We would soak fresh corn and roast them over the coals as we sat around the fire telling "ghost" stories. Being outside didn't feel as threatening when we talked about ghosts and spirits, but we didn't contemplate using the Ouija board again.

The playroom was also used as my mom's sewing room. This room would become the catch-all for toys, clothes needing mended, books and soon, became a storage room.

Woodburner aka my stepdad had an amazing vinyl record collection of 33s and 45s. We received a record player as a gift, so I'd listen to the records for hours. He told me I could have the 45s and I took them to my room with the record player. This is where I learned "Wake Up, Little Susie," "Oh, Suzy Q," "Peggy Sue," "Mr. Postman," and the greats by the Beatles, Eagles, Rolling Stones, Kenny Rogers, Hank Williams and so many more. My first personal record was Juice Newton, "Playing with the Queen of Hearts," and I played that for hours, mixed with "Mickey" by Tony Basil. Sorry if that song is now stuck in your head.

If you're not familiar with the chorus of "Mickey" it goes like this: "Oh, Mickey, you're so fine, you're so fine you blow my mind, hey Mickey. Oh, Mickey, what a pity, you don't understand, you take me by the heart when you take me by the hand. Oh, Mickey, you're so pretty, can't you understand, it's guys like you, Mickey, oh, what you do, Mickey, do, Mickey, don't break my heart, Mickey." That was especially for my mom, stepdad, and my sisters. My mom and stepdad hated it and my sisters loved it.

We were part of a large extended family on all sides and were constantly given random clothes to see if they fit any of us or that mom could use for sewing. There was a skirt I loved, even though I wouldn't wear it to school. I was not a skirt or dress girl, but I would wear it at home. The skirt background was white, with flowers of all colors, shapes and sizes and an orange ruffle that started at the waist along the split, down and around the bottom hem. I loved wearing it so I could spin around, and the bright orange split ruffle would twirl around.

When we had to replace the water heater, we were given the box to play with. That box was converted into a "dressing room" for outfit changes, usually my skirt, so we could attend our "concerts." Any large box thereafter was incorporated into our play.

Our concerts began in the kitchen while our parents were in the living room watching TV. The kitchen was great because we had floors that weren't carpeted so we could slip and slide all over while "performing." We learned how to do the "catwalk" after our mom started going to modeling school and had to practice at home. On Saturdays while she was gone, my sisters and I would practice our walk, turns, poses, and added our own flair. We found random things to make into dresses, scarves, hats, and outfits. My feet were bigger than my mom's so I could never wear her heels. I would use what I could, sometimes wearing my stepdad's black leather biker boots.

During our "concert" rehearsals, we had to have music as loud as possible so we could sing and add more sass. Saturday nights became our "performance nights," sometimes just for ourselves and other times, once we found the boxes for dressing rooms, the living room became our stage. That's when the parents suffered.

We used posters to decorate the inside of our boxes, used markers and paint for the outside, added cheap boa feathers to make it more glamorous and used a knife to cut a door into the long side of the box so we could enter and exit easier and with more flair. I couldn't sing even a little bit, but I had enough sass to make up for it or so I thought.

One of the things of farm life and rural living, especially growing up with only 2 TV channels, sometimes a 3rd, depending on the weather, how the antennae was positioned, the moon phase, and so on, our imaginations were limitless.

We created stories for everything, made up conversations between the cows, pigs, goats, and chickens. We went on adventures in our minds, expanding on each one, changing things up, looking in the encyclopedias for new things and places. Our reality was contained to the farm when we weren't in school or with my dad. Our reality was simple, feed animals, do chores, eat breakfast, go outside, and play 'til lunch, go play again, do afternoon chores and evening feedings, wash up for dinner, set the table, eat, dishes, go back outside to play, wash up and bedtime.

That simplicity changed one night when my mom received a phone call. Her sister was finally able to get away from her abusive husband in Texas and made it to NY, but she needed a place to stay with the kids where he wouldn't be able to find her. Since my mom and dad divorced and her and my stepdad hadn't gotten married yet, the abuser didn't know where my mom lived, and it was far enough away from the rest of the family that it was the best option.

We were also well armed, and we would know if a vehicle was coming down the hill, up to almost a mile away due to the way the house sat, and we could see about 1/2 a mile away from the other direction. The road we lived on was a small 2-lane route that connected a few small towns.

My aunt and her kids arrived at the house. It was dark out when the call came in and it must have been close to midnight when they arrived. They had nothing, but the clothes on their backs. All the kids slept downstairs in the living room. We spread all our sleeping bags out, so everyone had a spot to sleep and something to cover up with.

My mom and aunt sat in the kitchen with the lights low, quietly talking. I could hear my aunt crying off and on while they talked. I had to go to the bathroom and quietly walked into the kitchen to get to the bathroom when I heard my aunt say, "I was trying to get away after he hit me, over and over and pushed me down the stairs. I grabbed the gun and shot as he started coming towards me, yelling, 'I'm gonna fucking kill you, you won't ever get away from me.' I saw him stumble, grabbed the 2 younger kids and told the oldest to get in the car. I never looked back to see if he was okay or if he was still coming. I don't even know if I shot, I just know I had enough time during his pause to grab the kids and run like hell."

I don't think my aunt ever heard me or realized I was there. She kept talking while my mom rubbed her hand and arm. My mom saw me as I crept to the bathroom and nodded for me to continue as my aunt talked. They stayed up for a while longer. My aunt was going to sleep in my room, but she said she wanted to sleep with her babies to make sure everyone was okay.

We all snuggled in and slept on the outside of them, making a little protective barrier without realizing it. It was still dark out when someone screamed. I'm not sure if it was my aunt having a nightmare or if it was my oldest cousin having a nightmare. There were quiet murmurs and then everything was quiet again.

The next morning the phone rang. It was early. I jumped up to answer it when my aunt grabbed my arm and said, "No, don't answer it, it might be him looking for me, just let it ring." My mom heard the phone and came down the stairs when she heard what my aunt told me. I overheard them discuss not telling any family she was there in case he tried getting information from them. We stayed close to the house that day, letting everyone relax and settle in.

My stepdad came home from work, he generally worked from 11 P.M. to 7 A.M., and my mom explained what happened. He told my aunt she could stay as long as needed, not to worry about anything and he would make sure they were protected. She broke down again and kept saying, "Thank you, thank you," over and over. This is when I realized what an amazing man my stepdad is.

I went to the store with my mom later that day to get more food, basic hygiene items for everyone and undergarments. My aunt was able to wear some of my mom's clothes and the kids fit into what we had.

My mom and aunt could sew. They took the time to sew some summer clothes for the kids so they each had a couple things of their own. Slowly they started to relax and enjoy games and exploring with us. We picked berries, apples, and rhubarb to bake pies, make jellies and to keep busy. The farm and woods helped my aunt find new strength, courage, and determination. I witnessed a wilting flower begin to bloom and flourish again. Hearing my aunt and my cousins laugh, play, and find true joy in life was such an awe-inspiring experience.

They stayed with us a while, at least a month or so, before the rest of the family was told. They now had a safety net of family to embrace them. Soon my aunt was able to get her own place, not far from where she'd grown up. We visited quite a bit, spending many Saturdays there and sometimes the night. I learned about crawfish, crab legs, shrimp, and other tasty delights that I'd never eaten before. I started to realize that there was an entire world of delicious foods and sights waiting for me to experience.

I learned a great deal from my aunt without her ever realizing it. She was an inspiration of grit and perseverance. She was the first person I'd ever seen with a tattoo. It was a butterfly and it had so much meaning, especially after she escaped. Years later, she met and fell in love with a man completely different than her ex. They dated for a few years before getting married because she was hesitant. They were married a few years before she died during a surgery on her kidney. She will be forever missed but lives in our hearts and memories.

I had never heard the term "domestic violence" until I was older but hearing what my aunt and cousins lived through taught me no one had a right to ever lay a hand on me, control my thoughts, actions, how I dressed, who I talked to, where I went, how much money I had or spent. What I wasn't taught was how to recognize the early signs of domestic violence, including psychological abuse, until I was older. It's hard to see when you're amidst it and most get trapped before they realize what's happened to them.

If you're reading this, don't ever stay in a situation because you have kids, your family/friends tell you to stay and work things out, or because the person promises to change. They don't change. They get worse over time. There is help out there. Never doubt your own strength and courage or resiliency.

3
Small-Town Girl

I was used to fighting for what I wanted, protecting others, as well as protecting myself against bullies. I was raised with my uncles, where I had to fight for food and space. I was a tomboy, raised on a farm, with uncles that were always in trouble at school, fighting and causing a ruckus and I carried the same last name.

I almost failed kindergarten because I didn't like my teacher. She never smiled and was always comparing me to my uncles. We had reading groups that were fruits. As we progressed in our reading, we went to a new fruit group. I was fine with this until the end of the year when I reached the lemon group and I thought I needed to eat a lemon.

Eventually, I was convinced I didn't have to eat a lemon, but my reading issues and family name followed me into 1st grade. In 1st grade, I began getting into fights with the boys on the playground. There were several reasons. To defend my uncles and our family name, someone pulling my ponytail, or defending other kids being picked on.

My best friend and I spent nights at each other's houses and sticking up for each other. She had darker skin than me and I found out later that she is multiracial. Having her as my best friend taught me at an early age, we are all human, regardless of our skin color, religion, culture, upbringing. I embraced the beauty of who she was, her heart, her caring nature, and her strength of being comfortable in her own skin.

During the 1st and 2nd grades, I found myself sitting on the cold aluminum bench, next to my uncle, for fighting. I developed a "crush" and learned "sitting in a tree, KISSING, first comes love, second comes marriage, then comes baby in a baby carriage." Oh, my young, innocent heart. By the 3rd grade I started receiving letters, "Do you love me, circle yes or no," colored pictures of a house and family, and them sneaking quick pecks on the cheek as they walked by my seat to get off the bus.

Not only did I go to school with my uncles, 4 of them, but I also rode the school bus with them. Thankfully, our bus driver was a stern and Godly man. He enforced the no fighting or roughhousing on the school bus.

I liked to fight, therefore when a boy I didn't have a crush on had the nerve to kiss my cheek as I walked by him, he was not prepared for me to turn around and start punching him as I yelled at him. The bus driver, the only bus driver thus far, calmly put the bus in park, unbuckled his seatbelt and walked back. He gently removed me from the boy and started talking to me quietly. He told me I had every right to be mad and to want to protect myself and he didn't think the boy would ever try something like that again.

He was the first adult who allowed me to release my anger at being violated, instead of punishing me for defending myself. Not only was he the first adult, but he was a male. All my teachers had been females and they punished me for standing up for myself. At what point is it taught you can freely touch another person's body, whether it's pulling hair, tugging on ponytails, braids, or pinching their butt? Does this lead to the extreme of fully violating another person? My bus driver taught me the truth. No one had ever taught me this and it became a core part of who I was going to become, a protector and guardian.

My teachers were concerned with my reading, and I was sent to an after-school tutor. She lived next to the school. Her window overlooked the playground, and my bench. She had white hair, wore aprons because she was always cooking or baking, and smelled like cinnamon and vanilla. I loved her and her house.

I don't remember how long I went for tutoring, but I loved it. It gave me a chance to be me. No sisters, uncles, parents, teachers, or school kids around. She taught me how to lose myself in a book, to go on adventures in my mind, to live like "Dick and Jane." Reading became my lifeline, my solace, my escape. The books were my friends, and I became part of the story with my imagination.

After my parents separated and divorced and with my mom moving us to a new house, town, school, and "family," this opened the door to all sorts of new challenges. It was the middle of my 3rd grade year when I was introduced to my class at the new school. I heard whispers of divorced parents, welfare, not going to go anywhere in life. Unfortunately, most of the whispers were from teachers, staff, and other parents. I didn't understand what most of it meant, but it was unwelcoming and foreign.

With the stigma of divorce and welfare surrounding me and being a child accustomed to fighting, it was tough to make friends. There were stigmas from family as well. My step-grandmother that married my mom's father bet me $50 I would be pregnant before graduating high school. This was while I was still in elementary school.

Naturally, I gravitated to the games the boys were playing. Hopscotch, jump rope and double-Dutch were games commonly played by the girls and they were not familiar. Although I preferred the games the boys played, they weren't keen on me joining their ranks. Where did I fit in?

I slowly found a new independence away from my uncles. I learned the unfamiliar games. The boys soon realized I could beat them at arm wrestling and let me join their ranks. Slowly, I made friends and throughout the years I had some great teachers and coaches who saw the potential in me, rather than the strikes against me.

There weren't many kids in my class, and most of them had grown up together, were related, or their parents had gone to school together. There were a few girls I got to know better, and we became friends as they taught me the unfamiliar games. I began to meld with my classmates and found I got along with most everyone. I was the tallest and gangliest girl in my class, but I finally felt accepted.

One of the girls I became friends with lived in the same little village as me. Our parents knew each other, so we hung out on weekends. When I got a bike, with long handlebars, a banana seat, and a big orange safety flag on the back, I rode it up and down the dirt road between our house and our neighbors until I convinced my mom I could ride it up the road to my friend's house. Normally, I had to be home by dark and I would push the limits. It was nice to get away from the stress and tension in our house.

This friend moved when we were in 5th or 6th grade. By then I had gotten to know one of the girls that lived around the block from her, so I rode my bike to see her.

By the 8th grade, I was playing sports, and doing just about anything that would get me muddy or scraped up. I liked boys, but I was too shy to let them know. I also was not ready to stop being a tomboy.

There were nights when my mom and stepdad were gone, and we would have one of the local girls babysit us. They were a few years older than me. I thought I was grown, but I didn't want to deal with my younger sisters. My mom was likely afraid of what would be damaged or which of us would wind up with something broken. We were extremely rough on each other. Several items in the house were broke or damaged through the years.

We lived in an old farmhouse, with over 100 acres of land where my stepdad grew up. His grandparents used to own the house across the street from us and one of his brothers lived about a quarter-mile down the road. My stepdad went to grade school at the schoolhouse in the village before it closed, then he went to the school my sisters and I attended. He knew almost everyone. He was a wealth of knowledge and information, but I had to pry it from him, little by little.

Back to the babysitters. We terrorized the first girl that babysat us. After years of abuse from babysitters at our old house, my sister and I were rebellious hellions. Things got physical when she tried to tell us something or get us to go to bed. She only watched us a few times and cussed us out several times. Although she did not deserve our treatment, she taught me some of my favorite cuss words to use for emphasis. When she wasn't available, my mom hired one of the 3 sisters down the road. They were each vastly different in their temperament and patience.

The oldest one was calm and patient. We learned not to push her buttons, or we were not going to like her at all. The middle sister was quiet and more reserved, but she watched us without us knowing it. She seemed to shut us down before we got started. We didn't have her as a babysitter as often as the other 2. The youngest one was about 4 years older than me. She was the shortest of the 3 and had a short temper to match. However, she was the one I ended up learning the most from.

She was a cheerleader and the only sister still in high school. I never thought about being a cheerleader, but I loved to jump. I was loud and strong. I watched her practice her cheers/routine and asked her if she would teach me some cheers. I knew how to do a cartwheel and a roundoff, but I have no memory of learning how to do these.

She told me to show her what I could do. I started doing cartwheels across the lawn and completed about 12 or 13 in a row when I stopped. She told me to keep practicing until it was perfect, explaining about keeping my legs straight, how to get more air on a roundoff and that if I learned how to do a split, I could do a cartwheel or roundoff, into a split.

We practiced. She showed my sister and I cheers, taught us how to move, clap, yell from our diaphragm and to be seen, as well as heard. That year, I was old enough to try out for junior high cheerleading, so I did. I made the cheer squad. I didn't realize how much I would enjoy it.

The next year, my sister tried out and we were able to cheer together. She was smaller so we tried a lot of stunts together with me as base and her as the flyer.

Our cheer coach was also the school librarian and she learned how much I loved books. She gave me an opportunity to be a library aide, helping reshelve books, checking books in/out, learning the Dewey Decimal System and having a safe place to land when needed. I was able to read more books and assist with book sales during fundraisers.

We also had a town library across the street from our school. We were able to visit this library once a week and check out books. The town library was an old colonial-style house, with 2 floors. There were gorgeous hardwood floors, windows all over, letting in light and books everywhere. To see, touch and smell the books was a balm for me. I eagerly awaited library day each week.

As we got older and had to do history research, we found hidden gems at the library. History of our town, the surrounding areas, the oil booms, and a part of *The Wizard of OZ* that was shot in our town. A town with no traffic lights, few stop signs, and 2 main roads. If you blinked, you'd probably miss it.

While I was helping in the school library, I became friends with one of the other aids, Queenie. She was in my class and her mom was the computer teacher. We were complete opposites, I was tall, she was short. I was a beanpole with unruly hair. She was curvy with trendy haircuts. Our love for books and reading was something we shared. I started spending the night at her house. As the relationship with my mom grew more strained, I started staying more nights, then weeks, at her house. My real-world education started expanding with our friendship.

I was introduced to Dr. Ruth, a sex therapist, whom we listened to every Sunday night. We found a book she had written and started reading and learning all about sex. I also learned about woodworking, crafting, gardening, homemade wine, and so much more. I was introduced to the world of boxing and televised boxing matches. They only had 1 TV in the house, a small one in her stepdad's office and we could be found there watching the fights. I was definitely a fighter, but I learned that she was a mighty scrapper, too. She was tough as nails and didn't take crap from anyone.

We joined the soccer and softball teams together and most weekends, I was at her house or her parents' woodshop. The woodshop was located in the town where I used to live before the divorce. We would help in the shop, clean or wander around town.

In high school, I started spending time at another friend's, Hazel, before or after games, if it was late. The 3 of us could normally be found in mischief somewhere and we started our own acronyms that we still use today.

Dating and charting our courses for the future, would reduce our time together. There were a couple rough patches because of "boys," but our bond was never broken. A few times we were targeted by other girls in our school and from neighboring schools. The dispute was usually over sports or boys. Many of our friendships were with boys from our school, as well as other schools and this did not sit well with their girlfriends despite our lack of romantic interest.

I was friends with a boy 4 years older than me. Our families had known each other for years. He dated a girl from another school that we played against in soccer. Words were said on the soccer field and hostility grew. One day, after soccer practice, a couple of us were walking to a friend's house, near the school. When we came around an old, abandoned building, this girl and one of her friends jumped us. Although I was skinny, I knew how to wrestle, thanks to my dad. I was wiry from the years of baling hay, throwing hay bales, carrying firewood, and other physical jobs on the farm. I also knew how to throw my hip and use my legs as leverage, I mean, why would I be blessed with "thunder thighs" if I wasn't going to learn how to use them?

The fight didn't last long. I got her to the ground and after a few punches, the town cop pulled me off her. His house was next to the abandoned building, so he had heard and seen everything that happened. She was told to stay out of our town but the rivalry on the soccer field grew over the years.

Another fight was with a girl that I rode the bus with. I don't know why she wanted to fight me. She was dating some boy and I guess she was jealous because we were in a class together. I was good friends with her brother, but she wanted to fight me. So, I took the fight to her. After that she never bothered me again.

Fights were not just with girls. I wound up in fights with guys, with one ending in "ISS" (in-school suspension) and detention for all of us. I became the champion for the underdogs and hated mean people or to see anyone mistreated or picked on.

After several trips to the principal's office, we became good friends. He asked me why I always seemed to be in a fight. I told him I was taught to defend myself and others, to never throw the first punch, but never let them get a second punch in. When he found out what I chose to do after high school, he wholeheartedly agreed with my choice.

Before junior high and sports, I started having extreme knee pain. My knees hurt to be touched and there was a growth under both of my knees. We had a large trampoline, a gift from our dad and a luxury in our eyes. I spent countless hours jumping, flipping, and playing on it. Then it hurt to jump.

The doctor said I had a disease in my knees, called Osgood Schlatter's. Lots of running, jumping, activities during growth causes the growth plate, tendons, etc., to grow out instead of up. I had to sit out of gym class, all sports, and any activity other than slow walking, for 8 weeks. The doctor said if I didn't adhere strictly, that I would have to wear braces. He also said I should grow out of the pain in about 3 years. That did not happen. These 8 weeks should have taught me patience. It did not.

My dad moved to Texas, to find steady work for his trucks and eventually to Arizona where he would remain. I was used to spending weekends and weeks during the summer with him. I was devastated. The atmosphere and tension at home didn't help. My mom and I were always fighting, sometimes with her slapping my face. I punched a hole in the wall so I wouldn't punch anyone. I found ways to escape, other friends that lived close enough for me to ride my bike to, spending hours in my hiding places, reading, writing, or just daydreaming in the silence.

Before I reached high school, my sisters and I began going to a youth group, "The Good News Club," at the house of a local church member, Grandma B. Once a week we got off the bus at her house, along with her grandkids and a few other local kids. I was one of the older kids in the group and tried to keep an eye on my sisters. This was a way of escape as I was shy in close quarter settings.

We learned different stories of the Bible, played games, had snacks, and learned to socialize in a different setting. I was invited to Awana, a youth group at church, for school ages, to participate in different team games, Bible study and bookwork time, followed by a brief service with everyone together. After the service, the team that won the game(s) would be announced and they received chocolate, normally Reese's, as their prize. I was motivated to win!

My family never went to church, and I didn't own a Bible. I went for the games and candy. Now I understand why they waited till the end before you got a prize.

After being called up and recognized for the team games, receiving my candy, I went back to my seat. Most of the time, I waited until we were released, then left quickly. One night was completely different. Normally, I listened halfheartedly, counting the minutes until I could leave. That night was different. The pastor was talking about being saved, what it meant to be saved, to ask Jesus into your heart and to cleanse you of your sins. I went through the motions, but when it came time to pray, I paid lip service.

What I felt as he was talking is not truly describable, but after we were released, I just sat there, not really seeing or hearing anything. I'd always felt someone was with me, protecting me. I continued sitting in the pew as the church emptied. Grandma B quietly came and sat beside me.

She asked if I was okay, if I needed to talk or if I had any questions about what the pastor had talked about. I told her that I didn't understand what he meant by being saved. She sat down next to me and said that the stories we had been reading at her home were from the Bible. Each story in some way related to God and Jesus.

I told her that I didn't have a Bible and was confused. I understood the stories, what it meant to be a good person, but didn't understand how everything tied together, or what it had to do with what the pastor had talked about. She asked if I was saved. I had no idea what she was asking and told her I didn't think so. What did being "saved" mean? Who was I being saved from?

She said it was hard to explain in a short time but explained about asking Jesus to come into my heart, to cleanse me of my sins. She told me everyone was born a sinner and had to ask Jesus to cleanse their hearts of sin. I was still confused. Did it have something to do with washing my heart?

I think she saw the confusion and asked if she could pray for me and with me, for understanding. I told her yes. She grabbed my hand, bowed her head, and softly started talking. I was used to the gestures of praying because we started and ended every group time with it, but I didn't understand why or what prayer did.

Her nickname was "Grandma" even though most of us weren't related to her. I was comfortable with her, and I wanted to learn. I listened intently to what she was saying as she "spoke to Jesus." When she finished praying, she said "Amen" and when she looked at me, I told her that I wanted what she had. I wanted to have a heart like hers, I wanted to be able to talk to Jesus the way she did.

She said that if I was ready, she would help talk me through it, but I had to say the words and mean them. She told me that even though people were saved, they still sinned and needed to pray for forgiveness, guidance, and direction. She said the reason we sang songs in church and in our group at her house was a way to worship and praise God for all He's done for us.

I told her I was ready to ask Jesus into my heart and I wanted to keep learning. As we sat in the pew, with darkness settling around the church outside, the only sounds I heard were her voice and mine repeating what she said. I didn't just say the words, I felt the words. I felt warmth surround me, as if I were being hugged, from the inside and out.

We sat there quietly for a bit, her holding my hand. I cried and let some pain and hurt out. She whispered prayers while I rested my head on her shoulder. Her hands were thin and arthritic, but roughened and strong from years of gardening and hard work. There was a peacefulness I never felt before.

I had to get home and she let me know I could always ask her questions. She said she was proud of me and handed me a blue Bible. It was new. I asked her when I had to give it back and she told me I didn't. It was a gift for me to keep, to learn, to study and to share with others. I thanked her and hugged her hard before I left. I still have that Bible.

I got home, did my chores and homework, then began reading. I began to understand our group work in Awana, the books of the Bible for our bookwork. I learned scripture and I began to understand what I was reading. It would take me longer to understand what it meant to be a Christian. To live and believe, to have unwavering faith.

I had finally found the person who had been with me for years, keeping me safe, holding my hand through the tears, fears, and anger. I had found the one that walked me back to the light. I found Jesus. He was always with me, but now I found Him. He helped guide my steps, comforted me and no matter how many times I strayed, lost my way, He was there.

"Grandma B" was who I aspired to be like. She had a huge heart of gold, filled with love for Jesus and her "family." My heart hurts as I write this. She celebrated her 100th birthday, but her health declined. She was tired and wanted to go peacefully. I wanted to finish this before she departed this earth. She guided my wayward self towards Jesus. I'm so grateful to have been wrapped in her love. My heart would not be the same, if it hadn't been for "Grandma B." I am forever grateful and will carry her spirit with me.

The summer of 1985, my grandfather, my dad's father, passed away. A man of few words, but a man many people loved and respected. He was a hard man, with two volumes, loud or silent. He was a proud man. He loved my grandmother, his kids, and his grandkids. When I was younger, I was often curled up next to him in his chair, hearing his breathing and heartbeat, feeling loved and protected, while smelling the Swisher Sweets, always in his pocket.

I never understood how much he drank when I was younger. I was probably too young to notice. Now, I recognize the demons, frustrations, and memories he tried to drown in whiskey.

He was a man that took pride in everything he did. He drove a school bus during the day, snowplows during the winter, and after the kids were gone from school, he cleaned the schools, as a custodian. He was a World War II veteran, and no job was ever considered "beneath him." I learned to respect anyone who worked hard and took pride in the job they did.

I loved watching him and my grandma get ready on the weekends to go out square dancing. She was about 4 foot 11 and he was at least 6 feet. They made a striking pair and won several contests. I loved my grandma's dresses, the ruffles and lace that flew out as she spun. Some nights, they taught us the basics of square dancing and we would practice while they were gone.

There were also disciplinary lessons. You knew the lesson was disciplinary when the tone of his voice changed. Everyone immediately responded to his direction or commands when this tone was used.

He also had a booming laugh. It made you smile. After suffering a stroke, my strong and hardworking grandpa became a shell of who he was. It was a hard thing to see, especially when you didn't understand.

A couple years later he had another stroke and passed away. I cried along with rest of the family and friends. As I stood with my cousin and sister at his funeral, I looked at him, he still looked proud. He received a military tribute. I knew I had to do something to make him proud.

At the age of 12, I decided to join the Army. My dad was disqualified because of his asthma. After I told my sister and cousin, they said they would too. We all kept our promises!

After the funeral, I tried to find comfort in the Bible. I didn't understand how the Bible and my beliefs tied into my daily life. I struggled with the day-to-day fighting with my mom and my sisters and now, I didn't know how to deal with death. Little things became big stressors. The tension was unbearable. I had no idea how to cope or ground myself, I kept looking for a physical escape. There was never enough quiet to write and provide a release.

At times the pain, hurt, and feelings of hopelessness weighed heavier on me. The burdens I carried threatened to pull me completely into a darkness that might numb or end me if I just let it envelop me fully. Most of my free time was spent at a friend's house down the road from me.

It was easy to ride my bike down and many times I would spend the night. There I learned about Dungeons and Dragons, heavy metal, and how much I hate scary movies. The primary source of these lessons were my friend's older brother and his friends. However, I also found an outlet in my friend. We shared about the darkness that seemed to surround and follow us.

My friend's older brother and his friends tried introducing us to "weed," or marijuana. I hated the smell of it and somewhere in the back of my mind I knew that it wasn't a good thing to get into. I feared not being in control even though I was already drinking beer and liquor. The alcohol did not concern me, I felt I could control the effects by limiting my intake. Additionally, I had always been around alcohol. Marijuana was an unknown.

Neither of us fully understood or were able to describe the darkness. We did not recognize the trauma impacting our daily lives. We talked about different and painless ways of letting the darkness take us. Wondering if the pain would end. I don't think either of us genuinely thought about killing ourselves, we just didn't understand. We only knew the darkness seemed to be the best way to release the burdens and pain.

Through therapy, I have the ability to look back. I did not want to kill myself or be gone from the world. I wanted the pain to end and the memories to stop haunting me.

I used to think suicide was selfish. This thought may have developed from how family discussed my mother's brother killing himself and leaving his beautiful wife and children behind. My thoughts have changed. So many want to end the pain and the darkness that engulfs them. Some turn to alcohol, drugs, prescription drugs and/or risky adventures. We tried alcohol. It didn't help much, so alcohol use initially, was minimal.

We found new ways to distract ourselves from the pain. We explored on our bikes, played sports, and increased the amounts we were drinking. Our bike rides would take us by abandoned houses we thought to be haunted, different structures that were overgrown with weeds and forgotten, hills we could race down.

When I wasn't playing sports, I started hanging out with older kids. Access to beer and whiskey to help numb the pain was easier to obtain with older kids. I was averaging approximately 3-4 hours of sleep a night. I rarely did homework, yet managed good grades, except in math. I hated math. It required patience and thought.

I couldn't wrap my head around why the alphabet was mixed in with numbers, fractions, division, and word problems. Math equated to effort. I did not have a natural inclination for it like I did with the other subjects. I struggled with algebra 1 but was better with geometry. When it was time for algebra 2, I didn't even try. I did enough to get by with homework while in study hall. I passed enough tests to keep my grades up, but at the end of the year, I had to take a final and a regent's exam. Regents' classes and exams were a requirement in New York State if you were planning on going to college.

I wasn't planning on college, but my guidance counselor explained if something happened while playing sports, an injury could disqualify me from the military. He was like the devil and hoodwinked me into regents' classes.

I passed my exams, but my math teacher sat me down and told me I could do better if I applied myself. She suggested I go to summer school so I could learn in a different setting and then retake the regent's exam. While I contemplated the idea, a few of my friends said they had to take summer school for at least one class, so they could graduate the following year.

I decided it wouldn't be that bad and I would still be able to hang out with friends on the way to and from summer school and afterwards. I signed up and applied myself because it was 1 class for a couple hours each day. I still didn't enjoy math, but I did well on the retest. It worked out because the ASVAB would have algebra and geometry questions.

There were always keg parties at the local hangout, where teens of all ages could be found. At one party, at the ripe age of 13, I found myself talking with an older friend that I had known for years. He asked me to go for a walk. Soon, we were kissing, and he had me on my back, on the ground. Soon, he tried sticking his penis inside me. The pressure hurt and I squeezed my muscles tighter to keep him out. When I was finally able to use my hips and legs to knock him off me, I ran away towards the bonfire as I heard him laughing.

How does a 13-year-old fully understand what happened? Most adults don't process it until years later and this was someone I'd known for years. He hugged me at my grandfather's funeral and offered condolences. He was someone I saw every day in study hall. When we heard things about rape or sexual assault, it was always portrayed that this only happened by strangers.

It took me a long time to fully process what happened and even longer to trust. The first time I chose to have sex, it was because I wanted to have control over who, what and when. I was almost 16. I chose to have sex and intimacy with my boyfriend. I wasn't technically a virgin, but I wouldn't allow the molestations and sexual assaults take my virginity away from me.

My sport activities expanded as I tried out for basketball with my sister and our friend. I cheered and played basketball during my 7th- and 8th-grade years. I also discovered a love for softball. While in science class, after raising my hand to answer a question, my teacher commented on how big my hands were. He then threw me a softball that was always present in his hand or on his desk. I caught it, one handed, and he asked if I'd ever played. I hadn't, and he told me to show up for practice the next day.

I didn't have a glove and the only sneakers I had were the ones I wore for cheer. I didn't have athletic shorts, but I showed up. There was snow on the ground, so we practiced in the gym. Our school was small, we didn't have a JV or junior high team at the time, so I was practicing with upper classmen.

My teacher who told me to show up was the softball coach. He gave me a glove to use for practice and after showing me the form to throw, I was left to catch and throw with another girl. The sound the ball made as it hit the leather of the glove was something I fell in love with. It made me feel strong when I threw the ball and it hit its target. The coach called me over to where the pitchers and catchers were warming up. He showed me the basic mechanics of pitching, how and when to release the ball to hit my target, the catcher's mitt.

It took a while to find the coordination, comfort of my stride, and timing on when to release the ball, but I loved it. I threw several pitches to get the feel of the mechanics before I was called to the batting cage. Our batting cage consisted of a net that could be pulled out enough to encompass a batter, pitching machine and coach, but kept the balls from flying all over the gym. Batting was also a new experience.

We started off with stance and mechanics, when to swing, how to swing, where my hands needed to be on the bat, how they should line up and coordinating my step with my swing. I started hitting off a tee to get the feel of holding the bat, swinging, and stepping into the ball. After Coach saw I had the hang of it, we did some soft toss, where he threw a ball from the side, and I hit it. The crack of the bat as it smacked the ball soon etched out throwing the ball as my new love. Batting practice was my favorite part of practice.

As I progressed to the pitching machine, practicing seeing the ball, watching it all the way to my bat and getting my timing, I soon found my stride and kept knocking the ball to the opposite end of the batting net. After a couple weeks of practice, we had tryouts and I made the team, as a 7th grader. I practiced daily, with the team and at home. I didn't have anyone to catch for me, so I spray painted a square on the side of our barn. I had to paint several squares as I kept breaking the wood on the side of the barn. My sister, KJ, threw me pop flies, grounders, and line drives.

I told my dad I'd made the team, but I needed a glove. He sent me a box with my first ever glove in it, a Wilson. I still have it. He also sent me money to buy softball cleats. I oiled my glove and broke it in as I was instructed, to keep it in great shape. I ran sprints as if I were running bases and had KJ stand in as if she were a batter, while I pitched. That year, I was allowed to attend a pitchers and catchers camp at Cornell University. I learned new techniques, different ways to throw and how to control my throw.

I earned a spot on the field playing right field. I was used as a pinch runner when we needed to advance bases and score. Stealing and sliding into bases, calculated off the pitcher's release of the ball and the time it took the catcher to catch and throw the ball, was exhilarating. My sprints were paying off because I didn't get thrown out. I also had no idea that I was using algebra in my head.

Softball became more than just a passion; it was an obsession. I learned how to hit from the right and left side of the plate, how to hit the ball where I wanted it to go and when it was most effective to drive it hard for a home run. My 8th-grade year, I sat at the bottom of the batting order, but almost always got on base. The following year, I moved up to 4th batter, clean-up, due to the number of homeruns I was hitting by the end of my 9th-grade year. Batting became a physical release of the pain I lived with.

I pitched some games, depending on who we played, but as the seniors graduated, my speed landed me in left field and then centerfield because I could cover more distance. I loved outfield. I could see the entire field, anticipate where batters would hit, and change fields as needed to cover. My role, backing up 2nd and shortstop, was essential as well.

Sophomore year, I tried out for shortstop. The position between 2nd and 3rd base. It was a hot spot of activity for hits, to work as the cutoff for left field and covering 2nd base when runners stole bases. The team was young. The sophomores were the oldest upperclassmen on the team and many of us had been working together since 8th grade. We became a well-oiled machine and began winning. We ended up in the sectional finals again, winning cool jackets. This was the 3rd year our team won sectionals and my 3rd jacket.

I also started playing soccer my 9th grade year. Once I hit high school, I was playing a varsity sport in every season, soccer in the fall, cheer in the winter, and softball in the spring. I tried playing varsity basketball my freshman year. Basketball was a winter season sport, so it coincided with cheer. After the first game, and me getting 4 quick fouls, my coach (also my softball coach) sat me down. He said, "I can't believe I'm saying this, but you will be better off sticking to cheerleading and not basketball, you're too aggressive for this sport." I was grateful for his honesty. I liked cheer and put my focus there during the winter for the remainder of my high school years.

There are a few games that stick out in my mind, in soccer and softball. In one of our softball games, my 10th-grade year, I kept stealing 2nd base and my coach set a play for me to steal 3rd so I could be in scoring position. We were the visiting team, so we had to get another run and hold them from scoring the last inning. I took off for 3rd and before I slid into the base, I heard the other coach yell, "Take her out!" I went into the slide and as I was sliding on the ground, the catcher threw the ball to 3rd, but instead of the 3rd-baseman's glove, she threw the ball at my face.

I took a direct hit to my left eye. By the time I finished my slide and popped up on 3rd, I could see a huge protrusion from my left eye. I likely yelled a cuss word. My coach called time and checked my eye, asking me if I wanted a runner. I said, "Hell no, I'm scoring." The next chance I had to score; I took it. As I barreled down the 3rd-baseline, the only thing I had in my sights was home plate and the catcher. She didn't get out of the way, and I didn't try to avoid hitting her as I slid. My feet popped up as I slid across home and planted firmly in her chest protector, pushing her backwards into the backstop.

I have no idea if we won the game or not, but as I left the game, prom was on my mind. It was in 3 weeks, and I was going to have a shiner on my eye. The marks left from the stitching of the ball seam healed first, but the black eye and discoloration lasted a while.

During one of our soccer games, I was playing goalie and it was one of the few games my mom was at. We were playing her alma mater school. It was towards the end of the game and the girl took a shot on goal. As I dove for the ball, the kicker kept coming and kicked at the ball again, which was in my arms. Instead of her hitting the ball, her foot connected with my face, hitting my nose and my left eyebrow area.

I stood up with the ball and continued playing. I thought my nose was running and wiped it with one of my goalie gloves, which was bright yellow. When I pulled my glove away, the referee saw the blood and called time. He came and checked me out, I said I was okay and would finish the last few minutes of the game.

Adrenaline is what carried me through the rest of the game and the "good game" comments as we slapped hands with the opposing team, at the end of the game. I walked to the sideline and grabbed the medicine chest to help carry our equipment to the bus. Not even halfway across the field, I became lightheaded and unfocused. My friend Hazel helped me to the bus while my coach and mom talked with the other coach and referees.

I sat down once I got to the bus. I felt weird. After the bus was moving, Hazel told the coach that something was wrong with me. My coach checked me out and said she thought I had a concussion. She had me stand up and walk the aisle so I wouldn't fall asleep. The bus driver radioed the bus garage, told them to call the ambulance and have them at the school when we arrived.

My mom got to the school before the bus. One of the men from the ambulance recognized her and told her they were there to check me out for a possible concussion. When the bus arrived at the school, they checked my pupils for responsiveness. Not seeing the response they should, my mom said she would drive me to the hospital because she could get there faster.

Hazel rode with us, keeping me awake by talking to me and asking questions, while my mom drove. At the hospital, the only thing I remember is being afraid of the IV needle. My mom had a nurse tell me I didn't need an IV, which calmed me down. After answering a bunch of questions, I had an x-ray or some scan on my head. I had a concussion and needed to be monitored for the next couple days. My eyebrow was cut, and they put a butterfly Band-Aid over it.

I have a scar, camouflaged by my eyebrow, and my left pupil doesn't dilate or react to light the same as my right pupil. Close-up pictures clearly depict the difference in my eye dilation. I will always have side-effects, but I'm thankful for my hard head.

During the off-seasons, I worked on getting stronger and faster while working on my skills. I began riding my 10-speed bike to/from practice during the summer workouts. I swam for hours when I was in AZ, rode bikes and ran around the neighborhoods. This was something I could control and excel at if I worked hard.

The normal teenager behavior continued. Rebelling and talking back, pushing the limits enough to know they were pushed. Knowing wrong from right but pushing the boundaries of rules and laws. The town cop and a neighboring town cop knew me by name and sight. Sports kept me in school and out of real trouble.

The daily chores that came with life on a farm included chopping and carrying firewood, shoveling snow, mowing the lawn, gardening, feeding the cows, chickens, pigs, goat, dogs, gathering eggs, baling hay, washing dishes, laundry, sweeping, vacuuming, and so on. They all came before I could worry about homework. Not that homework was ever a primary concern of mine.

Late nights, early mornings, it didn't matter, homework and sleep waited until chores were finished. I quit doing homework. If there was something that needed to be done, I did it in study hall or on the bus. This allowed me time to read (for pleasure) for hours when I got to bed. I read because KJ continued doing her homework or studying and the light was on. I couldn't sleep much anyhow.

Up until my senior year, I had my own room with a door, but I could hear KJ in her room across the hall. As the relationship between my mom, me and KJ grew more antagonistic, the stress and fights continued to grow. My junior year and KJs sophomore year, she chose to live in Arizona with my dad. I thought about it, but I knew I would be leaving town sooner than KJ and I had learned how to avoid being home.

KJ came back my senior year, her junior year, because she wanted to be there during my senior year. We chose to share a room so we could spend more time together when we were home. By this time, we were both playing varsity soccer and softball. During the winter season, I was cheering, and she was playing basketball. The year she spent in Arizona; she developed her skills as a basketball player. She was more confident in other sports, too.

My senior year, I watched KJ play in a basketball tournament with the top players from other teams, she ended up being named MVP of the tournament and region. I couldn't have been prouder to be cheering for her. That night as we were driving home, I was driving our 1978 Ford F150 truck, with a friend and one of my younger sisters, KM, while KJ was riding with her friend, behind us.

It had snowed quite a bit and the roads were icy under the snow. As I came to the bottom of the hill and the stop sign, I hit ice and couldn't stop. We wound up crossing the main road, where we were supposed to turn. We hit a dirt road which was in worse condition than the main road. I knew I couldn't slam on the brakes. I had to get control of the truck before we hit the bridge, which would be iced over.

There was a chance we would drive off the side of the bridge. I used every technique I had practiced from doing donuts in parking lots, drifting, and what I learned about driving in snow and ice. I finally managed to get the truck stopped, inches before hitting the bridge and going in the water.

After we all caught our breath and I made sure everyone was okay, my friend said, "Wow, that was really impressive." KJ's friend pulled up beside us and after seeing we were all okay, we slowly drove home. KJ was shaken. She felt helpless watching us spin and slide. After our friends left, we crawled into my bed to help each other calm down.

That year, with KJ and I playing next to each other at shortstop and 3rd base, our softball team went to states and lost by 1 run in the semi-final game. It wasn't my best game, in the field or at bat. I carried the weight of that loss for a while. I don't think we lost 1 game during the regular season. We started the season off with a bang. I was the lead batter in the first game of the season, and I swung at the first pitch, hitting a home run. We won 36-19. This is one of the few articles I kept from the newspaper. The line that made me keep it all these years is this: "Greene homered on the first pitch of the game, opening the floodgates in a contest that saw 49 hits."

I had some great coaches, even when we didn't agree. I even got benched during a game for running my mouth. These coaches shaped me, on and off the field. They taught me sportsmanship, discipline, perseverance, and that hard work will always beat talent when talent doesn't work hard. Coaching is more than knowing the game. It's developing athletes' skills, building their confidence, inspiring a work ethic, and listening/observing what the athlete is messaging. These coaches not only taught me the love of the game, but also the love of coaching.

My softball coach typed each of us letters at the end of every season and I received my first one in 1986, after we won sectionals. It says:

"Dear Suzy;

I can see it coming, Suzy. The talent is there, it just needs a little refinement and lots of confidence. You have a great arm and super speed. We will work on the hitting and fielding. You know there are several open spots on next year's starting team. I am looking for you to fill one of them. Work hard on your game, Suzy, and you will not be disappointed.

You would be a super lead-off hitter. With your speed, a steal at second would be almost automatic.

I've enjoyed it, Suzy. I hope that you have had fun this season."

Not only did I have some great coaches, but my Superintendent that encouraged my decision to join the Army also sent my teammates and I letters for cheer my senior year, after our cheer team took first place in a competition:

"While on medical leave in mid-January, I was very delighted to receive the good news that you, the varsity cheerleading squad, placed first in the Pom-Pom competition.

I did not read about this happy event in the newspaper or hear about it from anyone associated with our school, but instead received a message from one of the judges in this contest. It was very gratifying to receive this information this way, from a judge who felt that the cheerleading squad stood out above all the other competing schools and were more than deserving of their first-place finish.

Congratulations to you, your fellow teammates, and your coach for achieving this honor. I'm sure that this award was the result of much hard work on all of your parts with the results, however, being extremely rewarding."

Then my final letter came from my softball coach, after losing in the semifinals, he helped me see the entirety of what our team did and my softball career in high school.

"I think one of my fondest memories of you is when as a skinny seventh grader you made the great hook slide into second base. At the time I don't think you understood what happened—I am not really sure you understand it yet!

You have had a great softball career. The last couple of seasons have really been super. You run exceptionally well, throw and field well. Your leadership and hustle are factors that don't show up on stat sheets, but they are every bit as important. I have been very fortunate over the years to have good athletes at shortstop and centerfield. You certainly upheld the standards at those positions. I have enjoyed almost every minute of our time together. I still regret the incident last season. I hope that you will let me slide by on that one. Thank you for all the great games and hustle. From a coaching standpoint, you have made my years with softball very enjoyable.

Sincerely,

Coach"

This man taught me so much, to include, but not limited to humility and being humble. I kept these letters for years, not to be braggadocios, but to read when I stumbled in confidence, to remind myself that I am more than just 1 thing, that with hard work, determination, and a great coach/mentor, I can do anything I put my mind to.

To Coach Skiv and Coach Harris, thank you for believing in me and helping me become the person I am. I have never forgotten the lessons I've learned on and off the fields. You both taught me I was more than a title someone labeled me with, I was more than my circumstances and I could rise above the limits others and myself tried to place on me.

Growing up in a small town, surrounded by small towns, you could go almost anywhere, and someone knew you or recognized you. There's definitely a lot to be said for growing up and living in small towns and on a farm. You learn how to live off the land, take care of animals, hunt, fish, and forage. There are many things to explore when you are surrounded by nature, completely alone but never feeling alone.

With 4 girls from my mom and a boy and girl from my stepdad, things tended to get rowdy on weekends, during summers and holiday vacations. The farmhouse had 4 rooms upstairs with a large open closet at the end of the hallway, beside my room. That closet held Army dress uniforms and many other treasures. It was big enough that we could sit in the closet under the clothes and read, color, or play games. My room faced the road, so my window opened above the porch. This allowed me to climb out the window and onto the porch roof. I sat up there for hours, listening to the sound of the 2 large maple trees rustle in the wind. During the summer, I was almost camouflaged from the road with all the leaves. The winter left me more exposed, but after 5 P.M. I had darkness to conceal me.

We had a hammock made of macramé that hung between the two maple trees during the summer. It was another spot where I spent hours reading, writing, and daydreaming. I read *Charlotte's Web* in one day lying in that hammock. I also perused magazines and gossip papers my grandpa (mother's father) would drop off by the bag full, almost weekly. He managed the laundromat and car wash across the street from his house and collected all the leftover items at the end of the week. When you live in the middle of nowhere, with no cable TV and only 2 basic channels, you read what you can get.

The maple trees were a huge part of our outdoor life. We made cities, towns, bridges, and construction sites, in the dirt surrounding the trees. We used Tonka trucks at times, when we needed to really move some dirt, but most of the time, it was Matchbox cars and Hot Wheels. We had a tire swing that hung from one of the huge branches and we used to see who could climb the highest. During the fall, we added leaves to the scenarios, raking them into different shapes, creating houses, with different rooms. The winter brought snow so we could make snow angels, build snow forts, igloos, snowmen, and walls to defend ourselves during snowball fights.

My stepdad drove truck for a grocery supplier and had to get up extremely early, usually between 1 and 3 A.M., so he would be in bed no later than 7 P.M., deemed "quiet time." That was hard for 4 loud, active, and rambunctious girls, especially during the summer when it was lighter longer. We found ways to entertain ourselves, away from the house because the windows had to be open for air circulation. They eventually invested in a window air-conditioning unit to help cover the noises of us running around like wild banshees, yelling, laughing, and screaming as we played hide-and-seek, tag, and jumped on the trampoline.

There was a camper shell for my stepdad's pickup truck and during the summers, it sat down by the barn, on blocks. My sisters and I started using that as our "schoolhouse" while we worked in schoolbooks that were no longer in circulation. I have no idea where they came from, but they kept us occupied and our minds working during the summer. My younger sisters loved "school" and working in the workbooks, I think mostly because we older sisters allowed them to hang with us. KM became a teacher.

It's odd we enjoyed playing "school" when I didn't care much for schoolwork and KJ seemed to struggle with it. Maybe it was the structure, something that kept our minds busy once chores were done and no adult was around to take us to the swimming hole (the creek that ran through the property). When the camper shell wasn't available and when we didn't have pigs, we would use the pigpen as our schoolhouse. After we cleaned it out really well, we would put the desks or tables and chairs in that my grandpa had brought over.

There were a lot of out buildings on the farm, the chicken coop, wood shop/wood storage, pigpen, garage, and the barn. The wood shop we tended to stay away from unless we were working on a specific project. We had to gather eggs every morning from the chicken coop and when we had the pigs, we made sure they were fed.

There were many access points to the barn and storage within. There was a backside storage area that we had the goats and the bottom part of the barn, under the main floor and hay loft, where equipment and hay was stored. This was also where the cows came in for feeding. During the summer they spent most of the time in the pasture, grazing on grass and the apple trees when they could reach them. The pasture and fencing ran from the barn to the property line of our neighbors, and up to the little dirt road that went between our house and neighbors. The pasture from the barn had a gate that we could go through to cross over to where "the lane" (walkway to the swimming hole) began.

There was a fenced-in area off the side of the chicken coop, by the lilac trees that butted up to the pasture fence. Sometimes we kept rabbits in there too. We tried ducks one year, but we lost one that wandered away, but the one we had the longest was named "Weiner." We had outdoor "barn" cats, to help keep mice and other pests from the house, barn, and hay field. And one house cat, we nicknamed him "Fat Cat," but his name was Smokey because of his gray and black color. He wasn't much of a people person and if you laid in his spot on the couch, he would lay on your back.

I paid dearly for sleeping in Smokey's spot. I was wearing a tank top and laid down on the couch after lunch, so Smokey laid on my back. We must have both been sleeping pretty sound when the phone rang. It scared us both. When I jumped up from the couch to answer it, he dug his claws into my back. There was nothing but skin for him to dig into. For the remainder of that summer, I sported scratches on my back.

We also had a family dog, Taffy. She had a golden color that reminded us of taffy. We had gotten her as a puppy. She loved following us around, messing with the cows and swimming in the creek with us. When I sat on the porch swing reading, Taffy would sit on the floor under my feet, or on the steps leading to the porch. When we got home from school, Taffy was waiting by the mailbox for us to get off the bus. Taffy was killed by a drunk driver when I was 21, leaving all of us heartbroken.

We had a large garden on the side of the driveway, where we grew all kinds of produce. The garden had to be tended daily during the summer, as produce needed to be picked. We would grab a head of lettuce, radishes, onions, peppers, tomatoes and whatever else we chose to add to a fresh salad for dinner. There was a strawberry patch and in October we were able to pick our own pumpkins we had grown. There was a corn field between the pigpen pasture and the cow pasture. It made a great hiding place during hide-and-seek. The rhubarb patch did, too.

When we had dry days with no rain in the forecast, us girls would head up into the woods to help our stepdad cut, chop and load wood. It was much cooler in the woods, and it was a great joy being surrounded by the smells and sounds of nature. During one of our "breaks," my stepdad was working on the saw, or refilling it with fuel, anyhow, we girls interpreted that as a break. My younger sister, SE, and I wandered around and stepped onto a pile of leaves, like we normally did, only this time it was an underground bees' nest. They came from all sides, stinging both of us.

Our screams could be heard over the running chainsaw and my stepdad came running to discover us surrounded by a cloud of bees. He told us to run to the truck and he gathered the equipment and loaded it quickly. We jumped in the truck. Once we got away from the area, he stopped and poured cold water on both of us to help rinse the stings until we got to the house.

When my mom saw the 2 of us, she started a bath with oatmeal to help take away the sting. Before we got in, she checked us over to make sure there weren't any actual stingers in us. We had at least 100 stings each. SE was more affected because she was younger and smaller. She welted up worse than I did. The next day I was back in the woods helping gather firewood, more cautious of where I stepped.

There were times we would try our hands at vehicle reconstructions, wood working, and building random things. My stepdad had an old Ford Bronco he used to pull the trailer with when we would get wood for the winter. My stepbrother suggested we take the doors off it to make it cooler. We set out to figure out how to get the doors off. I was on top of the hood by the window, holding the door up while my stepbrother was cutting the hinges. When I was getting off the hood, I planned to slide down the front to jump off. As I started sliding down, a piece of rusted metal cut my outer thigh, about 6-8 inches long.

I was wearing white shorts when it happened but had no idea how bad it was. Initially, all we could see was the white, meaty part of my skin. It looked deep, but there wasn't any blood, so I thought I was okay. Once I stood up and started walking, the bleeding started. Now we were all a bit freaked out. Mostly because of what we had been doing with the Bronco without permission. My shorts started turning red from where they skimmed the top part of the cut, and I couldn't stop the blood running down my leg. Everything else happened in a blur. My sisters grabbed washcloths and towels from the house, while my stepbrother ran to get my mom. There was yelling as we climbed into the vehicle to go to the hospital.

I ended up not getting stitches, although I probably should have. I had butterfly bandages lined down my leg with orange streaks from the iodine where we tried to clean it. I couldn't swim for weeks and had to be careful with all activities because the cut kept opening. But my cuts and scars weren't the only ones. KM fell while we were playing in the house, hitting her head on the corner of a chair. It split open and she needed stitches. My stepbrother put his top teeth through his bottom lip after going through the "poop shoot" and landing in a pile of hay on the barn floor. The "poop shoot" was the top level of the barn, also called the "hay loft" where we loaded and stored bales of hay during the summer, to be used for food during the winter.

We created an area under one of the beams by the open area of the barn to slide the bales of hay under to the ground floor, when it was time to feed the cows. It was a hay chute but without an actual chute. We started using the chute so we could slide from the second story into the pile of hay on the bottom floor. We spray painted the beam with green paint, so everyone knew it was the "poop shoot."

We had friends and neighbors that would come over to slide through the poop chute, a few of them wound up with scars under their bottom lip, too. Another activity in the barn was playing a game we called "deer." There was one hunter, with a BB gun and the rest of us ran around the barn, as deer. If we were shot, we had to sit out and the last "deer" standing, became the hunter. Surprisingly, no one lost an eye or was seriously injured.

We had a creek running through our property, about a mile from the house. The creek was like a border between the hay fields and where the hill started with all the trees. We could walk through the hay fields, to get to the creek, but it was frowned upon during summer and hay season. There was another way to get there, down a tree-covered, grassy path that we called "the lane." The lane was the border from our property and the neighbors. We would go berry picking along the lane for jams, pies, and other goodies. There were apple trees, and we could grab a snack while walking or out playing.

We dammed a section of the creek to make a swimming hole. This is where I learned how to swim. We found places to jump from, climbing higher every time to get an adrenaline rush. Our neighbors had a section by their house that was more like a mini waterfall. The water ran faster and was deeper in this area, making it more dangerous than other areas of the creek. It was covered by trees, branches and roots extending across the water to create the waterfall. After a hard rain, the water was like mini rapids, swirling and foaming. This section was also near the treehouse we built, so we were tempted to swim and play there.

The treehouse we built was at least 1/2 a mile or more from the house, making it a nice getaway from the adults, parents, and little sisters. We found wood from random places around the farm, to make a floor and build the walls. My stepdad brought aluminum home that they were no longer using for the signage on the side of the semis, which became our ceiling and some of the siding to help keep rain out. We used some carpet that had been pulled from the house, to cover the floor.

We took turns on the weekends that my stepbrother and stepsister came over. The 3 older girls would sleep in the tent, at the bottom of the tree, in the middle of the lane, while the boys, my stepbrother and neighbor boys, slept in the treehouse. Then we would switch on other weekends. One night, the girls were sleeping in the tent, and it was getting ready to storm. Just as we had settled down for sleep, the boys threw a firecracker outside the door of our tent. It was so loud; we came out of the tent yelling and ready to fight. At the same time, we heard someone yelling for us and saw a flashlight walking towards us.

We realized it was my mom. She didn't think it was safe for us to stay out in the storm because the creek was known to rise quickly and flood the area. We'd heard the boys snickering until we saw the size of the hole in the ground. The firecracker was an M80, a military-grade explosive. Not only did the girls get angry, but my mom did, too.

We all walked back to the house as it started raining, leaving our eggs and bacon we had planned for breakfast, in the creek to keep cold for the morning. After we all got back to the house, dried off and obtained dry bedding, we all crashed on the living room floor. Early the next morning there was loud knocking on the door.

When I took my bleary-eyed self to the door, there was a guy standing there, looking extremely official. I didn't recognize him, then he showed his FBI badge. My mom pulled into the driveway shortly after and greeted him. He said he had some questions for us as to our whereabouts the night before. I was thinking he was looking for us because of the noise from the M80. My mom said we had been camping until the storm came in and she came to get us, then we all slept in the house.

He asked more questions, and we all answered the same. When he asked about eggs, I said we had them tied up in a waterproof bag, tied to the tree so they could stay cold in the creek and didn't attract any critters. We didn't grab them because of the storm and were gonna go back to get them for breakfast if the creek hadn't flooded. That's when he told us that our neighbor's house had been egged on the inside. In the kitchen and side room where we hung out to watch TV. I have no idea who did it, even though one of the neighbor kids stayed in trouble, but I know suspicion was cast over all of us.

When the egging incident happened, we had been living next to our neighbors for years. They were like grandparents to us, and we loved their entire family. There were some friends of our parents we didn't enjoy, but we loved our neighbors. We would run over even if our mom wasn't with us. We listened to their stories, how they met, about World War II, and the struggles leaving their homeland and family to come to America.

The wife, Maria, was from Austria, growing up and living through the ugliness of World War II. Her tiny homeland was overrun with Germans as they looked for "Jews" to take to the concentration camps, or those who were harboring them. The husband, Rob, had been a soldier in the US Army, fighting in the war. There was so much love and respect for each other, as well as lots of lighthearted joking and kidding.

I loved listening to Maria speak in her native tongue while she worked around the big farmhouse. Their kitchen was the main hub of activity, there was always something simmering, baking or ready to be made. Rob loved to cook and bake too and would surprise us with goodies hot from the oven while we were there.

Most times when we came over, Maria was in the kitchen or in the tiny little room off the kitchen, where they had their TV. We would run in and give them both hugs, telling them about our day at school, if it was a school day. During the summer we would hang out on their huge front porch, sometimes playing under their big pine tree in the front. The pine tree branches came to the ground and was big enough that several people could sit under it comfortably where it offered shade and cooler weather.

When it was colder, we would hang out in the room that could be considered a parlor or maybe a music room. I loved this room because there was a dark red velvet chaise lounge in front of the bay window. I would curl up there to read a book, write in a journal or just daydream. Rob was talented and would play the violin for us. Most of the songs were fun and upbeat but some were haunting, filled with sadness.

Watching this big strong guy hold a tiny instrument and play it so magically helped me choose my instrument when we started band in 4th grade. I spent hours practicing with him, but I didn't have the patience or talent. He had to have been partly deaf to sit there with me as cringing sounds came from my violin, and I later switched to the clarinet.

They had 5 kids, 4 boys and 1 girl. They were all older than us. Two were in the Army, but they taught me how to shoot guns and get into mischief. The oldest would run past our house when he was home, with his long muscular legs, wearing his short shorts. This was next level crushing for me, not like the innocent crushes of my early grade school years. They were all charming and funny which added to their good looks. One became the town cop in a nearby town and the other joined the Army after he graduated high school.

The daughter went to college a couple hours away, but when she came home, I was able to spend time with her. I listened to her stories, watched her brush her gorgeous thick hair and banter with her brothers and parents. She was tough, like her brothers, and never backed down from a fight with them.

They all loved and adored their parents. Many times, we would find the boys helping in the kitchen, randomly hugging their mom and the daughter would be outside helping her dad with the farm. When they were all around the dinner table, sharing stories, jokes and messing with each other, you could hear the love for each other.

They weren't all together very often due to the military, but we had a chance to get to know their wives and soon their kids. There were stories of adventure, travel, different sights, and cultures as I sat and listened for hours. When I made the decision to join the Army, they were some of the first I told.

I can't imagine how different and boring it would have been living on a farm, with only 2 houses nearby, if they hadn't been who they were. There was no hesitation on them welcoming us into their home and hearts. When our duck, Wiener, went missing, we knew he would be found somewhere near their house.

To be accused of damaging their house was such an insult, but it also angered me to know someone did something like that to them. If it had been any of the kids that were at the treehouse with us that night, they got an earful from us. No one ever admitted to the damage, but it also never happened again.

They sold their farm to move south a couple years before I graduated high school. They had an older red MG convertible they stored at our house during the summer, until they had a place they could put it. It had to be restored and fixed up, but KJ and I would sit in that thing for hours, singing and acting like we were driving across the country. We would look at maps and chart our course, we would pack our small suitcase with random items, make signs about going to California and repeatedly sing songs by the Beach Boys.

Growing up in NY, California was such a different world for us. California Girls, Surfin' Safari, Surfin' USA, and Little Deuce Coupe were our favorites. Kokomo was added to the list after that was released. KJ and I have since made several cross-country trips, but we still haven't done our red convertible trip. That is in the planning stages now!

At the end of summer, the farm started to change. The leaves turned colors and then fell, the garden was mostly barren, jars of canned goods lined the pantry and cellar shelves. We sold beef cows and pigs, but also kept some for our family. There were days of cutting, chopping, grinding and sausage stuffing. During hunting season, there were deer to clean and dress, cut up and store for the winter. Most of the stuff we ate came from what we had raised and slaughtered, shot during hunting, or grew in the garden.

During the winter we rode the snowmobiles as much as we could, racing each other and pulling people behind the snowmobile on an inner tube. We had an Arctic Cat 440. Riding it was one time I really enjoyed being in the snow. We would take turns pulling each other on the tube, but I preferred to drive. We drove across the creek when it was frozen, sometimes stopping to ice skate or play a version of hockey.

One time, I was pulling KJ on the tube, flying through the hay field. There was quite a bit of snow. We didn't always know what was underneath. This time as I drove over an area, it took the snow and ice off what seemed like a little tree. By the time KJ and the tube hit it, it was standing straight up, still hardened from the ice, slapping KJ in the face, and forcing her off the tube. Luckily, no one was hurt other than some aches and pains.

We used to see how close we could get to the creek in an open area and turn fast to make the tube airborne over the creek. There were a few times when the tube hit the bank as it made its way back to solid ground. We felt invincible because we were bundled in so many layers of clothing, jackets, and overalls to stay warm.

After we were all chilled and our clothes were wet, we trudged into the house. We hung our wet clothes and boots by the fire stove. Once down to our bottom layer over our long johns, we were ready for hot cocoa and food.

We spent many hours around the kitchen table playing board and card games, while clothes dried, or storms and blizzards stirred. We only went out for firewood. There were times we tied a rope from the porch steps to the woodshed because it was a complete white out with snow, or the snow was so high that you could only see the pom-pom on the top of our winter hats.

Monopoly was one of the favorite games because all of us could play it and it kept us occupied for hours. There were times we would leave a game to go back outside, then come back in to finish it. As we got older, we found that each of us seemed to have a particular strategy to win. Acquiring all the railroads was a top goal and then trying to get St. James Place, the orange section, and the yellow section with Marvin Gardens. Boardwalk and Park Place were high value but didn't get as much traffic so those were added for bonus cash.

Candy Land, Chutes and Ladders, Sorry, Chinese checkers, Stratego, Battleship and Scrabble were other favorites. We had Operation, but we went through batteries too fast so that was a special treat. We played go fish, war and learned how to play Euchre when we were older because there was always a Euchre game going on at our house on the weekends or at a family friend's house. Playing Euchre enhanced my trash-talking skills.

I started dating my sophomore year and had a couple serious relationships. The first guy I dated, Colt, I had known before we dated. We initially met when I was in 6th or 7th grade because he was the brother of one of my friends, Lynn, but he didn't take notice of me until my freshman year when I started playing sports and became a cheerleader. He played soccer, basketball, and baseball so I saw him regularly.

At the end of my freshman year, his sophomore year, he signed my yearbook and said we should keep in touch over the summer, while I was in AZ visiting my dad. I sent him a letter first, to say hi, test the waters, and give him my address where I would be spending the summer in AZ. This was the start of our letter-writing campaign.

Our letters that summer shared our hopes, dreams, fears, and goals. We really got to know each other over the next 3 months. I returned to NY in time for the first soccer practice of the season. He also played soccer. I was finishing practice when I saw him for the first time after the summer of letters. We went for a walk and found we were as comfortable talking in person as we were via letters. When we were walking, he wrapped his hand around mine. I was taller than most of the boys and I usually felt like an amazon, but he made me feel tiny. Holding his hand felt natural and made me feel safe.

We created a lot of memories together over the years. When we started dating, we had outside forces, including his family, standing against us. His family didn't approve because I didn't come from the right type of family. Although Lynn and I had been friends, played sports together and cheered together, our relationship was strained our freshman year when I made the varsity cheer squad, and she didn't. This was exacerbated, when her father, a member of the school board, made an agenda item out of why his daughter didn't make the team, but I did.

I was the only freshman that made the varsity squad. I worked hard before tryouts. The judges were neutral, and no one knew who I was. I was judged off my performance and I nailed it when I finished my cheer with a roundoff into a split!

Colt and I were dating for approximately a month, when we got into an argument one afternoon before I went to soccer practice. He went home and then took off in his car, a beautiful classic car he lovingly restored for months. He crashed after losing control on a dirt road.

I heard the sirens during practice but didn't think anything of it until someone came and told his sister he had been in an accident. She looked at me and screamed, "What did you do?" Practice had just finished, and I heard them tell Lynn he was home and banged up. His car was totaled. He was lucky to walk away with bumps and bruises. Grabbing my bag, I ran from the field to their house. Their parents weren't home yet. I saw his car first, then I saw him and hugged him. He squeezed me tight. When his parents got home, I left to go home.

I struggled with the accident. Wondering if he intentionally tried to hurt himself, to get my attention, or if it was truly an accident. It broke my heart seeing his car covered with a blue tarp and as this was big news in our small town, there were all kinds of stories and rumors about what happened, whose fault it was. People knew I was nothing but trouble. Our relationship made it about 5 months before I tired of the drama. We both went on to briefly date other people. I dated Sam a few months, then Colt and I reconnected over the summer. We decided we had something real and wanted to give it another chance.

My junior and his senior year, we spent a lot of time together, at school, after school, before/after sports, and when he went to work, cleaning a shop after hours, I went with him, to keep him company and help him clean the shop. We would catch up on our respective day. I was at the Vo-Tech center the 2nd half of my school day and sometimes we didn't get to talk as much before games, so we caught up while he worked.

We became great friends while being a couple. We spent holidays together, went to prom and started talking about the future. He knew how much I loved photography and chose to go to college where I was actively looking, even though in the back of my mind, I was still thinking about the Army.

After he graduated, we spent some time together before I left NY. I drove cross country, in a semi with one of my uncles, to visit my dad and KJ. Once I got to AZ, I called Colt to let him know I made it and when I would be back home. A female answered his phone, but it wasn't his sister, Lynn. There were a lot of voices in the background, as if they were having a party. I asked to speak to Colt, and the girl laughed, said he was "busy."

As I hung up the phone, it felt as if I had been punched in the gut. No one was home except KJ. I told her who I suspected answered the phone, but she couldn't believe it. Whether KJ called Colt's house or Colt called, somehow, I wound up talking to him and letting him know I made it. He provided the standard, I love you, I miss you, blah blah blah. All I heard though was "he waited till you were gone, then gave in to temptation." I have no idea if he ever did anything. There were rumors. A few days later, I returned to NY to work our school's food booth at the county fair.

There were a couple schools that had long standing food booths at the county fair. Working the food booth allowed students who finished their junior year to earn credit hours toward their senior trip. If we had a parent or others work for us, their hours counted as our credits, too. There was a group of us who signed up for every morning shift, with our parents helping.

Each morning for a week, my mom and I worked from 6 A.M. 'til noon or 2 P.M., depending on how busy it was. A friend's dad ran the grill, frying eggs, bacon, sausage, pancakes, and potatoes for breakfast and switching to burgers, brats, and hotdogs with fries for lunch. We had a great crew. Everyone knew who was doing what, and who needed help with order deliveries or big crowds. It was fun, but exhausting. There were a couple days that I worked the morning and the night shift, which ended at midnight.

The hot, humid days zapped your energy, but our young age pushed us through. We even made time for rides, games, and the different exhibits. One of the nights I was working, I ran into Colt, who I hadn't talked to since the girl answered his house phone.

During one of my breaks, I saw Colt working at a booth that sold sports items. Whether it was habit, the friendship we'd had, or feelings we still had, I agreed to talk to him after my shift. I was nervous and excited to finally be able to talk face to face, but I was still carrying hurt and disappointment.

We talked for a few hours after my midnight shift ended. I went without sleep before my 6 A.M. shift started, but it was worth it. We worked things out and aired our grievances and hurt. It was the last day of the fair, so I could catch up on sleep after this last shift. We made a date for that night, not to do anything or go anywhere special, but just to sit under the stars and talk like we did before.

This was summer love; the kind stories are written about. Him going to college, making the best of every moment, knowing it will change. We swam in the lakes, went to the drive-in movies, drove aimlessly on back roads, made plans, and promises we wanted to keep, wondering if we would.

Although we spent time together before he left for college, I focused on having KJ home for my senior year. Both of us were preparing for soccer season. I had a regular gig babysitting almost every day. Colt visited me while I babysat, sometimes staying a few hours, waiting until I finished so we could do something together.

We started drifting apart as he prepared for college, and I focused more on conditioning and soccer practice. By the time he left for college, hopes of maintaining what we had or hoped to have again were dwindling. My focus turned inward as I began my senior year. I visited Colt a few times at college, but it was strained. Giving him my class ring to wear was likely a last-ditch effort to revive our relationship.

A war raged in my head, heart, and soul. Staying in NY and going to college meant a miserable life of petty jealousy and drama. I didn't want that for either of us. Too many people from this small town were stuck in their "glory days" of high school with nothing new to share. For some, personal growth ended after high school and most never discovered their true potential. I did not want to live with that.

Colt knew I was struggling with what I wanted to do after school. He suggested we go to college and get a place together, then he started talking marriage and kids in the future. I was suffocating. The pull of the Army grew stronger. I wanted a husband and kids someday, but I was not ready to start planning them just yet. If I chose him and college, I would ruin our lives. If I wasn't going to be true to myself, he would be married to a shell.

During my senior year of high school, I felt a stronger pull, almost a pulsing energy surrounding me and my thoughts, about leaving the small town, he said/she said drama and boyfriend drama. I had an appointment at the US Army recruiting station the day after Thanksgiving to take the ASVAB, to see where I scored and what kind of MOS, military occupation specialty, I would qualify for.

Ideally, I wanted to be a combat photographer. I had been taking photography/graphic arts at the local vocational/technical training center my junior and my senior year and thought it would be a great use of my skills. Capturing images that shared war stories, training obstacles, and daily Army life.

Unfortunately, that job was closed. I had to choose something else. I chose a job in communications for 2 reasons: 1) it was a shorter commitment, if I didn't like it, then I could reclassify/train for another job; and 2) it sounded cool. I needed to get a top-secret clearance to do the job because I would be seeing and hearing classified information.

This was before access to the Internet, Google, or social media, so what better way to be in the know, than to be on the front lines of it?

The week of Thanksgiving, Colt came home from college, but didn't tell his family. He stayed at my house. After he arrived, I told him I had an appointment to take the ASVAB test. It was what I needed to do.

Colt was supportive and went to the center, where I took the ASVAB, with me. I passed the ASVAB testing with extremely high scores and had my choice of job. We enjoyed the weekend together.

I soon learned about the Delayed Entry Program (DEP). Under the DEP, I could enlist, pick my job, get my ship date, and start the top-secret clearance paperwork. My recruiter said I could start as soon as my mom signed the paperwork, because I was 17.

The recruiter came to the house that night because I was ready. My mom tried playing a mind game, asking me, "Well, what if I decide not to sign?" It might have been my face, my tone, or her toying with me, but she finally signed the paperwork. I asked when I could go to MEPS and get started. The recruiter laughed and said he could take me the next morning, I was ready.

I officially joined the US Army, DEP on December 2, 1989, and for the first time in a long time, I felt a weight had lifted off me. The entire day was spent in Buffalo, doing the processing, interviews, and questionnaires. Some of my shenanigans in high school almost disqualified me for the job and clearance. Who knew mooning a bus load of soccer players would be frowned upon by the government? I was told to stay out of trouble, no more drinking, fights, mooning or other shenanigans.

As we drove home, it was dark, and had started snowing. While I was happy, telling Colt I officially became property of the US Army and wouldn't be joining him at college put a damper on my joy. I would leave for basic training within 3 weeks of graduating high school. KJ was excited it was official and said she would follow my footsteps the next year after she graduated. She also told me Colt called a couple times.

When the phone rang, I knew the time had come to tell him and break his heart and mine. He was mainly upset I hadn't told him beforehand, otherwise he was happy for me and told me I would do great. We planned to see each other the next weekend. I would drive up late Friday after our game or early Saturday.

At school, the news spread fast about my enlistment. Guys in my class asked about the process. I provided my recruiter's number and advised he would help them get started. The underlying buzz at the basketball game Friday night was my joining the Army. Yes, the one jumping, yelling, cheering, and prancing around as the captain of the cheer squad.

Several people came up to me after the game to shake my hand. I finally felt accepted in this small town. A town where I gave my blood, sweat, tears, laughter, and heart, on the playing fields and off. Small towns thrive on sporting events. When the town cheers for you on the field, you've won their respect. When they cheer for you off the field, you've won their heart.

As I drove home that winter night, I was warmed by the respect the community showed me. As I sat at a stop sign to head out of town toward the little village we lived in, I saw my ex-boyfriend, Sam, drive by. We were in the same grade, and he played basketball. We didn't talk much due to the relationship he was in, but we saw each other daily at school and/or games. We never spoke much, so it was odd our eyes met and held as he drove by, taking his girlfriend home.

After he passed, I made my turn and drove home. I stopped to get fuel at the general store, the only option in our village. A few locals talked about the game and me joining the Army. They shook my hand and said good luck. I drove the last mile home and as I parked the truck, lights pulled into the driveway behind me.

After the lights turned off, I saw it was Sam's car. Why was he at my house? He lived about 2 miles in the opposite direction. There was no reason for him to come by my house. I got out of the truck and stood with my arms crossed giving him a questioning look.

Sam heard the rumors that I signed up for the Army and he wanted to hear if it was true. I confirmed I was in the Delayed Entry Program, and I shipped out to boot camp on July 17th. Sam had been thinking about joining and asked more questions. Sam asked if I wanted to go for a ride so we could talk more. It would be warm in the car, and we wouldn't wake my parents.

We drove around the backroads, talked about the Army, and rehashed our dreams of getting away and doing something bigger. We stopped on a dirt road, halfway between his house and mine and talked for another hour or so when he asked me what Colt thought of my decision.

I shared how closed in I was feeling before I signed, but that Colt was supportive. We briefly talked about our relationship with each other, after dating for 6 months our sophomore years. Sam hated that we couldn't even say hi anymore. We shared jokes and memories from when we dated. The more we talked, the more our seats reclined watching the snow. We were both ready to be out of the small town. Something sparked physical contact, which led to intimacy or how we accomplished intimacy within the confines of a small car. Things heated up and we were sharing a front seat having sex.

Having sex in a two-door hatchback with a guy who stood over 6' was no small feat. Sam took me home and we didn't make any plans to talk or see each other, except at school. It felt like a goodbye.

Once home, I bathed and got ready for bed. I needed to leave in a couple hours to see Colt. After I arrived at Colt's college, we got some food, walked around campus, looked at the studios and dark rooms where he had been working. We went back to his dorm; I watched a movie and fell asleep while he did his homework.

I woke up a couple hours later with Colt snuggled up against me. I had to tell him I'd slept with Sam, his former teammate. The guy I had officially, though unofficially, gave my virginity to. Colt knew I saw Sam every day at school and that he lived about 2 miles from me.

This was a new situation. How do I bring it up? I didn't even know why I did it. It bothered me that I was going to hurt Colt, yet I didn't have regrets about Sam. Maybe I needed this extreme for Colt to understand I was leaving. In hindsight, this felt like my way of cutting the tie with Colt and avoid dragging out the pain over the next 6-7 months.

We picked up dinner and brought it back to the room so we could talk. We started with my enlistment, that I may be promoted if one or more of the guys joined before I left, and my interviews. He laughed about the shenanigans and how the guy doing the interview hadn't found any humor in it.

He could tell there was more. He told me he would love me regardless, but he needed to know it all. I explained how I was feeling trapped, like my life was being suffocated. He didn't know what it was to carry the stigma, of not fitting in, being talked about in a negative manner, that no matter what you did, how hard you worked, you bore the scars of your childhood. For him to fully understand, I shared what happened when I was younger, that my virginity was stolen from me when I was 5, when I was raped by a family member.

Colt didn't know what to say and he hugged me hard as the tears started falling. He held me and told me it didn't matter, I mattered. He listened. He didn't judge and he hugged me with all he had. He held me as I cried for hours, grieving the little girl that was lost. A childhood forever tainted with ugly memories. The beauty of who he was and how he handled my revelations initiated my healing.

Neither of us knew how defining those moments would be in our lives, but I will always be thankful he was the one that I was able to be completely broken with. I shared I had slept with Sam and how it felt like a goodbye. I couldn't continue to hurt Colt, I told him we needed to make a clean break. He would always own a big piece of my heart because of how gentle he was with it.

I stayed the night with him. We talked into the night as he held me. The next morning, I left before he woke up. The goodbye was going to be painful, and I didn't want to prolong it.

I was promoted the next week. My recruiter and another, drove me to the station in Syracuse for the official ceremony. I missed a day of school. We had a home game that Friday night, a couple days before winter break and all the college kids were home for the game. I didn't know if Colt would show or not, we hadn't talked since I left his room. After the game, I talked to a couple people in the parking lot while the truck warmed up. Conversation stopped and everyone looked over my shoulder.

They said hi to Colt, then bye to both of us. I turned around to face him. He stood there with a box of my stuff I had given him. It hurt to make eye contact. There was a deep sadness in his eyes. There seemed to be something else simmering, not rage or anger. He wanted to fight for us but respected the space I asked for. The only thing I wanted back was my class ring, the one thing I never got back. He told me he had lost it.

The holidays passed in a blur. We practiced for the cheer competition. We had placed and done well every year, but I wanted the championship. We had the squad and routine to do it. We practiced for hours. Timing, choreography, over and over, with music, without music. This was our chance.

School started again. It was still winter, but our class was in spring break and senior trip mode. We worked hard raising money and would be flying to Orlando, Florida, to go to Walt Disney World, Epcot, Universal and the beach. Final plans were made of who was going, who wasn't, and who might if they could get help to cover the cost. There was also prom, graduation preparation and more.

Most of the college kids were still home. Tom had graduated the year before with Colt. He had dated Colt's sister, Lynn, off and on, and apparently, they were off again. He was home from the military for the holidays. We knew each other, but usually only conversed when others were around. I was shocked when he singled me out during halftime at our basketball game. He was in the Army, and I figured that's what he wanted to talk about.

Instead, he heard Colt and I broke up and I was single. I laughed and confirmed we broke up, but I wasn't dating before I left for the Army. He asked if he could call me sometime and I said sure. I returned to the game and didn't think much about it, but other people saw us talking. Colt and Lynn heard about it.

I was used to rumors. My focus was on the cheer competition. We all stayed at one house the night before, got ready and went to the school to get on the bus. Nerves were stretched, but excitement was high. Individually and as a team, we had each put in the work needed to win and our confidence reflected that belief. Part of the excitement and nerves was due to the Buffalo Jills, cheerleaders for the NFL Buffalo Bills, were going to be our judges. That meant, judging would be neutral. Every team had a fair chance.

On January 26, 1990, our cheer squad took first place in the pom competition, with a routine to "Wild, Wild West" by the Escape Club. I have never been prouder of a group of girls than when they announced our first-place win. We had all worked hard, put in long hours enhancing and perfecting our routine, jumps, stunts and pyramids. One of the key factors in our success was each of us doing a toe touch at the same time. Some of the girls were not able to do the toe touch prior to the hours of practice. Another factor was one of our pyramids. We had the small girls, normally flyers, set up as the base and the bigger girls, usually a base, as the top of the pyramid.

A feeling of accomplishment settled over us. The effort, time, energy and sweat paid off. The girls glowed with pride. They had each given their all and left everything on the floor.

Reflecting back to when the idea of cheer occurred to me, all the practice and work to make the squad, and additional practice to advance to the varsity squad, I realized no one could take my accomplishment from me. No matter what I come up against, I can be stronger than the obstacle. That mindset has served me well and I continue to live by it.

I enjoyed the perks of being a senior and the freedom of being single. Sam and I continued to spend intimate time together. Our class set up a senior skip day, but those of us who played sports had to check in at school for a brief amount of time before we could "ditch." We went bowling, then found a bar open at 10 A.M. We hung out at the bar, then meandered to a friend, Liam's house, where we played cards, drank, and watched movies.

As the end of the school year neared, our class was ready for our senior trip to Florida. The Latin teacher going as an advisor for the boys, was attractive. Every afternoon when I got back to school from the Vo-Tech center, I spent in his office while I waited for lunch.

He had been at the school a couple years. He was the "tall, dark and handsome" I'd always heard and read about in romance novels. I was infatuated with him. It was a high school girl crush. Nothing would ever happen, but I enjoyed listening to him talk, especially when he spoke Latin. It was easy to crush on him because he listened to me and cheered for me.

Tom started calling and writing letters. He was in Texas. Not much thought or effort went into the letters, we didn't have a "relationship." In high school, I didn't like him much because drama and rumors seemed to gravitate around him. He was handsome, but a jerk. He had an attitude. He thought he was untouchable because of who his dad was.

Additionally, he had dated Colt's sister during high school. She and I had been good friends until the cheerleading incident our freshman year, but I remembered the times we spent together, cheering our 7th- and 8th-grade years, soccer, and we even tried to have a "seance" at her house. We almost burnt the chandelier in the dining room. When I dated Colt, we hung out watching movies and double dating. After her car accident she had issues with her back and was never quite the same.

By the time Colt and I broke up my senior year, Lynn and I we weren't speaking. We were cordial passing each other in the hall, but that was it. As we got ready to leave for our senior trip, the tension was so thick between us and others in our class. At some point she received dead roses from Tom, but I knew nothing about it until others talked about the incident.

It created a bigger barrier between her and I because she thought I was part of it. The trip was fun, but there was awkwardness and tension mixed throughout. I enjoyed myself, especially after working so many hours at the county fair to earn the hours to pay for it.

We returned home and went back to our routines. I was spending extra time in the dark room at the Vo-Tech center. I loved shooting in black and white and had some great shots from our property, as well as around the Vo-Tech center.

Mixing the chemicals in the dark room to develop my film, negatives, and photos was soothing. Capturing an image through the lens was one thing, but watching it slowly come to life in the developer was like watching my creation being born. I preferred being outside, capturing nature, random unposed shots, and the rawness of nature and people.

As graduation grew closer, our class did, too. Classmates who historically ignored each other were talking and hanging out. The senior trip brought many of us closer. We decided to have another senior class weekend before graduation.

A classmate's aunt owned a house on the lake. She invited us to spend the weekend. We took a huge tent and some smaller ones, we played card games, played in the lake, told old stories, shared funny memories about each other, drank wine coolers and for the first and last time, I smoked a cigarette. After a couple puffs, I decided cigarettes were not for me. The smell, taste and feeling were disgusting. The smell of the smoke, even on someone's clothes or in their house/car gives me a headache, making me nauseous.

I had gone to several proms, beginning with 9th grade. My sophomore year I went with Sam. That prom contains pictures of my black eye from softball.

The prom with Colt, my junior year, was the most memorable and enjoyable. We always had fun together. As prom approached, I was frustrated I couldn't find a dress I liked. I didn't want to wear a huge southern belle-type gown. I asked my mom to make me one. I found the pattern I liked, picked the emerald green, satin fabric and the black lace underlay for it. I felt grown up and sophisticated when I put it on during fittings.

I found all my accessories to wear; shoes, jewelry, hair pieces and added a touch of fun with elbow-length lace gloves. They were made from the same fabric as the underlay, with a thin band for the middle finger and a small rose sewn on top of the finger hold.

I kept my hair simple, pulled away from my face. We went for dinner and ice cream at our favorite place, before the prom. We had as much fun eating, as we did at the prom.

I felt comfortable in my own skin for the first time. My dress fit perfectly, I was with someone I loved and trusted, and I wasn't worried about what anyone else thought.

That was a night of growth for me. I realized without the dress; I was still the same person. I didn't have to get "gussied up" to feel like a different person. I just had to be comfortable and confident in my own skin. I didn't have to be part of a "couple" to belong, I could belong on my own. I was my own person, with my own personality, thoughts, dreams, and goals, it was time to be ME.

My journal entries from so long ago reflect this event as a turning point for me. I had always been shy and self-conscious of how tall and gangly I was. I never considered myself "smart," even though I was regularly on the high honor roll. I won the national spelling bee contest for our school, beating out "the smartest person." She was 3 years older than me, but I won. Instead of the teacher congratulating me, she asked how I cheated.

I didn't let that defeat me, but I never felt "proud" of my win. I had a vast vocabulary from reading adult romance "smut" books. I tended to see a word once and remember how to spell it. I did well in English, despite a contentious relationship with the teacher. She nicknamed me "Polly Perfect." Polly was short for Pollyanna.

I researched "Pollyanna" as I never heard the term before. There was a movie released in 1960, titled "Pollyanna," and the definition is "an excessively cheerful or optimistic person." Apparently, I rubbed her the wrong way. I strove to be more "Pollyanna" like because my locker was outside her classroom door.

I wore bright, happy colors and made sure to say things like, it's a great day today, what a perfect day to be in school, and whatever new "positive" thing I could think of. When we moved to the upper-class English teacher, I still made sure to share some sunshine when I saw her.

I didn't have much reinforcement or encouragement to believe in myself, which is why junior prom stands out. I found a new inner strength and belief in myself, not just in sports, but in all aspects of my life. It was within me, buried under the trauma, hurt, and mistrust.

A common theme, after my parents divorced, was my mom telling me how much I ruined her life. I was the biggest mistake of her life. This affected my self-worth and confidence, but I didn't see how much until that prom night.

I began taking control of who and what I was, who and what I was going to do and be. I wasn't going to let anyone control me, psychologically, emotionally, mentally, or physically. I was a caterpillar inside the cocoon. I saw glimpses of the butterfly I would be. It was a slow transformation, and I didn't know I was going through the process then. Something inside my mind had changed.

My senior prom, I went stag with KJ. I didn't want to share the night with anyone. We had fun that night with all our friends.

After prom, it was the last month of my senior year. It seemed to be in fast forward. We finished softball, took our class graduation photo in cap and gown, took our last exams, and anxiously waited to hear we'd all passed. Family was flying and driving in from all over the country.

Before and after graduation, our house stayed full as my mom and aunts prepped food for the graduation party. Our traditional meatballs were the main dish so people could make meatball subs, there were pasta, potato and macaroni salads and cheeses galore. My aunt that lived with us for a while made my cake. She was working as a professional cakemaker/baker and made me a gorgeous 2-layer cake.

The day before my graduation, my uncle got married and I was part of the wedding party. Tom and I were talking more. He was planning to be home for graduation and wanted to see where our relationship would go. He sent me a heart-shaped locket as a graduation gift. I wore it with my bridesmaid dress.

After the wedding was over, I walked outside the church, getting ready to head to the reception, when I saw Tom standing off to the side. He was wearing his Army dress greens. It stopped me in my tracks from surprise and he looked handsome.

He went to the reception with me, and I introduced him to most of my family. We talked about graduation, and my leaving for basic training in 3 weeks. We had fun dancing and talking, getting to know each other. He seemed more mature.

He drove me home after the reception and hung out at the house. After he left, I readied myself for bed and tried to process my feelings. I liked the new version of him, but I wasn't sure it was real or a game.

The next day, I got ready for graduation and had to leave early. It rained that day, and our auditorium was under construction, so our outdoor ceremony was held under a tent. I made sure I wore flat sandals to avoid sinking in mud or tripping. There were 21 kids in our graduating class and graduation didn't take long. Then I asked my step-grandma for my $50 because I wasn't pregnant.

After graduation, I drove home for my graduation party. There were about 6 of us having big parties, so I hung out at mine for a few hours, talking to family, friends, coaches, and teachers. I left once it started getting dark and made my rounds at the other parties, saying goodbyes to some of the parents I wouldn't see before I left for the Army.

The last party was the party we all decided we would end up at. It was a farewell party and last goodbye for some of us. Our graduating class had 5 of us departing for the military, including Sam, under the DEP. I was the first scheduled to leave.

Friends from other classes were there along with older friends who already graduated. After a few hours, I wanted to leave to spend time with my dad before he went back to Arizona. Tom was there and we talked, but it felt awkward being around other people. He asked if we could do something before he left.

I said sure and left with KJ, after we said our goodbyes. I have no idea if we hung out or if he stopped by briefly before he left. I was focused on my next chapter and making it through the last few days at home without getting into trouble. My alcohol intake my senior year was significant with the house parties, hill parties and bonfires. During the winter when it was too cold to be out, we played card games in the sugar shack where the sap would go through the evaporation process with heat to become maple syrup.

I eluded trouble with underage drinking, which was fortunate as I needed to get a top-secret clearance. I was doing good staying out of trouble until the last night I was home.

A group of us who frequently hung out decided to go to the basketball courts next to the school. This was a regular hangout place, whether you were there for a pickup game, a game of horse or you were just sitting around talking. The basketball courts were one of the few places in town that had lights that came on after dark and it was centrally located making it easy to congregate there.

The basketball courts were also located behind the town cop's backyard. He generally left us alone unless we were too loud, causing trouble or racing around town. There used to be an old bank on the corner which provided a barrier, but they tore that down to add parking spaces at the school.

None of us were juvenile delinquents, well, most of us weren't, but we tended to push our limits. We were most problematic on Halloween. We would raid our parents' refrigerators for eggs, or stock up at the grocery store, for that night. We didn't stop at eggs, we added shaving cream and toilet paper to the mix.

We used the eggs, as our "ammo" as we bombarded each other with them. Some threw eggs, some smashed them on the top of people's heads and others sprayed people with shaving cream or rubbed it in faces. The height of this activity was usually on the corner where the bank was.

The bank was an old brick building that was an original from when the town was homesteaded, and oil was found. The oil boom lasted for some time, but as with most towns, once the oil, copper or natural element runs out, the towns are left to die. The bank couldn't keep its doors open and when it closed, nothing took its place. It became our hangout. We could sit on the steps and watch traffic on the main road, wait for people before and after school, or hang out during lunch breaks.

This abandoned building became a battlefield. The sidewalk in front was wide. The bank's steps provided an advantage over taller people, or you could hide around one of the corners, waiting to ambush someone trying to escape.

The town cop knew his kids were part of the shenanigans until they graduated high school. His primary concern was that we were safe and not hitting cars as they drove by. We were good, but a few eggs missed their targets and went astray. The first year my class joined in, we were the targets. The next year, we changed our tactics.

We went to Hazel's house to prepare. We wore one-piece snowsuits over our jeans and sweatshirts. We put a hooded face mask over our heads and tucked the collar of our snowsuit under the mask. We wore thick rubber gloves to help us smear the shaving cream and give us a better grip on the eggs.

Once we were ready, we walked to Lynn's house on the way, to gather reinforcements for our ambush. When we got to her house, we didn't know there was a hole dug by the back corner of the house and we couldn't see well with the hooded masks on so when I heard an "oooofff" I had no idea what had happened. Someone started laughing and using my flashlight, I saw one of the girls had fallen into the hole.

We tried to stop laughing for 10 minutes before we could finally catch our breaths and help her out. When you're wearing a one-piece snowsuit, with clothes underneath, you don't want to laugh because it can trigger the need to go to the bathroom and possibly wetting your pants from laughing too hard. You can't escape the confines of the snowsuit fast enough when things become urgent.

After that obstacle, we rounded up the rest of our crew and supplies. None of the supplies were damaged during the fall. We made our way down to the meeting point, but we came from the back side, through the soccer field and playground so no one could see us. The plan worked perfectly! We spread out and hit almost everyone in the area with shaving cream and eggs.

No one could figure out who we were because we were completely covered until we started laughing. We had a lot of fun that night and helped clean up the mess we had made the next day. It became a tradition as did the cleanup party the next day.

During my senior year, we participated in the festivities, but something happened. A car stopped in the middle of the road screaming at us. We didn't know if it was hit, or they thought someone was getting hurt and stopped. As we tried to figure out what was going on, the town cop headed down the street in his patrol car.

The patrol lights came on, the siren started blaring and it took us less than a second to realize we needed to split up and get out of there. As we were running, we were shedding the bulk and letting it drop where it landed. The group I was with ran through side yards and backyards to stay off the main street and when we rounded the corner, we saw him with his spotlight.

The only place we had to go was towards him, or over the wrought-iron fence, into the cemetery. I have never been a fan of cemeteries. When we would visit my mom's dad, after he moved next to my aunt, they lived across the street from a cemetery. My grandma and uncle were buried there, and my cousin's dad was buried there so we would walk around looking at the gravestones.

As we got older, my cousins and sisters started daring each other to go into the cemetery when it was dark. I hated the eerie feeling that crawled over me and one of the nights we were running around when we all heard a noise and took off towards the road. While we were running, there was a freshly dug grave and I fell directly into it. I have no idea how I got out, but I didn't like it.

I felt as if my heart was going to come out of my ears it was beating so hard. That was the last time I went into a cemetery at night, until we were running from the town cop. Even though I hadn't done anything, I didn't want to be part of the suspicion so I ran as fast as I could towards the cemetery.

The only way in was over the fence because we were on the back side. The fence wasn't that high, but high enough that you couldn't step over it. The pointed decorative iron pieces on the top of the fence made scaling the fence tricky. It wasn't so pointy that it would cut you, but it was pointy enough that when I went over, my sweatshirt got snagged.

I was still trying to run and realized I wasn't going anywhere. Initially, I thought the cop had grabbed ahold of my sweatshirt, but I knew he wasn't close enough and I was the second person over the fence. I tugged on my sweatshirt and heard a ripping sound as it came free of the fence. I still have this sweatshirt, with the hole in it.

We continued running, through the cemetery and cut back across a yard towards the school again, staying in the shadows and close to the trees. I don't know how long he looked for any of us, but after hiding and working our way back to the school, we split up. That incident put all of us on the cop's radar for the rest of the school year. He would wave and say hi when he saw us at the basketball games, different events around school, but none of us sped through town again.

4
US Army

The night before I left for basic training, a group of us were hanging at the basketball courts and one of my friends was supposed to be coming to take me home. We lived down the road from each other and rode to school together most days.

I didn't know he was going to bring his car, which was an older rebuilt muscle car with a souped-up engine. You could hear it coming before you saw it and one of his favorite things was to squawk the tires and see how much smoke he could create.

Not only did he make a loud entrance, but he had a couple of our friends with him, alcohol in the trunk and some items that were no longer legal in our state. What I wasn't aware of was the trouble that he and the other guys had caused in the next town, less than 5 miles from us. There had been an ongoing rival between some of our kids and a group of theirs. It was never anything serious, but a few times punches were thrown between the groups.

This night there had been some instigation and taunting between the two. As it was starting to get physical, their town cop drove by and saw someone with a club. After he chased the other kids down, my friends came to the school to get me.

Just as I was getting in the car, the cop from the other town showed up, along with our town cop. Neither of them knew that I hadn't been with them, but I was seen in the vehicle when they pulled up. While we were being pulled away from the vehicle to be questioned and the vehicle searched, a couple state troopers pulled up.

I had a sinking feeling in the pit of my stomach. Something bad must have happened for this type of manpower. I prayed one of them wasn't the cop that was friends with my parents or the town cop that was our neighbor.

I was "sweating bullets" while I waited to hear what was going on. Each of us went with a different cop and placed in the back of their patrol car. I didn't recognize the trooper that I was "escorted" by. I felt defeated walking to the patrol car, and I dropped my head.

He put me in the back of the car as I saw the town cop pull a club from the back seat of my friend's car. I still had no idea what had happened but knew from the looks on their faces it wasn't a good thing. While I was sitting in the car, I saw them pop the trunk and find the beer. I yelled, "Fuuuuucccccckkkkkk," in frustration. It was 10 P.M. I wasn't 18 yet. I was out past curfew, and my recruiter was going to be at my house to pick me up at 3:30 A.M.

I leaned my head back on the seat and closed my eyes. I couldn't watch the shit show unfolding. I was a suspect. I heard the door open, but I didn't open my eyes until I heard a voice I recognized, call my name. I looked at him and said, "I don't know what happened, but I wasn't part of it. I've been sitting here at the courts since 8 watching the guys play basketball." He said they needed to ask me some questions to help sort the situation out and we would go from there.

The town cop that witnessed the altercation came over to ask me questions. We were not friendly. He was a bully with a badge, especially to those of us not from his town. I had to bite my tongue and keep my attitude in check when he questioned me, otherwise it would be worse for all of us.

He started out with "I'm not your biggest fan, you and your crew are troublemakers in my town, but I know you weren't in the vehicle earlier. I also know that you're shipping out to basic training soon, which I can't say that I'm sad about. So, here's the deal, answer my questions truthfully and I will get you out of here." I nodded my head and he asked, "Do you know where your friends were coming from earlier?"

I said, "No, and I didn't know the others were going to be with him." He replied, "Okay, did you know they were going to try to start something with the crew in my town?" Again, I answered, "No," and he asked if I had ever seen the club in the car before.

I told him, "We don't ride in this car, we're normally in his Bronco and I've never ridden in this car. Tonight was the first night I've been that close to being inside because he was supposed to give me a ride home. I didn't see the club in the car when I was getting in and wouldn't have known about it until I saw you pull it from the back."

He nodded his head and looked away towards the car, then looked at me again and said, "I appreciate your help and your honesty. I knew you weren't in the car because I only saw 3 heads earlier and the guys playing ball said you had been here since 7 or 8. The cop from here also vouched for you, he said you waved when you got here because he was in his backyard, and he didn't see you leave."

I nodded my head but didn't say anything as I looked at the guy I saw almost daily, patrolling our town, the guy that chased us during Halloween and saw him nod at me. I saw a guy that was honest and fair, that just wanted to make a difference in his town, and I was grateful for him.

The cop that had been questioning me asked when I was shipping out and I said in a few hours. He laughed and shook his head. "You're free to go once we clear here, but I want you to go straight home, so you don't find any more trouble. I don't want to see you in my town again, even when you come home on leave. I hope the military can make you a productive member of society. I want to thank you for choosing to serve our country, but I don't want to see you in my town again. Do you understand?"

I nodded my head yes and replied, "I don't want to see you again either and I have no desire to be in your town." He laughed again and said, "Good, we have a clear understanding. I'm going to finish up with these guys and cut them loose after I cite them. Can you get another ride home?"

I said, "Yeah, one of these guys can probably give me a ride, I don't want to risk having this guy dropping me off in his patrol car." They both laughed and he told me to get out of there. I walked up to our town cop and said, "Thank you, you're a good guy and doing a great job." He pulled me in for a bear hug and told me to go do great things. He said one of the guys volunteered to give me a ride home when I was ready.

I thanked him again, said goodbye to my other friends, wished them all well when they went to basic training, and I got in the truck. As we pulled away, there was a bittersweet feeling, knowing when I came back, everything would be different. I would be different. I left my troublemaker days on that court and had no regrets when we drove away.

When we got to my house, we were laughing about how close I had come to missing the most important date of my life. I told him I had done so good the last couple weeks and less than 12 hours before I was set to be picked up, I almost lost it.

An hour before my recruiter arrived, I thanked my friend and said goodbye before going in to get my bag. I washed up, changed my clothes, and climbed into bed with KJ. She asked where I had been, I laughed and said it's a long story. We laid there and talked some before we went to the kitchen and wait.

When I saw the lights in the driveway, I gave everyone hugs, said goodbye, grabbed my bags and walked out the door. My recruiter asked me if I had everything and put my bags in the trunk.

Most of the 3-hour drive, I stayed silent in the back seat, watching the farms in the moonlight, committing landmarks to memory, listening to the 2 recruiters talk quietly in the front.

I did all my final paperwork then waited to be officially sworn in with the others. They took us to a hotel where we stayed the night before picking us up to take us to the airport.

We were fed an early dinner then they read the roster of what time each person had to be ready. All our flights were for different times and places. They broke us into smaller groups for the rides to the airport. We were told where we needed to be for our time slot and not to be a second late. That was my first lesson in, if you're not early, you're late. I still arrive 30-40 minutes early for appointments.

I was exhausted after being up all night, but I was keyed up, nervous and anxious too. I wondered what would happen if I just didn't show up and left for home. I had never been nervous about my decision until then.

I called my dad and left a message. I walked around the hotel, through the gardens and decided to go sit by the pool. While I was sitting there, a couple other people leaving the next day stopped by. We talked about where we were going for basic, what our job was going to be, if we were going active duty or reserve.

We were all antsy and on edge, none of us having any idea what we got ourselves into. We had seen some videos, talked to people that had been through basic, but it didn't do anything to prepare us. The closest thing to what we were about to experience was being at MEPS with them yelling at us. Hurry up, sit down, wait here, be quiet, hurry up, let's go, get your head out of your 4th point of contact, etc. That didn't scratch the surface of what was to come.

I stopped by the front desk for any messages. They handed me a note, saying my dad called and he loved me, call if I could. I went to my room to get the direct number to my room, then walked back to the lobby to make the outgoing call. I left the number to call me back at in 5 minutes.

I ran back to my room to wait for their call. When the phone rang, I jumped on it because I needed to hear comforting voices. My dad's booming voice immediately calmed me. I laughed realizing I chose to do this and needed to stop freaking out.

We talked briefly because I didn't want to rack up their phone bill with long-distance charges. No one had cellular telephones in the 1990s. Most computers were huge, heavy monstrosities. Computers were not household items at this time. In high school, the computers were used to write codes, type reports, and play games on. What we had were telephones hard-wired to a landline, which was connected to the phone lines outside on the telephone poles that ran along the roads.

If you were saving money, like us, you had a "party line." That meant if you were on the phone, someone in your party could hear what you were saying if they picked up the phone while you had a call, in progress. Also, if someone else was on a call, anyone trying to call you would get a busy signal until the other line hung up.

If you needed to make a call and you weren't home, there were pay phones. You could put quarters, dimes, or nickels in them to make a call, but you ran out of time quick. You could also call a number collect by dialing 0 for the operator. The operator would ask for the number you wanted to call and what your name was. They would tell you to please hold while they connected to the party. Once your party answered, the operator would say, "Are you willing to accept a collect call from...." Once your party answered yes, the operator would disconnect and the person you called would start getting charged.

Collect calls were billed at a higher rate. Thus, more expensive for the person accepting the call. Sometimes I would call and have the other end say no to accepting the call, but they would know to call me back that way the call would be charged at a lower rate.

To help ease the long-distance costs, especially for college students and military, the phone company came out with a "calling card." It was the size of a credit card, and it had a number on it that you entered in before dialing the number you wanted to call. My stepmom got me one so I could call them without worrying about having enough change.

This came in handy in basic training when we were allowed to use the pay phones and when I was stationed overseas.

After the brief call with my dad and stepmom, I took a shower. I couldn't sleep so I grabbed my journal. I was at a loss for words to put on paper. I sat at the little table in my hotel room, staring out the window. I couldn't put pen to paper.

As I was about to put the journal down, the nerves came out in words. I wrote about the incident the night before, about being 17 and leaving for the Army, unable to think further than getting to basic training.

I relaxed enough to lie down and sleep. I slept for a few hours and woke up 3 hours before I was scheduled to be in the lobby. I showered again, got dressed and packed up. I went to the lobby and grabbed a light snack.

Approximately 30-45 minutes later, others in my group started showing up. The last one arrived about 90 minutes before our ride arrived. We all looked at each other and laughed. I said, "Well, I guess none of us are late."

I couldn't believe the time had finally come, to fulfill my promise at my grandpa's funeral. I was physically ready. I was used to playing sports, throwing hay, shoveling snow, chopping, and carrying wood, bike riding for miles at a time and running. Even still, the physical aspect of basic training was going to be grueling, every day, all day, for 8 weeks.

We arrived at the airport and checked in, dropped our bags, and made our way to our respective gates. I arrived in Atlanta, GA, to catch my connecting flight to South Carolina. This was only the 2nd time I had flown, the first was for our senior trip.

We had to walk downstairs, then outside to a little plane. It looked like we were flying in a toy plane. I stopped walking. My feet would not move. It's a can of sardines with wings. I heard someone say, "This must be your first time on one of these little guys, it will be okay, I fly them all the time."

It was the pilot talking to me. I laughed and said I didn't think planes were that small. He said, "You must be going to basic at Fort Jackson, we don't get many young people on our planes unless they're going for training." Then he told me he had gone to basic there, then got out to fly commercial planes.

His conversation brought me to the steps to climb into the plane. Claustrophobia closed in on me. Inside the plane was even smaller. There were 16 seats, 8 rows with 1 seat on each side of the aisle. We could see the pilot because there was no wall or barrier.

I slowly walked to my seat and tried to control my breathing. Once I sat down, I looked out the window and moved my arms around so I could feel the space around me and remind myself I was able to move. I could breathe. I wasn't confined.

The flight was short, just over 30 minutes. By the time we were up we started descending. It was dusk when we landed, and I was met by someone in uniform. They walked me to get my bag, then took me out to a bus. We sat there waiting for more recruits to land.

It was the middle of July, in South Carolina. It was hot and humid. We weren't allowed to talk to each other, the windows had to stay up and they were completely blacked out. It was stifling. Once we had everyone, we departed the airport. It was dark now.

The silence was heavy on the bus. I couldn't even hear breathing. It was the oddest feeling. We didn't drive in a straight line to the base. There were lots of turns before we arrived and were told to grab our stuff and get off the bus. We were told to be at the front of the chow hall in 15 minutes.

What the hell was a chow hall? It was sometimes referred to as the "mess hall" and after training it is called the D-FAC, short for dining facility. We grabbed our bags and got off the bus as quickly as possible without knocking each other over. It was dark outside, with a few outdoor lights and the moon to guide us.

We all gravitated toward the only building with a light on, which ended up being the correct building. We were now at the in-processing reception station. This is where all soldiers are brought when they arrive, prior to starting basic training. Reception is where we got our uniforms, boots, dog tags, ID cards, immunizations, and final physical testing before being allowed to move to our training company.

That first night, we were lined up near the door and there was a line of desks down the hallway. Before we went inside the building, we went by an "amnesty" box, which is where we threw any items considered contraband. Contraband was any food, gum, snacks, drinks, alcohol, knives, or other weapons. After the amnesty box, we had to go to the table marked with the first letter of our last name. I was at the 2nd table with the letter "G." There was one girl in front of me. They took her packet from MEPS, took some forms out, then filed the packet into another folder.

The girl was assigned to a building, room and bunk and told to go to the counter with an open window. I stepped up, she said, "Name," I told her, then she said, "Packet." I handed the packet to her, and she opened it, separated some papers then filed the packet.

I was assigned a building, room and bunk and told to move to the counter with the open window. I was given a punch card with my name and social security number, they told me that was the only way I would get chow, don't lose it. I was directed around the corner to an open door which opened into a huge cafeteria or "chow hall."

I stood in line, after my card was punched. I was told to move forward, grab a tray, and get some food. I had 10 minutes to get my food, eat and throw my trash away. I grabbed a small box of cereal, a banana, and some bread. I went to the next line and got some milk, peanut butter, and utensils.

I was directed to a table to sit and eat. I moved quickly trying not to spill my milk, sat and ate. I was used to eating fast. If you ate slow at home, you missed out on second helpings. I finished eating and stood to throw my trash away, drop my tray and dishes off and was directed to another door. She said, "Go to the counter, pick up linens, go to your building and bunk."

I grabbed my linens as I shouldered my duffle bag and carryon bag. I was directed outside the door. They had us lined up by building numbers. Once everyone was processed, done eating and had their linens, they took each group to their assigned building. We were told to make our bunks, put our bags in our wall lockers and then to go shower.

Formation was at 0600 hours. We had to make our bunks then clean the showers, bathrooms, and general area before we left for formation. We were only allowed to bring a couple changes of clothes, a pair of shower shoes (flip-flops), running shoes, hygiene items, sleeping clothes. All our underwear, socks and bras had to be white, and we had to have a pair of black shorts and white t-shirt to wear for formation.

It was late when I found my bunk. I was so tired. My bunk was on the bottom and my bunkmate was already there when I arrived. She arrived a few hours earlier. We introduced ourselves and I started making my bed the way they told us to do it. We talked a bit while I made my bunk, and the other girls were talking around us. Some of the girls knew each other from school and joined the Army together.

I made my bed as instructed. One white sheet on the bottom, tucked in all the way around. One white sheet on top, with the bottom and 3/4 of the sides tucked in. One green blanket went over the white sheet, tucked in the same way and the other green blanket was folded and placed at the foot of the bed. When we made our beds in the morning, the top sheet had to be folded down, over the top of the green blanket that was tucked in. The pillow was to be placed in the middle of the open spot on the bottom sheet, where the other sheet had been folded down. The open end of the pillowcase was to be tucked inside the pillowcase, forming a neat closure with the tuck.

I finished my bed, put my bags in a locker, then grabbed my sleeping clothes, towel, and hygiene kit so I could shower. The showers were open stalls, with half-walls between the showers. There were only a couple people in the bathroom when I went into shower.

I braided my hair before I went to bed. As I set my alarm, I saw it was only 10:30. The girl I shared a bunk with introduced me to some of the girls she had in-processed with, and we sat around talking till 11 which is when they yelled lights out. This girl would become a lifelong friend and my soul sister.

We all scrambled for our bunks before the lights went out. There were a couple girls that were on fireguard duty that made sure everyone was in their bunk and accounted for before they sat by the doors. Those on fireguard duty would ensure no one left and no one came in and if there was any fire or hazard, they would wake everyone up to get out. Fireguard was a 2-hour shift. They woke the next two girls when their shift ended and so on.

It was nice when you got the first shift or the last shift, but the shifts in the middle were the worst because you didn't sleep very well before or after.

My alarm went off at 5 A.M., right before the girls on fireguard duty came in to turn all the lights on and yell for us to get up. We had to get dressed, complete our morning hygiene, make our beds, make sure the bay we slept in, and bathrooms were clean, trash taken out and wall lockers locked. With so many girls going to the bathroom, this process took the longest.

Once we finished and a final walkthrough was conducted, we went down for formation. Most of us arrived 15 minutes early. We were marched to breakfast, where we had about 5 minutes to eat after we made it through the line. There was no talking. Eyes and head faced forward, and you ate what was put on your plate.

After chow, we assembled outside again in formation to march to the processing building. They broke us into groups to work everyone through the process quicker. We were issued our military ID cards, our dog tags, uniforms, boots, green socks, brown undershirts, brown towels and washcloths, uniform rank if other than a Private/E-1, which was lowest enlisted rank. I was an E-2 when I arrived because people enlisted on my referral. My rank was a solo chevron, which looked like an upside-down, wide V.

We were shown how to display our rank on our uniform collars. We walked around in our boots to ensure they fit correctly. Everything went into our duffle bags with our name stenciled on the outside. We stood in lines for several immunization shots, with an air gun. After lunch they sent us to our buildings to clean out our wall lockers, strip our linen from beds, change into our uniforms and make sure everything we had been issued that day was in our duffle bag. All our personal items went into our personal bags after another "amnesty" check was done.

We grabbed our personal bags and our green Army duffle bag and loaded onto busses with blacked-out windows. All the Army duffle bags were thrown in the back of the bus, each trainee taking a seat with their personal bag. There was a drill sergeant on each bus, making sure we didn't talk.

The heat on the bus was oppressive. The 100-degree temps mixed with the humidity was disgusting. Being packed on a bus with a bunch of other girls and our bags in the heat made us all antsy and irritable.

We arrived at our training barracks. All the bus doors opened at the same time and the world went crazy. There were drill sergeants all over the place, yelling at us as we got off the buses. Each platoon had 3 drill sergeants assigned with 4 platoons in a company. There is also a first sergeant and captain present.

Each drill sergeant was yelling commands, a mixture of males and females. It was made to feel like a crazy and chaotic scene, to induce pressure and stress. I reacted to the commands without stopping to think. This is now referred to as "shark attack." Basic combat training had begun and the yelling from the drill sergeants did not stop for 8 weeks, when we graduated.

"Get off the bus, let's go, what are you looking at, don't let those bags hit the ground, you're not at home anymore, Private"; the yelling became a blur of words thrown at us as we exited the bus. We were told to go to the back of the bus and grab a duffle bag and take it to the center of the concrete pad. As the bags started rapidly coming off the bus, it didn't matter who grabbed which bag, it just mattered that we grabbed a bag and quickly moved to the center of the big concrete area, outside the huge building.

As we were grabbing bags, there was a drill sergeant on the other side of the door, yelling things like "Hurry up, Private, grab that bag, don't you let my bag hit the ground." It didn't matter what we did, at some point between getting off the bus and making it to the bag drop, you were told, "Drop and give me 10, Private." Some were being told to drop more than a couple times.

After dropping the bags in a huge pile, we were all told to stand in one area until all the bags and trainees were off the buses. Once the bags were all thrown together, we were told to grab our bag. It was chaos. Your bag was somewhere amongst the hundreds of other green Army bags.

Now the drill sergeants swarmed around us, literally like sharks waiting for fresh blood and then they pounced. Even though there were hundreds of us, there were enough drill sergeants swarming to give the sensation there were hundreds of them. We found out later the drills from other companies came over for shark week because they were in a different cycle than we were, which doubled the number of drills barking at us.

When we located our bag, we had to grab it and run back to the formation where we had been standing, next to our personal bag. I lucked out and found my bag early, grabbed it and ran to my spot. There were only a couple drills next to the formation when I got there, but as more recruits grabbed their bags and ran over, the drills started splitting up. I felt like a statue. I was afraid to move, blink or make any noise. Good thing I played "freeze tag" for so many years with my sisters.

Some recruits took more verbal abuse than others for varying reasons. There was one girl in front of me that had 4 drills surrounding her, yelling, asking questions she couldn't answer, telling her she might as well quit because she was weak. As a group, they had us "open ranks, march" which meant each squad moved so we had enough room to do pushups, jumping jacks and other exercises.

After the "discipline," we had to grab our Army duffle bag then strap it on our back like a backpack or hold them in the front over their shoulders. I was grateful for all the heavy lifting, chores, and baling hay. I was able to throw my duffle on my back. My personal duffle bag and carry on, were around my neck and under one arm, crossways over my body.

Once everyone was reassembled, the first sergeant explained what was going to happen next. He told us to move at a rapid walk once we heard our name called and line up in the appropriate formation.

They started calling last names in alphabetical order and yelling which platoon they were assigned to. I heard my bunkmates name called because hers started with a B. Soon I heard my name called and heard "2nd platoon" which is where my bunkmate was assigned. We were excited to be in the same platoon, but we couldn't show it or say anything then.

My drill sergeant lined me up as the 1st person in the 3rd squad. I was right next to my bunkmate because she was the 1st person in the 2nd squad. We couldn't see how many were behind us because we had to stay facing forward, with each recruit lining up behind a squad leader. Soon there was a person at the head of the 4th squad next to me and our entire platoon was filled a few minutes later.

The drill sergeants told us that each squad would file out as soon as the last person in the squad before them had moved forward. We had a drill sergeant in front to show us which bay we were assigned to. There was a drill sergeant next to the formation telling the squad leaders when to go and the last drill sergeant was behind the line, making sure no one veered off from the platoon.

The building was set up with the bays on the 2nd story. Each one separate from the others, with shared outdoor stairs between the bays. The floor of the bays was the cover/ceiling for the concrete area on the ground, where we would have formation, some classes and where the main office was located for the company. The office is where the captain and first sergeant were unless we were away from the barracks for training.

The Army's rank was set up as enlisted personnel and officers, a system of hierarchical relationships. The military rank system defines authority and responsibility in a hierarchy. It is also referred to as the "Chain of Command." Enlisted personnel went through basic training, most straight out of high school, officers went to officer candidate school, OCS. In order to go to OCS, you had to have completed college with a bachelor's degree or higher. Most officers were part of ROTC, Reserve Officer Training Corps, a college program offered at many colleges and universities to help prepare young adults to become officers in the U.S. Military.

Some ROTC students received a scholarship to help pay for their college tuition, with a commitment to serve a certain number of years with the military. ROTC was also offered in some high schools, but that program didn't qualify anyone for entry into the military without completing college or basic training.

We had E-1 through E-4 ranks in our platoon, most starting as E-1. E-1s automatically promote to E-2 or PV2, private second class, after completing six months of service. They could promote earlier if they did something to earn it. Your rank indicates your pay grade and the amount of responsibility you hold. A PFC or E-3 is called a private first class and some trainees enter basic at this rank, if they've completed some college, high school ROTC program or began as an E-2 and referred another person.

If you entered as an E-1 and made E-2 after basic training or in 6 months, most earned the rank of PFC within a year, at the request of a supervisor. Soldiers serving at this rank are the backbone of the Army. Their primary role is to carry out orders and complete missions.

The next rank is E-4 or Specialist (SPC). Most can attain this rank after serving a minimum of 2 years, but individuals with a bachelor's degree who are looking to become officers via the Officer Training Course, come to basic training at this rank. They promote to the rank of E5/Sergeant when they successfully complete basic training. They go through OTC as an E5 and promote to 2nd Lieutenant after successfully completing the Officer Training Course. There are some recruits that enter basic training as an E-4, with a 4-year degree, but they intend to stay in the enlisted ranks. Officers are addressed as sir or ma'am.

You do not to call a sergeant, sir or ma'am. The standard response was "Don't call me sir/ma'am, I work for a living," indicating officers didn't, they just gave orders.

As the ranks progress, there's E-5, Sergeant (SGT), E-6, Staff Sergeant (SSG), E-7, Sergeant First Class (SFC), E-8, Master Sergeant (SGM), First Sergeant (1SG), E-9, Sergeant Major (SGM) and E-10, Command Sergeant Major (CSM). The highest-ranking enlisted rank is the Sergeant Major of the Army (SMA) and there is only 1 SMA. The SMA oversees all noncommissioned officers (NCO).

To be a drill sergeant, the soldier must be an E-5 or E-6 and complete a drill sergeant academy. A first sergeant (1SG) must obtain the rank of E-8, or be a SFC promotable, to be laterally appointed to 1SG upon selection by senior leadership at Department of the Army.

The 1SG is the highest US Army NCO rank position that is still in a direct "hands on" leadership setting. They are the senior NCO of company sized unit. Most soldiers refer to their 1SG as "Top" once they arrive at their permanent duty station. In basic, we saw our 1SG regularly, but didn't hear much from him.

The commissioned officer ranks started with Second Lieutenant (2LT), first lieutenant (1LT), captain (CPT), Major (MAJ), Lieutenant Colonel (LTC), Colonel (COL), Brigadier General (BG), Major General (MG), Lieutenant General (LTG), General (GEN), and the highest rank is General of the Army (GOA), only achieved in times of war.

There are also Chief Warrant Officers, CW1 through CW4, they do their own thing. Most of the pilots are CWOs, which is what the neighbor boys I had grown up next to were.

The only PFC in our platoon was chosen by the drill sergeants to be the platoon guide. The platoon guide took orders from the drill sergeants, then passed them onto the squad leaders. The squad leaders were responsible for disseminating the information to their squad. The platoon guide was the leader for each basic training platoon. It was a lot of responsibility.

It was Friday afternoon. Hot, sticky, and busy. We were led up the back stairs to our bay area where the drill sergeants assigned us to our bunks. Each squad leader was at the front of the bay, closest to the drill sergeant office. Our bunks were on the bottom, and we were assigned the first wall locker in the row.

1st and 2nd squad were closest to the door the drill sergeants used, with the shared outdoor stairs. 1st squad's wall lockers were lined up against the wall, with approximately 2 feet of space from the wall locker to where the bunks started. The bunks were in a straight line going towards the back of the bay area by the bathrooms. The wall lockers were lined side by side, against the wall, all the way to the back of the bay.

There was a walkway in between the bunks for 1st and 2nd squads, about 6 feet wide. The wall lockers for 2nd squad were set the same distance from their bunks, closer to the middle of the bay, backing up against the wall lockers for 3rd squad. 2nd and 3rd squad wall lockers divided the bay in half.

3rd and 4th squads were lined up the same way as 1st and 2nd, and situated near the drill sergeant office, and closer to the back stairs, which trainees used. There were 2 entrances to the bathroom, one from each side. The bathroom had 10 stalls and 10 sinks with an entrance to the showers off the side. There were 10 shower stalls, 5 on each side of the room. Each stall was open with a half-wall about chest high, separating the stalls. The entire bathroom was covered with small square tiles, including the walls of the shower stalls. The floors were a bigger tile, with drains in the middle.

The bay floor was a creamy white color, not stark white and not beige. It was white enough to show boot scuff marks and dirt/sand tracked in. The floor was a tile consistency and had to be waxed and buffed on a regular basis, which was a regular chore.

At the front of the bay was the drill sergeant office, about 10 feet in front of 3rd and 4th squads' bunks. There was a window next to their door, that looked into the bay area. Next to their office was a small room with a few weights but no one really had time to use it. This is the room we would sit in front of when the drill sergeants had something to share with our platoon, usually at the end of the day. This is the area we did mail call and the area where we got "smoked" if we messed something up.

When we got "smoked" it was a form of corrective discipline, while making us stronger. Most times it was pushups, but there were times it was also flutter kicks, jumping jacks (side-straddle hop) or holding the front-leaning rest position. The cycles could last until we all hit muscle failure, other times, it was a short burst of 20 pushups, then recover. Recover was when we stood back up from being smoked. The first couple weeks of training, if 1 person messed something up, the entire platoon was smoked.

When you had fireguard duty, you sat in a chair near that room, in the middle of the wall so you could see down both sides of the bay and both doors.

After we were assigned our wall lockers, we were shown how to set the wall lockers up, how to hang our uniforms, which drawer to put our socks, undershirts, bras, and other small items in. The top shelf of the wall locker was where we could store our personal items, like our hygiene kits, Bibles, letter-writing items and mail we received.

Most of us arrived in the afternoon and were assigned to our platoons. A few girls showed up right before we left for chow. These were the girls that hadn't been able to complete the push up test to leave reception. They were given another chance after lunch, if they passed, they were sent to their platoon for training. If they failed again, they had to stay until the week after, when they started another training cycle.

After we all finished getting our wall lockers set up, beds made and made sure we had everything we were allowed to have from our personal items, we lined up to put all our personal bags in a storage room. The room was a small area, big enough to throw all our bags in a pile. The door had a lock and was in front of the bathroom.

The drills inspected wall lockers, beds, and uniforms after we put our personal bags in storage. They gave us one last chance to get rid of anything we weren't supposed to have and put in the amnesty box. They said if anything was found after amnesty, we would be facing discipline.

As they checked our lockers and beds, they told us what needed changing and tips for keeping the bed sheets tight. They started with the platoon guide and the squad leaders. The platoon guide was in the first bunk with the 4th squad leader. After they checked ours, made corrections, if needed, they told us to help square our squads away before morning formation.

After the drills confirmed there was no contraband in the lockers, they had us all sit in the open area near the front of the bay, on the floor. They introduced themselves, went over their rules, expectations, date for graduation, if we completed the cycle, how fireguard duty would work, where and when we needed to be the next morning. We had 2 male drill sergeants and 1 female.

They explained how the chow hall worked. When you got to the door, yell your last name and last 4 of your social security number. This is how we were accounted for on the roster, at every meal. All the trainees would go first, with the squad leaders and platoon guide last. By the time the squad leaders got through the line with our food and drinks, we had approximately 2 minutes to eat and drink.

When the drills yelled chow was over, every trainee took their trash with them to throw away, placed the tray and dishes on the counter for the trainees that were working KP to wash. KP duty is "kitchen police" or "kitchen patrol" duty. Every trainee is assigned to KP duty at least once during basic training, to help teach teamwork and to help feed all the trainees.

Some of the KP duties are cleaning and mopping floors, after every meal, washing dishes, trays, peeling potatoes, taking the trash out and every other job that needed to be done in the kitchen and chow hall. When you were assigned to KP duty, it was for the entire day, showing up when everyone else was going to PT and staying until after everything was cleaned after dinner. KP duty kept you busy, but it was also a break from the mental, physical, and emotional aspects of training.

Our barracks and mess hall were set up with one half for the female company, with 4 platoons and the other half was the male company. The drills set it up so we would alternate which company ate first so there was no fraternization between the males and females. The only time we saw the males was if we worked KP or when we dropped our dishes off at the counter, and sometimes when we were cleaning the grounds.

We were forbidden to talk to any of the male trainees and when we were on KP duty, they kept us separate while we worked. A couple weeks into the training, I heard someone call my first name when I was going through the line to drop my tray. I looked in the kitchen area and saw a kid that I went to elementary school with. He was one of the boys that wrote me a "check yes or no" letter when we were in 3rd grade. After elementary school, we'd seen each other through the years at sporting events and at the Vo-Tech center.

I was the last in line as the squad leader and our female drill sergeant heard him call my name before I could react or respond. She was only about 5 feet tall, but she was a no-nonsense drill sergeant, tough as nails. Most of us were more afraid of her than the other drills in our platoon. She came flying up to the counter and asked the guy which platoon he was in.

After he replied, she asked him if he had forgotten about the no fraternization policy or, was he only thinking with his lower head. I felt bad for him because he was harmless and it took us both by surprise to see each other in the chow hall, so far from our small towns. He was punished.

My drill went to his drill sergeants and told them what happened. She was going to take care of him after dishes were done, before his KP duty was over. We were all sitting in the bleachers, under our bay, waiting for the next set of instructions, when I saw her come around the corner. She called me to the front where I stood at attention, waiting for my punishment.

She told me to stand at ease, which was the position of my feet opened slightly, hands resting lightly behind my back. When at the position of "at ease," we could talk and look around, unlike the position of attention or parade rest. Parade rest is like at ease, but the arms are behind the back, with the hands placed on top of each other, at the small of the back.

She asked how I knew the guy from the chow hall that called my name. I explained we went to school together until 3rd grade and saw each other at the Vo-Tech center our junior and senior years, as well as at sporting events. She nodded her head and said, "Okay, did either of you know the other was here or in the same building?" I replied I didn't even know he joined the Army.

She told me she would be punishing him for fraternization and reiterated I was not allowed to talk to him, until after graduation. I said, "Yes, Drill Sergeant," and she dismissed me to sit back down on the bleachers. She addressed the entire platoon and said if any of us were caught fraternizing, we would be disciplined in a similar manner as the trainee you're about to see.

We weren't allowed to talk, laugh, or say anything when we saw him. I had no idea what was about to happen after she left to go around the side of the building. When she came back, she was walking next to a guy that was low crawling around the building. She was yelling at him, telling him her soldiers were off limits and other things we couldn't hear.

We continued to watch as he went through our formation area, on his stomach, with left hand stretched out in front of the body, head tilted slightly up and to the right, the other arm bent to help pull himself along. The left leg was straight behind him with the right at an angle to help him push forward. The low crawl is meant to move you from position to position, without being seen by enemy, to stay under bullets flying above.

The high crawl is similar, but the arms and knees are bent under the body, with chest and butt raised to allow quicker movements. The type of crawl used depended on the situation.

To walk around our entire building took a few minutes, low crawling took much longer. The girls in my platoon watched silently. After they passed by our area to go around the back side, we all looked at each other with eyes wide open and lips slightly parted. The point was made, fraternization was bad.

The first official day of training started with a PT test, which consisted of pushups, sit-ups and a 2-mile run. You had 2 minutes to complete as many pushups and sit-ups as you could without lying down. You could hold the front-leaning rest position, if needed, which was hands on the ground, shoulder width apart, arms extended, body forming a straight line from your shoulders to your ankles. This is similar to holding a plank position with your arms fully extended instead of on your elbows.

To have a pushup count you started in the rest or "up" position, bent your elbows to lower your body as one unit towards the ground, maintaining a straight line of your body, until the elbows are parallel to the ground. To complete the pushup, you push your hands into the ground to push up. The body must maintain a rigid line, with no sagging or lifting, on the way down and back up, to count as 1 pushup.

The sit-up starts with the shoulders, butt, and legs on the ground, with hands behind the head or neck. The hands must stay behind the ear during the entire repetition to count. The shoulders lift towards the knees, bent at a

45-degree angle, with elbows touching knees, then lower the shoulders to the ground, to count as 1 sit-up. Your butt cannot come off the ground during the sit-up. The rest position for the sit-up is with the shoulders at the knees. Once your shoulders hit the ground, they must immediately come back to the knees without resting on the ground.

We did pushups first. You needed to do at least 19 to pass. Sit-ups were next and you needed to complete a minimum of 71. When everyone completed both events, we went to the track for the 2-mile run. We had a certain time to finish the run, according to age. My time had to be under 19 minutes, for a 17-year-old female. I was fast when playing sports, but I hated running long distance, especially when there was not a competition to win. I could run for 45 minutes straight during a soccer game but running for time was boring.

This PT test was a gauge where we were, what we needed to work on and provided a baseline to compare to our next test. To "max" a PT test for a 17-21-year-old female, you had to do at least 56 pushups in 2 minutes, 82 sit-ups in 2 minutes and run 2 miles in 15:36 or less. Each event you could score a max of 100 points, allowing for a 300 or "perfect" PT score.

My first test, I completed 24 pushups, 78 sit-ups and 17:44 on the 2-mile run. Only a few of us did more than 20 pushups. The 2nd squad leader and I compared scores when we were getting ready for breakfast. We were close in all categories. We high-fived each other as we finished getting ready then went to chow.

After we finished chow and showering, we began what was termed "hell week." I have no idea how many pushups, sit-ups, mountain climbers, flutter kicks, jumping jacks and other various exercises we did that day and the rest of the week, but my uniform dripped with sweat.

We had regular wall locker inspections to make sure we didn't have any food, gum, or other contraband. The inspections also checked wall lockers were securely locked. Each day a drill sergeant checked lock security. We would return to the bay some days to find wall locker contents all over the floor because someone didn't properly secure their lock. Even now I double and triple check locks on doors and vehicles. If there's an alarm on a vehicle, I hit the key fob lock 2-3 times.

Surprise inspections normally caught at least 1 person with contraband, crackers, or something else they smuggled from the chow hall and put in their wall locker. The consequences were not good. One girl in 2nd squad was always a problem. Once they found 5 packages of crackers, she had taken from the chow hall.

The first few offenses had the drill sergeants emptying her locker and throwing her mattress and bedding over the floor along with her personal items and uniforms. The last time she was found with the crackers, it was right before lights out. Everyone was in bed or almost in bed. We heard the drills come in as the fireguard yelled, "On your feet!" the command any recruit yelled as soon as they saw a drill sergeant.

We jumped out of our beds to the position of attention, heels touching, toes slightly pointed out at a 45-degree angle, arms down at your sides, with hands slightly curled, thumb touching the side of your outer thigh, head, and eyes straight ahead. The drill sergeants always started with the squad leaders' lockers first. After inspecting our wall lockers, if we passed, we followed behind them as they went through our squad's lockers.

Halfway down my row of squad lockers, I heard the drill on the other side say, "You guys handle this, or everyone will be punished for her willfully breaking the rules," and then all three of the drills surrounded her wall locker. One of them said, "Do you think you're above the rules because your daddy is a Chief Warrant Officer, because you're not and you will not like the consequences if this happens again. Do you understand, Private?"

There was not another sound in the bay, and I couldn't hear if she responded. All the drills left, and one told the 2nd squad leader, "You'd better handle this," then they said lights out in 5 minutes and left. Everyone finished their night routines if they weren't already in bed, fixed their wall lockers and made sure the lock was secured.

There was mumbling on the other side of the bay, but I couldn't see anything. I heard the fireguard yell lights out in 1 minute, get your stuff in lockers and in bed. I made sure my squad had their lockers closed and locked before I laid down in case there was another surprise lock check while we were sleeping.

I went back to my bunk and double checked the lock just as lights went out, then the 2nd squad leader came over and whispered, "We have to teach her a lesson, otherwise she's going to keep thinking she can get away with stupid stuff and my squad is tired of it." My bunkmate sat up and said, "We need to rough the princess up, Brooklyn style."

As the 3 of us went back around the corner, we heard muffled noises coming from the middle of the row. As we got closer, we could make out body shapes. There were 15 or 20 trainees surrounded this trainee's bed. Some were holding a blanket over her, to hold her down and restrain her. Others had pillowcases and socks and we could hear thuds. One of the trainees said, "We're done with you screwing around and acting like you're better than the rest of us," another said, "If you don't start acting right, the next time is going to be even worse than now."

We told them all to go back to bed. After the other girls left, my bunkmate said, "Hell yeah, that's how you get it done, quit fuckin' around, princess, and get your shit together, we're all in this together." I told my bunkmate to go to bed. The 2nd squad leader leaned down and told the girl, "I'm sure that really hurt, but you're lucky we were here this time, don't let there be a next time."

As we walked away, we could hear soft whimpering coming from her bunk. The next morning her wall locker was cleaned and organized. She was up and dressed for PT, physical training, her bed was made, and she was asking others if they needed any help before formation.

We all noticed it but said nothing. We finished getting ready for PT formation and made sure everyone was out of the bay, double checking wall lockers and locks. That trainee completely turned things around. She became one of the better recruits and shot expert during BRM, basic rifle marksmanship.

As the days went on, we started receiving letters and packages from family and friends. It was nice to have a touch of home and people to write to at the end of the day, but when someone received a package with candy or baked goods, we all paid for it.

The first couple weeks we worked on drill and ceremony, which includes marching as a platoon. We had left turns, right turns, about faces, counter columns, and other fun things to keep it from being boring. My marching band days paid off because I knew you always started on your left foot for any of the commands and how to march.

D&C, the sound of the boots hitting the pavement, the cadences, the precision of the group moving as one, were all things I enjoyed. We marched everywhere we went, and it didn't take long to perfect D&C. When we were getting ready to run, the command was "Double time, march" and when it was time for PT or to get smoked, the command was "Open ranks, march."

Many times, we heard "Open ranks, march" and knew we were in for a long smoke session. Open ranks allowed each squad to move to provide everyone room to perform the exercises without hitting each other.

We did numerous confidence building courses. These courses and exercises were meant to help trainees face their personal fears and build their confidence so they can learn to work as a team.

The first course was Victory Tower, which was a large wooden structure, 40 feet tall, with ropes and ladders on all sides. To begin the course, you had to climb a rope ladder up the side. Once you got to the top, there was a rope that you had to swing across the open hole, "Tarzan style," to get to the other side.

The feeling of flying across a completely open hole had my stomach in my throat, but I didn't look down as I swung across. On the other side of the platform, there were 3 sets of rope structures, all of them angled towards a lower platform. The first one, you had to lie down on the rope, on your stomach, hands in front of you, and pull yourself to the other side. One of your feet was hooked on the rope to help guide and balance you, while the other stayed off.

At the platform, you went around to a small wall where you were shown how to rappel, using a mini-wall. When the drill sergeants felt you understood how to do it, they would send you to the big wall. To get to the big wall, you had to climb up to the mini platform and walk on a rope bridge back to the top of the tower.

The rope bridge was 1 thick rope to walk on with a rope on each side to hold onto and ropes connecting the bottom rope to the sides, for stability. The rope bridge moved as you walked, and you had to use all your muscles to stay balanced.

As you reached the top of the tower, the drill sergeants hooked you up to the ropes and showed you where to place your feet, how to sit back into the ropes and guide yourself down the wall. I had never rappelled before, but I loved the feeling of floating down the wall.

After we finished, we sat with our platoons to cheer on the rest. While we were sitting and cheering, we started talking about where we were going to

AIT (Advanced Individual Training) for our MOS (Military Occupations Specialty). The 2nd squad leader and I were both going to Fort Gordon, GA, for the same MOS in communications.

Within 7 days, our bond had grown tremendously. It felt like we had known each other for years. I called her "Berryhead," and she called me "Greenie Wienie." As training went on, we found out we had so much in common and our friendship continued to grow. Soon we were more than battle buddies; we were soul sisters. We were inseparable. We trained together, worked together, helped strengthen the others' weaknesses, laughed, cried, and formed a lasting sister bond.

The drill sergeants noticed the bond we formed and decided to use it to push us harder, seeing we were both competitive. Soon we were racing each other everywhere, trying to do one more pushup or sit-up than the other. Even if we didn't want to compete, the drills made sure we would. If one of us was told to do something, the other was told, "Don't let her beat you," and we were off again, laughing the whole time, knowing neither of us would win.

As we finished whatever task we'd been given, the loser would be getting smoked, with pushups, sit-ups, flutter kicks, etc. The winner knew they would get smoked, too, so the loser didn't gain ground on the winner. It was a vicious, but fun cycle. It made us stronger, physically, and mentally, and sealed our bond.

2 weeks after the first PT test, we had to do another one, to see who had improved and where work was still needed. Berryhead and I both improved significantly. That spurred the drills to push us harder. If one of them was working CQ, Charge of Quarters, they made sure we were on fireguard duty together and kept us busy during the night. CQ is an overnight shift the drills had to pull, making sure if something happened at night, a drill sergeant would always be there.

Our first weeks of training were tough mentally, physically and for some, emotionally. It was the first time many had been away from home for more than a few days and for others, it was a reality check into who and what we were made of. Some started getting hurt on purpose, to leave basic and some were on "suicide watch" because they couldn't handle the stress and pressure.

Some girls were recycled to a later training date due to injuries if the injury was minor. A girl in my platoon fell while running up the stairs and broke her leg. She was recycled.

The first 2 weeks was called the "red" phase, where we learn how to become soldiers, adapt to Army life, learn proper dress, discipline, hygiene, build self-confidence, and hear briefings on first aid, sexual assault awareness and prevention. This phase also included physical readiness training, road marches, and an introduction into what was then called NBC, Nuclear Biological Chemical training. It is now called CBRN, Chemical Biological Radioactive and Nuclear readiness. NBC readiness taught us how to recognize any NBC warfare, how to alert others, what a gas mask was, how to use, clean and store it.

We also learned the levels of MOPP gear, level 0 to 4. MOPP is mission oriented protective postures. If you were at level 0, you had your gas mask with you, in its carrier, strapped around your waist and thigh, with all the gear on hand, ready to don. MOPP levels were based on current chemical and biological threats and could elevate in minutes. MOPP gear consisted of thick over garments, gas masks and hoods, boot covers and gloves.

MOPP level 1 requires the troop to don over garments because a chemical threat is present so troops must remain alert, as the hazard could escalate at any time. Level 2 mandates quickly putting on over garments and boot covers because the threat has increased. Level 3 must don over garments, gas mask and hood, and boot covers. At this level, the threat of contact with hazardous vapors is high. Level 4 is to don all, over garments, gas masks and hoods, boot covers and gloves. MOPP4 is to be worn when a chemical or biological threat is present in the area.

We learned how to use M9 paper, which can detect the presence of liquid chemical agents, like nerve agents, when and how to use atropine injections, how to recognize and alert others with warning signals. The basic types of warning signals are sound and visual.

Vocal is to shout "Gas!" as loudly as possible. Sound signals are a succession of short signals, either on a metal object or anything that produces a loud noise. Visual standard signal is to put on the protective mask, extending both arms to the side horizontally with doubled fists facing up, and moving fists rapidly up to the head and back down to the horizontal position, repeatedly. If in an area with chemical detection alarms, those would be a sound signal.

The atropine injection is an involuntary nervous system blocker. It can treat heart rhythm problems, stomach or bowel problems and certain types of poison, when injected. It is used in conjunction with 2-PAM-CI, pralidoxime chloride, as first aid, buddy aid or self-aid, against nerve agents. The injections were provided in 2 separate auto injectors, meant to be injected into the meaty area of the thigh. They have now made a model with both drugs in one syringe.

After the atropine was administered, we were to put the needle through the buttonhole of the soldier's top left pocket, bending the needle so it would stay. This would alert medics or other personnel that the medicine had been administered. For training purposes, we used the syringes without needles or drugs.

To help build self-confidence, we did the obstacle confidence course, bayonet drills and pugil stick fights. The obstacle confidence course had several obstacles, varying in construction. We had to climb, crawl, jump and run; over, under, and through different obstacles. Some of the obstacles were concrete drainpipes, back crawl under barbed wire, step over wooden fence-type obstacles, running through a rope weaved net, ending with a steep jump requiring you to tuck and roll.

Pugil sticks are heavily padded pole-like training weapons used since the early 1940s by the military in training for rifle and bayonet combat. The pugil stick is marked to indicate which end represents the bayonet and which is the rifle butt. These drills were to train us how to fight with our weapon if we were close enough to the enemy. Most of the pugil stick training has been replaced with hand-to-hand, combative training and bayonets are no longer used.

Bayonet training consisted of running towards stuffed targets representing the enemy and sticking them with the bayonet attached to your rifle. As we got ready to thrust the bayonet into the target, we had to yell, "To kill, to kill, to kill without mercy, Drill Sergeant."

All these drills helped boost self-confidence and build team camaraderie and trust. Although the training was tough and demanding, the courses were also fun, and we were able to release aggression and stress. Different charities, causes or fundraisers use obstacle course runs and events that mimic some of this training.

We had to memorize things such as the 3 general orders and be able to recite if any drill asked us. We must memorize the general orders and live them. Another item to memorize was the "Soldiers' Creed." Many times, we said it as a platoon while standing in formation.

General orders are used to describe the proper conduct of a sentry while on duty, in every possible operational scenario. The Army uses a condensed version of the 11 General Orders. The 3 general orders are:

I will guard everything within the limits of my post and quit my post only when properly relieved.

I will obey my special orders and perform all of my duties in a military manner.

I will report violations of my special orders, emergencies and anything not covered in my instructions to the commander of the relief.

Training went late one evening. After we finished, we went to the bay area to clean up. Our female drill sergeant was on duty that night, but all our drills were in the bay area. It was August 2, 1990, and they told us Operation Desert Shield started. Desert Shield was the operation for the buildup of troops and defense in Saudi Arabia, which was followed Operation Desert Storm, the combat phase. The troops were part of coalition forces from 35 nations, led by the United States, in response to Iraq's invasion and annexation of Kuwait arising from oil pricing and production disputes.

As we sat there in awe, thinking about war stories from history classes, grandparents and parents, the drills told us there was a possibility they would have to leave and go back to their units. Our 2 male drills were airborne rangers, special forces and air assault and the female said she probably wouldn't be sent because her husband was part of the deployment.

They asked if we had any questions. Some asked if they could volunteer. They said with us being in training and still having to complete AIT, we probably wouldn't be seeing any war. There were a couple more questions, but as the reality of what we were training for hit us all, we grew quiet and somber.

Before the drills left, we did mail call which is normally a time we all look forward to. That night was different as we thought about what our parents, family and friends were thinking as they watched the news. We thought about our own friends and family possibly being deployed.

After the mail was passed out, the male drills left. The female drill was still there, and we could tell she was sad, not her normal feisty self. She asked if any of us had questions or concerns before she went to the CQ office. No one said anything, then I asked her if she was okay.

She did a half-smile and said she was processing the fact her husband was on a plane to the Middle East. He had called her late the night before and told her he was leaving, and he loved her. She hadn't seen him since our training class started because he was at a different duty station. She didn't know when she would see him again.

She asked if any of us had friends or family possibly deploying. I told her my stepbrother and a guy from high school. One was in transportation and the other was a combat engineer. The guy I knew from school, Tom, had written a couple times, so I was waiting for a letter to find out.

During red phase, the only contact we had with family and friends was via letters. Upon completing red phase, we moved to white phase and were allowed a 5-minute phone call, using the pay phones, on Sundays. That weekend, after our second PT test, our platoon had passed all tests to move to white phase and we made our first phone calls home. By then I received a letter saying both were deploying. When I talked to KJ, she told me Colt asked about me, so she gave him my address.

White phase was a continuation of red phase with more road marches and BRM, Basic Rifle Marksmanship. BRM familiarized us with our weapons, the components, how to take apart, clean, and put them back together. It also covered firearms safety. We learned about sight picture, sight alignment, steady position, breath control, and trigger control.

We had timed drills of who could take their weapon apart the fastest and who could reassemble it the quickest. That led to who could disassemble and reassemble the fastest, then who was fastest blindfolded. The smell of gun oil became a constant aroma.

After we familiarized ourselves with our weapons, we learned how and why to zero our weapons, we practiced sight picture and sight alignment and did hours of dry firing, firing a weapon without any ammunition. Dry firing is a great technique to practice the skills needed for accuracy during live fire.

The first day on the live fire range, we zeroed our weapons in preparation for our qualifications. To zero a weapon, you use 3 bullets, holding the same position, sight picture and alignment. The purpose is to find your grouping so the rifle could be dialed in to your sight. I was able to zero mine after the first try and was told to go sit in the shade area. Each platoon was assigned a shade area to sit once they completed their zeroing.

Before coming off the range, a drill sergeant or officer had to check our weapons for any brass or ammo. We had to make sure the ejection port cover was open with the charging handle pulled back and the bolt catch locked. We had to yell, "No brass, no ammo, Drill Sergeant!" as we rotated the open bolt action so they could see it. They stuck a long thin rod into the barrel as they looked, to make sure nothing was stuck. Before we left the range, we all had to make sure we had no brass or ammo left in our cargo pockets of our BDUs, Battle Dress Uniforms.

My drill asked if I'd already finished and I told him I had, and on the first try. He laughed and asked where Berryhead was. Soon after I sat down, Berryhead came over because she had zeroed hers quickly. As others started trickling in, we made sure everyone stayed hydrated, safe and had no brass or ammo stuck in their pockets. After most of our platoon was done, the drills came over to our shade and asked Berryhead if I had zeroed before she did.

We both laughed because we knew what was coming. We both stood up from the bleachers and went to the side of the shade and started doing pushups. We kept pushing and were laughing at the same time until our drills finally said, "Get your asses up and back into the bleachers."

Before we started to file out for the march back, each squad leader had to double check their squad, for brass or ammo and then yell their squad number and "No brass, no ammo, Drill Sergeant." After most of the platoon had left the shade area, my drill pulled me aside and told me I was going to be the new platoon guide. I said, "Yes, Drill Sergeant," as I wondered why. The drills told me I had shown leadership skills, had a loud commanding voice and was leading the platoon in testing, in many areas.

They took the squad leader patch off my arm, which was a black band held together with Velcro, with 2 chevrons on it. They replaced it with the platoon guide patch, which had 3 chevrons on it and told me to take charge. It was a rewarding feeling knowing my hard work was noticed, but also overwhelming. I now oversaw 4 squads, instead of 1. As the platoon guide, I was now the last to eat at every meal.

One of the cadences we used regularly was "shoot, communicate, move on out" which was a reminder instilled in us as to what our basic roles were as a soldier, no matter what our MOS. We learned when, why and how to use communication equipment, learned topography map reading, how to use a compass and other skills to pass land navigation.

BRM took up most of our 2nd phase, we did our qualifications, night shoots, threw live grenades, learned how to shoot the LAW, Light Anti-Tank Weapon or Light Anti-Armor Weapon, the grenade launcher and how to set up a claymore mine. We also had to go through the gas chamber for our NBC training. We wore our gas masks and hood for the gas chamber.

Upon entering the chamber, after a group was squeezed in, a drill sergeant would give instructions. Even though our masks were on and sealed, you could smell and feel the CS gas seeping in. Some of the typical effects of CS gas are burning, watery sensation in the eyes, difficulty breathing, chest pain, excessive saliva, skin irritation, runny mucous from the nose and a heavy exposure can induce vomiting.

After the drill explained the instructions, each of us had to lift our mask, breaking the seal, say our last name and last 4 of our social security number. If they were satisfied we had been exposed enough, they would open the door to let us out of the chamber, 1 at a time. If they weren't satisfied, they would ask more questions. I had to say my hometown, in addition to my last name and SSN.

As the platoon guide, I was able to lead the platoon in more marching and call cadence. I also got punished more. After I left the gas chamber, I walked waving my arms to air out. Snot was running out of my nose; my eyes were watery, and I felt like I was going to throw up. I was called back in for a second dose. Surprisingly, the second dose didn't affect me as bad as the first.

As soon as I was released from the chamber the second time, all the drills came out and left the doors open to air the CS out. I kept walking to the formation area while decontaminating myself as much as I could and kept myself from throwing up. I believe that's what they were hoping to see. There was a photographer and videographer capturing footage, but I never knew until I saw the video after graduation. There I was with snot running out of my nose like a busted faucet.

During our BRM quals, we had to shoot at 40 popup targets varying from 80 to 327 yards. We had to shoot from the prone position and from the fox-hole. We had to qualify with our weapon to graduate, which consisted of hitting at least 23 of the 40 targets. To qualify as marksman, you had to hit 23-29 targets, 30-35 for sharpshooter, 36-40 to qualify for expert. If you hit 40 out of 40, you earned a Hawkeye badge with your expert.

During our initial phase of BRM, we learned about function checks, correcting malfunctions (SPORTS), front and rear sights adjustments. To correct a malfunction, we were taught to remember the steps using the acronym SPORTS; Slap, Pull, Observe, Release, Tap and Shoot.

The SPORTS steps consist of:

Slap upward on the magazine, to make sure it is properly seated.

Pull the charging handle all the way back.

Observe the ejection of the case or cartridge, look into the chamber and check for obstructions.

Release the charging handle to feed a new round in the chamber. Do not ride the charging handle.

Tap the forward assist.

Shoot. If it still doesn't fire, determine cause of stoppage, and take appropriate remedial action.

Broken down in the civilian world you may hear a simplified version, Tap, Rack, Shoot. For a double feed, also called a Type 3 malfunction, there is a different process.

To clear a Type 3, with gun still aimed towards target, look at ejection port for any visible malfunction. You will know it's a type 3 when you see a round still in the chamber and the next round in the magazine, hard up against it.

If there is an indication of Type 3 malfunction, hold the rifle steady and still aimed at the target, lock the bolt back to the rear to release the tension on the round trying to move into the chamber.

Release the magazine and let it fall to the ground. Rack the slide three to four times to clear any debris, casings, or dead ammo from the chamber. If racking doesn't remove objects, you must physically remove them by reaching through magazine well or ejection port.

Once objects are removed and chamber is clear, load a fresh magazine or the one you retained into the rife. Rack the slide to chamber a round and prepare to fire another shot.

During my qual from the foxhole, I had a double feed. I started SPORTS and as I got to the observe step, I saw the 2 rounds, so I quickly shifted to type 3 malfunction drill. After I cleared my weapon and inserted a new magazine, I finished my qual. When you clear a double feed, if it's 2 rounds trying to enter at the same time, you lose both rounds when you clear it and can't pick them up. Due to the targets being on timers, I missed a target as it popped up while clearing my type 3, and I lost 2 rounds.

I qualified as expert with a score of 37 out of 40. Instead of being upset about the two lost rounds, I was impressed with my ability to clear my malfunction under stress and still hit the targets for a score of 37. We did most of our BRM during the day but there was a night shoot, which was completely different and fun.

After all our quals, we did more night movements, one of them was low crawling and high crawling under live tracer rounds, shot overhead. It was cool to see the different colors fly over as you were crawling but also added to the adrenaline rush.

During white phase, we were allotted more personal time on Sundays. Some people chose to go to church, some went shopping at the PX for supplies, some caught up on letter writing, phone calls home and laundry. We still had our duties, consisting of stripping, mopping, waxing, and buffing the floors, cleaning the bathrooms and other common areas.

I went to church one week, but I realized by the time I was back to the bay, I had lost time I could have done laundry or made phone calls. We didn't have to get up as early on Sunday, but we still had to eat meals as a platoon. I started getting up earlier on Sunday so I could start my laundry, and have it finished before we went to breakfast.

If you've never lived somewhere with high humidity, you won't understand the frustration of washing and drying clothes yet having them still feel damp. Or taking a shower and never fully drying off. Our uniforms and towels took on a musty smell. No matter how many times you washed and dried them, the smell never quite went away.

While my clothes were in the washer, I would make a phone call because no one else was up. After I received the letter from Colt, where he wrote his new phone number, I called him, just to say hi. He had left college and moved to Florida to do construction. He said he was happy to hear from me, asked if it was okay to continue writing me and he told me he was proud of me.

We talked longer than 5 minutes because no one was waiting for the phone. I apologized for how things were left between us at Christmas break and after I graduated. I missed having him as a friend and confidant. We continued our letter writing and I called him weekly after that.

I called my dad and stepmom each week because I had the calling card. My dad was working nights, so he was up. I called my mom later and talked to my sister mostly. I told her about Colt. She always liked him the best, so she was happy.

When I put my clothes in the dryer, I would write my letters for the week, rereading the ones I received. Most times Berryhead would join me, and we would share our news from home, who we had talked to, received letters from and things we wanted to say, but didn't want to write in a letter.

As our platoon qualified at BRM and passed the other weaponry courses, we were able to move to blue phase. Blue phase consisted of final testing on all the things we had learned in first phase, our FTX, field training exercise, 15-mile ruck march, "war" games against the other platoons, to capture their flag while protecting ours.

Before we left for our final FTX, we had to pass the "Superbowl" testing. This consisted of completing a final PT test, demonstrating proper use of our protective mask, setting up a claymore, administering CPR and first-aid skills, completing land navigation with proper use of map reading, demonstrating how to use the LAW, and other drills.

To round out the final FTX, we had to complete a tactical foot march, with full ruck, weapon and LBE, Load Bearing Equipment. Our march was at least 15 miles long. We arrived at our destination during the dark. We put up our tents, dug our trench, and established guard duty all while maintaining light and noise discipline.

The drills scouted our final location prior to the march, keeping us separated from the other platoons. As the platoon guide, they allowed me and the squad leaders to set up guard rotations, determine where to dig fox holes to best protect our encampment, and devise plans to capture the other platoons' flags while maintaining a defensive protection.

It started raining before we arrived at our final destination, and it was about 1 or 2 A.M. We quickly set up tents and dug our trenches I already set up the schedule for guard duty and had others help set up the tents for those pulling duty.

I didn't sleep because I patrolled our inner camp to make sure tents were secure and troops were staying as dry as they could. The ponchos we had to protect us from the rain weren't waterproof, they were more water resistant. Once they were wet, they didn't do anything but keep you wet and cold or wet and steamy.

The squad leaders made sure their squads were set up for the night, had MREs, hydrated and refilled their water canteens. I made sure those pulling guard duty were doing the same. We were covered by lots of trees, which helped, but it didn't block the rain.

As the first shift ended, I made sure the next shift was up and ready to take their shifts. We had "miles gear," multiple integrated laser engagement system, to simulate actual battle. The new version uses lasers and blank cartridges, and soldiers carry small laser sensors scattered over their bodies, which detect when the soldier has been illuminated by a firearm's laser.

Our version was an early version where we had laser emitters attached to the rifles' barrels and the laser receptors were on the soldiers' helmets and harness, LBE. When a blank shot was fired by a weapon, it causes the laser to fire a coded burst in the direction the weapon was aimed.

If the burst sensed another soldier's receiver, the "hit" soldier's gear beacon made a beeping noise to let them know they were "hit." The problem with the early version of MILES was that it allowed the person hit to still fire their weapon, and some soldiers were tempted to "cheat" by turning the receivers off and on again, resetting their system.

There was also no data about the engagement so drills couldn't determine who had shot whom, a critical component for FTX. During the FTX, we always had to keep our MILES gear on our equipment. There were many times that the gear failed but overall, our platoon kept our flag and maintained our position with no casualties.

FTX lasted 3 days, with no chow service in the field. Our water was from a "lyster" bag, hanging from a tree. One of our last breakfasts consisted of scrambled eggs and something else that were in "mermites," military food storage containers. The eggs were runny and made from powdered eggs, re-hydrated with water. They were supposed to resemble fluffy scrambled eggs but were more of green, runny, wannabe scrambled eggs.

I was tired from offensive movements, keeping the guards taken care of, helping dig foxholes for better defensive positions, dealing with heat during the day and the rain and cold at night, knowing other platoons were trying to attack and take our flag, I couldn't relax enough to sleep.

By the last morning, after 3 nights with no sleep, as I was waiting for the guards to change shifts, I was standing against the tree holding the lyster bag and fell asleep standing up. One of my drills started talking to me, thinking I was awake because my eyes were open. When he realized I was asleep, he called my name. It registered that my name was being called and I had to close my eyes and open them again, to wake up.

My drill sergeant was laughing and exclaiming he'd never seen someone fall asleep standing up, with their eyes open. Berryhead was next to me, and I heard her laugh, too. Our platoon ate breakfast and then we tore our tents down and packed everything up. I think a bus or cattle truck picked us up to drive us back, but I honestly don't remember because I was so tired.

When we were back at our barracks, we had to lay all our equipment out to dry, where we had formation, then we took showers in shifts, making sure someone was watching the equipment, at all times. Some of us started washing our clothes, washing the mud off our boots and equipment.

We had to clean our rifles, the miles gear, our e-tools, and our other gear. After we cleaned our gear, we did inventory and turned the gear in that had been assigned to us. The last couple days were spent cleaning our bay thoroughly, making sure our equipment and uniforms were in order, and practicing for graduation formation. Everything had to be done by Tuesday night because Wednesday was family day, after a final graduation practice in the morning. Graduation was Thursday.

Family day was a day we could all reconnect with our family and friends that came in for our graduation, a day early. We had to stay on post and were limited to the places where we could visit. Most of us hit the PX so our families could get souvenirs and we were able to see more than just our training area. It was a surreal feeling to be around people that weren't part of your platoon or company. People in regular clothes who didn't smell musty. People that didn't wear wide brown hats, "smokey hat" symbolizing a drill sergeant.

My family wanted to get some shirts and I had to pick up the shirts I had made for them. One of them said, "My daughter wears combat boots," another said, "My sister wears combat boots," and I had an extra platoon sweatshirt printed that said "Commandos" with our platoon logo.

After shopping and picking out new supplies, we went to McDonald's for lunch. My mom, stepdad, 3 sisters, dad, stepmom, and grandma were all there for family day. It felt so odd to be talking to them in person, after talking through letters and over the phone for so many weeks.

I had to make myself slow down while eating and I hadn't had any type of fast food or greasy food, in 8 weeks. I mostly ate French fries, so I didn't upset my stomach. We went bowling after lunch for a few hours, enjoying the coolness of the AC before we headed back to my barracks. Family day ended around 4 or 5 P.M., but we were able to show our families where we had formations, did PT and our common areas. We weren't allowed to take them to our bay area but some of us were able to introduce our drills to our family.

Berryhead and I met each other's family, feeling as if we were all family after all the letters and stories about each other. We took pictures with family and each other as we sat in the formation area, talking, laughing, and relaxing. We were nervous about leaving what had become home, to head to AIT, but we were also excited to be done with basic combat training, "Boot Camp."

The next morning, we were up early, made sure all our bags were packed and on our empty mattress, linen turned in, wall lockers completely empty and cleaned before we got ready for graduation. We put on our class-A uniforms, light green short-sleeved shirts, olive green polyester blend pants, black dress shoes and hair neatly pulled away from our face, off our collars.

We were bused to the graduation field, Hilton Field, where each company graduating, male and female, lined up in a huge formation on the field. We had speakers sharing about the training we had gone through, to be able to graduate and be called a "soldier." As the speakers continued, some of the recruits locked their knees and passed out. We were warned about not locking our knees and if someone did pass out, no one could move.

Because we were so far away from the stands and such a large formation, I don't think any of the family could see what happened. Soon it was time to do our final march, showing off the drill and ceremony we had practiced for days and weeks. There were so many emotions running through me as we marched in front of our families, the feeling of pride, accomplishment and knowing I had become a United States Soldier.

As soon as each company had marched by, we were able to meet up with our family briefly before getting back on the bus to go back to our barracks. Our families met us at the barracks where we grabbed our personal bags if we had a pass to stay off post. Our military duffle bags were left in our wall lockers so we could retrieve them before leaving for AIT.

My aunt and uncle lived north of Columbia, about 90 minutes so we drove there to spend the night. We ate, told stories, talked about what was going on in the Middle East with Desert Storm. I felt relief basic training was over.

The next morning, we got ready to drive back to Ft. Jackson so I could get my bags and get on a bus to drive to Ft. Gordon, GA, where I would begin AIT. We all said our goodbyes before I had to leave, and my family drove or flew home. Our platoon said goodbye to each other and our drills before some of us boarded buses to Ft. Gordon and other bases nearby, or to the airport to fly to their base. Some of the recruits would stay at Ft. Jackson for their AIT and they were taken to their training barracks.

The bus ride to Ft. Gordon seemed like it took hours, in reality, it was only a couple hours. Berryhead and I sat together on the bus, and we recognized a few girls that had been part of our company, but in other platoons. When we arrived at Gordon, we were driven to our companies to in-process. We were assigned to our platoons within the company, each platoon representing a different phase of training.

Our group was assigned to the same platoon and the guys that just graduated arrived soon after us. The sergeant working CQ told us we would have formation at 6 P.M., to be in BDUs, in front of the building. When we in-processed, they ended up assigning Berryhead and I to the same room and we were bunkmates again. The girl we had met on the bus from our company was also assigned to our room. Our room had 3 sets of bunks on each side of the room, for a total of 6 bunks.

The other girls were in different phases of training, and some had off-post privilege. We were told how our wall lockers needed to be set up, how our laundry bags needed to be tied on our beds and some other inspection tips from our roommates. AIT allowed us to personalize our space a bit more, we could put pictures on the inside door of our wall lockers, and we could have civilian clothes.

I only had 2 changes of civilian clothes and there was a weekend before training started on Monday. We found out that we could take a taxi on post, anywhere, for $1.00 each person. The taxis were old station wagons and could fit several of us in one, most of us didn't have personal vehicles and taxi was the only way around post.

We met our drill sergeant at our formation. He was more intimidating than our basic training drill sergeants. He gave us the rules for phase 1, what our school schedule would be and what time we had to be in formation Monday morning. He told us we couldn't leave post, but we could go to the PX, uniform store and the fast-food places on post.

After we were released from formation, we met some of the other soldiers assigned to our platoon and company. We found our way around the barracks and talked to guys, for the first time in 8 weeks. We all felt uncoordinated as we learned how to talk to each other again, without worry of getting into trouble for fraternizing.

The dayroom had a TV, pool table, and tables to play games or eat. This is where we spent most of our down time the first couple weeks. There were picnic tables outside, around the barracks and on weekends, we could stay outside later.

I washed my uniforms twice to see if I could get rid of the musty smell. The next morning, after breakfast, Berryhead, Skaggs and I took a taxi to the PX, which was much bigger than the one we went to for basic. We each bought civilian clothes, new running shoes, hygiene items, laundry soap and snacks, then we went to the uniform store to buy a couple new BDUs and PT clothes. When we got back to our barracks, I threw my old uniforms away.

While we were in first phase, we had to wear PT gear or BDUs around the barracks. On the weekends, most of us were in PT gear. We started forming into little groups and hung out on the picnic tables during the day sometimes eating pizza for dinner and stayed outside until well after dark.

We didn't have a time limit of when we had to leave the chow hall after dinner. We could take our time eating and talk to each other. They had ice-cold chocolate milk I could get by the glass, it was exciting. I got 2 chocolate milks and a water to go with my meals.

School started Monday morning at 8 A.M. If we wanted breakfast, we had to be up by 6 to eat and be back in formation, at 7:30 A.M., to march to school. The first day of school was a breakdown of our schedule, the testing and what we needed to graduate. We did typing tests, for speed and accuracy and to familiarize us with the machines we would be using. We learned how to read and send messages, the different message classifications, and other communication stuff.

Initially, we spent more time in the chow hall after dinner, sharing stories about each other and getting to know each other better. One Friday night we were telling stories about laughing so hard that food or drink came out of your nose. I told them about being at summer camp, laughing during breakfast, and a Cheerio with milk come out of my nose.

We were laughing with tears when I finished, and Berryhead yelled, "OMG, I'm gonna pee my pants," to which we all laughed harder. She was not exaggerating.

We made a circle around Berryhead as we walked back to the barracks to change. We made it back to the barracks, showered and Berryhead threw her clothes in the washer. We finished taking care of the stuff in our room and went downstairs to the picnic tables. I made a comment about needing to go to the PX for a couple small things knowing the taxis would be busy taking soldiers off post.

While we sat and tried to decide if we wanted to go that night or wait until Saturday morning, we heard "Ice, Ice Baby" playing loudly and saw a car pull up. Someone said my name. It was the guy from the chow hall, Tyrell, that I met after some non-verbal flirting. He asked what we were doing, and I told him we were debating about going to the PX.

He offered us a ride so we didn't have to worry about a taxi, then my Saturday would be free to hang out with him. Berryhead urged me on and said let's go. Tyrell hung out with us most of Saturday and Sunday at my barracks.

After a couple weeks, after moving to the next phase, we were allowed off post on the weekends, if we didn't have fireguard duty. Some of the others had been off restriction longer, told us to hop in the taxi with them to go off post.

That weekend led to almost every weekend of going off post on Friday night, as soon as formation was over, to one of the local motels for drinking and partying. I don't know who was old enough to buy alcohol, but we always had some. Berryhead and I usually split a large bottle of Everclear mixed with a 3-liter of 7UP.

One of the weekends, I met up with Tyrell and he drove Berryhead and I to the motel. Someone handed us cans of beer before we walked up the stairs. As I got to the top of the stairs, to turn down the hall to our room, a girl was standing at the railing and told Tyrell, "Now I see why you wouldn't go out with me, you're with a dumb white hoe."

I'd been called names before, but when she chose to refer to me, the way she did, I had to stop. I looked at her, then at Berryhead. Tyrell told me to ignore her and then I swung as I turned and punched her in the nose. She fell to her knees, crying with blood all over the place. I told her she could call me dumb, white or a hoe, but she couldn't call me a dumb white hoe.

I went to our room and waited for the cops, Military Police, or even a drill sergeant to show up, while I ate pizza and sipped on my Everclear and 7UP. We played cards for a few hours, and no one showed up. On Sunday, we went back to our barracks, to get ready for the week and I wondered if I would get in trouble once I got back on base. I found out she wasn't allowed to be off post and if she reported me, she would have gotten in trouble.

AIT progressed with school during the days, every now and then doing PT, drinking on weekends and towards the end of AIT, more vaccinations, and shots. I had orders to go to Germany after AIT, so I had to get extra shots. While I was getting the shot in one arm, someone else looked at my records and said, oh, you need a tetanus shot, and then BAM, they were giving me a shot in my right arm at the same time as my left.

The shots were referred to as POR shots. Everyone said they would hurt for a few days. Pushups were recommended to help move the medicine through the arm and reduce soreness. After they gave me both shots, another guy waiting for his looked and said, "Damn, they got you on both sides, at the same time." I took my records and immediately did 20 pushups because both arms were stinging.

That weekend we stayed in the barracks because Berryhead was sick, my arms were killing me and none of us felt like doing much. I did extra cleaning in the room, spit shined my boots, made sure my class-A dress uniform was crisp and ready for inspection and graduation. We had been told that our drill sergeant would climb on top of the wall lockers during inspections and if he got dusty, we failed inspection.

I cleaned the top of mine and Berryhead's wall lockers, got her soup and crackers, went for a run, and laid in my bunk, listening to music. Knowing that I was going to Germany in a few weeks was somewhat overwhelming. Berryhead still didn't feel well but went to class on Monday. She had bought some "NoDoz," which are caffeine pills to help keep her awake.

Monday night I had fireguard duty, from 2-4 A.M., so I slept a few hours, then went to relieve the girl on duty. I wrote some letters, read, and did crossword puzzles, in between doing my room checks. At 3:45, I gathered all my stuff together so I would be ready to go to my room when my relief arrived.

At 4:05 A.M., my relief still hadn't arrived, and I didn't know who it was. I called down to the CQ desk to let them know so they could make sure she was okay. She never showed up for guard duty. I had to stay on duty until 6 A.M. We had a test that morning, so I grabbed a bottle of Dr Pepper from the vending machine to keep me awake during the test.

We finished our test about 8:30 A.M., had a break at 9 and went back to class. By the time our 10 A.M. break came around, I was falling asleep. I grabbed another Dr Pepper and Berryhead told me she had some NoDoz left. I took a couple of those and washed them down with my Dr Pepper. By 10:30, I felt like I was coming out of my skin and my hands were shaking so bad I could barely keep my fingers on the keys. At 10:45, my instructor noticed and asked me what was wrong.

I told him about not being relieved from fireguard, missing breakfast, then drinking 2 Dr Peppers to stay awake and taking the NoDoz. My heart was beating rapidly, and I felt hot all over. He told me I looked like I was vibrating and to go to the bathroom to splash water on my face. I went in, splashed water, and ended up lying on the tile floor because it was cold.

Berryhead came looking for me at 11, during a break and found me on the floor. She said we were breaking for lunch and the instructor told her to make sure I got some food in my stomach. Lunch helped calm things down, but I still felt odd.

After school one day and while we were in final formation, the drill sergeant said something, and I made a comment under my breath. He heard it and somehow knew it was me and Berryhead.

He dismissed formation and told us to come forward. He told us to start pushing. While we were doing pushups, we started laughing and he said, "I'm gonna smoke you like a cheap cigar!" We did pushups, then flutter kicks, then donkey kicks, which made us laugh even harder because Berryhead had a larger chest. Then the DS yelled for us to cross our arms over our chests. Neither of us was getting tired and couldn't stop laughing. A crowd formed around us, and the DS was pissed. He made us do pushups again until he was frustrated because he couldn't break us. He told us to get out of his face.

We finished AIT in December, Berryhead left right away because she was in the reserves. I was supposed to go to Airborne school, but one of my drill sergeants told me to seriously think about it because it would wreck my knees and back. He said that if I wanted to be able to walk at 40 then I should pass. I ended up not going and now that I'm 48, I'm glad. I had to wait a couple days until my orders were finished so I was transferred to a small room by myself.

I hung out with Tyrell each day and he was set to leave that Friday because he was in the National Guard. I left Wednesday, flew home, to NY for a couple days before flying to AZ for Christmas with my dad.

I had to leave NY on December 29th, to fly to Germany. I got back to NY on the 27th, said goodbye to my family and went to Niagara Falls with Hazel, Queenie, and others from school. They were taking me to the airport. We went shopping to buy jeans and other warm gear for Germany. One of our friends had an apartment we stayed at that night, so we hung out, drinking, and playing card games before I went to the airport at 5 A.M.

I flew from Buffalo to Philadelphia where I had to wait over 12 hours because a huge snowstorm had everything grounded. We flew to Newfoundland to refuel and then to Frankfurt, Germany. I watched the screen for our flight time. It turned blue while flying over the Atlantic Ocean. Our flight was over 6 hours and by the time we landed in Germany, it was the next evening because of the time difference. As we got off the plane and grabbed our bags, all the military personnel went to one area.

We listened for names being called and told which company we were going to and where we would be picked up. My group was called last. There were 8 of us. After our names were called, he said, "Don't bother unpacking your bags because your unit is leaving for Saudi Arabia in a few days."

We stood there in shock and disbelief. A van picked us up and he told us the unit was set to leave January 6th. We would have to do all our in-processing, in a couple days because everything was closed Monday, for New Year's Day.

The ride was long and quiet. Each of us lost in our thoughts as we watched the scenery go by. The scene that kept playing in my head was calling my dad and telling him I would be going to "war" after saying that I shouldn't because I had just finished training.

We arrived at our post, a barracks building and offices, built inside caves. We were assigned rooms, our linen, and CQ took us to our rooms. I was last because females were on the 3rd floor. When he knocked on the door and it opened, he told the girl, PJ, I was their roommate until we left.

She wasn't mean, but her and the other girl, Tasha, asked why I was assigned to them and not another room. He said he didn't know and for them to help me settle in and show me around. There was a bunk and wall locker near the door that were empty, so I set my stuff there while they peppered me with questions.

They were from deep Louisiana, and they both had "Jheri Curls." PJ had a gold tooth with a heart-shaped cutout. She also snapped her gum when she chewed and would snap with emphasis when she was asking a pointed question. The door was still open, and the girls next door, Q and Felicia, heard them, so they came over.

Now I had 4 girls looking at me, all of them from the South. I had the lightest skin and hair in the room, and I was a Yankee. I laughed and unpacked my uniform and sleep clothes. They showed me the showers, where to find vending machine, phones, and food. I showered and came back to the room to find the door open. There were guys in our room, one was sitting on my bed.

With attitude, I told him to remove his ass from my bed. He laughed and got up, telling me I had spiciness. I grabbed my wallet and went down to the vending machine, where I was able to get soda, snacks, and beer. I had to buy one, because I could.

I grabbed my crackers and drinks, then called my mom and dad. I called my dad first. It was going to be the hardest. After he answered, I told him my unit was leaving for Saudi Arabia on January 6th. I heard the air leave his lungs. I told him I didn't know anything else, but I would call him before I left with more details.

He told me he loved me, to stay safe and to come home soon. I hung up and called my mom. I didn't talk to her long, but I talked KJ, who was a senior. She said she was excited and nervous for me. She told me I better not miss her graduation in June.

Our first formation, I walked with the girls because I had no idea where to go and the caves were long with random turns and offices. Once we started in-processing, everything was a blur. We had to do paperwork, get equipment, rifles, more gear, and other items on the Army checklist. We had to do wills, power of attorneys and another round of shots for the Middle East. The "peanut butter" shot was a thick substance shot into the biggest part of our butt. I could feel the serum as it went into my tissue because it was so thick.

January 5th, we finished our in-processing. I was assigned the M60, the general machine gun. It was heavy and there were small legs that folded out to help hold it up. The armorer was the assistant and was responsible for making sure the ammo belt was ready to be fed, as needed. We had formation at 3 A.M., Saturday, January 6th. There was a bus that took us to the airport where we loaded the military aircraft.

We were all in full uniform, Kevlar helmets, LBE, weapons and ruck sack. Our duffle bags were loaded in the back of the plane while we sat in the cargo net seats. There were seats that lined the walls of the plane, with 2 rows in the middle, facing the walls.

The flight time was roughly 6 or 7 hours. We arrived in Dhahran, Saudi Arabia, during the night, and close to a 100-degree temperature difference from Germany. It was crazy, though, because some nights were warm, and some were frigid when the sun went down.

We loaded on buses to go to our camp, "Camp Messenger," outside of Dhahran. The camp consisted of old single-wide trailers, some smaller trailers used as offices and storage, and restrooms constructed out of plywood, 2x4s and thick black plastic. There was a row of sinks outside the bathrooms, with sinks on both sides and across the dirt area was a row of showers, made from the same material as the bathrooms.

Inside of the trailers they were divided into rooms, using plywood as dividers and thin doors. We were in the first trailer because we were HHC, headquarters and headquarters company, with Alpha company in the trailer next to us. Charlie and Delta arrived the next day because they were coming from northern Germany. They were in the last two.

Most of the rooms had multiple sets of bunkbeds, to house more soldiers. The female soldiers were in one room that had cots. There were 6 females assigned to the room and I tried to stay out of it as much as I could. These were temporary quarters until our equipment arrived on the boat.

The first morning, we woke up to "hueys" and chinook helicopters flying overhead. We had boxes of MREs for the first few days until our MKT, Military Kitchen Trailer, arrived. We ate our MREs while we set up guard duty positions along the perimeter. The perimeter had large concrete barricades between positions and a fence that surrounded the entire compound. We were assigned groups to work together to build barricaded defense positions, digging and filling hundreds of sandbags.

Some worked harder than others. While we were setting up, we saw a white truck headed down the dead-end road, directly towards us. Only those that were assigned to guard duty at the time had ammo in their weapons and it was only 3 rounds. Rumors were someone made threats against the company commander, and he didn't want anyone to have rounds unless they were on guard duty, then they gave their rounds to the oncoming shift.

Those with ammo, I was one, took position behind the concrete barricade in the event the truck stopped and had guns. At the last minute, the truck skidded to a stop, turning sideways, right next to the fence. None of us moved or said anything, waiting.

No one got out of the vehicle, and it was too far away to see how many people were in it. After 5 or 10 minutes, the vehicle sped off the way it had come from. When all of us started breathing again, we started filling sandbags again. This time everyone was working and working quickly.

The SCUD attacks started while we were at Camp Messenger and continued nightly. The first night, I was showering when I heard the alarms. I didn't even put my uniform on, I just put my MOPP gear on, while I was soaking wet.

One morning, I went to shower and smelled something disgusting, like hot blood, mixed with body odor and goats. As I walked around the end of the trailer to the showers, I saw a Saudi man standing next to a goat raised in the air, with its throat cut and slit down the stomach. The stench was amplified because of the heat and became a regular occurrence.

Groups of us went to the makeshift PX, where we could use the phones, buy snacks and hygiene supplies. I called my dad and told him he should receive a letter soon but that wouldn't be my permanent address. Due to security, I couldn't tell him where I was.

I told him we were in range of the SCUDS and wore our MOPP gear every night. I went in the PX, which was a big warehouse structure, lined with snacks and random items down both sides. I bought some SPAM, Vienna sausages, beef jerky, crackers, and a small box of Chips Ahoy cookies. I only ate 1 can of SPAM before all SPAM was removed from the country because it contained pork and we had to abide by their religious customs.

This was the first "meat" I had eaten in weeks, and I almost cried when we had to throw it away. We traded items in our MRE or bartered if they had something else. I hated the Kool-Aid, Charms and Jolly Ranchers and traded them for peanut butter and crackers or the cheese. My favorite MRE was the spaghetti and meatballs. We left them in the sun during the day to warm up.

We made a makeshift volleyball net, and someone found a volleyball so we could play for hours. One of our sergeants set up races, for PT and conditioning as well as preparing us in case we had to do rescues. We did races with fireman carry and sandbag carry/drags.

The SCUD alerts and attacks continued nightly, multiple times a night. The air war began January 17, 1991. I can't remember how we found out, we were isolated like a desert island, cut off from the world. We heard the jets and helicopters daily but had no idea the war had begun. The only communication we had was the Armed Forces Radio and Television Services, AFN.

The next weekend, January 27, 1991, was the Super Bowl, with the NY Giants and the Buffalo Bills. I wasn't a fan of either, the Denver Broncos had my heart, but the Bills were closest to my "hometown" team. Most of us were excited to listen because it was different than the constant news of war.

Several of us had wagers on the game, snacks, candy, and items from our MRE were some of the contents wagered, along with how many SCUD attacks we would have during the game. I bet on the Bills. Most of my family were Bills fans, especially KJ. She loved Quarterback Jim Kelly. Broncos QB, John Elway, was my love, but he wasn't in it this year, so I rooted for her team. One of the guys I became friends with, Chip, was from NYC. He messed with me about being from the country part of NY and he was a Giants fan.

The anticipation, trash talking, and wagers continued to grow daily, while we brushed our teeth, guys shaved, females braided or did their hair in the mornings. It continued as we played volleyball, while we were on guard duty, in MOPP gear, in the chow line, it was a much-needed distraction.

Finally, it was Super Bowl Sunday. We had fresh batteries and extras on hand. All of us were wearing our bulky MOPP gear, with gas masks strapped to our hips. Kick off was at 6 P.M. in the United States, which was 1 A.M., Monday morning for us. We were used to being up in the middle of the night from the Scuds.

The game was close and came down to the last few seconds. Giants were up by 1, but the Bills had the ball. Kelly moved his team toward the end zone but was unable to get a touchdown. The Bills set up for a 47-yard field goal attempt, with 8 seconds left. If they made it, they would win. As we all listened intently during the 3 seconds, waiting to hear, "It's good, the kick is good," we instead heard what would be termed "wide right." The announcer said, "No good... the kick is no good, it went wide right." The Giants won, 20-19. I lost beef jerky, peanut butter, and crackers on that game.

While waiting for the boats to arrive with our equipment and vehicles, we were ordered to line up for a mandatory vaccine. We were threatened with an Article 15, which is a form of punishment where you can lose rank, part of your pay and/or extra duty, if we didn't get the shot. The shot, anthrax vaccine, was never noted on our shot records, but the commander had a list of names of every person in the unit and checked us off as we went through. We were also given tiny white pills, called PB pills that we were supposed to take, to help offset if we were hit by gas. I took mine for a few days before I thought if I was hit, I wouldn't want to suffer through the side-effects.

Some of our equipment arrived and our chief told my squad we were being attached to a unit out of Ft. Huachuca, AZ, to run the TYC-39a equipment, in Riyadh. Our chief was the only one in theater that knew how to set it up, run and maintain it. The rest of our unit was heading to KKMC, King Khalid Military City a forward support base, to set up communications support.

My unit consisted of 4 privates, 5 sergeants, 1 staff sergeant, 1 sergeant first class and our chief warrant officer. The convoy to Riyadh was blistering hot driving a 5-ton truck, with a trailer. The 5-ton was a 3-axle, 6-wheel truck with a Cummins engine. The MPG for a 5-ton was 5-8 miles per gallon. It took us several hours to make the 5-hour drive because we had to get diesel, 1 of the trucks had a flat tire, there was a massive dust storm and traffic stopped each time the locals stopped on the highway to pray, which occurred 5 times a day.

Each call to prayer is known as Salat times and lasts 5-15 minutes. Life came to a halt, vehicles stopped no matter where they were, and shops and business closed for Salat as soon as the local Mosque called for prayer.

Driving in the desert, we had no warning for Salat. Luckily, our trucks only went 55 MPH, and we were limited to 40 MPH due to issues with the trucks, but it still took time to get the 5-ton truck with the shelter on it, pulling a large generator, stopped.

One of the problems with the 5-ton truck was the lack of anti-brake systems. When you hit the brakes hard to stop suddenly, it would cause the truck to lock up. You would lose power steering ability, the engine stalled and it became a hot mess of issues. I liked driving and enjoy road trips, but this convoy sucked.

We arrived at our compound, Eskan Village. We were hot, sweaty, dusty, irritable, tired, and ready to get to our barracks, but had to set up the equipment and trucks. Once we decided on the best location, we started to set up.

We unhooked the generators, backed 2 of the 5-tons up to the backs of the 2 other 5-tons, placed a large steel platform in the middle, that was raised off the ground, to allow us access to all 4 shelter equipment vans without having to climb up and down. 1 van was the message and data van, with all the computers and recordings, that had to always maintain a temperature of 65 degrees. The van across from it was where the teletype and printers were, in case the messaging switch, nodes or one of the modems went down. Another van was the maintenance van, where 2 of the sergeants worked out of and the last van was our administrative and breakroom van.

We put camouflage up, carefully placed the concertina (razor) wire around the perimeter and finished securing our equipment. The chief and the sergeants worked to get us online. We had a door to enter/exit the compound that had to be manually unlocked by a key from someone on the inside. No one was allowed in our compound unless they were on our approved list, which required a Top-Secret security clearance and need to know access. The generator was placed outside the compound so it could be refilled.

It took 96 hours to get our equipment online and keep it online after all the test messaging. Our equipment was the main messaging center between the Pentagon and US Forces in the Middle East. We received messages from the Red Cross about family emergencies and/or deaths that we had to pass to the troops. We received basic messages and confidential messages about troop movements, the ground war and other pertinent mission information.

Our equipment was set up outside the building that housed the headquarters of ARCENT-SA or the Army Forces Central Command-Saudi Arabia and the offices of General "Stormin'" Norman Schwarzkopf and General Colin Powell. Third U.S. Army/U.S. Army Forces Central Command (ARCENT) established their main headquarters in August 1990 with the start of Operation Desert Shield which preceded the Persian Gulf War in 1991. The main headquarters of ARCENT-SA was in Riyadh, Saudi Arabia, with responsibilities for the soldiers deployed into the theater throughout Operations Desert Shield, Desert Storm, and actions following the cessation of hostilities.

The ARCENT compound was surrounded by a tall concrete wall, with a gate for vehicles to enter/exit. The headquarter building looked like a palace. From our platform, we could see the fence perimeter around Eskan Village, the high-rise towers, and villas. There was a smaller concrete building in the corner of the compound and another communication switch, called the TTC.

The TTC was run by the unit we were attached to and acted as the operator/phone system for Eskan Village and surrounding areas. They could patch a call from the US or from the front lines through to the command staff. Our equipment was set up closer to the back wall, across from the entrance. We could see all around us, but it was hard for people to see us inside the camouflage.

Eskan Village was originally built in 1983 for the various Bedouin tribes who lived in the desert. Eskan Village consisted of 44 high-rise towers and 841 villas or housing units. The Bedouins chose not to occupy the village and the Saudi government offered Eskan Village to the US Military coalition forces. Eskan was 20 kilometers from Riyadh air base, so the Air Force occupied most of the compound. We had access to a small PX, some fast-food places inside a building turned into a mini mall and food court, an MWR (Morale Welfare Recreation) tent, and a dining facility tent.

After the ground war, we had access to tennis courts, near the mini strip mall, but if you hit the ball over the fence, you couldn't retrieve it because it was outside the wall perimeter. After hitting several dollars' worth of tennis balls over, I decided tennis was not my game. The shopping area, dining facility and ARCENT compound were located several blocks from the high-rise towers, where my squad was housed.

We didn't have transportation and walking from our tower to our compound was a hike. We normally left an hour or two before we had to start our shift. This allowed us time to get across the village, go to the PX for snacks for the nightshift and get dinner if we chose. They made boxed lunches for those working shifts so we would pick those up for our "lunch" at midnight.

One of my favorite places was the Baskin Robbins ice cream counter, located in the food court. I don't know how I managed to stay skinny and fit because I ate the 5-scoop sundae, daily, once they opened. There was a chicken sandwich place I started ordering from instead of eating at the DFAC. My go to shift snack was a 6-pack of Mountain Dew and a can of beef jerky.

It was late January when we arrived in Riyadh. The days were hotter, but the nights were still cold. It was early February by the time we had our equipment online and running smoothly. Our chief became a heavy cigarette smoker, from the stress and lack of sleep. He wasn't alone in the lack of sleep.

Every night we were awakened by SCUD alerts and attacks. When I was at work, we had to monitor the data and message traffic for top secret information or "flash" messages, which were time sensitive and important. The anxiety and stress of the SCUDs, 12-hour shifts 7 days a week and the constant "head on a swivel" for anything suspicious, was draining. I couldn't shut my brain off when it was time to sleep, and I needed the caffeine to keep me awake during shift.

I was never a coffee drinker, even though my mom and grandpa drank it like water, all day. I requested hot chocolate in my care packages to help stay warm in the 65-degree work van and decided to mix the cocoa with coffee. It took me a few days to get used to the taste and slowly decreased the amount of cocoa mixed with the coffee. It took me years, but coffee is my blood type now.

Our routine was work 7 P.M.-7 A.M., walk home, shower, sleep (try to), up at 3 P.M., watch a movie, read mail, get ready for work, leave for snack loading at 5 P.M., get to work about 6:30 P.M., repeat. We knew things were ramping up based on troop movements and the daily briefings from ARCENT.

Along with the air strikes, there were troop movements from all the coalition forces along with the US Military as they crossed the border into Kuwait. The Ground war began February 24th. On February 27th, Iran agreed to the allied terms for a cease-fire. President Bush ordered a halt to hostilities, exactly 100 hours after the G-day campaign began.

A massive amount of information came through our message center. The Iraqi forces were completely overrun and outmaneuvered, but the numbers continued to rise from American casualties and coalition forces. February was a busy month of monitoring, delivering, and receiving messages.

Another message center was set up in Riyadh. Some of us were sent to help set it up, train the operators and monitor. It was the first time I left Eskan Village since my arrival. This new location was out in the public world. Most days, we drove to the site, worked, and drove back home. On February 24th, things changed.

On the way to work, there was an accident on the freeway. My sergeant stopped to make sure everyone was okay, while I got out but stayed with our vehicle. Once it was determined everyone was okay, my sergeant called for me to help him move the tire that was blocking traffic. As I approached him, a group of Saudi men that stopped to help realized I was a female soldier.

I was in full US Army battle dress uniform, but once I was close enough and they saw my face, their demeanor completely changed. I was about 3 feet from reaching the tire and my sergeant when 10-15 Saudi men started coming towards me. They were waving their arms and gesturing towards me with their hands, yelling things in Arabic.

I stopped walking and took my rifle off my shoulder where I had slung it. I started to feel closed in and pressure was rising in my chest. My heartbeat was racing. I couldn't breathe. I was going to fire if they put their hands on me.

The incident seemed to last forever, but in reality, it was only a matter of seconds before my sergeant ran in front of me, facing the men, yelling, "American soldier, US Army, American!" while gesturing that we were wearing the same uniform. The men slowed down their advance towards me and I slowly moved backwards and get in the vehicle.

I reached the vehicle and jumped in the passenger seat. My sergeant ran back to the vehicle and put it in drive as soon as he jumped in the seat. We were moving before his door was fully shut, merging into traffic that was driving around the accident.

As we drove by, I watched the men and noticed 2 females in the backseat of one car, with a goat in the front seat. I was working to get my breathing under control. My hands were firmly gripped on my rifle to keep them from trembling. This was my first encounter with locals not associated with our bases.

Once we were off the freeway, headed to the other base, my Sgt. told me not to go anywhere by myself, on and off base. He heard about some of the locals and their reactions toward American female troops, but that was the first time he witnessed it. Even wearing the same uniform as the males and doing the same jobs, females were treated differently.

I couldn't respond. I looked out the passenger window, so he didn't see the tears silently rolling down my face from the panic attack of claustrophobia.

When we arrived at the message center, I had composed myself. We were briefed on things that happened, what times troops were expected to move and the daily items. I took the first shift in the van, closing the door behind me and started working.

A few hours later, the air raid sirens started to wail. The equipment started moving as the others jumped up and ran to put their MOPP gear on. I heard my sergeant yell out, MOPP4. Immediately my body changed, as the underlying panic of claustrophobia set in. I had been through this exact drill, sometimes 4 and 5 times a night. It should have been easier to work through.

I grabbed my gas mask out of its carrier, where it was strapped around my waist, on my left hip. As I stood up, I flung my head forward to put the mask on, sealing the mask before I flipped my head up and pulled the hood over. I heard more yelling and panic. I opened the door to see people pointing at the sky.

I grabbed my gear bag and looked up, to see a SCUD headed in our direction. I quickly donned the rest of my MOPP gear. There was a lot of activity around us as people ran toward bunkers and equipment.

We watched as the SCUD, waiting to see the patriot intercede it. Thoughts were racing through my head as we realized we were the target. In January, there had been a direct hit on Riyadh, killing several civilians and we drove by the destruction every day.

There was a chair by the side of our van. I grabbed for it as I felt the darkness of claustrophobia close in on me. I tried to gain control with breathing techniques, but I was losing. People yelled amidst the roar of noise around us, but the noise started to fade. The patriot interceded, but SCUD debris landed a block from where we stood.

The next thing I remember, was sitting on the platform, next to the chair I was grabbing for. From the platform, I could see over the wall, as people ran from our compound. There was debris all over, dust and dirt clouds floated around. We finally heard, “All clear.”

The rest of the night passed in a haze and the drive home, quiet and somber. No one had been injured or killed, but the reality of war was all around us. On February 25th, there was a SCUD attack on Dhahran. I saw the message come across; almost 30 were killed and 100 injured. There was a direct hit on the barracks that housed a National Guard unit, that just arrived in country.

It was heartbreaking reading the messages to the Red Cross to be delivered to family members as they named the deceased.

Troop activity was in high gear, with troop movements all over. There were so many messages about Iraqi soldiers surrendering en masse, US military and coalition forces arriving to engage, injuries sustained, troops killed in action. I didn't have time to stop and think about what was happening. The mission came first, and we were a huge part of it with the communications.

The ground campaign was halted on February 27th, but there was still fighting and activity into March. We finished the training for the center downtown, and I went back to work on ours in Eskan Village. Each unit had to provide a soldier for 2 weeks, to pull guard duty. We had to work 2 hours on, with 4 hours off.

One day on my way to work, I saw a bus dropping soldiers off at a high-rise tower, near ours. I asked one of the soldiers where they were from. They said they were a reserve unit out of Pennsylvania. I was from Western NY and asked what part of PA. They told me the area and I immediately stopped. My Berryhead was in a reserve unit there.

The guy walking to work with me knew her from AIT and told me to ask CQ if she was there. I went inside the building and asked the CQ if she was in the unit and in country. She looked at the roster and said, "Oh, yeah, she just went by with the Lt." I asked if I could leave a note for her and as I bent down to write, I heard the CQ say, "Here she comes right now."

I looked down the hallway and knew it was her, from her walk and laugh. I couldn't speak. She was here and this close to me. As she got closer, the CQ told her someone was here to see her. She laughed and said, "Who, we just got here." Then I said, "My Berryhead," and she stopped. Her face in disbelief, then she ran to me, yelling, "Greenie Wienie," and we embraced.

There were tears while we laughed. She introduced me to her friends in the unit. I was on my way to work and would be done by 7 A.M. She had volunteered for a guard duty assignment for the next 2 weeks, so I volunteered for it, too.

When I told my sergeant I volunteered for guard duty, he looked at me like I had lost my mind. The guy that had been with me laughed and told him one of the girls from our AIT class, was here and working it. The sergeant had been one of our main class sergeants in AIT and remembered her.

I packed my extra uniforms, books and crossword puzzles, my sleeping bag and alarm clock to head to my new home for 2 weeks. It wasn't far from my high rise, but they wanted everyone in the same area, to make sure no one was late or missed a shift. There were cots all over the place and we were told to pick one because it would be our "home" for the next 2 weeks.

Berryhead and I chose 2 in the corner, next to each other and were assigned the same shift rotations. A couple shifts we were able to work in the same bunker together, but most of the time we were by ourselves. The bunkers were on the outside of Eskan Village, to guard the wall from being breached.

The guard duty was comprised of US and coalition troops, along with the Saudi Arabian national guard. The Saudi troops patrolled in vehicles, outside our bunkers, along the barbed wire fence. I recognized a couple of them from the PX and on post, but for the most part, they kept to themselves.

We normally walked back in a group, after we were relieved. One of the teams hadn't been relieved and they told us to go so we could get some sleep because those 4 hours were valuable. It was the last day we had to work and even though I knew I wouldn't sleep well, I wanted to try.

I didn't hear or see Berryhead come in before I left for my next shift and her bed hadn't been slept in. It was one of my last shifts. I was excited to be done. I walked with the group and started hearing words like, assault, beaten, raped but they didn't penetrate the sleepless, numb haze I was in. I finished my shift and went back to try to sleep before my last shift.

When I got to my cot, I looked around because Berryhead wasn't there. Her stuff was gone and someone else was in her cot. I didn't want to wake anyone because we were all like zombies by this point. I couldn't sleep and conversations I overheard earlier started to replay in my head. I hoped Berryhead hadn't been attacked.

When I walked to my last guard duty shift, I asked one of the guys that had been talking about the assault if he knew anything else. He said he didn't know much but heard one of the US females was hit in the head by Saudi guards and raped. Someone that was on shift heard noises and ran to see what was going on.

I went by Berryhead's building when I was done with my shift, and they said they couldn't tell me anything. Something was wrong. I felt helpless and guilty for leaving that shift.

I grabbed all my stuff to go back to my quarters and try to sleep before my regular shift that night. Thoughts of Berryhead being hurt prevented me from sleeping. I never saw her again, while I was in Saudi Arabia. A part of my soul was missing. It wasn't until years later that she told me what happened.

By March, they were slowly trying to send troops home. My chief told me I would be leaving in a couple days, to go back to Germany. I asked him why me and he said I had worked hard, but I wasn't sleeping. He didn't feel it was safe for me as the only female on our squad. I said being female shouldn't be held against me. He told me he didn't want to but knew how much the sexual harassment from one of my sergeants, when we first arrived in Riyadh, had bothered me.

We went back and forth, but my name had already been submitted. I was being banished from the island and the activity. I packed my room and gear up, said goodbye to my roommates, grabbed my 3 VHS tapes and went to work for my last shift.

I was driven to a small remote airport. There were several US troops waiting to board the plane. The temps were now regularly in the 100s during the day and the building was just plywood walls, mostly dirt floors and a couple outhouses for restrooms. We had water available, but no food. There were phones. I called my dad and left a message.

It was about 5 P.M. when a plane arrived. There were troops getting off, but most of the plane was stocked with equipment and supplies. We were called to line up and hand our bag off to be loaded before we boarded the plane. I was in the middle of the group with last name beginning with "G."

We were on the plane, waiting to take off, when someone came on the plane and talked to the pilots. I was in an aisle seat and closed my eyes to try to nap when I heard my name being called. I was sitting toward the back of the plane. Someone was walking down the aisle, toward the back, saying my last name.

Two of us answered to that last name. They looked at the paper and said my first name. They said I needed to get off the plane. They said one of the sergeants got a message that his son was really sick, and he needed to get back ASAP.

I walked to the front of the plane, where I saw one of the sergeants from my squad. I hugged him and said I would see him soon, then left the plane.

Someone from my unit in KKMC was on the way to get me. I saw a vehicle with our unit stenciled on the bumper after about 30 minutes, pull up to the building. The driver was one of the sergeants I met briefly before I went to Riyadh.

He loaded my bag and told me I was going to KKMC until they could get me a ride back to Riyadh or back to Germany. He said, KKMC is a big sand pit, surrounded by miles and miles of sand.

It was about 6:30 P.M. when we pulled up to KKMC. I could see tents for miles, surrounded by nothing but desert sand. I was shown to the tent I would be staying in with the rest of the females. They shouted and hugged me, asking questions.

I explained what happened, that I didn't know how long I would be at KKMC. At dinner, I ran into more of my unit, and we sat around telling stories.

The next morning my platoon sergeant told me I would be going back to Riyadh, but he didn't know when a ride would be available. I had no job, but there were shifts for KP duty or "shit"-burning detail, if I wanted something to do. I volunteered for shit-burning detail, I had no desire to prepare food and wash hundreds of dishes.

I was shown what to do by the guys on shift that evening. The bathrooms AKA latrines were 2 separate plywood buildings. 1 was for females and the other for males. The buildings looked like a chicken coop with a sloped roof and the bottom part had a small door with hinges that opened upwards. This door allowed us access to the barrels which accumulated the shit during the day.

There was a door on the side of the building with spring hinges so it would close and stay closed even during dust storms. There were 2 steps up into the building and there were 6 stalls, each one with a hole cut in the top of the plywood "seat" to sit and urinate/poop. Each stall had a plywood divider but there were no doors so when you had to take care of business, you were open to others entering to do their business.

During the detail, we had to pull the barrels out through the bottom door, sliding them through the sand with a long stick. We did 2 barrels at a time so people could still use the bathroom, if needed. Each barrel was a steel drum barrel, cut in half.

After we pulled the barrels out, we put diesel in the barrel and lit it, so it smoked and smoldered but never caught fire. The diesel fuel helped mask the smell of shit burning, but the fumes, smell and smoke were enough to knock you out. We pulled our neck gaiters up over our nose and mouth. It didn't help much.

Each barrel burned/smoldered for 10-15 minutes. Once there were just ashes in the bottom, we would slide the barrel back under and grab the next. Because there were 12 barrels, the process normally took a few hours. It was a shitty job, but someone had to do it.

I was at KKMC for almost 2 weeks before I had a ride back to Riyadh. I was glad to get back to our "cushy" living, with running water, air-conditioned rooms, a bed with a mattress, a laundry/dry cleaning facility and a PX with ice cream. Each tower had several floors, each floor had 6 suites, 1 on each end and 2 in the middle, on each side of the hall. The bottom floor had a suite on each end, a huge lobby in the middle and a suite on each side of the lobby.

One of the suites on the bottom floor housed a mailroom, laundry drop-off/pickup and a small PX for essentials. The females were housed in the end suite next to the mail room. There was a door to the stairs and an elevator. You could go up the stairs or outside through the back door. When we had SCUD alerts, everyone had to gather in the area outside our suite for head count. The females were allowed to stay in our suite, with the door open.

Each suite had at least 4 bedrooms. Our suite had 4 rooms and 4 bathrooms, with 3 of the rooms having their own bathroom attached to the bedroom. I was the last female to arrive, so I was assigned the room next to the main bathroom, but we didn't have guests, so I was the only one that used it after my roommate went back to the States.

My roommate and I both worked nights at the same compound. When I got back to Riyadh, we would try to sleep for a couple hours in the morning, then go to the roof and sunbathe. We usually fell asleep again and we had nice tans when we left. The guys asked how I was getting so dark, and I told them about the rooftop. They started joining us.

We started taking lunch up with us and over time, our group grew to the entire compound that worked nights, except supervisors.

We were allowed to leave base to go shopping and visit other places around us. Initially, the female soldiers were told to cover their heads and wear long gowns, to cover arms and legs, if we were out of uniform, to abide by Saudi customs. After a few of us met with the generals, regarding our thoughts, they changed the policy. We told them that just because we were female, we were still US soldiers and shouldn't have to abide to all customs when the male soldiers didn't have to. We no longer had to cover our heads but if we were wearing shorts, we would cover our arms and legs, out of respect.

The first time we all had the night off together, we went downtown. The shuttle picked us up on base and dropped us off. It waited for us to bring us back to base, driven by US military, for safety reasons.

There were 5 females and 15 or 20 males. All the girls stayed together as we shopped because we knew it was going to be weird for the locals to see us. Each of us had long hair, 3 of us were blonde and the others brunette. We wore our hair down since it was always pulled back and pinned up when we were in uniform. The 2 big stops for us were the perfume store and jewelry store. We could buy name brand perfume and cologne for 70-90% cheaper than in the States.

We could by gold jewelry super cheap and knew we would be leaving the country soon. We bought necklaces and charms for family and ourselves. Afterward, we met up with some of the guys at the food court before we had to get on the shuttle.

We were walking from the food court, towards the shuttle, when a group of Saudi men started rushing towards us, yelling, and pointing. One of the guys with us was an interpreter and told the girls to hurry to the shuttle because they were talking about us with our heads and faces uncovered. Some of them wanted to touch our "gold" hair and others wanted to cut it, to keep as souvenirs.

Our guys jumped in front of us, to form a barrier from the locals and the females started sprinting toward the doors. Soon it was a mob of locals yelling and running after us. The driver had the doors open for us and as the last person cleared the door, the driver hit the gas to drive away. The rest of our group had heard the commotion and ran out of the shops, so we were all on and headed straight to the base.

My father sent me a tape of him talking to me and he sang a new song, by George Strait, "Daddies don't just love their children every now and then, it's a love forever, amen." He would record messages to me while he was driving to work in the mornings. It was March when I received the tape that captured him telling me about his day prior and in the middle, he heard the song that reminded him of us. When I heard his voice on the tape, then the song, I was homesick, but grateful to hear his voice whenever I wanted.

I missed him. He had always been my rock, even thousands of miles apart. Even 30 years later, I still get misty-eyed, thinking of how much I missed my dad and how the tape made me feel.

I found out I could patch through to a military base, closest to my family, and they would connect me from there. Luke AFB was in Glendale so it would be a local call. Fort Drum, NY, would be a long-distance call to call my mom and sisters, but it wasn't as bad as calling collect.

That night I went to work, feeling excited. I would talk to my dad soon. I patched a call through and asked Luke to connect me to a local number. I gave them my dad's number and they patched me through. When he answered, he was surprised to hear from me. I told him I would call more often now and thanked him for the tape, as well as the goodies.

My unit found out it would be rotating back to Germany in May. My squad was still attached to the other unit so we didn't know when we would leave. Jack was a member of my squad, and we first met in AIT. While in Saudi, we became friends. We hung out on the roof together, worked the same shift, and spent most of our waking time together.

He had a crush on me, but I was cautious of getting involved with someone I worked closely with. I was also writing and receiving letters from Colt and Tom. I didn't know where that might lead. Jack was from Chicago. While we had a lot of things in common there were also many differences.

My squad was told we would be done in Riyadh, May 19th, then we would have to drive our equipment to the docks so it could be cleaned and loaded on the boats. We packed up our rooms and were ready to leave Riyadh as soon as we went offline and packed up the equipment.

The convoy to the docks was worse than the one to Riyadh. The temperature was disgustingly hot. It was close to 130°. We left at 3 A.M. so we could drive when it was cooler, before the sun came up. When we arrived at the docks, we had to drive our equipment to the wash racks to be washed and sanitized before it was allowed on the boats. There was sand in every crevice of our equipment.

We cleaned every inch of the equipment. There was sand stuck in the grease and oil for the axles, in the motor, in the seats. It felt like we were never going to get it clean. There were inspectors walking around. Before we left the wash racks, they ensured the equipment was fully cleaned. No one passed the first time because there was sand in places no one thought to check.

We were only allowed one bag on the flight home. If we had more, we had to load it on the boat with our equipment. I needed my military stuff, so I packed my civilian clothes and personal items and put them on the boat. One of the items was my Pentax 35mm camera and lens. Even though they were in a case, inside a bag, there was enough sand inside to corrode it when it mixed with the sea air.

Luckily, I packed all my film to be developed in my military bag, but my camera was a loss. Some of the pictures are still hard to look at. Some I haven't looked at in years. Some of them I've never shown anyone else. These memories are disturbing.

5
Soldier Mom

We arrived in Germany at the end of May. We were sent to a different base. The base was a small, historical base. It used to be a military hospital. The location we had been in before (the base in the cave) was turned back over to the German government.

My room was large, but I'd have a roommate assigned to me eventually. The other rooms were single-person rooms with a shared bathroom or their own bathroom. I used the main bathroom and shower, but normally had it to myself. All the females were on the top floor.

We were told we could take leave and go home because we didn't have any equipment yet. I was excited because I was going to make it home for my sister's graduation. My flight was booked for the middle of June.

My flight home departed from Frankfurt, Germany, with a layover and connection at JFK airport, in NYC, then flying to Buffalo, NY. I would be arriving late into Buffalo and my aunt said she would pick me up. I was happy to fly in civilian clothes and to see my family. I had a small carryon bag that contained a sweater, book, journal, pens, and alarm clock.

My flight from Frankfurt was delayed due to a bomb threat at the airport. When we arrived in JFK, I had missed my connecting flight by 5 minutes. It was 9 P.M. and there were no more flights until the next morning. They told me that I could go to a hotel and come back in the morning, or I could sleep in the airport. I chose the airport because I had never been to NYC and had no idea where to go.

I called my mom and aunt to tell them what time I would be in the next day. I told them that I was going to find a place to curl up and take a nap. My aunt told me to be careful because people could come in off the streets. This was prior to 9/11, when people could come to the gates to meet planes or say goodbye to family and friends.

I went to the bathroom to wash my bits and pits, as best I could. As luck would have it, my period started, a week early. I had no feminine products. The machine in the bathroom had 1 tampon left in it, which cost me $.15 cents.

I left the bathroom and the airport looked like a ghost town. There were no passengers, no employees and every shop was closed. It was eerie. I wandered around to find a spot I could sleep but didn't leave me exposed.

I found a counter near my boarding gate that allowed me to see outside, but there was a wall that hid me once I crawled under the counter. It was a small space, wide enough to curl up in, but not wide enough to stretch my legs out. I laid my sweater down and used my bag as a pillow. I set my alarm clock for 5 A.M. and curled up.

I couldn't sleep. I could still see the windows, but I was concealed. There was enough light that I read for a while, but soon lost interest. I watched people walk by outside.

My vivid imagination made the airport experience nerve-wracking. I started writing in my journal, wondering how things would go when I got home. Colt and Tom were both going to be there. Tom's unit had come back from Saudi Arabia, too.

My feelings were all over. I had been writing to both. Colt still had my heart, but Tom was new. Tom had written about his feelings for me, he wanted us to try a relationship when we were both home and he carried a picture of me with him.

I didn't know who I was anymore. I wasn't the same girl that left a year ago, or even the girl that came home at Christmas. I felt older than 18. I'd seen and learned much. Some experiences I hadn't processed yet.

I had feelings for Colt, feelings were developing for Tom, then there was the friendship Jack and I formed while we were in Saudi Arabia. It was a trifecta of emotions.

Some of my confusion was assisted by my period hormones. It was the first period since January. My body was completely out of rhythm. I was sleep deprived and I had post-traumatic stress, which wasn't recognized in 1991.

Even if I had known the symptoms to look for back then, I wouldn't have been able to step outside of myself to recognize them.

Before I left Germany, I was promoted to E-4, a specialist. It meant a little more money, with more responsibility. Although I felt ready for it, it was additional stress. Then there were 3 different guys vying for my attention, which added to my stress and confusion. One I had a past with another I worked with, and the other I would only see at random times when we were both on leave. Each offered something different.

As the hours slowly ticked by, I sat and pondered. Thoughts would come and go. I curled up about 2 A.M., hoping to get a little sleep. I drifted in and out of sleep until 4:30 A.M.

My flight was on time, but the tampon dispenser was not re-stocked, and the stores weren't open. There were risks leaving a tampon in longer than a few hours, but I was not flying without one. I added toilet paper, folded into a thick layer to serve as a liner for my underwear. I could change the toilet paper out as needed, on the plane.

My aunt and mom were waiting at the gate when I arrived. They wrapped me in hugs, and I relayed the fiasco with my untimely period. The bathroom in Buffalo was also out of tampons. There was still a 2-hour drive before getting home. I wanted to shower, brush my teeth, and lay down when I got home.

Hazel planned on stopping by but didn't know I was just getting home. She was in the driveway when we pulled in. I was happy to see her and after we hugged, I told her I needed a tampon. We laughed. It was like high school all over again when we borrowed tampons from each other or checked each other for "leaks."

My leave was for 2 weeks. I was scheduled to return to Germany at the end of June. Our house was busy leading up to graduation. I tried to figure out how I fit in. I felt out of place. Most of my friends seemed young and immature. My family treated me like a child, and it was difficult to have a conversation with someone that had depth.

People talked about the war, asking me questions, but cutting me off by filling in what they'd seen or heard on CNN. Most didn't notice I stopped talking or quietly slipped away. My uncle and grandpa, both war vets, saw I was struggling and diverted the conversation.

My dad and stepmom were there for the graduation and party but weren't in NY long. I spent as much time as I could with them before they left. KJ, and I went to a couple graduation parties, she was saying goodbye because she would be leaving for basic training soon.

The week after graduation was the start of dairy week. There was always a parade to kick things off. Dairy week was huge for the local dairy farms and factories. Our family went to the parade, then stopped by my stepdad's sisters house, which was near the parade route. They hung out there while I took my younger sisters to the fair.

After taking them all home, KJ and I went back to the fair that night to meet up with friends. We had a great time and KJ got drunk, which she didn't do often. As I helped her up the stairs to bed, she kept saying, "Shhhhhh, don't tell Mom," while trying to hold her index finger in front of her lips. I tried not laughing out loud, but halfway up the stairs my mom said, "I can hear you," and we all started laughing.

A couple days later, Tom flew home. They had a welcome home parade for him with the fire engine, ambulance, and other vehicles. His parents invited me to it and to the surprise party at their house.

I wanted KJ to come with me, but she was busy. I was nervous and didn't know what I was feeling. She told me to go, to see how it was in person and go from there.

There was fanfare and cheering when he got home. He was the "hometown hero" and first one home from that town. It was good to see him, but awkward. He came up, hugged me, and kissed me in front of the entire town.

I was shocked. He invited me to his house so we could catch up and hang out. His mom sent me to the house with the others invited to the surprise party, while she distracted him. Most of the people at the party were people I knew, but never spent much time with. When Tom arrived, I was standing off to the side.

He was surprised and after a couple hours, I said I was heading home so he could catch up with his family. He asked me to stay because he really wanted to be with me. We were standing at my car, and I felt overwhelmed with guilt for wanting to leave. His mom asked me to stay. People were leaving and soon it would be mostly family.

I stayed but felt out of place. Guilt and confusion kept me there. I knew his family. Tom had an older sister that I played softball with for 1 year before she graduated. Tom's older brother I knew from school and sports. I didn't like his brother. He was cocky and egotistical. Granted he was good at sports, but he was an obnoxious jackass.

We went into the house; the family and friends were asking us questions about the military and being deployed. We hadn't told each other specifics about our respective experiences, but Tom had been in Saudi Arabia since August. Everyone treated us like a couple; asking about our plans while we were home if I would be stationed with him.

I relayed I was leaving in a couple days to go back to Germany, where I would be stationed for at least 3 years. The only time people get stationed together was if they were married and "that's not happening any time soon." Tom looked at me saying, "It could."

Whatever my expression showed, Tom didn't push the subject and changed the topic. He put his arm around me, resting it behind my lower back and hip, while he held my hand with his other. There was static in my head. My thoughts were scrambled.

I needed to go to the bathroom. Tom showed me where it was. When we got to the door, he turned me around and pinned me against the wall. He said he dreamt of doing that for over a year, then kissed me. The kiss started aggressively, with no control, then softened. I responded to the kiss, the intimacy. I savored the moment, then got lost in the kiss.

I forgot I had to go to the bathroom. Tom's erection pressed against me. My body hadn't been touched in months. The feelings assaulted my senses. He ran his lips and tongue down the side of my neck, whispering in my ear. My flesh tingled with anticipation and my lady parts throbbed with desire. Then he asked me to stay the night.

I went to the bathroom, and he waited for me. I told him he couldn't come in and he said, "You're right, the first time shouldn't be in the bathroom." As I shut the door, I realized what I agreed to. I thought, *Fuck it, it's 1 night, we would see what happened.*

Tom provided me one of his shirts and shorts, to sleep in. Before we walked down the hall, he pinned me again, rubbing against me as he kissed me. The kiss was slower, softer, teasing, as he ran his tongue along my lower lip, gently nipping it, then taking my mouth fully, again.

My heart was about to explode and my knees ready to buckle. Someone started down the hall. Tom pulled back and whispered, this is just the beginning, then grabbed my hand and walked me back to the living room.

I was apprehensive about staying the night. Tom and I had never been on a date and our conversations were mainly through letters. I didn't really know who he was. I didn't know who I was. This was unchartered territory. I tried to embrace the moment.

After the friends left, his parents went to bed, his sister went home, and his brother went out. My thought, *Shit, it's just us.* Before my thoughts spiraled and took over, he pulled me down on the couch next to him. His mouth was taking over, crowding out my thoughts.

The night continued until early morning, exploring each other's body, learning intimate physical details, releasing pent up frustrations. While Tom claimed I was more than he ever dreamed of, I chalked it up to sexual depravation. I returned home as I had an interview with the local paper, and I needed to start packing.

Tom asked me to stay, until after the 4th of July, when he was scheduled to go back. I didn't know if I would be able to but said I would let him know.

As I drove home, I was conflicted. What had I started? It wasn't a relationship. There was no need to feel guilty, but I felt off. After I showered and got ready for my interview, my recruiter called and asked if I would be home for the 4th of July. I told him I was supposed to leave in a couple days but asked him why.

They were doing a huge parade in the city where his office was located. They wanted as many soldiers as possible that were returning from Saudi Arabia that they could get. I told him I would see if I could extend my leave after my interview.

My sergeant allowed me to extend my leave. He said he would take care of the details, then I called my recruiter and told him I could participate in the parade.

I was told to let others know that were home. Did I want to call Tom and tell him? He deserved to be in the parade. I left a message with his mom with the info.

I changed my flight to the 8th so I would be back by the 10th. After the interview, I went inside, feeling lost. I looked out the bay window. I felt out of sorts. Nothing was planned because I was supposed to be packing and leaving. KJ came home and I told her I was staying 'til the 8th. She jumped on me, hugging me, and screaming.

My mom and aunt came in from picking berries and heard KJ. She told them I was staying until the 8th. They looked at us, wondering what was going on. After explaining the 4th of July parade planned in Olean, my aunt lifted her eyebrows, wiggling them and asked if that was the only reason I was staying or if last night was part of it.

I laughed and explained Tom had asked me to stay, but I wasn't considering it until my recruiter called. I asked if they were making a pie for me, to change the subject. They laughed and started washing the berries.

KJ was asking how things went with Tom, when the dog started barking and we heard a car pull in the driveway. My mom asked if I knew anyone with a blue sports car. KJ and I both said no. It was Tom getting out of the car.

I walked outside and he leaned against the car, crossing his arms, with a smug look on his face. I laughed and asked why he was in my driveway. He just bought the car and came to take me for a ride. My mom and aunt were saying, "Go, have fun," and KJ said, "Well, I guess that answers my question."

I grabbed a sweatshirt and hat. The car had T-tops and Tom had them out for our ride. We didn't talk much; the wind was loud. It felt freeing as the wind blew through my hair.

We drove through small towns, took back roads, and explored familiar places together. We stopped for lunch and drove more. He drove to one of the lakes. We sat there listening to the water, watching the stars, sitting in comfortable silence. I felt peace.

We made love in the moonlight. We reveled in the moment, creating memories to replace memories of war. We bonded over our shared experience, grateful to be alive and home.

Over the next few days, we camped with friends, participated in the parade, then spent the 4th of July at the lake together, knowing both of us may be affected by the fireworks. We spent every day and most nights together until we left the 8th.

Tom came by my house before we left to say our final goodbyes. He told me to seriously consider what he had said the first night he was home, he wanted to marry me. I told him I would, but I wasn't ready for a commitment that big yet.

He told me several times he loved me. I liked him and cared for him, but I didn't love him, I was trying to love myself. He kissed me thoroughly, then drove away towards Texas.

After I signed in from leave, I called my mom, leaving the number to contact, in case of emergency. She told me one of my friends called and needed to get ahold of me. She gave me her number, then I called Tom. He verified my address before we hung up. Next, I called my friend, Shannon, excited to say hi after we had spent time together camping.

She told me it was hard to tell me something, but she didn't want me blindsided or decide without knowing. She went to a friend's house that morning and her friend was giddy and wearing a set of dog tags around her neck. She had "whisker burn" on her face.

Shannon continued. Her friend said Tom stopped by her house on his way out of town, spent a couple hours there and gave her his dog tags before he left. They had written while he was overseas, and she saw him a couple times while he was home. Tom wanted to see her again and she was in love and couldn't wait to see him again.

Gripping the phone tight with my hand. My gut wasn't wrong, but I didn't listen to it. I thanked Shannon and asked her not to let anyone know she told me. I hung up slowly, feeling nothing, no anger, no jealousy, nothing.

People were getting ready to go out to the club. The building I was in, housed males from HHC and Alpha company and the CQ desk. There was a hall at the end of their barracks that connected to the main part of the hospital, and the wing where my room was located. Normally, we didn't use that hall because it was creepy and took longer than going out the front, cutting across the lawn and entering the side door.

That day, I chose to walk through the hall. As I walked towards the back, one of the doors opened and some of the guys saw me. They started yelling my name, asking when I got back and what I was planning to do that night. They gave me a glass of vodka with juice, told me to start pregaming because we were going to the club, they would come get me in a few hours.

I took the cup and drank as I walked, thinking of the past few days, the lies I had been fed. I was done. I was going to enjoy being young and single. I went up the stairs towards my room, saw Q and PJ, told them I was pregaming for the club. They squealed with delight. Hugging me while each talked over the other, about their time at home, asking about mine. I joined in their laughter while we all got ready to go.

A few days later, I received mail and care packages. One of the packages was from Tom. I put off opening it. After dinner and a shower, curiosity got the best of me. There was a long letter, a T-shirt from his unit, a couple other items and a small box, wrapped in paper.

I set everything down and unwrapped the box. Before I finished, Q knocked on my door. She was asking me something while I continued unwrapping. It was a velvet box. My heart was pounding. Hoping it was a necklace or earrings, I delayed opening it. I stared at the box as if something was going to jump out and bite me.

Q stopped talking when she saw I wasn't listening. She saw the velvet box I was holding and squealed with delight and yelled at me to open it. She asked who it was from, what did I think it was, and several other rapid-fire questions. She drew the attention of other females on our floor and before I knew it, there were 4 more girls in my room.

They all yelled, open it, open it. Slowly, I opened it with my eyes closed. They started shouting and clapping, telling me to open my eyes. There sat a beautiful diamond-shaped solitaire diamond ring, glittering and beckoning me to put it on. I stopped breathing after I gasped and dropped the box, as if it were burning me. He had lost his mind sending me an engagement ring.

Thoughts were racing through my head. Why did he do this? What kind of game is he playing? Am I a pawn in a bigger game? Am I supposed to be the "good" wife while he cheats and screws around? Did he expect me to give up my career?

Q told the other girls to leave, and she shut my door. She asked if I was okay. I looked like I was going to be sick. I couldn't believe what was in the box. There was a letter, but I couldn't read it, I didn't want to see it in writing. Q said she could read it to me.

I left the ring on the floor and stood at my window, looking out but not seeing, as she read the letter. The gist was his professed love for me. He asked me to be his wife, talked about us starting a family, buying property near his parents' new place, blah, blah, blah.

Q asked what I wanted to do. I asked her to pick the box up, close it and put it back in the big box it came in, along with the letter and other items. I wasn't even 19 yet. I had no desire to get married, let alone to someone that cheated on me the day we left home.

Q gasped when I revealed the cheating and placed her hand on my shoulder, offering silent support and comfort. I told her about the phone call I received the day I got back to Germany, the promises and lies he fed me for 2 weeks, in person, and for almost a year in letters. I wanted to be in the Army, make a career out of it and here he was, not even considering that. It showed me how selfish, controlling, and self-centered he was. There was no way I could spend my life with him. He was not worth me giving up my career.

She put the box away, tucked it in the bottom of my wall locker, covering it with another box, shoes, and boots so I wouldn't have to see it. She grabbed me by the shoulder, turned me around, gripping both of my shoulders, looked me in the eye and told me to get dressed because we were going out.

That was the last we talked about it. She must have warned the other girls because it was never brought up again. As we were walking down the hallway to leave that night, the CQ runner came over and told me I had a call from a guy. I told him to take a message and tell the guy I was out.

There was a level of alcohol intake over the next few months that exceeded rational behavior, but every night there was something to drink for, a club to go to, a card game or a mixture of jungle juice at the barracks. On the weekends we explored the areas around us. We were only a few miles from the French border, a couple hours from other countries and surrounded by so much beauty.

We found an indoor waterpark with several pools, waterslides that looped outside and back in, a pool that you could swim from inside to outside. We could go any time of year, which we did on several Saturdays. We partied with the locals at the bars, danced for hours at the NCO clubs, visited other towns, and tried to stay out of trouble.

I drove on the Autobahn, which has no speed limit. I enjoyed driving fast. The feeling of freedom from being able to drive, wide open, appealed to all my senses. I couldn't get enough. One weekend, we rented a car to drive north, where the rest of our unit was, in Bremerhaven. I was sitting in the backseat, enjoying the conversation and scenery, until we started passing acres of cornfields.

My active and vivid imagination overtook me with a vengeance. Recalling the movie, *Children of the Corn*, I imagined children coming out to snatch us, our car breaking down and not being able to get away. By the time we made it past the cornfields, I had everyone in the car freaking out with me. Each of them grew up in the south and believed in spirits.

One weekend, there was a huge fight at the NCO club, involving our friends, which led to arrests by the Military Police and stitches. Q was in the middle of it because the guy she invited started the fight, hitting one of our guys, Chip, in the head with a beer bottle. We all wound up in front of the MP station, waiting for Q and PJ. The girl with Chip, started cussing me out, saying it was Q's fault for inviting the other guy. After telling her to shut up, she responded, "Fuck you, you're just a dumb white bitch," and lunged at me, grabbing my hair and one of my hoop earrings.

I punched her in the face and tackled her to the ground where I continued punching her. I was in a haze of red when I felt myself being lifted away from her. My guys were yelling at me to stop and 4 of them were holding me. As they set me on the ground, we heard the station door open, and Q asked what was going on.

The guys told her to take me inside before I got arrested. The MPs finished their questioning about 20 minutes later and asked me what was going on outside. When I said I didn't know, an MP said, "Well, you're missing an earring and your ear is bleeding." I shrugged my shoulders and asked if we could go.

I told Q what happened outside the station. I think I broke the girl's nose. We found out later she never reported anything because she attacked first, was underage, and using a fake ID to get in the club.

There was another night we all went out, but I don't recall what happened after we left post. I woke up sitting on the floor next to my door. My black skirt was ripped, one shoe was off, and my body hurt. Later I was informed that I jumped from a moving vehicle for unknown reasons.

Our routine was set, we started drinking after our 4 P.M. final formation. We drank until early morning most nights, falling asleep in our PT uniforms, rolling out of bed at 5:45 A.M. for PT formation at 6 A.M. My 19th birthday was on a Thursday and a group decided to go to the club in K-Town to celebrate. The celebration lasted until 3 A.M. We had a 90-minute drive back to the barracks, then PT at 6 A.M.

That morning after we had finished a 6-mile battalion run and were being released to get ready for formation at 9 A.M., our platoon sergeant told us to stand fast after the battalion was released. He made us do pushups, sit-ups, side straddle hops and other exercises until most of us collapsed. Before he released us, he told us he could smell the liquor seeping out of our pores and wanted to teach us a lesson.

We were covered in sweat, mostly liquor sweating out of us as we walked to our rooms to shower and get breakfast before formation. We messed with each other about how bad they stunk before going our separate ways. That afternoon our platoon sergeant dismissed us for the day after 1 P.M. formation. The first thing we did was taste the jungle juice that was fermenting since Thursday night and began a crazy weekend of celebration.

Some group donated trips to soldiers that came back from Saudi, a tour bus ride and all-inclusive weekend at the Berchtesgaden resort. Anyone could go, but the bus was leaving at 6 A.M. I was relieved from CQ duty at 5:45 A.M. I sprinted to my room and pounded on Q's door. I was stripping out of my uniform along the way. She opened the door and I told her to pack a bag, get dressed and be ready to leave in 5 minutes because we were going to a resort, all-inclusive for the weekend.

She was looking at me like I sprouted 2 heads. I told her to stop thinking, just do, because I wasn't leaving without her. I threw clothes and hygiene items in a bag, ran to Q's room, and threw some stuff in a bag for her, told her to change or not, she was coming.

She changed quickly and we took off running for the main building to get on the bus. We were the last 2 to board. We had no idea who else was going, but we made it at 5:59 P.M. Once we settled down and Q stopped calling me crazy, we found out who was on the bus. Q had a tooth worked on Thursday in preparation for a root canal on Tuesday, so she was in pain.

We arrived at the resort about 9 A.M., checked into our rooms and I took her to the bar to take some whiskey shots to help the pain. The bartender made us a special shot called "Sandstorm" because we had been in the Gulf. It was made of Kahlua, baileys, and vodka, and tasted like chocolate milk with a kick. We were drunk most of the weekend but had a great time. We took over the stage where the band was playing Saturday night. We left Sunday afternoon so we could recover Monday, but it was a fantastic weekend.

One of the females in our company left for another unit. She had a room with a bathroom. The girls with more seniority moved to that room, which enabled me to move to a room with a connecting bathroom, shared by Q. I bought a stereo system, with 6-disc changer, decorated my room to make it more personal. It was like living in a college dorm, without all the schooling.

The first trip to the class 6, the base liquor store, I stocked my fridge with wine, beer, MD 20/20, malt liquor, whiskey and premixed bottles of Long Island iced tea. We were also allowed to have microwaves in our rooms, so I added some microwavable meals and snacks for the weekends when I didn't make it to the chow hall.

My squad was temporarily assigned to a unit that ran the messaging center in Pirmasens, where we worked 12-hour shifts, 4 days on, 3 days off, then rotated the next week with 3 days on, 4 days off. Each month we switched day and night shift but kept the same days off rotation.

I played softball and soccer for the Army travel team, traveling around Germany and other countries for tournaments. Belgium and Amsterdam were 2 of my favorite places to visit. The celebrated Oktoberfest. There were street parties every night and festivals with live performers every weekend. We walked from tent to tent, tasting beer, eating sausage, fries, and other delicious treats.

In November, we found out our unit was leaving Germany in December, as the US downsized units in Germany. We would be heading to Ft. Gordon, GA, with small groups leaving in waves, beginning the first part of December through January, with the expectation the entire unit would be moved by the end of January.

I panicked. I would no longer have an ocean between me and my final decision with Tom regarding the engagement. I called him and told him I received the box, but before he could say anything about the ring or my answer, I said it was a bad connection. I avoided calling him again, writing instead that I was busy with work, travel, and sports.

The box stayed in the bottom of my wall locker until I was told my rotation from Germany would be December 27th, with allowance for 2 weeks of leave and reporting to GA by January 5th. The time had come to make the call.

I pushed it off, partying the thoughts away. I told Tom, via a letter, I would call the day after Thanksgiving, while he was at his parents'. I would tell him there was no engagement and figured he could "lick his wounds" by visiting his other girl, if he hadn't already.

I called from a payphone in my building. He started talking as soon as he heard me say hi, it's me, happy Thanksgiving. I cut him off, told him I needed to tell him something and needed his undivided attention.

After several months of thought, I couldn't accept his ring or his proposal. There was too much left to do in my career and life before I married and settled down. I apologized for allowing it to go this long, but it was a big decision. I wasn't ready to say yes. I mailed the ring back on Monday, to his parents, so it should arrive before he left.

He said something about me being so far away, we could talk more when we were together in person, long-distance relationships were hard. He asked if I would be home for Christmas. I told him I would be home and afterward I would be stationed in GA.

He said that worked out even better because I would be in the States when he got out of the Army. We would be able to spend more time together. I told him my answer was still no, there was going to be a lot of upheaval in my life, adjusting to a new assignment.

I was still unsettled that he wasn't accepting my answer.

The remainder of my unit still in Germany participated in a reforger event, a large training exercise, with several other units, for 2 weeks in December. We didn't have equipment to "train" with because everything was sent to GA the first part of December, but we went.

We stayed in military tents, with woodburning stoves in the middle, in the attempt to keep us from freezing. We couldn't train and other than being assigned to KP duty or guard duty, we did what we could to stay warm, in between meals. Most of us played cards, huddled around wood stoves, inside the tents. We were in northern Germany, near an Air Force base close to the sea. There were snow drifts taller than me, around us.

The temps didn't get above freezing and the wind chill factor kept the temps below zero. When we had guard duty, we were in a military vehicle, by the front gate. We couldn't turn it on because we had no way to refill the fuel and the heater didn't work. I was assigned to KP duty twice and guard duty once. We had the MKT set up for meals and a large tent with tables to eat, but we had 55-gallon steel drums to wash and rinse dishes in, which were outside the tent.

By the end of my first KP duty, my hands were almost raw. We had to rinse the dishes in hot water, then wash the dishes in the next steel drum, with water temps just below boiling. After washing, there were 2 rinse barrels, to fully get the soap off, before placing the dishes in the drying area. Putting your hands in and out of hot water, followed by ice cold wind blowing over your hands while they're wet becomes painful quickly.

The only good thing about the hot water was it kept my fingers from getting frostbite. Guard duty on the other hand brought me close to frostbite on my hands and feet. I was assigned the 2 A.M.-6 A.M. shift and the walk to the front gate was about ¼-mile.

Once we arrived and started our shift, there was no way to warm up. Our boots, gloves and "cold weather" gear was not enough to keep us warm in the below zero temps. I had brought extra thermal underwear, just in case and wore a thick sweater under my uniform but the wind cut through all the layers. The one thing that helped some was the long parka I had acquired while we were in Saudi Arabia.

After we left reforger, I vowed I would never live in a region with snow and extreme cold temps.

Mail was waiting for me when we got back. There were letters from Tom, mostly saying he couldn't wait for me to be home, and we could discuss things in person. We had been reassigned to different rooms because we were downsizing. I packed what I didn't need for the next few days while still making my room warm and cozy. Now, I had a room with my own bathroom. There were only 3 females left.

The guy I had become good friends with while we were in Saudi, Jack, openly made it known he had a huge crush on me. After we'd been in the field and our assignment at the messaging center was done, I invited him to my room to watch a movie. Most of the time we watched movies in his room because it was bigger and a group of us would hang out.

One day, I fell asleep watching a movie. I started dreaming about home on the farm and when we would mess with the cows to get them to moo. I woke myself up as I said, "Moooooooo," and found Jack staring at me before he started laughing.

This time we were in my room, and I had bought a sexy, silk, purple camisole and shorts set. I was playing with fire, but I needed to stamp in my head I was free to do as I pleased. I was leaving the next day and he was leaving the day after me, why not? There was a mutual attraction, along with a strong friendship and I decided to give it a go.

When Jack got to my room, I was wearing sweats, my normal movie watching attire. I put the movie in, started popcorn, gave him something to drink and we settled in for the movie. I got up to go to the bathroom and changed into my new set. I came out and asked him what he thought.

The look on his face said more than words would ever say. We didn't finish watching the movie. Things heated up when I told him I had condoms in my nightstand that would go to waste. We spent the afternoon and night together, consummating our "friendship" before I left. We knew we would see each other in a couple weeks and left it at that.

I was done with Tom. As I flew home, I felt lighter than I had in a long time. KJ, was also going to be home from training, and we were excited to spend time together. She was going to be stationed in NC, 3 hours from me, which we were both ecstatic about.

My younger sisters didn't know I was coming home so we surprised them at the house. I spent time with family, catching up on sleep from jet lag and enjoying the warmth of being snowed in with both wood stoves burning. We were snowed in for a couple days and I was planning to go car shopping, if the snow stopped, and roads were cleared.

It was another day of being snowed in before I could car shop. I wanted a convertible, something sleek and fun. At the Lincoln-Ford dealer I saw my car as soon as we pulled in. It was a 1991 Mercury Capri, candy apple red convertible, 2-door.

It had a backseat that was big enough for a small child, but tight for an adult. It was an automatic with the option to shift manually, electric windows and other fun gadgets. I drove slowly through the parking lot to the main road, then I floored it.

I loved the way it handled, and the smoothness of the ride. The speedometer went to 140 mph, and it got 24 mpg. It had a slight purr when idling. I pulled over to put the top down, then drove a few more miles before heading back to the dealership.

The car had a hard top that could be attached. I was ready to start talking price when we got back. I told them I wouldn't pay more than X amount, with monthly payments no more than $225/month. I would walk away if the agreement didn't work. He had less than 30 minutes before I left, and I wasn't going to haggle price.

He came back with his manager, who had the final say on deals. I asked if the agreement was ready with my conditions, if not, I was leaving. The manager shook my hand, said congratulations, the car is yours. He told me the final price with financing, with monthly payments at $221, financed through Ford Motor credit, all I had to do was sign.

I thanked him but informed him I would be putting a large down payment towards the car. I saved my combat pay and most of my pay while in Germany. I drove off the lot with a brand-new sporty red convertible with monthly payments less than $200.

I drove around, visiting friends and family, testing out the speed capabilities, before I went home. I had to meet with Tom, face to face, before I left, but I didn't want to deal with it yet. I planned to leave NY after the New Year. I wanted to take my time driving back and stop in NC to visit KJ at her new duty station, before driving to my duty station.

Before I came home, my sister had run into my ex, Colt. He asked about me and she told him I would be home soon. He said he would love to see me. I called Colt and we set a time for a casual meeting.

I decided to get the meeting with Tom over with before I met with Colt. I didn't want any unresolved issues between Tom and me. I called Tom and let him know I would be over about 6 P.M., giving me time to leave by 7 and meet Colt.

KJ called to give me her number and where to meet her when I got there. I promised to call her after I met with Tom and Colt. She was excited for me to meet with Colt, she had always liked him the best.

It was only a 12-minute drive from my house to Tom's parents'. It took me almost 30 minutes as I purposely tried to delay it.

I parked and walked to the door, where Tom was standing, with a smug look on his face. He tried kissing me when I walked in, but I ducked out of the way, walking toward the living room. Tom shut and locked the door. I didn't think anything of it because there was so much going on in my head.

He came into the living room, asking if I wanted something to drink. I told him no, I wasn't going to be there long. He told me to sit down so we could talk because I was pacing the floor. I sat on the edge of a chair, with my trembling hands between my knees.

I stood by my decision of not getting engaged or married, we were at different points in our life, and I wasn't ready for a commitment. He came over to where I was sitting, knelt in front of me, grabbed my hands and said we didn't have to rush marriage, we could do a longer engagement. I didn't want to get married; I didn't want what he wanted, and I didn't want to marry him.

I wanted to travel and explore the world. I wanted to be well-rounded and well-traveled before I had children. As I explained all this, I felt the pressure on my hands grow as he squeezed harder.

I tried removing my hands, but Tom wouldn't let go. He was hurting me. Fear and tension bloomed in my stomach. I asked where his family was, hoping they would be home soon. They had gone to their property to work on the house and would be staying the weekend.

I tried to stand up, but he held my legs down with his arms as he continued to grip my hands. I asked him what the hell he was doing, he needed to let me go. He said I was his. He could do what he wanted. If he wanted to take what was "rightfully his," then he would.

He told me I was lucky he had chosen me to be his wife. I continued trying to stand and get my hands free while he said awful, hurtful things, but he wasn't budging. Tom was at least 75 pounds or more, heavier than me. I couldn't get my legs under me for leverage.

He kept talking as if he were in a trance, then I felt his hand at the waist of my pants. He tugged at the snap as I squirmed backwards, but he was leaning fully on my thighs, pinning my legs. He still had my hands with one of his, squeezing. I had no feeling in my fingers.

The more I struggled and squirmed, the more leverage he gained. I screamed for him to get off me. He laughed and said there was no one to hear me. I was scared. I started struggling with everything I had. I got a hand free and hit him where I could. He laughed harder as I fought. I fell out of the chair onto the floor. I kicked at him trying to get away.

He continued talking, calling me names, and other condescending things, playing into the things I had heard my entire life.

He pulled on my pants that had been unsnapped and the zipper was down. Suddenly his weight was on me, his bare skin and erection pressed against my thigh. Screaming, I tried to get on my knees to stand, but he grabbed my waist, pulling himself closer.

I was that young child again and I felt the fight leave my body as his weight pressed down on my hips, pushing me down to the floor, with him between my thighs, one of his arms still holding me around the waist, pinning my hips. He told me most people thought we were engaged so if I said anything, he'd say I was mad he had broken off the engagement.

Only a few people knew something happened, but not the details. Reliving the details for this book was excruciating. Remembering the feel of his weight on me, the brush burns on my body from the rug, the bloody lip and swollen eye from hitting my face on the floor, the overwhelming feeling of panic and claustrophobia.

I look around at the beauty of nature surrounding me, the pine trees, the wind blowing lightly, my dogs lying next to me, reminding myself, I'm safe.

He got off me and walked to the bathroom. My keys were digging into my leg. I moved as fast as I could. I rolled over, pulled my pants up and got to my knees, using the chair to help me stand. I ran to the door, realizing it was locked. He locked it after I came inside.

I was pissed. He planned this. I unlocked the door and threw it open against the wall, not caring if the window broke. I grabbed the keys out of my pocket as I ran to my car.

I put the keys in, started the car and put it in reverse without shutting the door. I backed up without looking behind me, not caring if I hit anything, then put the car in drive and hit the gas. I didn't stop at any stop signs, I just drove.

When the adrenaline wore off, I stopped to figure out where I was, not recognizing what was around me. I saw streetlights in the distance and drove towards them. I stopped at a gas station and saw I was in a small town in Pennsylvania, about 70 miles from my house. It was after 9 P.M., I missed my meeting with Colt. I had to leave, ASAP.

I drove home, grabbed my suitcase, and left a note, telling them I had to leave early. I grabbed snacks, threw everything in my car, and drove towards the freeway. I chose to drive the truck route one of my uncles told me about. I drove as fast as I could, being mindful of the weather and deer.

I turned the music on loud, trying to drown out the noise in my head and soul. I found a truck stop, refueled, and paid to use one of the showers. Trying to wash away the disgust, hurt, trauma and memories, I showered for a long time. The water and soap stung my brush burns. I could taste the blood in my mouth and felt the swelling under my eye, but I couldn't stop scrubbing.

When I got out of the shower, I pulled my hair into a ponytail, put jeans and a t-shirt on, then got my boots and winter coat out of my car, where I had thrown them. I grabbed my toothbrush and toothpaste and went back to the restroom. Looking in the mirror for the first time, I saw the aftermath of a fight I didn't win. I vowed he wouldn't win the war.

I purchased a six pack of Mountain Dew bottles, beef jerky, Twizzlers, M&Ms, and water before departing the truck stop. I drove a couple more miles before I saw the exit for the truck route and headed south.

It was freezing outside, but I put my windows down to feel the fresh air against my raw skin. I cracked open a Mt. Dew, grabbed a piece of jerky and let the music take over.

I drove through Pennsylvania, West Virginia and entered Virginia, watching the scenery fly by. I was at ¼-tank of gas and started looking for a gas station. This was before you could pay at the pump with a debit or credit card. I passed several gas stations, but they were all closed. I was driving through small towns.

Nerves started eating at me. The tank was on E, and I didn't know how many miles before I ran out of gas. It was 26 miles before my car sputtered and died. It was the middle of nowhere and 1 o'clock in the morning. There was no other vehicle on the road. I let the car coast to the shoulder, put my hazards on and contemplated my options. Walk the main road, looking for a gas station, or walk through the hay field toward the farmhouse.

I chose the farmhouse. Grabbing my hat, gloves, and flashlight, I started walking. There was a tractor in the field, and I could make out a building before the farmhouse. The building was small. I looked in the window and saw it held gas cans, diesel, tools, and other items. I checked the door, which was unlocked, walked in, and grabbed a gas can. I would refill it and bring it back, or leave it with a $20 bill, in the field by the tractor.

I was about to leave the field and walk through the trees to my car, when I saw flashing blue lights by my car. In NY, flashing blue lights were cops and flashing red were firefighters. I was in trouble. I dropped the can by the edge of the field and yelled out, "Officer!" when I heard someone yell, "Hello!" He was a volunteer firefighter.

I came through the trees and told him I ran out of gas, taking a route my uncle told me about, not thinking about the small towns closed at night. He said I would be mad when I learned how close I was to a gas station and freeway connection. I was less than ¼-mile from a 24-hour 7/11 and ½-mile from the freeway.

I started laughing. He had a gallon of gas in his truck to help me get to the gas station. I thanked him and asked if I could pay him. He said no thanks and followed me to the gas station to make sure I made it okay.

I filled my tank, used the restroom, and called my uncle from the payphone, to yell at him for telling me to take this route. He laughed and asked why I left in the middle of the night. During the day, the gas stations were open.

I started driving again. After going down the rabbit hole, thinking I survived a war and basic training, but couldn't defend myself against an asshole who believed he was entitled to whatever he wanted, I started feeling more control again. I turned the music up and lost myself in some of my favorites,

Boyz II Men, Heavy D, Whitney Houston, Alabama, Lisa Lisa and the Cult Jam and my longtime favorite, Prince.

It was about 8 A.M. when I drove onto my sister's base in NC. I hadn't slept in 24 hours, I looked like I was in a bar fight, and I was hyped up on Mt. Dew.

After spending a couple hours with my sister, I left to get to my base, get checked in and unpack. She knew I wasn't okay but didn't press. I would tell her when I was ready. We made plans for me to visit every couple weeks or at least once a month.

It was dejá vu being back at Ft. Gordon, where I had done my training. I settled in and explored the surrounding areas. I visited Alabama with Q to meet her family, explored Atlanta, and went to my first NBA game.

One morning, I woke up for PT, and immediately ran to the bathroom to vomit. It was 5:30 A.M. on a Monday morning. I hadn't done much on Sunday, except laundry and getting uniforms ready for the week. I had watched movies, ate, and laid low for the day.

I brushed my teeth, which made me sick again, wondering if I had the flu. I went back to my room, across the hall from the bathrooms and got dressed for PT. I looked at the calendar and realized my period was supposed to start that morning but hadn't.

My period was like clockwork now. It started early morning on the 24th, each month. I went back to the bathroom and put a pantyliner on. I ran down to formation for PT. The 1SG announced they were doing a urinalysis that morning. The urinalysis was to check for drugs, which had become a problem after returning from Germany and the war.

Looking back, many of us were suffering from undiagnosed PTSD, using drugs, alcohol, and sex to cope. We never knew who was being tested until the 1SG pulled numbers from a hat. If your SSN ended in that number, you were tested. While everyone was tested, the rest of the company was released for the morning, to PT on their own, get breakfast, go back to sleep or whatever they chose before formation at 9 A.M.

My number was called. There were only 14 females in my company, so our line went quick once we felt the need to go. Our problem was it took most of us at least an hour before we needed to pee, because we normally took care of business before the PT formation. We couldn't leave the sight of the sergeant administering the test or the sergeant in the day room, where most of us waited until we could pee.

I bought a couple bottles of water, but the first drink of water made me nauseous with a violent urge to vomit. I ran to the bathroom, found an empty stall, and threw up again. The sergeant, who was one I bunked with during the reforger training, asked me if I was okay. After explaining I had been sick since I woke up that morning and the water made me sick again, she laughed and jokingly said, "Maybe you're pregnant and it's morning sickness!" Before I could think, I was vomiting again. There was nothing left in my system, it was all bile. My throat was raw. I had no energy to stand up.

Slowly, I sipped water, not wanting to vomit again, waiting to do my test. I finished a bottle, felt nauseous again, threw up, and this caused pressure on my bladder. I was able to urinate in the cup, handed it to the Sgt. and started walking out. She sent me to sick call and said she would let my platoon sergeant know if I wasn't back for formation.

I went to my room, grabbed my sweatshirt and pants, ID card and some saltines. I nibbled on the saltines as I walked to the sick call clinic, which was across the street from our barracks.

It wasn't a far walk, less than ¼-mile. I felt fine when I came down the stairs of the 3rd floor. However, when I walked outside, I was sick again. I ran to the side of the next barracks and threw up in the bushes.

I rinsed my mouth out with water, waiting for the nausea to pass, when I heard a male voice ask if I was okay. It was still dark out, with only amber streetlights by the admin building, but I recognized my captain. I told him I was not feeling well and on my way to sick call. He told me to check in with him when I was done, to let him know how I was.

I started walking again and nausea overwhelmed me. There was a heavy smell in the area that contributed to the nausea, which I found out later was a paper mill. I made it to sick call, signed in and wrote my symptoms before I sat down in a chair.

There were only a couple of us in the waiting room and I heard my name called after 5 minutes. The nurse told me to pee in a cup, put it on the tray outside the restroom then sit in the waiting room. It had been less than 30 minutes since I did my urinalysis.

I peed in the cup, washed up and set the cup on the tray. When I opened the door to go to the waiting room, someone opened the main door and the odor I smelled earlier had me running to the bathroom again. I had thrown up more than 10 times in 90 minutes.

I was pregnant. I had never been sick like this, even when dangerously intoxicated. There were no other symptoms. I hadn't been sick with the flu or a virus since elementary school and I hadn't started my period. Calculating backwards, Jack and I had sex, 1 month ago. Tom assaulted me, 26 days ago. I was pregnant.

The nurse called me back. After checking my vitals and reviewing my chart, the doctor came in. He said he had the results back from my urine. Before he said anything else, I blurted, "I'm pregnant!" He laughed and said, yes, you are pregnant, approximately 1 month, according to your last menstrual cycle.

He would send my records to the OB/GYN to set up my prenatal appointments. He estimated my due date to be the beginning or middle of October, but I would know better when I had an ultrasound. I could still do PT, for now, but come see him if my "morning sickness" was aggravated with PT.

He wrote me a profile to let my command staff know I was pregnant and to monitor my condition during PT. I stood up to leave, barely making it through the restroom door before I vomited again. The doctor followed me and asked how many times I was sick that morning. I told him that was 11 times since 5:30 A.M. I had nothing left to throw up. I was dry heaving because there was no more bile.

He told me to take the next couple days off. He was going to get me into the OB/GYN before the end of the week. He rewrote my profile, stating I needed to be off rest of the week, until I went to the obstetrician.

I left the clinic, preparing myself for the onslaught of the (paper mill) smell. My head was spinning, processing I was pregnant. This was definitely not part of my plan. Pregnant at 19, a mom at 20. I was grateful I was in the Army with access to healthcare and a steady paycheck, but I was scared. I had babysat for years, including new infants but I wasn't responsible for their entire wellbeing 24/7.

I walked across the street, to the orderly room to see the captain and 1SG. I handed my profile to my captain. His eyes seemed to pop when he read it, looked at me with a questioning look on his face, looked at the profile again before handing it to the 1SG.

The captain told me they were going to need a new orderly room clerk in February. The 1SG said I would be a great fit. I was smart and organized. It would be a huge asset to the company if I took the offer. 1SG explained I would be put on another profile the more my pregnancy advanced and my work hours decreased to 4 hours a day the last few months.

While they were talking, my chief came in the back door, yelling good morning. My captain yelled for him to come to the office, he had something to tell him. My chief came down, saw me, and immediately asked what was wrong. 1SG laughed and said nothing's wrong, except he would be losing a soldier on his team if I chose to take the clerk position.

My chief peered down and looked me in the eye, asking me, "Why would you be offered this position? What's going on? You love what you do!" I told him I was pregnant and when I brought my profile over, they offered me the job.

My chief responded, "Pregnant? Like a baby and you're going to be a mom in 9 months?" I laughed and said, "Yes to all the above." Chief asked a one-word question, "Jack?" I said I wasn't ready to disclose that info, yet. He said he respected that. The orderly room job would be a good fit for me, allowing me to still do some teaching on our equipment.

I decided to take the job. Taking control of something in my life, I told the 1SG I would come in the following week to start training. They told me they would send someone to check on me in a couple hours and over the next couple days. I thanked them and left.

It was now 8:30 A.M. I saw a couple guys from my squad, including Jack, waiting for formation at 9. They asked if I was okay. I said I was, but I needed to talk to Jack.

We walked to the back side of the barracks, and he asked why I had gone to sick call. I was approximately 1 month pregnant, I said. He stopped. "Is it mine?" I told him I wasn't sure. He already knew what had happened with Tom. Jack pulled me into a tight hug, telling me whether he was the father or not, he wanted to raise the baby as his.

I needed to absorb everything before making any big decisions but thanked him for stepping into a role that may not technically be his. I wasn't ready for this, but I wanted to do the best I could for the baby, vowing the baby would always know how much I loved him or her. Jack promised to check on me at lunch and to talk later that afternoon, then he hugged me again, kissed me on the forehead and told me I knew how he felt about me.

I went to my room, grabbed my favorite sweatshirt and sweatpants, and took a long hot shower. I cried tears of joy for a baby, of frustration for a life turned upside down, and of fear that Tom was most likely the father. I felt overwhelmed, exposed, and raw with emotion. This was an unplanned change in my life.

I heard voices in the hallway, which meant formation was over and people were going to work. Someone entered the bathroom. Q yelled my name. I responded, "In here, will be out in a minute." I took time to compose myself, knowing my eyes and nose would be red from crying and my face blotchy. I was an ugly crier and it stayed with me for hours.

I walked out of the shower, put my sweats on and wrapped my hair in a towel. I set my tote on the ledge under the mirror, grabbing my toothbrush and toothpaste, to brush my teeth, again. Q came out of the bathroom stall and went to the sink to wash her hands. She was telling me something, then realized I was in sweats and not my uniform.

She asked what was wrong as I bent my head into the sink to brush my teeth. Before I could shake my head, put a finger up indicating, hold on a minute, I felt the nausea rise. I dropped my toothbrush in the sink, put my hand over my mouth and ran to the first stall, where I proceeded to vomit, again.

Q followed me in and held my towel on my head while I was sick, then she sat on the floor with me when I leaned back against the stall divider, after she dampened a paper towel for me to wipe my mouth with. She asked if I was okay or needed anything else. I laughed, "I'm fine, the sickness will go away in 9 months!" She started to laugh, then stopped and looked at me, with eyes wide, her mouth in the shape of an "O" and I said, "Yup, you're going to be a godmother in October, I just found out this morning."

She grabbed me in a hug and rocked us side to side, while she went through a vocal course of shock, disbelief, excitement, then questions. She knew about Jack, and I couldn't fathom saying Tom was likely the dad out loud. I didn't want to make it true. Q knew I had seen Tom, things were sexually aggressive on his part, then I left and drove to NC. I didn't share all the details because I wanted to block it out. Even if I told authorities, what good would it do? It wouldn't take the action back; it wouldn't erase the memories, or the trauma and it would be an ugly mess I didn't want any part of.

Jack started spending every free minute with me. He brought me crackers, ginger ale, mashed potatoes, and other bland foods. Morning sickness was lasting all day, every day.

I had an OB appointment that Thursday and my blood tests showed I might be anemic. The OB gave me prenatal vitamins, iron pills to help with the anemia, a follow-up appointment in 2 weeks to make sure the iron was working and figured my due date, October 1st. She told me I should be done with morning sickness by the end of March, beginning of April, to stay hydrated as best I could. She smiled, patted my leg, told me it sucks, but the result would be worth it.

I went back to my room and cried at the possibility of 2 more months of this. I crawled into bed, pulled the covers over my head, curled into the fetal position. All I did was cry, vomit, pee, and sleep. How was I going to keep the vitamins in my system long enough to work? I brushed my teeth in the shower because leaning over the sink made me sick.

The smell of perfume, cologne, most foods, and some of the shampoos made me nauseous. I was a train wreck between the emotions, hunger, and vomiting. I prayed the baby wasn't going to be fussy or high maintenance because of my pregnancy.

Jack came into my room to find me curled in the fetal position, which immediately caused him to panic, thinking something bad happened. He woke me up, asking if everything was okay, with me and the baby. I cried and yelled, "No, everything is not okay because the doctor said my morning sickness will last until the end of March or April."

He stepped back at the volume of my voice, then said, "Damn, that sucks!" I rolled back over towards the wall, "Yeah, it does, but the dr. said it will be worth it when the baby is born. It doesn't make me feel better right now, though, and I pray the baby is calm, otherwise, I may lose my damn mind, if I have one left by then." He chuckled and laid down next to me, rubbing my back until I fell asleep again.

We both woke up to loud knocking on my door, not knowing who it was. The CQ was there, with my sister and her friend. I squealed and hugged my sister hard, started crying and pulled her into the room. She was looking at me with questions in her eyes and her friend looked at me like I was crazy. I sat down and told her I needed to tell her something.

I introduced Jack to them then I asked if he would get us some food. My sister sat down, and I told her she was going to be an aunt in October. Her jaw dropped open. I found out Monday after the doctor confirmed it with a pee test.

I wanted to tell her in person and the only ones that knew were my command staff, Jack, and Q. She asked if Jack was the father and I said I wasn't sure. She asked if I was going to tell Tom and I told her I didn't want to, but living in a small town, word would spread fast. She agreed and said she would hold my hand when I was ready to call him.

I called my dad Sunday night, to let him know he was going to be a grandpa. I gave him the basics. He asked if I was keeping the baby. I absolutely was, I hadn't even considered abortion or giving the baby up for adoption. He said he was glad to hear that, said he loved me, was proud of me, and very happy to be a grandpa.

I called my mom next. She assumed Tom was the father and asked if we were going to set a date soon, now that I was pregnant. I rested my head against the wall of the payphone, shaking my head and quietly saying, "Mom, Tom and I are not together, I told you I never accepted the ring and had no intention of marrying him, even with a baby." She responded, "Have you even told him? Does he know, what about his family?"

Emotions welled up. I said I had to go because I was sick and that my pregnancy wasn't for her to share. I needed to tell Tom but couldn't bring myself to do it. There was no rush, it's not like he could do anything. Tom was in Texas. I heard the phone rang and the CQ told me I had a phone call.

I assumed it was my mom calling back, so I answered, "I don't want to talk about it right now," then heard a male voice say, "It's not your mom." I dropped the phone. I heard him ask if I was pregnant. I said yes, then hung up the phone.

The next couple of months were a blur, mixed with confusion, guilt, fear and uncertainty. My hormones were out of control, my morning sickness continued daily, and I was moving out of the barracks, to a townhouse. I drove to Texas during the long holiday weekend in February, to see Tom.

I don't know what was going on with me. Jack and I argued because I wasn't ready to commit to him or accept his offer of helping me raise the baby. Me driving to Texas in the middle of the night may have been an attempt to escape one situation for another I was familiar with, no matter how much it terrified me.

Tom had written several letters, telling me how happy he was for the baby, for us to start a family, how sorry he was for the way things happened in December and how excited he was to be a dad. I was not rational at this point. I had lost almost 20 pounds and I was physically and emotionally exhausted with no control over my body.

I spent the night with Tom, at his friend's house, off post, after driving over 100 mph most of the way there. What should have been a 15-16-hour drive took me less than 12. I wasn't intentionally being reckless, but I didn't realize how reckless I was until I looked back at it. I raced a Camaro in the rain as I drove through Louisiana at 1 A.M. I tested the limits of my speedometer, hitting 124 mph before I slowed down for traffic.

When I look at the PTSD questions now, I hit every factor mixed with pregnancy hormones. The time with Tom was uneventful. I was numb most of the time. His touch didn't repulse me. It didn't do anything to me, as if I had blocked him from my senses.

I left Sunday so I could be back Monday and get some rest. After I left post, I drove by a bar and decided to stop. I couldn't drink, but I wasn't ready to get on the road where my thoughts would intrude on me for hours.

I went in. It was standing room only. As I made my way through the crowd to the bathroom, I saw posters for a wet t-shirt contest being held that night. I looked around. It was mostly a military crowd of men. After using the restroom, I was washing my hands and saw another poster by the mirror.

I hadn't really looked at myself for the past couple months. As I studied myself in the mirror, I realized how thin I was, but my boobs were bigger. One of the waitresses came in the restroom and told me I should enter the contest, there was a $500 cash prize for 1st place, and I had a real chance of winning.

I decided, what the hell. I was there, $500 cash would be huge as I prepared for a baby, and I had the boobs for it. She showed me where to sign up and get ready. I was wearing blue soccer shorts, a tight white t-shirt, and a light jacket. A couple of the girls had bikini bottoms on, but my legs were stronger and more muscular. I pulled my shorts up a bit higher, took my bra and jacket off, tied the lower part of my shirt into a side knot and let my hair out of its ponytail.

No one knew me in the bar, "Scandalous," and it would probably be the last time I would be able to enter a contest like this. There were 7 contestants, and I was the last one to go on. I chose "Pour Some Sugar On Me" as my song to enter the stage. They explained they would pour water on us after we entered and be given a minute to dance and show off to the crowd. The crowd noise was going to be a huge factor on who won. I used some of my cheer/dance experience and did a mental routine in my head while the others were called.

Providing a fake name for them to announce me, I waited to be called. I stretched my legs, did pushups and squats while I waited, to help showcase the definition. They announced my fake name and the music started to play.

I ran out, dancing to a song my sister and I had danced to for years. I heard the crowd noise rise in appreciation. The water was cold and plastered my shirt to my chest and stomach, which caused the noise to rise more.

I danced, jumped into a toe touch, did a one-arm pushup and ended with a split and my arms extended upwards in a V, as the spotlight emphasized my wet t-shirt. The crowd went crazy. The waitress that told me to enter was standing on the bar cheering and a few of the contestants were cheering, too.

There were 3 of us pulled to the front of the stage. I was the last one they spotlighted and the entire bar erupted in noise. The judge announced me as the winner, and I gave a little performance as a thank-you before I left to collect my winnings. The waitress gave me a hug and told me to come back the next week for the grand prize contest of $1000.

I let her know I lived in GA and was only in town for the weekend, leaving that night to drive back, and I stopped on a whim before driving for hours. She hugged me again and told me to drive safe. I grabbed my jacket while waiting for a to-go order of French fries.

One of the bouncers escorted me to my vehicle when I had my food, which I was grateful for when I heard the catcalls from the crowd. I left immediately and drove about 20 miles before I stopped to change my t-shirt, put sweatpants on and grab a couple drinks for the drive.

In the spring, I drove to NY for a baby shower at my mom's house. Everyone assumed Tom was the father and we were engaged. My friend Hazel was the only one that knew the truth. I was too exhausted to repeat myself.

I was moving into my townhouse June 1st and Q was moving in with me. We shopped for beds, dressers, and household goods. I was able to eat mashed potatoes and drink sweet tea from KFC without getting sick. After one of the shopping trips, I stopped to grab my "go-to" dinner before going back to the barracks.

As I sat at the stoplight next to our barracks parking lot, I felt the familiar nausea hit me hard. I opened my door and threw up everything I had just eaten before the light turned green. After I parked my car, I was sick again and threw up before entering the barracks. I left my purchases in the trunk and ran to the bathroom.

I was sick the rest of the night, into the early morning. After going to sick call, they sent me to the hospital where I was admitted for dehydration. I spent a couple days in the hospital. I called KJ to let her know. She called our parents.

When I was released and back at the barracks, I had a message from Tom, saying he was driving out to see me because he heard I was sick. I crawled into bed and slept off and on for 2 days. I told BR, one of the guys I had been in the Gulf with that Tom was coming to see me and I didn't want to be alone with him, in a hotel room.

BR told me we could stay at their apartment, they had an extra bedroom, and their daughter could sleep in their room a couple days. I told Tom where to meet me.

No one could tell that I was pregnant, the baby was growing like it was supposed to, but I had lost more weight from being sick. I spent most of the weekend in bed while Tom was there. I told him there was a chance the baby wasn't his because I slept with Jack in Germany. He said it didn't matter, we should just get married and not worry about it.

I was not getting married because I was pregnant, we still wanted different things and a baby didn't mean I had to quit my career. He left early because he was mad and said we would talk later. I was done with Tom. I didn't tell him where or when I was moving.

I stayed another night with BR and RR, did a final walk-through on the townhouse, which was in the same complex as BR and RR, then signed the contract. I would be moving that weekend. Several people helped us move and the items we had ordered were delivered.

We moved Friday, set everything up that night and had a party Saturday. PJ and Q taught me how to make southern fried chicken, collard greens and homemade macaroni and cheese. I couldn't eat much of it, knowing that I would be sick, but I did a lot of sampling.

People played cards, dominoes, and told stories. Guests were in and out most of the day, with a core group who stayed later. I loved having Q as a roommate. We each had our own room, but after a few weeks, we realized we were both used to having our own space.

Jack and I had started talking again. Trying to decide what our relationship was going to be. He stayed over a couple nights before Q moved out and told me he would stay there to help me with expenses. I needed some time alone to think about it, but wound up in the hospital again, 3 days later.

I decided it would be better if someone was there with me, in case I got sick again. Jack was only living there a week or two before he was deployed to Kuwait, with our squad.

One of the girls, a tiny thing from Hawaii, checked on me daily, when she got back from Somalia. She always called me "cuz" which meant close friend or buddy, in Hawaii. I was 5'8", she was 4'9". Her mom sent me chocolate-covered macadamia nuts, weekly, when she found out how much I liked them.

Cuz spent the weekends with me while Jack was gone. She came by every night when she was done with formation. I went in to work at 4 A.M. to do the personnel reports and daily tasks, then left at 10 A.M.

I started watching BR and RR's daughter a couple hours while RR went to college. We hung out at the pool every day. It was the tannest pregnant stomach my doctor had seen.

One morning, while the unit was in the field, I was finishing my reports before leaving and started feeling sick. I had been sick twice that morning. I ate a banana nut muffin, to get something in my stomach and had kept it down for over an hour. I ran to the restroom, which was near the stairs by the 1SG office. I threw up several times and had nothing left.

I was hot from the summer humidity and couldn't stand up. I crawled to the door and made it partway out when I collapsed onto the floor, from exhaustion. One of the command staff came to the orderly room daily, to update me on personnel status in the field, before I left for the day. I don't know how long I was on the floor before the Lt. came into the office. He called my name, but it sounded far away. I couldn't respond, my mouth was dry, and throat was raw. He found me in the bathroom doorway, on the floor.

He picked me up and carried me outside, where he put me in his car and drove me to the hospital. I was admitted again, for the 3rd time, in a couple months. After I was alert, my Lt. said he would be back, after he let the commander know what was going on.

The doctor put me on a liquid diet. Jell-O being the only "solid" I was allowed to eat. They gave me suppositories to help with the nausea and something in my IV bag as well, but nothing helped. I threw up for 2 days, every 30-60 minutes and the doctor was worried about me going into early labor because I was violently ill.

My unit came back from the field and Cuz came to see me. She knew I loved Samoa Girl Scout cookies and bought a box from the table set up outside the main entrance before she came up to my room. She didn't know I was on a liquid only diet and I was starving.

I ate the entire box while we talked. When the nurse came in and saw I'd eaten the cookies, she ran for the doctor after yelling at me. I told Cuz I wasn't supposed to eat anything other than Jell-O but that made me sick, too. The doctor asked me what I was doing.

I told him that I ate the cookies, they were all gone, there was nothing he could do about it. He asked, "The whole box?" and I said yeah. He asked how long it had been since I started eating them and Cuz told him she had been there for almost an hour, which is when I started eating them.

He checked my vitals and asked if I'd been sick at all. I felt better than I had, in a long time. He looked at my chart, checked to make sure I hadn't dilated. After a thorough exam he asked Cuz if she would buy more boxes, handing her a $20 bill.

I was released from the hospital the next morning. I was almost 8 months along and my morning sickness had finally ceased. Every 2 weeks, I went in for checkups and watched my stomach grow. I went home for a quick visit. The pregnancy was not obvious. It just looked like I had a basketball stuffed inside my shirt.

While I was home, I told my mom there was a possibility Jack was the father. I explained I didn't want a relationship with Tom, in any capacity, and Jack had moved in, before he was deployed to Kuwait. She needed to prepare herself because the baby might be mixed because Jack was Irish, Native American, and African American.

When I returned to GA and signed into the barracks at the CQ desk. The CQ told me I had a message from someone in Texas. I rolled my eyes, shook my head, and decided to call Tom back after I went upstairs and went to the bathroom. There was a phone on the 3rd floor by Q's room, which would give me privacy.

I called Tom, sitting down, leaning my head against the wall. He started yelling and cussing at me. He asked if it was true that I might be carrying a "N***er baby." I've never said the word and can't type it now. It's an ugly word and our country was experiencing violence over racism and inequality with the Rodney King and Reginald Denney case.

I reminded him that he knew I slept with Jack. And my child may be mixed, but I wouldn't allow him or anyone to talk about my child like that. I called him ignorant, more than I originally thought and to never contact me again.

He said he couldn't believe he slept with a "N lover" and he was going to kill me so no one knew that I may have a "N lover and N baby." I began shaking, crying, and told him to stay away from me. "Fuck you, I'm gonna take care of you both," he said as he hung up.

I dropped the phone and felt Q's hand on my shoulder, asking me if I was okay. I wasn't okay. I was afraid to go to my house. I relayed some of what Tom said. He was supposed to be getting out of the Army for good to be home before his brother got married.

There was a real possibility he was out and headed to GA because his brother's wedding was in a few days. Q told me to go in her room and wait while she let the CQ know what was going on. The CQ, Jayce, who was a bodybuilder, came up and told me to stay in his room that night, while he was on CQ, and he would make sure no one came in the building.

I described Tom's car, what he looked like, that he possibly had a gun, but I wasn't sure. I went to Jayce's room. Q got me food and some movies, then hung out with me while we waited. Jayce let the command staff know they were locking the barracks down, for precautionary measures, only people in our unit would be allowed in.

Jayce took my keys to hide my car in our motor pool, which was fenced with camouflage netting covering the fence. A couple guys went to my town house, even though Tom didn't know where I lived, he knew where BR and RR lived. BR was in Kuwait, but I called RR, to alert her, in case she saw him or the vehicle.

I don't know if Tom ever came by. I stayed a couple nights in the barracks until I knew Tom had to be home for the wedding. Cuz stayed with me a couple nights after that at the town house and I went to Atlanta for Labor Day weekend. I hoped if he hadn't shown up by then, he wouldn't come back.

My mom and sisters came to GA the end of September. Jack got home from Kuwait, the afternoon of the 30th, in time for me to go into labor early morning on the 1st of October. My water broke at 3:30 A.M., the normal time I was up for work, and I was at the hospital by 4 A.M. I delivered my healthy, beautiful baby boy, October 1, 1992.

The next couple months were an amazing adjustment, being a mom, watching my baby boy, DJ, grow, learn and all the baby snuggles. I was able to enroll him into the daycare on base, 5 minutes from the orderly room. I dropped him off at 4 A.M., went back to feed at 8 A.M. and then at noon. I fed him again, before we left for the day. I loved knowing he was so close, and I was able to continue the bonding, while also working.

After a couple months, we had all adjusted to the new life. DJ was sleeping through the night, I had started playing soccer again, Jack and I were enjoying family life, exploring new areas with DJ, and hanging out with friends. I broke my elbow in January, while playing soccer and my ETS, End of Term of Service, was approaching quickly. I hadn't decided if I was going to reenlist or not. I loved being a mom, the baby coos, smiles, smells and having someone I could love without boundaries.

6
You Have Cancer!!!

March 29, 1993, I had my ETS physical, which included an x-ray of the chest, to make sure you didn't have tuberculosis. I signed in at 9 A.M. and waited for my name to be called. There were several soldiers waiting. They would go back for their x-ray(s), wait approximately 5 minutes in the waiting room afterward, then the tech came out, called their name, said, "You're good," and the soldier was done.

Approximately 10 minutes after signing in, my name was called. I went to the room, had x-rays, and went back to the waiting room. By 9:20 A.M., I was the only soldier left.

I went to the reception desk and asked if they forgot about me or if I missed my name being called. She said they would be with me in a minute. I sat back down and a couple minutes later, heard my name called. I stood up, waiting to hear, "You're good to go." Instead, the tech said, "I need you to come back for more x-rays."

I asked why I needed more, and he said I may have breathed or moved during the first ones, and he needed to take more. I did not breathe or move, I wanted to know what was seen before I did more. The tech said his job was to take the x-rays, so I asked him to get the person that reviews them and makes the decision.

He left the room and came back a few seconds later with the doctor that read the x-rays. The doctor overheard me saying I wanted to know what was going on. He put my films on the screen and turned the light on. There was a black mass in the midst of the white.

The doctor wasn't sure what it was, which is why he wanted more x-rays. I complied and he called me into his office after he reviewed the new x-rays. I asked if the mass was cancer. He couldn't tell; said I needed to put my ETS on hold, while I underwent tests.

My first test was an endoscopy. A flexible scope with a camera on the end, went up my nose and down my throat, to the mass. The test was inconclusive. I had labs, nuclear testing, a full-body scan, MRI with and without contrast, ultrasound, bone marrow, and several other tests. For 2 weeks, I had tests every day with no answers.

I met with a surgeon. He said all the tests were inconclusive, but I needed surgery ASAP. The mass was on my right lung, the size of a goose egg and if it wasn't removed soon, it could collapse my lung. The doctors were talking about sending me to Walter Reed Memorial for surgery and treatment, but I didn't want to be away from my son.

Surgery was scheduled for April 12th, the day after Easter. I was scared, assuming the worst. It was my baby's first Easter. We spent it with our neighbors, BR and RR, and they were watching DJ that night. I had to be at the hospital later that evening to get checked in and prepped for surgery the next morning. This was the first time in 6 months I wouldn't kiss my baby goodnight, or be the first face he saw, when he woke up.

I tried to keep a happy face, so I didn't upset DJ because he picked up on my moods. After we said our goodbyes, Jack drove me to the hospital. They gave me my scrub stuff I needed to shower with that night and in the morning.

I had to be ready by 5 A.M. Surgery was scheduled for 6 A.M. I didn't sleep well, was up by 4 A.M., showered and ready to go. My anxiety was through the roof. It took the surgeon talking to me prior to surgery, to help me calm down.

Initially, the surgeon wanted to cut from the middle of my chest, below my collarbone, coming down and underneath my right breast. I asked him if we could try a different route that wouldn't be as visible because I didn't want people asking about the scar for the rest of my life. It wasn't vanity. I knew how most people are when they see scars, wounds, etc. I didn't want the pitying looks, or the "I'm sorry!" sentiments.

The surgery went according to plan. The surgeon was able to go in from my right side, under my armpit, between my ribcage. I had never been under anesthesia before, and it took longer than it should have for me to come out of it. The medical staff was concerned until I started stirring.

When I woke, I looked around, confused. There were tubes coming out of me from all areas. I had to pee and when I went, I didn't feel a warm wetness. I had a catheter in.

I was hospitalized for 14 days because I got pneumonia. They kept me on oxygen and took x-rays every 20 minutes, making sure it didn't get worse. I was confined to bed with my chest tube, which gave me a 3-foot radius, enough that I could get to the sink to wash my hands, face, and brush my teeth.

My face was dry from the morphine, my hair needed to be washed and I wanted a shower. Unfortunately, I couldn't shower or wash my hair because of my chest tube. I couldn't lift my arms without pulling on my staples holding me together.

I was miserable. I hadn't seen my son, DJ, in over a week. I hadn't had a real shower and my hair had not been washed in a week. There were only a few channels to watch on TV.

One day, I fell asleep with the TV on. I woke up to yelling and gunshots. There was a siege being covered by the news. It was a compound in Waco, TX, and the occupants inside the compound were firing shots at the police and FBI. The scene was surreal, as if it was a movie. Soon the compound was on fire, the gunshots stopped, and people were led out.

I had no idea what had led up to the Waco incident and never researched it further. It triggered too many memories from being in the hospital for so long. The Waco incident was still on the TV when the doctor came in a couple hours after lunch. I felt him sit down on the side of my bed and put his hand over mine, which was bruised from the IV.

He told me the results; the tumor was Non-Hodgkin's Lymphoma. He said it was cancer, appeared to be contained to the tumor. The prior tests indicated no signs of cancer. He told me about the follow-up treatment, as a precaution, in case any cells from the tumor had spread to surrounding tissue.

I would be non-deployable for 5 years and only be able to PCS, permanent change of station, if I was close to a cancer facility. He said he would set everything up and I should be allowed to go home by the end of the week. Before he left, he asked me if there was anything he could do for me.

I looked at him with tears in my eyes and said, "I need to see my baby." He squeezed my hand again and said he would make it happen. That afternoon, Jack brought DJ to the hospital. I just wanted to hold my baby, smell his hair, and hold his hand while looking into his beautiful brown eyes, with flecks of green.

DJ was smiling when they came into my room until Jack turned all the way around. DJ saw the tubes coming from my body. He started screaming and crying, but I kissed his face, told him I loved him and had Jack take him home. I didn't want DJ traumatized.

I turned the TV off and laid in the bed, looking at the ceiling with tears running down my face. The doctor said I had a 50/50 chance of surviving 5 years. I prayed and asked God why he would bless me with such a beautiful baby if I wasn't going to make it. I told God I just wanted to see my baby boy grow up.

The doctor came in that evening before he left for the night, to check on me again. I thanked him for allowing me to see DJ. He asked if I was okay. I was going to be. Praying brought me peace. I would be grateful for every day I was blessed to be DJ's mother. I explained why I sent DJ home, so quickly.

He squeezed my hand again; told me I was tough and wise at my young age of 20. He said I handled the news better than people who lived full and long lives. We sat in silence for a short time, before saying he would be back in the morning to check on me.

I cried tears of joy when I finally heard the chest tube could come out and the pneumonia was better. Once the tube was out, I could shower. Relief and emotions coursed through me. I was grateful. I had taken enough GI baths to last me an eternity.

I rolled onto my right side so the doctors could access the chest tube. One would pull the stitching together to close the scar up as soon as the tube was out. He said it wouldn't hurt, but it might feel funny as the tube came out. I held onto the bedrail to keep myself on my side and felt him grab the tube. He counted to 3 and yanked hard.

Some of my skin had healed around the tube and it pulled on the skin. It hurt but the feeling of something inside being pulled out, felt like a snake slithering through my lungs, ribcage and body. It felt like my breath was being pulled out of me until the entire tubing was out. I took deep breaths while they pulled my stitches together and put a waterproof bandage over the tube wound.

I rolled back over to see the tube being stuffed into a clear bag. It had a little blood on it, but it was remarkably clean which seemed odd because it had come from inside my chest. The doctor said a nurse would be in shortly to help me shower. He would be back later, to make sure I was still stable.

The nurse shampooed my hair 4 or 5 times because I told her it didn't feel clean yet. She put conditioner in and let it set while I washed the rest of my body, while sitting in a shower chair. The warm water felt so good that I didn't want to get out.

Once I was clean, back in a clean bed with my hair braided, I fell asleep and slept hard, for the first time, in over a week. I decided then I was going to get out of the Army, as much as I loved it, because I wanted to spend as much time as I could with my son. I brainstormed ideas on what I loved to do and ideas for possible careers.

My top-secret clearances afforded me several jobs, one with a national company, based out of Atlanta, GA, starting at $75,000 a year. I had no desire to live in Atlanta, or anywhere in GA, and the idea of a "normal job" didn't appeal to me.

After several pages of pros and cons, I narrowed my career choices down to: librarian, English teacher or cosmetologist. Being a librarian would allow me to be surrounded by books, working in an environment I was familiar with. The biggest downfall was the 4-year degree requirement. I wasn't interested in college, which also knocked English teacher off my list. I settled on cosmetology school, which would take approximately a year, but would allow me to "beautify the world" and expand my natural talent.

After 14 days, I was released from the hospital, to continue healing at home. I was limited on how much I could lift, carry, hold, or do because I had over 50 staples holding my incision together. DJ was just under the weight limit, but I still had to be careful.

While I was at home, we soaked up all the time we missed. I couldn't get enough of seeing his little face, hearing his baby talk and watching him crawl. He had been on formula since I had gone into the hospital and was also eating some baby food. We had a routine every day and I didn't realize my heart or love for him could grow.

I was scheduled to start radiation the middle of May, finishing the end of June. My profile was extended through August, after I completed treatment. The first appointment; I had to be lined up perfectly on the machine, with my head, arms and legs strapped down tightly. They measured and remeasured where the radiation grids would be, before drawing the temporary markings on my face, neck, and chest.

I had blue marker all over my face, under my chin, down my chest and around my breasts. It looked like small targets drawn in certain areas, all connected by lines. Jack had a softball game that night. Normally, I cheered in the bleachers, but I chose to sit in the car.

The only people who knew I had cancer were BR and RR, a few family members, and my command staff. Saying "cancer" caused a crazy reaction from people. Some acted as if it was contagious and backed away, while others treated you as if you did something wrong to get it. There were also the ones that immediately got a look of pity in their eyes, expecting you to drop dead any minute.

Telling others you have cancer is an exhausting experience. The pity, concern and reaffirming you're okay takes its toll. I didn't feel weak. My mind, will, and desire for life were all very strong. My cancer experience was isolating. There were times when I was surrounded by people but felt alone.

The next day I went back to the clinic where they remeasured me again using the previous marks they made, then permanently tattooed little blue dots on my chin, neck, and chest. Once I was tattooed, they did my first treatment, which lasted no longer than 10 minutes.

I had treatment every day for 6 weeks, including weekends and holidays. I scheduled all my appointments for 1 P.M. so Jack could bring DJ home from daycare during his lunch. Jack drove me the first week until I could drive and lift DJ out of his car seat.

The staff at the radiation center told me I could bring DJ with me to my appointments. There was a play area where he could play, and staff watched him. By the end of the first week, he had the staff eating out of his hand. He was the highlight of their day.

The radiation specialist said there was a possibility of losing my hair, especially the areas where I received radiation, which was the front from chin to breastbone and same location on the back side. The first couple weeks, I felt fine with no side-effects.

DJ was trying to walk. Crawling didn't get him to the places he wanted to go fast enough. After my treatments, we came home, had a snack and I sat on the floor so he could practice walking to me. I loved watching the glee in his face as he reached me.

I was into my 3rd week of treatment when we went through our normal routine. DJ was walking better so I put more distance between us. I had my hair down, instead of in a braid because my head was tender from the treatment. DJ started walking towards me and as he reached me, he started to fall. He grabbed my hair with both hands, to help steady himself, but he fell on his butt, holding 2 fists full of my hair.

We looked at the hair, then he looked at me and started screaming. I don't know if he thought he had hurt me or if it felt weird holding all my hair in his hands. I started crying and grabbed DJ in my arms, rocking him. I sat on the floor holding and rocking him until he fell asleep in my arms, then I laid down on the floor with him, crying myself to sleep.

I finished treatment right before July 4th, in time for us to drive to Chicago to visit Jack's family, so they could meet DJ. I had lost hair on the back of my head, from the top of my ears and occipital bone down, my throat was burnt on the inside, and it looked like I had dirt on my neck/chest from where my skin burned.

The second day we woke up to extreme heat warnings, high humidity and the air conditioner stopped working. I was miserable. My neck itched all the time from the sweat and burns.

We planned to visit downtown Chicago. I had a new video camera, which was as big as DJ, but that was technology in the 90s. Downtown was fun to see. We sang "Love and marriage, love and marriage, goes together like a horse and carriage. This I tell you, brother, you can't have one without the other!" from *Married with Children*.

We drove near Cabrini Greens, known from the show *Candyman*. The producers and directors had to work out a deal with the gang members that controlled the housing project to help keep violence down.

The other show *Good Times* wasn't filmed on location, but showcased Cabrini Green as the "set location." If you've seen neither, it's a wakeup to the racial injustices that are real, even now, especially those in poverty areas.

We stopped at a pizza place downtown with some of the best pizza I've ever had, drove up and down Michigan Avenue, near the lake and outskirt areas. I ate at White Castle for the first time, running for a bathroom soon after. If you know, you know.

We were in Illinois for over a week. The AC was out the entire time. It was fixed the day we left. The technicians were busy due to the holiday and record heat. It also took time to get the new AC unit. If you have dogs, put a gate, or fence up around the AC unit. If the dogs pee on it enough times, the components will rust, and need to replace your AC unit.

The summer passed in a blur, DJ and I spent most of the day in the pool splashing around. When he napped, I napped. I was fatigued all the time. I celebrated my 21st birthday by buying alcohol, legally, even though I couldn't drink it. My meals consisted mostly of scrambled eggs and milkshakes because my throat was raw.

By DJ's first birthday, I was down to 113 pounds. I looked like a skeleton. KJ said I looked like a zombie. I was pale even though we were in the pool during the day. There was peach fuzz on the back of my head where my hair had fallen out and growing back.

We celebrated with neighbors, friends, and KJ. DJ didn't have much interest in the presents. He wanted to play with the basketball hoop. The cake was a "Teenage Mutant Ninja Turtles" theme with DJ wearing most of his on his face, hands, hair, and shirt.

I was assigned to a "medical hold" unit, comprised of soldiers with medical issues. Anything from broken bones, pregnancy, psychiatric issues to cancer and other diseases. After returning from an appointment, I saw the television showing the news in Somalia.

We all had friends and/or family over there. They reported soldiers were pinned down, with Blackhawk pilots trying to rescue them, as we sat glued to the TV. I felt sick. One of the neighbor boys would probably be amid it all because he was a pilot.

Helicopters were being shot down. Information on survivors was unknown. There were soldiers fighting for their lives and running out of ammunition. As we watched, in utter silence, the news showed a pilot being dragged through the streets by the Somalis.

He was bruised and bloody, covered with soot. We couldn't make out who it was. It wasn't my childhood neighbor. Later, I learned the neighbor that used to run up and down our road in his short shorts, helped teach me how to shoot and I crushed on, was killed in action that day. He was one of the pilots that flew directly into a combat zone, to rescue soldiers. "NSDQ" – Night Stalkers Don't Quit.

Those images are burned into my memory. Chief Cliff "Elvis" Wolcott is remembered by family, friends, and comrades. There is a plaque in his honor in the school we attended and on a huge rock, in the town next to us. His bravery and courage will live on through those of us that continue to share his heroism.

I soon received clearance from my doctors to get out of the Army with continued follow up at the local VA where we planned to move. Jack was out of the Army, too and we chose Charlotte, NC, as our home. It was close to NY and Chicago and in a warm climate.

I chose the date I wanted to get out. It gave us enough time to secure a place in Charlotte, look for work/school and out-process. My last date wearing a US Army uniform was November 13, 1993. I ran into Q at my final sign-out. She was getting out, too.

After we talked about our plans, I left to begin the moving process. We had a U-Haul that Jack and some friends packed. They drove to NC to help unload it. DJ and I were in my car so we could get our keys before the office closed for the day. Jack was in his car, following the U-Haul and another friend drove a car, to take our helpers back to GA.

DJ and I were on the road by 11 A.M., after I changed my uniform, for the last time. The drive was about 3 hours. I stopped for a Happy Meal for him and vanilla shake for me. It was still hard eating and swallowing.

We had a two-bedroom apartment on the second floor. I was glad we had extra muscle carrying boxes and furniture. After everything was moved in, we ordered pizza and wings.

It was a surreal feeling, being out of the Army, no job or income, in a completely new state where we knew no one, except each other. We were exposed to the culture change. On and around a military base, we were insulated from the non-military communities. We quickly realized the military had been more accepting of interracial relationships. Additionally, Jack and I were northerners. We were "Yanks" in a non-military southern community.

We didn't go to many places together when we first moved to NC because he was going to school in the morning and working swing shifts. I was working in SC where my aunt worked. I did administrative work during the day, waiting for school to start. I was registered at a cosmetology school in SC where I would get state licensing in NC and SC, once I passed my state boards.

A week after we moved in, I got a phone call from Q, asking if she could visit. I was surprised, but excited to see her. She came over with her husband and told me they moved to Charlotte. They had their keys to an apartment and were moving in the next day.

My sister from another mister, Q, was going to be living 15 minutes from me. After helping them move and settle in, we saw each other almost every Friday and/or Saturday night, for movies, dinner, cards, and dominoes.

The month of December was rough. Our paychecks were smaller than our Army ones. We were paying more in insurance because we weren't married. I was using more gas because I had to drive to the VA, 3 hours away, weekly.

We were used to getting paid at the beginning of the month, taking care of all the bills, and putting money aside for budgeted food and fuel. Now we were getting paid weekly, but all the bills were still due at the beginning of the month, and we made less money.

We discussed what we should do if something happened to me. I wanted to make sure DJ was taken care of and Jack wanted to raise him. We talked about the legalities, cost of insurance, and the details most don't think about before death or illness.

Many laws have changed since the 90s, but at the time, if I had gotten sick or injured, Jack wouldn't be allowed to make decisions for me or DJ, because we weren't married. We made the decision to get married.

We chose December 22nd. We were both off at the same time and it was before the end of the year. A justice of the peace performed a quick wedding in a small room in his house. It had started snowing on our way. It was early evening and the flakes sparkled in the lights. All the houses were lit with Christmas lights and DJ loved it.

After a quick ceremony, with DJ standing between us, we went back to my aunt's house for cake and ice cream. I can't say I was "in love" with Jack, but I cared for him.

I started school in January 1994. My aunt set me up with the daycare her kids had attended, only 5 minutes from my school. School started at 8:00 A.M., and done by 3:30 P.M., Monday through Friday, until we finished the first semester. The next semester, we would move to Tuesday through Saturday. Saturday was open for the public to get discounted services by students.

School was 45 minutes from our apartment. We were always on the road by 7 A.M. DJ got breakfast and lunch at the daycare, so he normally ate a piece of toast while I got ready. If it was nice out, we drove home with the top down so DJ could feel like he was "flying."

He had started talking and putting more words together. He was developing a southern accent when he talked, especially when he called me "Momma."

I loved his little voice and how curious he was, always wanting to explore and see new things. If I drove home or to school a different way, he wanted to know where we were going, why we were going that way and how long it would take. Our car rides were filled with us talking, laughing, singing and his wonder at the world around him.

Every trip the to the VA for bloodwork and scans, DJ was with me. The first few visits, all the older vets always asked if I was there with my dad or husband. For them, seeing a young female vet at the VA was uncommon. Seeing a young female vet at the VA in the oncology department was rarer.

We got to know the regulars, heard their stories and soon they were bringing small toys for DJ. His obsession was Matchbox cars. He usually came home with a new car or truck. The guys weren't used to having a little one around. They loved talking to DJ because he was so inquisitive and attentive. Even playing with toys, he was still asking questions.

As they moved the appointments back to monthly, over time we had to say goodbye to friends that passed away.

My aunt asked if I would go to her house after I finished school for the day to help keep her teens from fighting until she got home. She had a maid that came in to help with light cleaning and laundry. I offered to clean, do laundry, and start dinner, and she could pay me instead of a maid, to help supplement my GI bill.

Soon, DJ and I were headed to my aunt's house daily, after school. He loved playing with his cousins, running wild, wrestling, playing basketball and jumping around. I loved getting to know my cousins and spending more time with my aunt and uncle.

My great-grandma and grandpa always called me by my aunt's name when they saw me because they said I looked exactly like her. I was her "mini me." We spent time together in the evenings and weekends. I loved helping take care of their house and knew having dinner ready when they got home from work was appreciated.

Soon after I started school, Jack invited a friend to visit. We both worked with him in the Army, but I didn't spend much time with him. I thought the visit was going to be a couple days, but it turned into 2 weeks. I was coming home to dishes in the sink, laundry needing to be done, and dinner to prepare. There was also the grocery shopping.

My "quiet" evenings with DJ disappeared and I grew resentful. That visit opened my eyes to how different Jack and I were. We wanted different things, enjoyed different things and were more like roommates than husband and wife.

I came home on a Friday, changed clothes, then DJ and I went grocery shopping. I found a great Chinese food place. This became our Friday night ritual. DJ picked a movie at Blockbuster before we ordered food, bought groceries, picked up our food and went home.

After we put groceries away, I showered, then gave him a bath. We put our pajamas on and settled in my room with our food and movie. With Jack's friend visiting, he had taken over DJ's room, so DJ slept with me.

One Friday, after getting groceries, Jack was home instead of at work. I was stunned at first then asked if he was okay. He became defensive and said, "Can't I take a day off sometimes?" This stopped me in my tracks. DJ ran up to him to give him a hug and I went into the kitchen. Dishes were in the sink; I smelled liquor and became more irritated.

Jack said they were going out and didn't know when they would be back. I asked if he was going to clean the kitchen before he left and he yelled again. I told him to leave, and I didn't care if he came back or not.

They left and I cleaned the kitchen, got DJ's bath started, showered, wishing for a bottle of wine. After eating, I snuggled with DJ trying to push the hurt out of my head and heart.

The next morning, there was no sign of Jack or his friend. DJ and I got laundry started, vacuumed, and dusted. After getting dressed, we went to the library for story time, wandered around Target, our new obsession, then went to the park.

Normally, I packed a lunch, so we didn't have to go home when DJ got hungry, between story time and Target. By the time we got to the park, his lunch had settled.

If no one was at the park, I would play with DJ, running around, pushing him on the swing and merry-go-round, up and down the slides, across the monkey bars and kicking a soccer ball around. When he got tired, I would read 1 or 2 of his books to him, but he never took a nap or wanted to nap. He wanted to get all his playing in before the sun went down.

If there were other kids at the park, then he would play with them while I sat at the picnic table with a book or journal. I could always hear him laughing and talking while he played, and he was never more than a few feet from me.

That day I had bought a new journal while we were at Target because I needed to get my thoughts out of my head and on paper, to move on. DJ immediately took off when I unbuckled him from his booster seat to play with his friends. I grabbed my bag and headed for the table.

I wrote for almost an hour with tears running down my face. It wasn't until DJ came over for some water and touched my face that I realized I was crying. His little hand was on my cheek, and he was looking up at me with his big brown, questioning eyes. He asked, "Momma, you okay? You okay, Momma? Do you have a booboo and need kisses?"

He melted my heart, and I vowed no matter what happened between Jack and I, or anyone else, nothing would come between me and my precious little boy. I put my journal away, took DJ to the bathroom, then we ran around and played.

We came home from the park about 4:30 P.M. so I could start dinner. Jack's car was in his parking spot. I prayed for patience and wisdom before I got out of the car. DJ saw the car and kept saying, "Momma, Daddy home."

We went upstairs and inside. Jack and his friend were knocked out in the living room. I could smell the liquor and on their clothes. I didn't allow smoking in the apartment.

I quietly shut the door as DJ ran over and jumped on Jack. Jack woke up and instead of happily greeting DJ, he yelled at him, making him cry, then cussed at me for "slamming the door" and being so loud. I told him to kiss my ass and went to the bedroom with DJ, shutting the door.

I gave DJ a bath and he stayed in longer than normal, distracting himself with his toys in the tub. "Momma, why Daddy mad?" DJ asked a couple times before I told him sometimes people are tired and can't control their emotions as well. I told him it wasn't his fault, Daddy wasn't mad at him, but he had to be careful when he jumped on people.

Keeping the peace when I was fighting so much anger inside me was difficult, but DJ didn't need to hear bad things about someone he worshipped.

After his bath and my shower, he was on the bed with his hands behind his head, feet crossed at the ankle, watching his movie. He was so grown sometimes. My baby was becoming a little boy.

I stood in the doorway, staring at him, finding my peace when he grinned and said, "What, Momma, what?" in his little southern drawl voice. My heart kept expanding with so much love for this little guy. We snuggled during the movie, me listening to his little voice recite almost every line, then giggling as if he'd seen it for the first time.

My heart was racing, from anger, after Jack showered and left. I was angry from the unknown future, the situation and because I was a coward for not confronting Jack. As I lay there, I promised myself I wasn't going to allow the behavior to continue, and Jack's friend needed to go.

I didn't see Jack the rest of the week. He slept on the couch and left for school/work before we got up. I stayed later at my aunt's that week and left a letter for Jack when I left Friday morning. The letter said his friend needed to be gone by the time I got home that night; otherwise, DJ and I would be finding another place to stay.

I didn't care what he did, but I wasn't going to live that kind of life. It was his choice as to how we proceeded. I left the letter in an envelope taped to the mirror above his sink, with my wedding rings inside.

I stuck to our Friday night ritual because DJ and I were tired. We stopped for groceries and dinner first, so we didn't have to leave again. We had been talking about DJ being a big boy and going potty in the toilet for a couple weeks. He was telling me when he had to go, but I didn't want to chance him not being in a pull up while at daycare or driving.

Driving home, I asked him if he was ready to be a big boy and get rid of the diapers. He yelled yes and clapped his hands. We stopped at Target before going to the grocery store. He picked out Batman and Goofy underwear. We would start that night after we got home, but we weren't going to the park that weekend so he could practice. "Okay, me big boy, Momma," he said while we checked out.

We stopped at Baskin Robbins for ice cream as a treat and we rented extra movies, knowing we would be in the apartment for the next 2 days. While we shopped, we talked about the things we were going to do while we spent the weekend inside.

We got home and after putting food away, I threw a load of clothes in the washer, and went into DJ's room to get his pajamas. His room was empty, except for his stuff. I was overjoyed. After bathing, I told him we were going to have a slumber party in the living room that night and we could build a fort if he wanted.

We ate, built a fort, and put blankets and pillows on the floor underneath. I gave him a flashlight and we settled in for the first movie. He told me he had to go potty, and I told him to grab his flashlight so we could go.

That became the routine. We made it a game. We woke up Saturday morning and we both jumped up with him yelling, "Potty, Momma, potty, me big boy." I told him that he could run around all day with just his big boy underwear on. He loved not wearing clothes while we were home.

We set up a racetrack for his cars, made a bigger fort, using towels and blankets. I had a timer that went off every 30 minutes to ask if he had to go potty. We went to the toilet each time, to try, so he got used to knowing when he had to go and when he didn't.

The next day, we did much of the same. I read the paper, making my grocery list for the week, while he ran around playing, bouncing his ball off the ceiling and walls, crashing cars, and stopping to tell me he had to go potty when it was time.

That night I asked if he was ready for big boy underwear every day now and he said yes, "Me big boy, not a baby." I packed extra clothes in his backpack, just in case and let the daycare know, to keep an eye out.

We never looked back, and he never had an accident. I was so happy to save money from not buying diapers.

Tuesday morning, I woke up to find Jack in the bed with DJ and me. I didn't say anything. Before DJ and I left, Jack came out, said he was sorry, he wanted our marriage to work, and he would do better. I said, "Okay," and left.

When I got home, my rings were on my counter with a note asking me to put them back on. We didn't talk about the incident. I didn't ask questions. He started spending more time at home in the mornings before we left because his school schedule had changed. He was still working swing shift, but we saw him briefly in the mornings and he would go back to sleep after we left.

I started school 6 days a week, 10 hours a day, with my aunt watching DJ on Saturdays. I did this so I could graduate sooner and start making money. We were barely making ends meet.

6 weeks before I graduated, I got a call that DJ had fallen and cut his head open. One of the ladies from daycare drove him to the hospital, while another held a cloth on his head. I met them there because it was closer. He had been standing on the bench in the back play area and leaned over to grab a ball. He lost his balance, falling over the back of the bench, hitting a small piece of concrete when he landed. It cut the top of his head and he got 5 staples but was okay.

A week after his staples were taken out, I got a call again that he had fallen. I rushed to the hospital and freaked when I saw all the blood on his face. My aunt met me at the hospital because she was an emergency contact. He had 2 slices in his forehead, right above his right eye.

I calmed him down, but he needed stitches because the bleeding wouldn't stop, except with direct pressure. The doctor told me they would strap him to a board, similar to a papoose, to keep him from flailing around while he stitched. He wasn't going to like being restrained, but it had to be done.

They strapped him in, while I stood near his left side so he could see me. He was good until they put the numbing shot in. He screamed bloody murder and flailed his little 2-year-old body around like a madman. The doctor asked to me to lay on him, holding his arms with mine and my chest on his lower torso. My aunt grabbed his head, and we were both talking to him, telling him it would be done sooner, if he helped and stayed still.

I told him we could go for ice cream on the way home if he stayed still. We had been working on numbers and I asked him to count them with me. I told him the doctor would be done by the time he got to 20.

Thankfully, the doctor worked quickly and had him stitched up in record time. As soon as the stitches were done, DJ instantly calmed down and said, "Momma, I good boy, ice cream now?" I laughed through tears, "Yes, baby, you're a good boy, let's get ice cream."

He ended up with 27 stitches. I hated letting him out of my site. We celebrated his 2nd birthday a couple weeks before the first fall. It was a Friday night. We stopped for ice cream, then went to my aunt's house before we drove home. I wanted to make sure he was okay before we drove longer.

He ate his ice cream and started running and playing as soon as he saw my cousins. They told him how strong he was and what a big boy he was, and he yelled back, "I know!" We couldn't help but laugh.

My uncle ordered pizza and we watched a movie so we could all unwind before I drove home. When DJ crawled on my lap and put his head on my shoulder saying, "Momma, I tired," I buckled him in the car and drove home.

Jack lost his mind when he saw the stitches after he came home. I told him to calm down, so he didn't upset DJ. We found out later a kid pushed DJ in the back, causing him to fall into a plate glass door which is why there were 2 cuts.

I needed to look for a daycare closer anyhow. I was almost done with school and would be working closer to home. DJ had the stitches in for 2 weeks, then we went to have the outside ones removed. The others had dissolved. It was a Friday and I promised him ice cream.

I had 3 weeks left of school and it was 1 week since the stitches were removed, when I got a call, again. DJ had fallen again and hit his head. I was livid. This time DJ stayed calm for the stitches, knowing it would be over soon.

The cut crossed the 2 previous cuts, making it look like an X, with part of the cut going through his eyebrow.

This time the doctor asked what daycare he was at, who the provider was and why each event happened on Friday. The provider was still at the hospital when we finished, and I asked the same questions.

I told them DJ would not be back, and I wasn't paying for the open slot or 2-week notice. I enrolled DJ in a daycare, a couple miles from the apartment, which was more of a preschool setting.

I finished school and waited to take my state exam. We got a letter from DCS explaining it was the same child that pushed DJ the last time into a chair. When DJ fell, he hit his head on the wooden leg, splitting his head open. They said they would monitor the facility, especially on Fridays.

DJ referred to his new school as a big boy school. He came home every day with a folder of papers and daily progress. He would get mad if I arrived early to pick him up, especially if he was in the middle of "homework."

I was hired by a smaller upscale salon in the "Old Money Historic District," shampooing hair, mixing colors, cleaning, and keeping track of inventory, while I waited to take my state exam. I had learned how to do scalp/neck massages from one of my instructors and started adding that to my shampoo routine. The owner added it as a service that customers could pay for, and I would massage for 15 minutes.

Clients' faces would relax when I massaged their scalp and neck, then their entire body relaxed as I worked the tension out. Soon I had stylists telling me their clients requested I shampoo them. Some clients paid for the extra 15 minutes, which added more to my paycheck.

I discussed doing facials and makeup with the owner after I passed the state boards. He had a room already set up, but no one to do the services. He told me if he liked the facial I did for him, then I could do it. I started booking facials during the week and kept Saturday open to help shampoo when it was busier.

My paychecks were growing, and I was able to save money. Soon I was doing facials full time and putting color in clients' hair. The stylists taught me tricks to doing foils and highlights, how to mix color to get the best gray coverage and let me practice on them.

I met a lady who volunteered with the American Cancer Society, ACS, while she was getting her hair colored. She was lying back with her head in the shampoo bowl and asked me about my ink dots on my neck.

After telling her I had been diagnosed 2 years prior and they were my radiation tattoos in case I ever had to get radiation again, they could line everything up. She told me about a program the ACS had, partnering licensed cosmetologists and estheticians with cancer patients getting ready to start treatment, during treatment or finishing treatment.

The program was called "Look Good. Feel Better." I volunteered weekly at the local hospital where they held the classes, sharing my knowledge about skincare, the changes your skin goes through during and after treatment and dealing with hair loss.

We taught them how to make head turbans out of soft t-shirts so the fabric wouldn't irritate their head, we had wigs they could try on and keep if they found one they liked. Each lady was given a beauty kit upon arrival, with skincare products donated by most of the large named beauty companies.

We went through the kit. They could trade items if there was something they didn't want or need. We started with the skincare routine, then proceeded to show them how to use an eyebrow pencil to add eyebrows after they lost them.

The program educated them about their skin and the additional care it required. We helped them with wigs, turbans, and hats, but most importantly we let them know there would be times you didn't want to look in the mirror, show your face in public or get out of bed. It was when they were having these moments, they should make an effort for themselves. We showed them how making the effort to look good, for yourself, can help you feel better.

There's a psychological factor behind what we see in the mirror. It affects us mentally and emotionally. I could relate because there were still days I hated standing in front of the mirrors at the salon, not seeing ME, only cancer.

I was ready to put down roots. I contacted the VA about using my home loan and they explained the process. I wanted to get out of the apartment and get a puppy for DJ. I found a community close to our apartment and DJ's daycare. I chose the lot, style of house, colors, and upgrades.

We broke ground in April, visiting the site regularly, walking through the house that was only staked out and recording the progress. We got a puppy for DJ, a golden Labrador we named Max, and made sure he was housebroken before we moved to the house.

My 2nd youngest sister, SE, graduated from high school in June and we had a family reunion. The Park had a sprawling lawn, significant parking, historical cannons, and a reception hall with a kitchen, bathrooms, and plenty of room inside in case it rained. There was also a large, covered pavilion with picnic tables underneath that would fit most of us, if we ate in shifts.

We had a volleyball net set up, kids were kicking the soccer balls, others were grouped together catching up, with people pitching in to get food ready and set out. Everyone seemed to have a good time. Some were meeting each other for the first time, others seeing each other for the first time, in years.

We ended the night with singing, dancing, a bonfire, and hayride. DJ fell in love with the John Deere tractor, which he hasn't outgrown. A few of us drove to Niagara Falls. My husband and son had never been.

The lights behind the falls were on, set up for the 4th of July light show. DJ was mesmerized and wide awake. He was running around with his cousins, playing in the water and mist.

SE moved in with us before we left the apartment. She worked at a craft store down the street from me. We carpooled, before deciding to go to NY, to go to college in January.

We moved into the house the end of September, right before DJ's 3rd birthday. I loved my home. I was a first-time homeowner at 23, giving DJ a place to run, grow and call his own.

Soon after moving into the house, I found a new salon, closer to the house, where I could grow and expand my skills. The first place had given me a solid foundation, but the owner got sick and had trouble keeping the salon open.

I was an apprentice, with a 50/50 commission rate, but the training I gained was unbelievable. Within 6 months I moved from apprentice to master stylist, with a 70/30 commission structure. I made great money and fell in love with helping people find something that worked for them, their life, hair, and face. I helped enhance and highlight the natural beauty they already had.

DJ and Max loved the freedom of our backyard, rolling in the grass, wrestling in the house, and snuggling together watching TV. Max was [not] a normal puppy. He ripped the tie down stake(s) out of the ground when he was outside, snapped the cables of the tie down, broke his chain, etc.

He chewed the carpet or linoleum if left in his crate while we were gone, tore the garage doors up, ripped the carpet in a spare bedroom and dug out of a kennel with a concrete pad. He drove me crazy, but DJ loved him. Their bond was more important than material things.

Jack's cousin, Kiki, more like a sister, moved in with us, the end of January 1996, after she dropped out of college. I shared my car, again. She worked at a business near my salon, so it worked out better, but not having my car, drove me nuts.

I went to the VA for my 3-year checkup in March 1996. The doctor said everything looked good, I was cleared for yearly checkups, but I needed to hold off on trying to get pregnant for a couple more years. I was on birth control pills, not ready for another pregnancy.

That week I broke a back tooth that the Army had fixed, or made worse, but I had to take antibiotics and pain meds, because it was abscessed. I worked Saturday and came home after my last appointment, took my meds, a shower and crawled into bed.

I spent the next day in bed, in and out of medicated sleep. Jack was working for the post office with Sundays off. Monday morning, I felt better and caught up on my chores.

I was obsessed with vacuuming my carpets and vacuumed daily. I liked seeing the vacuum lines in the carpet. DJ stayed home with me on Mondays and went to preschool Tuesday-Friday. My aunt, cousins or Kiki watched him on Saturdays.

I loved having the house to myself on Mondays. Kiki was dating a guy and he was staying at our house with more frequency. I liked the guy, but I was irritated with so many people in my house, no one else doing dishes, helping with cooking or grocery shopping. The couch and recliner were always full when I came home from work, so I spent more time in my bedroom and kitchen.

I worked late on Tuesday and Thursday nights, getting home about 7, depending on the last appointment. I had to make dinner, bathe DJ, wash dishes and get ready for the next morning. I hated coming home to dishes in the sink. I've never liked dishwashers; the smell from the heat and steam makes me nauseous. I know now it's a PTSD trigger smell.

After a couple weeks of this "routine," I had a client cancel on Saturday, my last appointment of the day. I left 3 hours earlier than normal, excited to spend more time with DJ. When I got home, I opened the garage door, entered the kitchen, and saw the back, sliding glass door, wide open. DJ and Max were outside, both muddy and DJ was standing on top of the doghouse.

There were dishes on the counter and in the sink, the trash needed to be taken out and I heard loud music coming from the back bedroom, which was DJ's room, but Kiki had taken it over. I got DJ down from the doghouse, took his muddy clothes off him before we came in the house, threw the stuff in washer, and walked him to the bathroom.

I passed his room and saw Kiki inside, folding her laundry, while her boyfriend, laid in the bed. I turned around and took DJ to my shower, while I packed a bag for him and myself, then I showered, and we left the house.

I was furious at the entire situation. I hadn't been part of the conversation for her to move in with us. I stopped to get gas, some Chick-fil-A, and started driving. I didn't know if I was going to the beach, my sisters, or a random location, each was a 3-hour drive.

It started storming so I decided my sisters was the best option. I pulled into a fast-food place with a play area, DJ and I used the bathroom, then he played. While I waited for the storm to let up, it gave me time to calm down, think things through and write about it.

I stopped at 5 P.M., called KJ, and told her I was driving to her house. We were 30-45 minutes away. She said Jack called to see if she'd heard from me. I told her I would explain when I got there, but I didn't want him to know I was coming.

I was going to stop to get food for dinner, breakfast, and lunch, before we arrived. She was not much of a cook. I decided to show her how to make spaghetti/pasta, from beginning to end. She was in a house with 3 roommates from the Army, but they were gone.

While making dinner, I told her what I saw when I got home, and the past weeks of frustration. I felt like I was going crazy, and I was angry all the time. Jack and I barely talked, we weren't having sex and I felt like we were two separate units in the same house. I hated who I was becoming in the situation.

After I let it out, we ate dinner and turned the ringer off the phone. We watched movies, ate popcorn and ice cream, played a game with DJ, and made a bed of pillows, blankets and sleeping bags. I slept peacefully.

We went to the park the next day after breakfast. She showed us around base, introduced us to some of her friends, went to the PX to browse, then back home for dinner. She had to work the next morning and we were leaving when she did.

We listened to the messages on my sister's voicemail. Jack had called. The messages began with wondering where we were, then they became angry messages. My sister called him Sunday night, said we were fine, and I didn't want to talk.

We had entered the age of the Internet and world wide web, with the ability to send emails. After I got home, I sat down and typed out how I was feeling, my frustrations and unhappiness. I saved it as a reference for myself if I needed it.

I needed to find a physical outlet. I heard someone was looking for people to play softball and had been given my contact information. The games worked with my work and volunteer schedule, and I needed to be on the diamond again.

Our routine became uneventful. Jack got home, ignored me, gave DJ a hug and went to shower. He came out later, sat in the recliner, watched ESPN while eating dinner.

I made dinner, cleaned the kitchen, then went to get DJ ready for bed. I laid down with DJ in my bed to watch a movie. I was asleep before Jack came to bed and he left before I got up for work. I decided to send Jack my email because talking wasn't going to work.

In the email, I said Kiki and her boyfriend needed to find their own place in the next 2 weeks, otherwise I was moving. They weren't paying rent, bills or even gas when she used my car. We couldn't afford to feed and house everyone.

I spent more time away from the house, with DJ, softball, volunteering, and work, to keep my stress down.

Kiki and her boyfriend found a place and moved out, but Jack and I still maintained our "normal" disconnected distance. I enjoyed the silence because I talked and listened to clients, all day long. DJ and I continued our Friday night ritual and Jack started participating after Kiki moved out. We found a place that sold subs, pizza, wings, and pasta, so we switched between that and Chinese food.

We didn't eat at restaurants because of my IBS (irritable bowel syndrome). I had to take prescribed meds 30 minutes before I ate any meal, to help prevent it. The pills were hit and miss, but I had found, through trial and error, what foods made it worse.

One night, I woke up feeling like I was going to be sick. I felt nauseated, with the urge to vomit, but then felt like I needed to pee/poop, with nothing happening. I had chills, then felt hot, there was pain in my back and stomach. I couldn't get comfortable.

I went from the toilet to a hot bath, to the toilet, to lying on the cold floor, to the toilet, to the bath, for a couple hours. Jack must have heard me and came in the bathroom, where he found me lying on the floor, crying from the pain. After he found out I had been in there for 2 hours, he helped me get dressed, got DJ out of bed, and drove me to the ER.

I could barely stand, it hurt to sit, and I was feeling ill. The nurse had me do a urine test, then we waited in the waiting room. I was called back to a room, where they started an IV, to get fluid, pain meds and antibiotics in me. The doctor said I had a UTI (urinary tract infection), a kidney infection and I passed a stone because it was crystalized in my urine.

I started feeling a little better with the pain meds but was groggy from lack of sleep and the physical exertion of trying to vomit and poop so much. Jack and DJ were in the room with me. We were all relieved it wasn't a serious illness. Then the doctor looked at his chart again and said, "Oh, and you're pregnant!"

I sat straight up in bed and yelled, "What? I'm on birth control and I haven't had sex in weeks." I looked at Jack, who had a weird look on his face. The doctor asked if I'd been on antibiotics for anything because that affects the efficiency of the pill.

I backtracked to March, when I'd had my tooth infection and looked directly at Jack. "What the hell did you do when I was knocked out?"

The doctor looked back and forth at us, then said he had discharge papers for me. I could leave soon. I kept asking, "What did you do?" while tears streamed down my face. My soul felt crushed.

On the drive home, Jack said, "When you were on the pain pills, I thought you were awake, and we had sex. I didn't think anything about the birth control not working." I felt violated, again. "You heard the doctor tell me not to get pregnant in the next couple years. You took advantage of me when I was knocked out from the pain meds."

Neither of us said anything the rest of the drive home. I went into work after we got home, thankful I only had a few appointments. I was still in pain and shock, trying to process I was pregnant. There were a lot of emotions, fears, and anxiety about the pregnancy, my body, immune system, and cancer.

The owner could tell something was wrong. When we both had a couple minutes between clients, I told him what happened, being at the ER, kidney issues and finding out I was pregnant. He was just as shocked by the look on his face. He had the receptionist reschedule/rebook my Saturday, so I could get rest and process everything.

Fridays were a shorter day for us because Saturdays were always busy. I left at 3, picked up DJ and went home. Jack and I went through the Friday night ritual, but I fell asleep on the couch without eating.

I slept most of the weekend. I was feeling better by Monday. I worked through the tumultuous emotions. Although I'd planned to be cautious, I was excited. DJ talked about having a baby sister and I asked what if it's a baby brother. He put his hand on my belly, "No, Momma, I get baby sister from your belly," then he leaned over and kissed my belly.

I didn't plan to find out the sex of the baby. I continued to get sick from kidney infections that never fully cleared up. The hospital did more ultrasounds to make sure the baby was okay. After the third kidney infection, at 5 months pregnant, the doctor put me on a daily, low-dose antibiotic.

I had morning sickness, not like I did with DJ, but I was more tired than I had ever been. I would go into the breakroom, where we had the washer and dryer, sit on the dryer to lean against the wall and fall asleep. I scheduled my appointments with longer breaks between so I could nap.

In June, we drove to NY for my 3rd youngest sister's high school graduation. KM was the youngest of my parents' kids and the last child to graduate high school for my mom. We visited some of the local places that were my favorites when I was growing up.

Berryhead was getting married the weekend after my sister graduated and we drove to PA before heading home. She was so excited I was pregnant. We hugged and loved on each other for the first time in 5 years, introduced our kids and spouses. Her parents enveloped me in hugs and introduced me as their Army daughter.

By my 24th birthday, I was feeling better. I had some energy, and it was time to get maternity clothes. I had to elevate my feet more often from the pregnancy and the kidney issues that caused so much inflammation.

I needed shoes with better arch support, a cushioned heel, and closed toe. In 1996, there weren't many cute options for women. As I gained more weight, I was also getting busier at the salon with back to school, homecoming, and holidays. My feet hurt more. I hadn't had the pain in my feet since the military. The cushioned fatigue mats only helped some.

Years later, I discovered I had plantar fasciitis, aggravated by long periods of standing, lack of arch support and heel cushioning. Combat boots were not equipped with any support, and we did a lot of marching and standing.

KM was graduating basic training at the end of September. I invited my mom and stepdad, my dad and stepmom and sister to stay at our house, then drove 1½ hours to Ft. Jackson.

My stepdad had to work, but my mom came down with a friend and her daughter. The day everyone arrived, a hurricane warning was sent out for the area. They canceled family day for the recruits and graduation was moved indoors the next day. We were only able to spend a few minutes with KM after graduation because the Army was transporting all the soldiers to their AIT, before the storm hit.

We drove back to my house, making sure we had enough supplies in case we lost power or took a direct hit from the hurricane. We filled the tubs with water, just in case and had plywood ready to cover the windows, if needed.

We played games, watched movies, and told stories, waiting for the heavier rain and wind to hit. Late that night, early the next morning the eye passed by to the east of us. Charlotte and surrounding areas sustained some damage from winds and flooding, with some power outages, but we were lucky.

I was happy with how well everyone got along while under one roof, cooped up with no escape. There were some snide remarks and sarcastic comments, but for the most part everything was peaceful.

My due date was December 13, 1996, and other than extreme fatigue along with kidney issues, my pregnancy progressed with no other issues. DJ rubbed and kissed my belly daily, telling me that he couldn't wait to have his baby sister.

We celebrated his 4th birthday with a small celebration at home, with friends and family. We bought him a bike so he could learn to ride. While we were putting it together in our room with the door shut, DJ was up early, peeking under the crack between the door and floor. I heard, "Momma, is that my bike?" That was when I truly understood, how resourceful and smart this kid was and is today.

I stayed busy at the salon. I was still playing softball and volunteering.

DJ loved hanging out at the field and was soon playing catch with other kids. I bought him a glove and baseball so we could play catch together at home. Soon we added a tee, bat, and net so he could practice in the backyard. Max had to stay in the house; otherwise he chased the ball and ran off with it before DJ could get to it.

KM finished AIT and began college. KM was in the Army Reserves. She came down to stay during her winter break from college after she finished her drill weekend. She was excited to be there during the delivery and to help me with DJ and the house.

We also found out that our other sister, SE, was pregnant and due a couple weeks after me. KM was going home after Christmas so she could be there for SE when she gave birth.

My due date of Friday the 13th passed with no contractions or labor. I saw the doctor on the 16th, and he said if I didn't go into labor by Thursday the 19th, I would go to the hospital for an induction at 7:30 A.M. Everything was fine, but I was starting to lose amniotic fluid and the baby was already over 8 pounds.

I worked all day Tuesday and Wednesday, in preparation for birth the next morning. My hair was a short pixie cut. I did my hair and put some makeup on. I figured I would try to look good while dealing with the labor pains.

We were assigned a room, which was huge, and waited for the party to begin. Jack and DJ sat on the couch, watching ESPN while KM and I played cards. They started the IV with Pitocin, to help start uterine contractions at 7:30 A.M.

At 9:30 A.M., I wasn't having any contractions and I hadn't dilated much. The nurse said she was going to give me the "San Antonio" special to help. I still have no idea what that was but it's something that has stuck in my head.

At 10:30 A.M., I was feeling slight contractions. The doctor tried breaking my water, to speed things along, but it didn't break. At 11:30, he tried breaking my water again with no luck.

I was hungry. I wanted to eat, but they were afraid I would be sick if I went into labor. I noticed my stomach started rising and falling, like a wave was cresting. It wasn't painful, but it wasn't something I'd seen before. Baby girl must be on the move.

At 12 P.M., I started to feel more pulls and contractions, labor was beginning. The nurse asked if I was sure I didn't want an epidural. I was good. The doctor came in at 12:30 P.M. for the 3rd attempt at breaking my water and was successful.

Once the water broke, it felt like all hell broke loose inside my body. Now the contractions were strong and painful, lasting for a couple minutes, with about a minute in between each. KM was holding my hand, while Jack was wiping my face with a cool cloth. DJ was standing on the chair next to the bed, near my head, watching and waiting.

I told the nurse I needed to push, but she told me to hold on, I wasn't fully dilated yet. The contractions were coming faster and harder, I was covered with sweat, cussing at Jack, with ESPN on in the background. I kept telling the nurse I had a strong urge to push. It was harder to stop. She sent another nurse for the doctor, I was dilated to 8 cm, but had to get to 10.

I couldn't stop my body from pushing. I had no control. Just as the doctor was running into the room, with one glove on, I yelled and pushed. The doctor sat down with his hand on the baby's head and told me the baby was crowning. He was putting his other glove on when the contraction brought me to an almost sitting position, and I pushed with everything I had.

The doctor had gotten his glove on just in time to catch the baby and finish the birth process. It was 1 P.M., December 19, 1996, when my baby girl, LJ, entered the world. DJ helped cut the umbilical cord while I held her in my arms. She was 8 lbs., 14 oz. and 21 inches long. She had a full head of hair and was absolutely beautiful.

After she was weighed, the nurse noticed she wasn't fully responding with breathing, and they rushed her to the NICU. While they warmed her up and took care of her, I was pushing the afterbirth out before the doctor could stitch me up. I had to get 14 stitches in my perineum because I tore it from giving birth so fast to a big baby.

The nurse was massaging my stomach/uterus to get everything out. It felt like she was pressing through to my spine. Several large clots came out and I was bleeding heavy. They kept massaging, with clots the size of melons coming out along with so much blood.

I started to become incoherent with the blood loss. The clots wouldn't stop. They stood me up to see if walking to the bathroom would help release everything. I saw the clot that came out while I hovered over the toilet. I couldn't believe how big it was and started feeling dizzy.

They took me back to the bed and gave me a shot to help stop the hemorrhaging. My temperature dropped rapidly, and my body was shaking from the cold. They brought heated blankets in to help warm me and had Jack lie partially on top of me for body heat.

The last reading I heard was 92 degrees. I felt like I was in a different world, hearing from far away. Someone yelled to bring the baby in to see if nursing would help me start contracting and stop the bleeding.

I had heat packs all around my body and covered with a stack of blankets. Someone reclined the bed to more of a sitting position and a nurse helped me hold the baby for nursing. It had been less than 30 minutes since I had given birth, but it felt like an eternity had passed.

Nursing helped the bleeding and my temperature slowly started to rise. I was starving, my body was sore from labor and hemorrhaging and I was sick of hearing ESPN. I told Jack to take DJ for lunch. KM turned the TV off and hid the remote.

Once I was stable, I was moved to a smaller recovery room. I could barely walk because the stitches pulled and were painful. I was still bleeding heavier than normal and had to change my pads every 30-45 minutes.

I ate some food and nursed. I couldn't stop looking at how precious and beautiful this little girl was. I tried nursing every 2 hours and soon found that my right breast wasn't releasing milk the same as my left. It was engorged and painful.

I told the nurse, and she could feel how hot it was. She told me my surgery scar had probably caused some nerve and muscle damage, which affected the milk let down in that breast. She wet a couple pads with warm water and placed them under my arm, on the side of my breast, to help expel the milk.

I nursed the baby while the pad was on to help increase the flow, but she couldn't get a good suction on that nipple. Soon the nipple was raw, and I had to manually expel by squeezing and working the milk out.

We went home the next day. I was nursing more often from my left breast, and it was soon raw. I was trying to use the breast pump on my right in between to relieve the pressure.

I had to take a sitz bath, with Epsom salt and warm water, 5 times a day, to help with cleansing and healing my stitches. I found a shower helped my right breast expel milk. Sometimes I would bring LJ in with me, to bathe her, but also to help nurse on my right breast.

LJ was gaining weight, so we knew she was getting enough to eat. Her checkup was good, but I told the doctor about the trouble nursing. She told me it was okay if I needed to supplement with formula, to help me heal and allow the baby to sleep more, so I could.

A week after I gave birth, I got sick. My body was completely run down and exhausted. I had some formula saved that I pumped, but I could barely get out of bed. Jack would bring the baby to me in bed, help her latch on, then let us sleep.

I was sick for almost 2 weeks, the doctor said I was anemic and prescribed iron pills. I started feeding LJ more of the formula. I was afraid she wasn't getting enough nutrients from me.

She was a fussy baby. When she was really bad, she would only burp and go to sleep if she was lying on Jack's chest. She began a continuous cycle of ear infections, which was why she was fussy. The antibiotic got rid of the infection, but the fluid wasn't coming out. At 18 months, she had surgery to have tubes put in her ears. What a relief that was.

She was mostly a happy baby and DJ loved holding her and reading to her. Soon she was crawling after him and trying to pull herself up by holding onto the furniture. She started daycare at the same place DJ was when I went back to work, and her personality started showing.

She was a handful, full of energy, laughter, playfulness and had the softest hair full of curls. On the flipside, she was stubborn and if she didn't like something, she let you know.

I went back to work, early 1997, after 8 weeks off. I loved being back at work, working towards normal and going home to my babies. However, I was having trouble losing the baby weight. I was as heavy then as I was pregnant. I didn't have energy or patience.

I started going to the gym, doing kickboxing 3x a week and being more careful about what I ate. The only thing that happened was my body was more toned, but I couldn't lose the weight. I had gone from 140 pounds before pregnancy to 194 before the baby was born and now hovered at 196.

I became frustrated, angry, and depressed. We started going to a church closer to our house, with a smaller group of people from our big church. I went to women's ministry at night, Sunday school, and volunteered in the nursery. I couldn't stop the feeling of swirling out of control.

The only thing I seemed to be in control of was work and volunteering. Shortly after returning to work, I had a lady come into the salon asking to speak to me when I had a couple minutes. I finished with a client and had 15 minutes before my next client.

She worked for ACS and heard about me from the lady I did "look good, feel better" with. They were starting a new fundraising community event in Mecklenburg County called Relay For Life. It would be a 24-hour, overnight event, where community members could make teams, fundraise, and then camp out at the high school track during the event.

She told me the event was based around 3 main things, to honor cancer survivors/patients, to remember loved ones lost and to be able to fight back against cancer, through fundraising, research, programs, awareness, and education. She told me she had a 5-minute video to watch if I had the time to watch it.

I had a small TV/VCR combo near my station and sat down to watch. I was hooked. The event had begun in 1985, by 1 man, a doctor that ran/walked the high school track for 24 hours, to raise money to fight back against cancer. I leaned forward in the chair and tears were running down my face. I had to be part of this event, it felt like I had seen home.

I started a team, started fundraising in the salon and invited Berryhead to come down for the event. She was diagnosed with the same type of cancer that I had approximately 1 month after I was diagnosed. She would drive down with her son, 6 months younger than DJ and spend the weekend with us.

I found that if I stayed physically busy and kept my mind busy, I was able to stave off the dark hole of depression. I volunteered to be the Team Recruitment lead for the Relay, which kept me busy on weekends and evenings.

We drove to PA to see Berryhead following a surgery on her wrist for a cyst that was most likely cancer. I took my foot bath, and pedicure stuff so I could give her a pedicure while we were there. She was in a good mood overall, but I could hear the stress in her voice. She was living at her parents', trying to work, go to school, take care of her son, dealing with the VA and lumps growing out of her in random places.

The salon was busy, and the owner asked if we were interested in going to New York City for an international beauty show at the end of March. The salon covered the costs and 2 of us went with the owner. He was originally from Long Island, so he was our tour guide.

We stayed in a hotel right across the street from Madison Square Garden. The Chicago Bulls played the NY Knicks that weekend. It was a huge rivalry game. The show was fascinating. I learned techniques I could incorporate when we went back to work.

We ate in Chinatown, had dessert in Little Italy, rode the Subway to SoHo, a lower part of Manhattan, and visited the Empire State Building. While I loved the lights, I was overwhelmed with the smells, people, and noise. When we boarded the plane back to Charlotte, I was overjoyed to leave NYC.

The weekend of the Relay For Life event was gorgeous. We arrived at the track Friday afternoon to set up and be ready for opening ceremony at 6 P.M. We decorated our tent to look like a race car, we were "Racing for the Cure." My 2 younger sisters, KM and SE, came down for the event and Berryhead arrived about 4 P.M.

The event kicked off with the opening ceremony, a welcome to all the participants and visitors and a big thanks to the sponsors. A cancer survivor shared her story and how she benefitted from the ACS-funded research and programs offered. She had participated in the Look Good. Feel Better program and I asked her to speak.

After her speech, the survivors were called to the track, given a medal and purple balloon. We were kicking off the event with the first lap, the survivors' lap. While we walked the track, Berryhead and I holding hands, with tears running down our faces, each of us celebrating 4 years since diagnosis; the caregivers were handed white balloons and would join us on the track for the next lap.

I pushed my 6-month-old baby girl, LJ, and held DJ's hand as we walked the track. He had been my hope and strength during and after treatment and LJ gave me renewed hope, not just for surviving, but to fully live and enjoy every moment of life I was given.

Berryhead held her son's hand during the lap, grateful the cancer didn't cause her to lose the baby. Neither of us would have ever guessed we would go from reception station, through basic, AIT, the Gulf War, to celebrating our survival from cancer, together.

At 9 P.M., we held a luminaria ceremony, a time to remember our loved ones no longer with us due to cancer. It was also a time to honor cancer survivors and those still fighting. People were able to purchase white luminary bags, decorate them, put pictures on them, the names of the loved one(s) they were honoring or remembering. The bags were lined around the football field, on the inside of the track. Each bag had a candle inside, held in place with sand.

A lady that shared the story of their loved one who had passed on several years ago. They thanked the ACS for allowing them this time to honor and remember them, sharing their story of strength, courage, and bravery during their fight against cancer.

After the speaker finished, the lights were turned off and they asked all participants to come to the track for a silent lap of remembrance. I will never forget hearing "Every candle has a name," recognizing the power of this ceremony, the power of 1 candle, 1 flame, 1 name, lining the track with hundreds of others.

Relay For Life was celebrating, remembering, and fighting back. Its mission was growing and expanding to every state, thousands of communities and later, into 14 other countries. It was an amazing and powerful event. It would become a difference maker in the fight against cancer.

We took turns through the night walking or running the track and purchasing items being sold by other teams as part of their fundraising strategy. Berryhead and I walked and talked through most of the night, catching up with each other, laughing, crying, hugging, and sometimes just walking in silence holding hands, knowing the other would always be there, no matter what.

After the event, we packed everything up, grabbed pizza and headed to my house for showers, naps, and relaxation. Berryhead was aware of the strained relationship between Jack and I, how I got pregnant and the depression symptoms. She could see and hear the tension. I tried to keep a positive attitude, but a part of me was dying every day.

We made it through the weekend and settled back into our routine. DJ would start kindergarten in August. We were spending more time at church, Sunday mornings, evenings, and Wednesday evening services.

My energy was lessening daily. It was hard to get out of bed in the morning and even after sleeping I felt tired. My hair started falling out and becoming brittle. My nails were breaking, and my skin was dry. My hormones and moods were on a roller-coaster with no end to the ride.

DJ started school and I volunteered every Wednesday morning. I met a lady that was talking about football and practices on the school field. She had been volunteered to be the cheer coach because her daughter wanted to cheer. I offered to help her. I finished work at 5 P.M. and practice started at 6 which gave me enough time to get the kids. DJ went to the daycare after school, so I picked both kids up from the same place.

I fell in love with coaching, the girls and the mom who told me about it. I adjusted my work schedule, working Mondays, so I could have Saturday off. This allowed the salon to be open 6 days a week instead of 5. I continued coaching through the next season, 1998. We had sleep overs and self-confidence building exercises, we talked about "girl" stuff and life.

During one of the spring games, DJ and other kids were running around playing behind the fence and bleachers. The 4th quarter had started when I heard a scream. I knew it was DJ. He came running over with blood running down his face, from his cheek. He was crying but told me he was hit by a kid with a golf club while they were playing.

The other mom took over coaching. The only thing I had to stop the bleeding and hold pressure was a clean diaper. I grabbed LJ in her carrier, told DJ to keep pressure on the diaper and we walked quickly to the car. He had 7 stitches, his cheek was swollen, but he wanted to play after he was stitched up.

I continued coaching the cheerleaders for a few more seasons, helped grow the Relay For Life event(s) in Mecklenburg County, went to church and played softball.

I was diagnosed with hypothyroidism in 1998, after my gynecologist saw I still weighed the same, even though she knew I was active. She ordered a blood test to check my thyroid levels. I was relieved to have an answer to the crazy I was feeling and living with.

I started medication and started feeling better. I tried to show passion for my husband, but it wasn't there. I prayed. I had others pray. I did Bible study groups, specifically for women struggling with marriage. I did devotionals and journaled, but there was too much distance, disconnect and lack of trust on my part.

I was financially responsible for the mortgage, insurance, utilities, my car, fuel, daycare, and groceries. Jack was responsible for his car; a couple credit cards he had and miscellaneous small things. One day, he came home from work, but he didn't have his car. I asked him how he got home and what happened. He told me he sold his car to a guy at work. In the meantime, he would use my car, drop me off at Caribou coffee in the mornings, drop the kids at daycare, go to work, pick up the kids, then me.

This changed my schedule drastically, but I adjusted and made the best of the situation. I had fallen in love with the Caribou Coffee shop, even though I didn't drink coffee. The general manager came in to get a haircut and after talking about what they served, he brought me a large white cocoa with a shot of raspberry and white chocolate shavings on top of the whipped cream.

It was like heaven in a cup and my relationship for Caribou coffee began. I usually arrived at Caribou at 6:20 A.M., after I'd gone to Bruegger's Bagels for my breakfast sandwich. I switched between the white cocoa with raspberry to the white cocoa with mint, which had Andes candy mints in the bottom.

I did a lot of my journaling, devotional work and studying while waiting for the salon to open. We started opening at 8 A.M. I had clients that traveled, and the earlier time worked better for them and helped my bank account.

I arrived at 7:30 A.M. and got everything ready for the day. I enjoyed the earlier mornings alone in the salon. It also allowed me to leave earlier on late nights unless I purposely booked a late appointment.

Life continued with work, planning, and fundraising for Relay For Life, church, coaching, softball and visiting my aunt and uncle. Our marriage wasn't great, I wasn't happy or passionate as a wife, but we were comfortable with each other, and the kids were happy. We had a roof over our head and food on the table, so we continued as we were.

Our salon went to NYC again for the international beauty show in March 1998. I shared my passion about color with other stylists and my clients. I changed my hair color to reddish auburn in beauty school and kept it red for a couple years. I started experimenting with colors, styles, and cuts on myself, ranging from the darkest to the lightest and various ranges in between.

I loved what I was doing, but things changed at the salon. Something was going on with the owner. He started micromanaging the stylists and was in a perpetual bad mood. Eventually, I hated working with him. It was hard to get through the day. My clients noticed and felt the tension. They also noted he seemed different.

The Relay For Life event continued to expand. We had some fun events planned. Berryhead and my sisters were coming down. Our team was "Hoopin' for a Cure."

Berryhead stayed an extra day, and I took Monday off so we could stay up late Sunday, knowing that it would happen regardless. The kids were in bed, and we were sitting in the living room, talking, and laughing. I was on the end of the couch, and she was in the recliner when Jack came out of our room, got in my face, and started yelling at me.

I was shocked and confused. I had no idea what he was going on about. He had his finger in my face, telling me it was my fault things were the way they were, I was the reason bad things happened, then he accused me of cheating on him.

Berryhead was sitting in the chair with a look of shock and disbelief on her face. I pushed as far back into the couch as I could, but anger boiled to the surface, and I told him to "get the fuck out of my face." I was done with the BS, our marriage and him.

He went into our room. I stayed up after Berryhead went to bed, writing and planning what to do next. I was unhappy at work, at home with my marriage and decided to make a change. I was going to move to AZ with the kids, where my dad, stepmom, and sister, KJ lived. KJ moved to AZ after she got out of the Army in 1996 and although I had seen her a couple times since then, not seeing her at least once a month was hard.

I started saving money from tips and my check, to put towards moving across the country. I didn't want anything in the house, and I didn't care what Jack did with it when we were gone. I hadn't told anyone about my plan. I started booking haircuts while my clients were processing with color, to make more money.

I started taking appointments at 7 A.M., adding more money to my savings. I started doing special events, weddings, rehearsals, prom, on Saturday/Sunday if it was a long-time client. I charged more but went to the client and did makeup along with their hair.

We had 1 car for 6 or 7 months before Jack came to pick me up in a green VW Jetta. I asked him where my car was and he said it was at the house, the guy at the dealership followed him home to drop my car off, then took him back to get the Jetta. I was grateful to have my own car back and the Jetta was a 4-door instead of a 2-door, which made it easier with the kids.

I was close to my goal of having a couple thousand extra dollars saved, I had my car back and started planning for the move. I wanted to wait until DJ was done with school before we left. I also had a couple big appointments on the book for weddings in June. I booked myself out for vacation in July, giving clients enough time to be rebooked after I left.

I was close to my breaking point at home. Jack accused me of cheating on him since LJ had been born and thought I still was. I was tired of defending myself against the accusations and didn't engage his stupidity, which I realized later was jealousy. I was making more money than him, had bought the house, my car and took care of all the bills.

I came home after a long day at work. I was quiet when I came in the house as the kids would be asleep. My client had brought me dinner, so I didn't start any food. I didn't turn any lights on, planned to do laundry in the morning. I was tired and wanted a shower.

I heard the TV on in the bedroom, with the lights off, except the closet light. I figured Jack must have forgotten to turn it off and fell asleep. I walked towards the closet, when I saw Jack, sitting on the floor, with my box of journals open, reading them.

He violated my privacy, my innermost thoughts and I sat hard on the bench in our room, letting the unshed tears roll down my face. He heard me sit down and tried closing the journal quickly. The look on his face showed all the guilt of what he had done.

He could have asked me, and I would have let him read them, but to invade my privacy, without asking, like he was looking for evidence, broke me. I didn't say anything else. I went to the bathroom, shut the door, and ran the water for a bath.

DJ finished school the next week. The big event was the weekend after. I decided to leave earlier than planned. My soul hurt and I had no idea how to heal. The day we were leaving, I packed the bags and had them in the hallway to take to the car. I told the kids we were going on an adventure after I showered, and Daddy got home.

When Jack came home, I was sitting on the bench in our bedroom. The kids' suitcases were loaded in the car and mine was next to me. The kids ran to him, yelling, "We're going on a venture with Momma." He came in the room with a smirk on his face when he saw me, then the look became disbelief when he registered the suitcase next to me.

I told him I was leaving. I was miserable and I didn't want the kids to grow up in that kind of environment. I could no longer "fake" a marriage. I told him I would call him when I got to my destination, but we were leaving that night.

He told me I couldn't leave, telling me he was sorry, he wanted to make things better between us, he'd been acting stupid and so on.

We were in the master bathroom when I told DJ to use the bathroom again, while I made sure LJ had a clean diaper. Jack was in the bedroom talking to someone. We finished in the bathroom and walked into the bedroom. Jack was sitting on the bench with the phone stretched out toward me. He said the phone was for me and handed it to me.

I said hello, then heard my dad's voice. I sat down on the bench, feeling the emotions rise again. He asked me what was happening because Jack called him. Jack asked him to talk to me because I was going crazy. I could only shake my head. I told my dad I had to leave for my sanity. There were too many things that led to this moment, but the invasion of privacy and disrespect pushed me over.

I talked to my dad, feeling defeated, lonely, and broken hearted. He told me to bring Jack and the kids to AZ for a couple weeks. He said it was worth at least another shot to see if Jack and I could repair our marriage, we had 2 kids, a house, careers, and 5 years invested.

He said he would help pay for the plane tickets, so we didn't have to drive. I hung up and told him I would sleep on it. The phone rang again, and I heard KJ's voice. I broke into sobs as I told her I was so confused, filled with guilt, but hating my husband and marriage.

We talked a while longer before I told her I was going to take a bath after I put the kids to bed. I shut the door and slowly went through the motions of starting the bathwater, adding soap, lighting a candle, then I stared at myself in the mirror.

My eyes, nose and cheeks were red from crying, my hair was messy from running my hands through it and I saw an old woman standing in front of me, with no light or laughter in her eyes. I was 25 years old, soon to be 26 and I felt like I lived a lifetime. I sat on the side of the tub, as the memories of the past few years swirled inside my head.

Later that week, I met a lady, Marsha, that offered a booth at a day spa, where I would pay rent for the space, but kept everything I made. They had a receptionist that covered the entire spa, which offered skincare, massages, nails, and they wanted to add more stylists. I thought about the clientele I had built, the freedom to work when and how I wanted, additional services that my clients would have access to and the ability to work for myself.

I decided to visit the salon the next day and see how I felt in that atmosphere. It was a Saturday so I could get a feel for clientele, traffic, and customer service from the others in the salon. I took the kids with me because I wanted their opinion and to see it themselves.

It had natural light, a bright open space, floor-to-ceiling windows in the front and relaxing aromas. There was conversation, laughter, and lighthearted banter between clients and nail techs. The receptionist was friendly with a beautiful smile. She was stunning.

She showed us around, showing me which booths were available for stylists, the room for facials and skincare, the massage room, and the breakroom/storage. I loved it all. It was calming. There was plenty of space, no one would be stepping on each other. There was one booth that called to me. It was on the back wall, with the mirror facing the front windows and the entire salon. I could see everything behind me while facing the mirror.

The kids oohed and aahhed. There was a room next to the booth to store color, supplies and other items I would need. I could add my little TV and make a small kids' area with books, videos, a small rug, and bean bags.

The owner, Marsha, finished with her client and gave me a hug. She had a warmth that enveloped you and when she smiled, her blue eyes sparkled. My kids and I fell in love.

We sat down, talked numbers and when I could start. I went to work Monday and started calling my clients in between my appointments, letting them know that their appointments would still be the same time and day, but at a different location. Most knew how unhappy I was and weren't surprised to hear I was leaving.

By the end of the day, I had contacted all my clients on the books, I was booked out for 2 weeks from the salon. I told the other stylist, Judy, about me leaving, the new place and the peace I felt knowing I could walk away from the tension, anger and walking on eggshells.

I knew Judy was unhappy, too. She had been in several arguments with the owner. She asked if there was another booth available. If she decided to leave and join the same salon I was moving to, we could share start-up costs on color, then each of us would reorder what we used.

She went to visit the salon and decided she was leaving, too. We planned to leave the same day, she would start immediately at the other salon, and I would start 2 weeks later, when I returned from AZ.

I felt bad leaving the way I was, but at the same time, I knew if I told the owner ahead of time, he would start calling my clients or would fire me. I had a separate appointment book from when I moved all my appointments and kept it with me.

After I left, I never talked to the owner again and our paths never crossed even though we were in a small town. He was able to grow his salon, moving to a bigger space in an upper-class area with clients ready to spend high-end dollars.

We left for AZ. It was a quick nonstop flight and the kids slept through most of it. Jack and I did not talk much, most of our conversations were through the kids.

We arrived in AZ, excited to see my parents and KJ. We rented a car so we could sight see and go to Las Vegas, where my dad was working. We went to the stratosphere, Treasure Island to watch the outdoor show and wandered the streets of Vegas.

The last day my dad worked, we went to the Clark County Museum, which showcased the early settlers and the Hoover Dam workers. We went on the "hard hat" tour, where we were taken down into the dam, where all the turbines, generators and mechanical components were.

The history of the Hoover Dam still amazes me. The ingenuity of the workers and engineers when we didn't have the technology and equipment we have today. The tour guide shared specifics about the dam, the workers and walked us through the tunnels and small passageways inside the dam.

We went outside on the bottom deck of the dam, to see how far down we were from the top of the dam. While we were outside, they opened the jet flow gates, for the first time, in the dam's history. They were testing the gates and the amount of water coming out of all 4 at the same time could fill an Olympic-size swimming pool, 500,000 gallons, in three and a half seconds.

We drove back to AZ before we flew back to Charlotte. I enjoyed the time with my family and was excited for my new salon and workspace.

I bought crayons, coloring books and games to put in the kids' area. I set the TV up and put the videos in a cabinet next to the TV. I put some books out, had a rug and blow-up chair for the kids. After everything was set, I picked DJ and LJ up from daycare to have them test the kids' room.

Life continued into 1999. My business was booming, DJ was in 2nd grade and LJ was growing like a weed. I became more involved at church, in the youth group, coaching the men's softball team, playing softball, coaching cheerleaders, volunteering for ACS, and keeping myself busy with the kids, away from the house.

I started going to a weekly women's devotional study group, with a smaller group, which was more intimate and eye opening. I worked through the book *Power of a Praying Wife* by Stormie O'Martian, *Lord, Give Me Grace* by Kay Arthur, and many others. I was trying to find something that just wasn't there.

I talked to Jack. I wanted to move to AZ. My allergies required me getting shots, but my eyes still burned/itched. Several times, I had to pull over on the side of the road and put a cold cloth on my eyes. I was miserable from allergies and the humidity was bothering me more because I couldn't regulate my body temperature with thyroid issues. I wanted to be near my family, for me and the kids.

June 1999, we drove to AZ for a 2-week vacation. I 26, mom of 2, cancer survivor, Gulf War vet and I felt like I was 40. Listening to Shania Twain reminded me I wasn't 40 and I could still be young and carefree, regardless of my age. Jack and the kids slept through the night while I drove and sang, loving the open road. It took us 30 hours to drive from Charlotte to Phoenix.

KJ came over after work to visit. The kids wanted to go camping with the horses and we decided to go that weekend. We drove north of Phoenix where the temps were cooler.

After we arrived and set up, we had dinner, S'mores, and settled in for the night. The next morning after breakfast, my stepmom and I settled in our chairs in the creek, to read while the kids splashed around in the creek.

We decided to drive to San Diego, when we got home from camping, to go to the zoo. KJ came with us, and we arrived in San Diego at 1 A.M.

The next morning, we went to the zoo, rode the trolley, and explored the jungle-themed areas. After we finished, we drove to the beach so the kids and Jack could see the Pacific Ocean, for the first time.

We hopped in the van to head back to Phoenix. My dad had taken time off, so we stayed at the house to work with the horses. He had a stud horse named Buster, a full-size Belgian draft horse.

LJ and DJ each sat on Buster while my dad led Buster around the yard. DJ was afraid of heights and didn't enjoy it because he was so far off the ground. LJ was so small that her legs were almost sticking straight out to the sides while she was sitting on the horse.

We worked with the other horses, explored my dad's "treasure island" of things he had acquired over the years. Most people would refer to it as junk, but my dad calls it treasure and has Greene Engineered many projects over the years. Those projects still stand and/or work today.

We drove around the area, looking at houses, schools, and job opportunities. I was set on moving to Phoenix, with or without Jack. I told him I was going to put the house on the market and give us time for DJ to finish the school year in NC.

7
Career Change

I put the house on the market the end of October 1999 because I didn't know how long it would take to sell. I spent time off painting walls, cleaning trim, getting carpet fixed, shampooing carpets, and downsizing for the move. Jack finally realized I was serious.

Another kidney infection/stones hit me in November 1999 while I was at work. I started feeling sick in the morning around 7 A.M. By 9 A.M., I could barely stand. The receptionist called my doctor and she told me to come right in.

I drove myself. I was in so much pain. It was 10-15 minutes from the salon, but by the time I got there, I was shaking and incoherent from the pain. The doctor had the nurse take me to an exam room, start an IV after she collected a urine sample and start pain meds.

My urine showed kidney infections, stones and UTI. They added an antibiotic to my IV bag and more pain meds because the pain was worse than labor and didn't stop. The doctor said I was probably passing a stone and the pain should lessen once it passed. They kept the fluids running through me, trying to push the stone out and at some point, I passed out.

The doctor had called Jack to pick me up because I was in no condition to drive. She told me I needed to make sure I was using the bathroom more often while I was at work, even if I had to set a timer to remind me. She took me off the iron pills because she wanted to make sure they weren't part of the cause.

I took the rest of the week off and slept as much as I could. The infections had knocked me on my butt. I didn't make a turkey or anything for Thanksgiving, we didn't go anywhere and had no one over.

I decided I would finish the year out at the salon, but stop work after the first of the year, so I could pack, get the house ready and take care of everything we needed to get done. We had a few showings, but the market was saturated with so many brand-new builds and communities that there was lots of inventory, but few buyers.

I threw a surprise birthday party for Q's 30th. We spent more weekends together, soaking up all the time we could. The youth group was fundraising to go to a Kidz Kamp that summer. I was volunteering at the church office on Fridays, putting the programs together for Sunday and entering data.

We started a Weigh Down Workshop group at church, focusing on whether we were hungry when we found ourselves standing in front of the fridge or cabinets, or if we were bored, eating our emotions or habit. We had daily and weekly journals to chart our progress. We had cassette tapes to listen to for each week, meeting as a group 1 morning a week.

We learned to eat when we were hungry, stop once the hunger was gone, even if we left food on the plate. To start it off, each of us fasted, as long as we could, so we could recognize true hunger. We had to write, pray, listen to the first tape and every time we thought we were hungry, we had to set a timer for 5 minutes, then write or pray. If we were still hungry, then we could eat, but only until we noticed the hunger was gone.

I found out how much I wanted to write a book during this time and how much of my life was passing by in an unhappy marriage. The pastor overheard me talking to one of the other ladies about having a testimony. Another lady from church shared her testimony at our Monday night Women's ministry group, and I couldn't stop thinking about it.

I didn't feel like I had a testimony, I didn't do drugs, hadn't been unfaithful, didn't have an abortion, wasn't an alcoholic or any of the things I had heard testimonies about. The pastor was walking by the office and stopped when he heard me.

He came in and said, "You have more of a testimony than you can imagine. Your strength and courage of facing cancer at 20 years old, with a 6-month-old son, with no family around is a testimony. You also willingly joined the Army at 17, found yourself amid a war at 18 and are now struggling to fix an unhappy marriage."

I still wasn't convinced. He asked me to pray about it. When the time was right, I would know my testimony and it would be heard by the people that needed to hear it.

Jack was using words from the Bible and sermons to manipulate me, changing them for his advantage. After a few weeks, I just didn't care to fight him any longer. I was doing hair for clients at their houses while DJ was in school, to keep income coming in for myself.

In May 2000, Jack told me per the Bible and what the pastor said, he was the man of the house so he should be taking care of things like our finances and decisions. I told him he was more than welcome to start paying the bills, budgeting for groceries, fuel, and extras.

I handed him the checkbook on May 1, 2000, telling him the mortgage payment had been sent and would process Friday. There was enough in the account to cover the mortgage, with $60 left until payday. The car, insurance and other bills were all paid for May, so the next stuff was due in June.

The kids weren't in daycare any longer and that was a huge savings for the budget. I had been approved for 30% disability rating from the VA for the mantle radiation I received in 1993, so I had a few hundred dollars to cover me not working.

We spent an amazing four days with kids from 7-16 years old at "Kidz Kamp." The counselors were great, and the kids said the fundraising and hard work was worth it, while some parents enjoyed 4 days with no kids.

I loved watching DJ grow, as seeds continued to be planted in his heart. I took the time to sit back, observe and photograph what would be lasting memories. I rewound myself to when I was in 7th grade and went to a youth church camp with one of my aunts and cousin.

I remembered the questions, the trust fall, the homemade waterslide, and new friends. That was the morning we were laughing during breakfast, and I had a Cheerio come out of my nose. This caused stories being shared about food or liquid coming out of our noses, followed by more laughter, until the counselors kicked us outside.

I had a crush on one of the boys, "Bungy," his nickname. My first kiss happened the last night we were at camp. We wrote to each other off and on when we returned home.

These memories of the young girl I was, the hope I had in my heart, and realizing I wasn't living the life I had planned. It was time to figure out, one way or another, what I was going to do with my marriage. Parts of me were broken and gone.

At end of June, we drove to NY for my youngest sister's graduation, RD. She was my dad's daughter by a lady he dated, after my mom and before he met my stepmom. We had spent weekends and the summer at their house before they split up and saw RD at school. She was allowed to come to AZ with us once or twice.

When she was little, her older sister, a year younger than me, was accidentally shot and killed, while sitting in their living room. Her mom had a difficult time with the loss and my sister became her lifeline. She was no longer allowed to visit my dad.

We had picked KJ up from the airport in Pittsburgh on our way up, so she didn't have to rent a car and were dropping her off on our way back to NC. Jack and I didn't talk to each other much during the drive, but DJ and LJ talked about everyone they'd seen and couldn't wait to move to AZ. Jack clenched his jaw when the kids talked about AZ, but I didn't ask why. I didn't want to get into another argument.

We went to Q's for a 4th of July party after we got home. We started talking about leaving and it would be a while before we saw the Atlantic Ocean again. We knew the hotels were booked for the weekend, but after everyone left Q's, we decided to drive to the beach.

If a hotel was available when we got there, then we would get a room, if not we would sleep in the car to watch the sunrise together.

We packed their SUV, grabbed swimsuits and towels, and jumped in, with DJ riding in the back. We stopped to get drinks and snacks before we left town, then settled in.

It was 2:30 A.M. when we arrived at a deserted beach and open parking lot. We parked close to the beach and after walking to the water briefly, we climbed back in the SUV to take naps.

I couldn't sleep and heard Q moving too. We got up and walked down to the beach. We were down there when the others woke up and came down to watch the sunrise. We took a picture with just the two of us, with the sunrise, capturing the moment forever. We look completely different with skin color, hair, and other physical attributes, but we have a long-lasting connection, and she will forever be a sister I chose.

The summer was busy with packing the rest of the house, house showings, back to school and time to share my testimony. I was permitted 45 minutes. I shared my faith giving me the strength and hope, to power through a lonely, scary cancer journey. Without faith, hope cannot grow because the garden needs to be watered, weeded, fed, and loved.

Sharing my testimony was difficult, being vulnerable among others. I've never wanted to be perceived as a victim, or as weak. At the time, admitting I was dealing with undiagnosed depression, was a weakness in myself. Years later, I realized I was weak because I didn't address it. I wasn't the strongest version of myself because I ignored the problem.

I shared my daily struggles, to include my marital strife. It became harder to pray for someone that disrespected you. Instead of sharing about what transpired in our marriage, I shared about learning to pray for my heart change, first, then to pray for my husband.

I prayed for Jack's overall health, finances, work, social, dreams and goals. I didn't pray for our marriage. My prayers were for individual needs, not our marriage. We were both dealing with unresolved issues and trauma without knowing it.

Jack and I didn't talk much about what I shared, but many friends and strangers thanked me for sharing a powerful testimony. My testimony was recorded on a cassette tape that I've never listened to. I didn't write anything down. I let the words come from my heart and God. I don't recall everything I said, but it was what was weighing on my heart.

There were a couple offers on our house with closing scheduled for mid-September. DJ would have to start school in NC, but I had a date to work with. As much as I had wanted to leave earlier, God had other plans for me in NC. Jack sold his Jetta, so we only had to worry about 1 vehicle for the cross-country drive.

I was packing boxes, after walking DJ to the school bus stop, when there was a knock on the door. I opened the door to a Mecklenburg County Sheriff's Deputy. She verified who I was, then told me that I was being served with foreclosure papers for my house.

I was stunned. I couldn't comprehend what she was saying. As she was talking, I read some of the documents, I saw the mortgage hadn't been paid since May. I nearly fell to my knees with disbelief, anger and hurt.

She asked if I was okay, before she left. I was. The house should be sold before it went to foreclosure auction, then it would be over, along with my marriage. The deputy was empathetic, but I didn't cry and declined her offer of coming back when Jack was home.

I started calling the banks, credit card companies, auto loans and utilities, to find out what hadn't been paid. The check I had written for the May payment, when I gave Jack control of the finances, bounced because Jack spent $150 on a damn golf club.

He never took care of the payments. The car he told me he "sold" a couple years prior had been repossessed. The last call I made was to the finance company for the Jetta because something didn't feel right. They asked if I wanted to make a payment to get the car back because the vehicle was repossessed. The vehicle was purchased with my SSN, as the main account holder.

I was numb by the time I finished the phone calls. I couldn't process anything. I sat at the desk, looking out the back window, feeling hollow and empty. Jack was playing golf that night with guys from work. I did what I could to salvage the finances.

We needed to rent the U-Haul, get fuel and food during the trip, then I would worry about things after we closed on the house. I called my parents and asked for a loan, telling them I needed money for unexpected closing costs, to finalize the closing.

I kept the money separate and closed the account so Jack couldn't use the debit card. There were a couple friends from church that were going to drive to AZ with us. They were going to school in Phoenix, so we planned a caravan.

I signed the closing paperwork and finished packing, Jack worked his last day at the post office, DJ finished his last day at school, we said goodbye to friends and family, then started the journey. The plan was to drive straight through because everyone was on a limited budget. We would rotate drivers so everyone could get some sleep.

Jack had to go to the post office in AZ once we got there, so we pushed to make it by Sunday morning. That would permit him to get some sleep before he went in. I planned to look for a salon and get my license transferred to AZ.

I would enroll DJ in school on Monday and figure out the childcare situation after. My parents let us stay at their house, they had a large family room/dining room they didn't use. We moved our stuff in, set up beds and made a "home" until jobs were secured, then I could look for a place to live.

KJ told me I could work in the mail room at the firm where she worked as the current mail clerk was going on maternity leave until after Christmas. Jack kept telling me there was an issue with his transfer paperwork at the post office when he came home early every day.

After a couple weeks of him not working, I started working at my sisters' firm, to have some money coming in other than my VA disability. I hoped to have a place by Halloween, but as the days progressed, I knew that wasn't going to happen.

KJ, her friend, my stepmom and I went to Vegas the day after Thanksgiving for a couple days. KJ had set up a girls' weekend at the spa. Jack and my dad were at home with the kids, so I was really looking forward to some time away with my sister, with drinks and laughter.

We checked in Friday, late morning, went to lunch and dinner then KJ decided we should go dancing. There was a little place off the strip she had been to, and we could walk to it.

We danced, drank, laughed, and had a great time. My stepmom went home before us so she could call my dad before he went to bed, and she could get some sleep. We came back a couple hours later.

The next morning, we had appointments at the Hard Rock hotel spa, beginning at 10 A.M. My stepmom said Jack called her cell phone, several times while we were out. When she called my dad and asked if anything was wrong, my dad said no.

We finished at the spa and went to the room to get ready for dinner. I was staying at the hotel to read and relax, instead of going out with KJ and her friend. My stepmom had her phone off most of the day and after KJ left, she checked her messages before calling my dad.

Jack had left several messages, some of them were extremely ugly with the things he said and accused me of. My stepmom couldn't believe the things he said in the messages, especially on her phone.

She called my dad to say goodnight while I grabbed my book. I fell asleep after a few minutes, then she woke me up because Jack had called again. Before I could say hello, he started cussing at me, accusing me of "screwing around" while I was there. I hung up.

He called back and my stepmom told him I was in the room, in bed, reading. She asked him not to call back and she was turning her phone off so we could get some sleep. I apologized for how he talked to her and for all the messages.

We talked for a little bit. She didn't know how bad it was between us until now. I told her I was going to look for another job that had good benefits and pay. I was going to do a separation. I couldn't live with it anymore.

Jack got a job with Nike, but he was spending most of his paycheck on his obsession, shoes. I was working until after the holidays, where my sister worked, but my credit was shot. I couldn't buy a house. I talked to my parents, and they told me we could stay there as long as we needed to get on our feet.

Most of my dad's siblings came into town for a wedding. We had a bonfire the night after the wedding before everyone left. Jack came home from work and came out to the fire to say hi to everyone before going in the house. The temps dropped rapidly, and we all went inside after putting the fire out.

My dad was making and drinking frozen or in his words "frogan" margaritas, so everyone was feeling tipsy. The laughter and stories continued as we moved into the house. The kids had fallen asleep watching a movie. I snuggled into one of the chairs, to listen and join in the laughter.

As the conversation started to quiet down, Jack came from our sleeping area, spun my chair around and started yelling at me, while pointing his finger in my face. He said everything was my fault, him not working at the post office, not having our own place, and other things, because of me.

I hadn't done or said anything to provoke him. He had been joining in on the conversations. While I processed the verbal attack, my dad calmly said, "Son, you need to step back and regroup."

The room went silent as the tears of humiliation and hurt rolled down my face. Jack went into the other room, and everyone went to bed. KJ hugged me, told me I had her support, and it was time to take care of myself and the kids. My dad hugged me and told me he was sorry because he hadn't known things were this bad.

I knew that things would only escalate if I didn't change things. I was done feeling guilty and feeling like a failure because my marriage didn't work. I put what I had into it. There was nothing left to give. I didn't want my kids growing up in that environment or for them to think it was okay to verbally abuse anyone.

I grabbed a blanket and curled on the couch. I prepared a "to-do" list in my head. First, find a job that could support me and the kids, with benefits. I would go through the paper the next day, after Jack went to work, to see what was in the classifieds.

I set a 6-month timeline to get my finances together for a vehicle and my own place. I slept on the couch. I couldn't stand sleeping next to Jack.

I found a job listing with the sheriff's office, as a 911 emergency dispatcher. It was full time, good pay, and great benefits. It was a job doing communications, which was my background in the Army. I thought it was a perfect fit.

I applied right before Christmas and looked at a few other options while waiting. We celebrated LJ's 4th birthday with a small party. Christmas was a small family affair with lots of food and laughter. New Year's Eve 2000, we were in bed by 10 P.M.

I received a phone call to set up an interview the following week at the sheriff's office. I was confident in my answers and looked forward to a new career. I never considered working in law enforcement and thought it would be a challenging but rewarding career.

I started working, the end of January, with a 3-week dispatcher academy. We had to learn all the major streets in the county, with their numbering system, to be able to quickly identify the beat area. We had to memorize the incident codes, beat areas, call signs for districts, deputies and distinguish between day, swing, and night shift.

There were call signs for each specialty division, detectives, chiefs, and captains. We learned north, south, east, and west, the numbering system for addresses, to identify if a house would be on the north or south side of a street, or an east/west address.

It was an intense 3-week academy, with tests daily. With only 1 vehicle for me and Jack, I used an old truck of my dad's, to drive a couple miles to the bus station. I was at the bus station by 4:20 A.M. to catch the bus that would get me downtown before 6 A.M.

I used the time on the bus to study and memorize everything we needed to learn. A friend of the family, Clara, watched LJ during the day and my step-mom was making sure DJ left for school on time.

It was a crazy time, but I was excited for the new job, new opportunities, and an entirely new career from doing hair, makeup, and skincare, to helping the citizens of Maricopa County.

8
Single Mom Life

I finished the Academy, top in the class and had first choice of shifts. I chose to work the graveyard shift, 10:30 P.M. (2230 hours) to 6:30 A.M. This would allow me to be home with LJ during the day, have dinner with the kids and put them to bed before I went to work.

I was used to operating on a couple hours of sleep and knew LJ would let me sleep a couple hours in the morning, after she was fed, and I put a movie on for her to watch. Sometimes she would nap with me, but she let me sleep.

Jack and I had gotten into another fight one morning, before he went to work, and LJ saw me crying. When I laid down, she put her little hand on my cheek, looked into my eyes and said, "It be okay, Mama, I love you." My heart hurt, knowing that even through the anger, hurt, disappointment, depression, and frustration, my baby girl still had a beautiful and caring heart. It was time for me to move forward and allow my heart to heal.

By then, I had been working for a couple weeks. I told Jack he needed to find a new place because I didn't want to live with him. I knew it would take him time to get the money together and find a place, but I wanted a separation and couldn't live with him any longer.

We had been sleeping separately since the night I slept on the couch, and we didn't celebrate our 7-year anniversary. I told him he could take the car and I would figure my transportation out. His schedule was never the same because he was working retail, but we worked it out so he could spend time with the kids. I had 2 days off and I made sure I had them, then he could choose from the other days.

For the first couple weeks, I drove my stepmom's vehicle, getting home before she had to leave for work. My aunt and uncle moved to Arizona and stayed at my dad's, living in their RV, outside of the house. I worked out a deal to use my aunt's vehicle, paying for her fuel and maintenance. She left for work after I got home in the mornings, and it helped me get through the first couple months of training.

I knew I would switch to day shift training in June and would be working the radio, communicating directly with the deputies, instead of the public, answering 911 calls, if I finished my 911 training on time. I was saving every extra penny to get a vehicle in June.

My sister, KM, graduated college in Ohio, the end of May and we decided to get an apartment together. She had come out for Christmas, then for spring break and found a teaching job so she would move to AZ in June.

I was looking at apartments, close to my parents, and others that were closer to the school KM would be teaching at. One Sunday I was sleeping when Jack brought the kids back home. They were outside, when he came into the room, woke me up and told me he was taking the CDs on the table. I didn't care. I needed to go back to sleep.

I sat up in bed to say hi to the kids and hug them before I went back to sleep, when Jack threw a glass of ice water in my face. I saw red and took off after him. He ran to the door and pushed my stepmom out of the way. My dad saw him push my stepmom and told him to go to the garage.

I was angry. My dad could see it on my face. He told me to lie down and get more sleep, he would take care of it. I walked back in the room and saw Jack had thrown all the CDs on the table and floor. Several were cracked. I picked them up so no one cut their foot.

The kids hadn't seen Jack throw the water in my face, but they saw me chasing Jack. I cussed at him, telling him I was done with the bullshit, and I was going to kick his ass. I didn't tell them what happened, but they knew I was angry, but not at them.

I decided to get the apartment close to KMs school. I wasn't going to tell Jack the address. We would use my parents as the drop-off/pickup point, so we had someone to referee, and I didn't have to worry about him showing up unexpectedly or doing something stupid at the apartment.

I bought a Jeep Wrangler the beginning of May. I put a deposit on the apartment the next morning, after I got off work. I asked Clara to watch LJ until I got home so I didn't have to drive back and forth.

The kids were with their dad when I moved into the apartment. I had a table, bedroom set, sofa, entertainment center and TV to move. I rented a U-Haul and had a friend help me move when I finished work. I loaded the U-Haul the night before I left for work and would be off for 3 days as I transitioned to day shift.

It was different being in the heart of a city, with so many things within walking distance and all the traffic, but it was a new start. The kids were excited for the pool, park, and playground. Our apartment was on the ground floor, and the back patio faced the pool.

KM moved to AZ the following week and watched the kids for me during the days I worked, when they weren't with their dad. He had every weekend off. We met Friday afternoons, when he got off work, and I picked them up on Sunday evening, after I got done with work.

The arrangement wasn't perfect, but it worked, allowing the kids to spend time with both of us, without disrupting their schedule when they started school. I felt safer with him not knowing where I lived. LJ didn't turn 5 until the end of December, but in AZ, as long as they turned 5 before the end of the year, they could start kindergarten.

KM took the kids with her while she worked on getting her classroom set up and decorated. We spent afternoons in the pool when I got off work, exploring our area, camping and last-minute decisions to drive to the beach.

KM met a guy, and they were dating steady. He had a street racing bike and rode with a group of guys in the evenings on the weekends, when it was cooler. KM and I started going with them Friday nights, having breakfast at Denny's Saturday morning, grocery shopping, then hanging at the pool until we went riding that night.

I started work at 6 A.M. on Sunday, normally on a couple hours sleep. We picked the kids up, grabbed pizza or something quick for dinner so we could go to the pool as soon as we got home.

Monday nights, KM and I started playing coed soccer and then started playing softball. The team we played for was the firm where KJ worked, and

I knew most of the players. We needed more guys, so I recruited some deputies I worked with and had gotten to know.

That led to playing softball a couple nights a week along with soccer on Monday nights. I loved being active again, not having to worry about someone questioning my whereabouts, spending more quality time with my kids, and feeling my heart start to heal. I was finally smiling, laughing, and enjoying my life again. I felt happiness for the first time in years.

September 11, 2001, our country endured a devastating tragedy, and changed our lives, significantly. I was getting ready for work when we saw the news, where the first tower of the Twin Towers had been hit by a plane. We were all in disbelief, then we watched live as the 2nd plane hit the 2nd tower. I had to kiss my babies goodbye, with tears running down my cheeks, as I left for work, knowing we were going to be busier than ever.

I finished my training and was approved to work by myself. I was assigned to graveyards to fill a hole until the next shift change rotation. I started picking up overtime, to help pay down the debts I was left with from my husband and to build my savings back up.

One night at work, I was working the west side radio channel, dispatching calls to deputies. One of our 911 operators had received a call of someone getting shot at. She found out it was my sister, KM. The operator notified my supervisor when she found out it was my sister. My supervisor contacted one of the deputies on duty, to come to the dispatch center so he could pick me up and drive me to our apartment.

I didn't know what happened until the city police department was with KM and she was safe. My supervisor had someone pick up my channel so she could tell me what happened. She told me KM called 911 because the guy she was dating, saw her with another guy and started shooting at her when she got in her car at our apartment. She kept driving to avoid him, but he continued shooting at her, while she was on the phone with 911. They told me she was safe, and a deputy was going to drive me home, to make sure we were all okay.

The deputy, Patrick, was one I had done a ride along with, just a couple weeks prior so I knew him better than some of the others working. When we got to the apartment, he waited for me to pack a bag for myself and the kids and for KM to pack a bag. Then he drove KM and me, to my dad's house for the night until the suspect was in custody.

My supervisor told me to take the next night off too, so I could make sure everything was taken care of at home and with my kids. I received a notice from the apartment complex that we had to move immediately because the shooting was a breach in our lease, even though my sister was the victim.

We moved into my dad's, again. Me, the kids, and KM, with all our stuff, right before Christmas. KM found an apartment and soon moved out, but I decided to stay at my parents. Paying for the breach in contract cost me more than expected.

I was getting ready to start working swing shift, from 2:30 P.M.-10:30 P.M., and my stepmom said she would help on the nights I worked. I kept the kids enrolled in school, even though we had a 45-minute drive every morning.

I started working construction for the company my dad worked for, helping unload the belly dump trucks in the morning so the material was ready and stocked for paving that evening.

The kids and I left the house at 6 A.M., drove near their school and got breakfast at McDonald's. We caught up on the prior day/night while we ate. The kids played for a bit, while I looked over homework, before leaving to drop them off at school. I cherished these times with the kids and looked forward to our morning drive and breakfast. I was spending more quality time with the kids, and they were happy.

I dropped the kids off for school then drove to the construction job site, where I worked from 8 A.M. until 1 P.M. I then drove to KM's apartment, showered, and drove to work at the sheriff's office until 10:30 P.M., or sometimes until 2:30 A.M., if they needed help.

The overtime helped, along with the construction job, to pay off debt and rebuild my credit. Working in jeans and work boots was a different look for me, but I appreciated a man in jeans and work boots, so I embraced it. In the afternoons, Clara picked her kids up from school, then drove to pick my kids up. She either took them back to her house or dropped them off at my parents.

This was our schedule for 6 months until the kids finished school, then I enrolled them in the school that DJ previously attended when I lived with my parents. I continued working the construction job through the first part of summer. I transferred back to night shift and stopped working the 2nd job.

I had Tuesday/Wednesdays off when I worked swing shift, then Wednesday/Thursday off when I went back to graveyards. I started coaching a youth soccer team and LJ decided to play. DJ was playing flag football, so every Saturday, we were busy with games in the morning as soon as I got home from work.

We had practice in the afternoons, which allowed me to sleep while the kids were in school and I would try to get an hour or two, after we got home, ate, showered and ready for bed. I left for work at 10 P.M., which allowed me to put the kids to bed and say goodnight.

I was playing softball with my sisters, in a couple different leagues on Monday, Tuesday, and Thursday nights, then started playing on Friday nights, before I went to work.

We were active, but we did everything together. The kids came to all my games, and I coached and went to theirs. We went camping, explored Arizona in the Jeep, and took trips to San Diego and other random places. The kids and I found our new normal.

My dad hooked his horses up to a wagon for Christmas eve in 2000 and we went around the little community singing Christmas carols. The wagon ride grew as did the amount of people joining us each year. Our route became bigger, with Santa and Mrs. Claus making an appearance for the night, along with their elves. We handed out candy canes, took pictures with families as we drove by, and our family tradition began.

After Christmas in 2002, my dad and stepmom went to NY to be with my stepmom's mother whose health was failing. My kids were spending time with their dad during the break, and I picked up overtime, helping work the DUI task force and covering for those that wanted time off for the holidays.

December 29th, 2002, I was working the switchboard, transferring calls to the jails, crime stop, other agencies or answering basic questions. It was a slower night at work. It was just my supervisor and one of the girls that trained me, working the 911 desks that night.

We had been at work for a couple hours when I received a switchboard call. I asked how I could direct the person's call, he told me his address, which wasn't being recognized in our system as being in our county. I asked him to reverify his address and confirm if he was in our county or the one next to ours.

He reverified his address, then he told me the only reason he was calling, was to let us know he shot his wife, 2 stepdaughters and was about to shoot himself, but he didn't want the bodies to stay out there and rot.

The moments that came after will haunt me for the rest of my life. Therapy helps, but it is forever burned into my memory. My supervisor could tell something was wrong when I kept asking to confirm the address. She got the other agency on the line to let them know there was something going on at the address.

Before she clicked over to listen in to my conversation, to update the other county, the man told me again he shot his wife, his 12-year-old stepdaughter and the 8-year-old. He said, "The 8-year-old is looking at me for help so I'm going to have to shoot her again," then I heard a shotgun blast.

I was aghast. He shot the 8-year-old girl again while I was listening on a recorded line. I kept the man on the line. I knew units were on their way to his house and I didn't want him to take the easy way out by committing suicide.

I heard yelling in the background and the guy being taken into custody. I don't remember if one of the deputies hung up the phone or told me they were code 4 before hanging up.

The rest of the night was a blur for me. I had no idea what I was thinking, if I was processing, but I pushed everything away, to answer the next call. My supervisor told me to take a quick break, use the restroom and if I wanted to go home, she would help cover.

I went to the restroom. I was in shock. I couldn't process what I heard was real. I grabbed a snack from my locker and my stress reliever box, which had crayons, coloring books and "Hot Tamales" to pass the time in between calls.

I told my supervisor I was going to stay because sleep would elude me when I got home. Besides, no one was at home. I finished the night and told my supervisor I needed to listen to the recording before I saw the news if she could have it ready when I came in that night.

I wanted to listen to the call to make sure I hadn't missed something and to know I did everything I could possibly do. I drove home and sat in my driveway looking at the house, but I couldn't get out of the car.

My phone rang, which startled me, and I answered it, knowing it was Patrick headed home from his shift. As soon as I answered, he could tell something was wrong. I couldn't get the words out and kept repeating, he shot her.

We didn't live far from each other, but I told him not to come over. I was going to shower and try to go to bed. We planned to talk on my way in to work that night, so he knew I was okay.

I went into the house, showered, and crawled into bed. I didn't sleep well and put one of my favorite movies on for background noise. My 3 go-to movies to help me relax were *Pretty Woman*, *The Little Mermaid* and *Top Gun*. *Top Gun* and *Pretty Woman* helped me get through Desert Storm and felt like old friends.

I slept off and on the entire day. I talked to the kids briefly and told them I would see them the next day, then went back to sleep before getting ready for work. I didn't turn the news on in the house, but I knew the news would be on when I went to work. It was always on in the dispatch room, which was next to our locker room.

I mentally prepared myself to listen to the call when I got to work. I went in early to listen to it. My supervisor let me into the tape room with the recording cued and ready.

She put her hand on my shoulder saying, "Child, I don't know how you listened to this the first time because I couldn't listen to it." She squeezed my shoulder and told me to come out when I was ready, she would be right outside the door.

I put the headphones on and pressed play with shaking hands. My heart was racing. I focused on steadying my breathing. I didn't want to have to listen to it again. I heard the little girl in the background, asking him to help her, before he shot her.

I talked to a real-life monster and in this job, I was going to deal with more. I finished listening, grabbed my stuff and walked out of the tape room. I walked to the dispatch room and stood in front of the TV. I needed to see the pictures of the girls, knowing the news would run the story.

I needed to see their faces to be able to grieve them and allow them to be more than an age or gender. I needed to see his face, to see the monster I talked to. They looked normal. You never truly know what is going on behind closed doors, inside someone's mind or heart. I couldn't have done anything more to save those girls or their mom, but I kept the coward that shot them from ending his life. He would live with what he did.

That night was busy. I worked the radio, so I didn't have time to think. I had to deal with the here and now, the new emergencies that were happening. Life kept moving.

KJ had been telling me I needed to divorce Jack so I could move on. After I filed my taxes in 2003, as head of household, with 2 dependents, I received a notice from the IRS that someone already claimed my kids. I went to the courthouse that day and filed for divorce.

I don't know if I was mad at his audacity to use our kids for his monetary gain or that he was that selfish. I was paying for everything, including the car he was driving and the insurance on it. He had moved back to Chicago, and I was ready to close that chapter.

I looked at houses so the kids and I could move into our own place. Jack wouldn't be able to take anything else from me. The paperwork was filed, Jack was served, and a date was set for the finalization.

My dad asked if I would stay at the house longer because he was going to be working out of town and wanted me to help my stepmom. After much debating, I decided to stay. It would help save money and they were helping with the kids.

Family members were living in their RV on the property, and I was adamant my kids were never left alone with them, for any amount of time, because of what happened with KJ and me.

After years of fluctuating hormones from birth control, the doctors advising me not to have more kids after my daughter was born, and the side-effects of hypothyroidism, I decided to get my tubes tied. It took me months to convince the doctor.

I told him that if I ever decided to be in a serious relationship again, that it would be about us, not about having kids. There was no way I was going to risk my life to have another child. I had two children that needed me.

In June of 2003, I had my surgery. I missed playing one of our softball games. I still went to the game to support the team and my team knew why I was sitting out, but rumors began flying, on top of the hundreds of rumors that had already been going around.

One of the worst was that I got pregnant by a married deputy and had an abortion. It took me a while to find out who started that rumor and how they pieced their beliefs together, but the saddest part was I had never met the deputy that started the rumor.

By now, 2 ½ years into a job with people working in close quarters, few women and lots of men, things were extremely catty and petty, with rumors, lies and gossip. I decided to stir the pot. Unfortunately, that pot stirring landed me in the supervisor's office with an oral reprimand.

The guys that were in on my pot-stirring were like brothers. I didn't hang out with many people outside of work except those I played softball with, and they became family.

One of the girls who played ball with us and worked with me part-time, Goldie, became a great friend. No one knew how much we hung out, away from work, except my sisters because they played ball with us.

We started doing ladies nights, on Wednesday nights, after the kids went to bed, at a local sports bar. We would shoot pool, have a couple drinks, dance, flirt and laugh. Ladies' night stayed the same base crew, but sometimes we had guests that would come hang out with us.

The summer of 2003 brought more family parties, camping, beach trips, lake days and a freedom I hadn't felt in years. My divorce was going to be final in September, the kids were flourishing, and I had hope in my soul again.

One of our party crew ladies, Eileen, said she wanted to go to Cancun, to celebrate being single, away from her kids and job. I wanted to celebrate, too. She found a great deal with an all-inclusive resort and airfare for 8 days/7 nights, the first part of September.

I was in!! We were able to make payments, instead of paying in 1 lump-sum. I couldn't wait! Clara watched the kids, making sure they all got to and from school the one day, otherwise they were all hanging out for Labor Day weekend.

When we arrived in Cancun, the humidity made my skin glow. It was late night, early morning, but we were able to check into our room, shower and get some sleep hours earlier than expected. After a couple hours of sleep, I got up and walked through the resort to the beach to watch the sunrise.

There was a small bar on the beach, which served alcohol 24/7 and the dining room was next to the bar. I grabbed a pina colada from the bar to watch the sunrise and listen to the ocean lapping at my feet.

Afterward, I grabbed breakfast, then found a lounge chair by the pool to do some reading and people watching. Eileen came out and we chilled by the pool for a couple hours. There was a swim-up bar, as well as servers all around so we sipped pina coladas most of the day until it started raining.

We didn't want to stay in the room, so we went to the bar on the beach, which had a large overhang from the roof and started making friends. We were under a hurricane watch, but the rain wasn't bad, and the temperature was perfect.

We met professional soccer players from Brazil, Holland and the Netherlands that were in town for the world cup in Mexico. We told stories and listened to theirs. We didn't leave the bar until 3 A.M. We slept a couple hours and were back at the pool by 8 A.M. with pina coladas and people watching.

We played beach volleyball, played in the ocean, drank, and laughed. One game, I went for the ball, stepped on the out of bounds rope, which was a couple inches thick and rolled my ankle. It instantly swelled and I couldn't put weight on it. One of the Brazilian soccer players picked me up and carried me to the bar, where he got ice and put it on my ankle. He had my ankle and leg on his lap and told me to keep it elevated.

I couldn't understand much of what he said, but he was a gorgeous specimen. Over 6 feet tall, thick dark hair, hard muscled with a sculpted body, darkened by the sun. There was a sprinkling of hair on his chest. I was mesmerized by his dark chocolate eyes and smile. Slightly buzzed from the sun and alcohol already, I felt downright tipsy and giddy sitting with him. Eileen and I sat there for hours.

Every day/night rolled into each other. Up at 8 A.M., drink, laugh, meet people, play on the beach, in the pool, and roll into bed about 3 A.M. We went to dinner at a sister resort one night, where they rolled fresh cigars in the lobby, outside the restaurant. I bought a couple to smoke on the beach after dinner.

The last day we were there, I got my first tattoo. I found an American guy, referred by several people and went to his shop. I explained what I wanted, a heart-shaped wreath of tulips and leaves, with the names of my kids on top of each side of the heart.

When I went home, I felt something new. I felt sensual, and strong in my own sexuality, choosing me, for me. The goddess within was emerging with strength, love, sensuality, passion, and desire. Sex had been dimmed for me as an act of disgust or duty. The light was back on, now renewed.

I began exploring where I liked to be touched, what I desired to touch. I allowed my senses to come alive, not for the act of sex itself, but allowing myself the freedom to find me, and to fall in love with myself. Learning to love my broken, scarred, and damaged parts, physically, mentally, and emotionally. I was all I needed and wanted. I began to grow and revel in it.

Soon, I shed the skin of "wife" and embraced being single. I was always a "flirt." In high school, I was voted "biggest flirt." However, during my marriage, the flirt in me was suppressed. Jack was jealous of everything and everyone. I couldn't be kind or nice to the opposite sex, let alone smile and say hi, without being accused of sleeping with the person.

As the months went on at work, I decided if I wanted to talk to someone, date someone or just have sex with someone that was my right as a single lady. I didn't care what the gossips said about it. The downfall...feelings!!!!

Just as I would get to know someone, start enjoying their company, they would say, "I'm starting to have feelings for you," and I abruptly severed the connection.

Feelings were tiring and exhausting, especially as I was learning to experience my own feelings. I didn't have time or energy to worry about someone else's. I joined a gym, not far from my house, for a release after work. I loved lifting weights and pushing myself physically, wondering what my limits were.

I met one of the trainers, we flirted, and he asked me out to dinner. I knew it wasn't going anywhere when we ate at Outback Steakhouse and he ordered a steak, broccoli, and a baked potato, with no butter or salt. He told me I looked good, but I would look "great" once I lost 5-10 lbs.

I laughed, finished our dinner, then smiled and waved when I saw him in the gym. I couldn't imagine giving up flavor or fun, with eating or anything else. After being caged in a "perfect little wife" role, faking the smiles, the emotions and life in general, I was not rejecting fun to be anyone's idea of "great."

I met guys, went to the movies, played pool, but mostly kept to myself and my kids. I didn't feel worthy of love from someone else because I wasn't fully in love with myself. I was 31 years old and had never learned to love myself or to fully experience emotion, feelings, and healthy coping mechanisms, other than journaling.

As 2004 approached, several friends were encouraging me to go to the deputy academy. Being a single mom with young kids and having trouble with my lungs, I didn't feel it was the right time. There was also fear of getting pepper sprayed and going into a full-blown panic, not being able to breathe.

The change in the weather and environment kicked my allergies into overdrive that turned into a sinus infection, subsequently losing my voice for nearly 2 weeks. As my voice started coming back, I tried going back to work, but it was making things worse and extending my downtime. I took the time off, rested my voice and caught up on sleep.

I was back to work a few days and working the west side dispatch channel, with my favorite squad, 2/4. We had been slow most of the night and the deputies were catching up on paperwork. Our policy was to check on the deputy every hour if we hadn't heard from them. I finished my checks and was talking Sgt. Shanley, on the "hotline," the phone that connected directly to the district, updating him of calls that weren't priority.

While I was on the phone with him, I heard a click in my headset and looked at the radio tower which showed the channel we were working on, volumes and if the equipment used to key up was a personal radio, base radio in a patrol vehicle or from the district.

The mic click came from a vehicle and after I did a search to see who was driving it, I called for that unit over the radio. No response. After attempting to clear the unit a couple more times, I sent him a text through our paging system, knowing we had spotty coverage in a lot of the rural and county areas we covered.

Sgt. Shanley stayed on the line with me and called the personal cell of the deputy. Still no response. I asked his beat partner if he knew his last location. They recently left the school where they did report writing, headed back to the district.

Shanley had me call the deputies mom, to ensure he hadn't stopped there. As soon as his mom answered, she asked me what was wrong because we wouldn't be calling that early in the morning if everything was okay.

Meanwhile, other units were sent to the last known location of the deputy, driving different routes, to see if they crossed paths with him. I launched a helo from a nearby agency to search the area as well.

27 minutes after the mic click, one of the deputies located the deputy and his car. He hit a berm, causing his patrol car to go airborne, then flip before it landed on its tires. The deputy was found outside the vehicle, leaning against the passenger side back tire.

He was flown to the hospital via helicopter as I already had it in the air, and he wasn't responding. We figured he was ejected and when the vehicle flipped his mic hit the ground or something, causing it to key up.

Sgt. Shanley picked up the mom from home, to take her to the hospital. As the next shift came on, his squad headed to the hospital, where he was in a coma, with swelling on the brain and multiple cuts/contusions.

I called my stepmom so she could get the kids to school, then drove to the hospital with a couple of the girls that helped with the incident.

That was my "weekend," so I stayed at the hospital most of the day, waiting for updates. I met his mom and sisters and we set up a phone tree to update everyone as we took shifts sitting at the hospital with the family.

One of the days I was sitting there, Sgt. Shanley told me they opened the hiring process for deputies again and I should apply. He had been telling me to apply since I did my first ride-along in 2001 with him. I laughed and he read me the testing dates before I left.

KJ stopped by the house, said she passed the entrance test for the FBI and would be starting the hiring process in the next couple weeks. I was happy and excited for her. As everyone hugged her, I knew it was my time to step up and expand my career.

I was going to apply for the deputy academy. She was ecstatic. We could train together, go through the process together and potentially both of us wind up as cops.

I filled out the application when I got to work. Nervous and wondering if I was crazy, I sat down with the kids the next day, after school, asking their thoughts about my decision and getting their input.

We talked about their fears. The more we talked, they both said they were excited for me to do it, as long as I always wore my bulletproof vest. I received an email stating the physical and written testing would be in 2 weeks.

I had to do at least 17 pushups in a minute, 30 sit-ups in a minute and run 1 ½ miles, under 15:30. I called one of the guys that I had become good friends with, Kurt, and told him I had to test in 2 weeks. He came over that night and we set up a plan of attack.

KJ and I started running and sprinting at the park as the kids rode their bikes, encouraging us. I was so nervous for my test. However, I excelled on the run, then we went inside for the pushups/sit-ups. I counted I had done 29 pushups, but the girl counting my pushups wasn't counting most of them and I missed the pushups by 1, according to her count.

A couple of the deputies and recruit training officers told me I had it, but her count was official. I was furious, knowing I passed everything, but not getting credit for it. The captain told me to come back and retest in 2 weeks and not to give up because I had it.

I kept training, pushing myself harder, stopping by the hospital, even if it was for an hour or 2, sleeping, then training when my kids got home from school. KJ's first physical test was after mine, and we pushed each other daily. We shared a strength trainer at the gym, set our daily/weekly and monthly goals, being accountable with each other.

I went back for the test, 2 weeks later, after working all night, determined no one was stopping me. I shaved 2 minutes off my run time and did more sit-ups and pushups than on the previous test. I was on cloud nine.

The written test was after the physical. Those that passed went into the auditorium to hydrate and prepare for the written. I knew the test would probably be similar to the military ASVAB, with math, comprehension, and logic testing. I didn't waste time on the math, if I didn't know it, I went with "C" as the answer. I would make up my score in the comprehension and logic portion.

It took a couple weeks to get our results back to determine if we would continue with the background checks and polygraph. I got my results letting me know they were moving forward with my background check. The good thing about already being an employee was they had my background packet up to 2001.

My sister and I both moved forward in our testing processes. We met to hike every Saturday morning and we did a mountain trail run every Wednesday morning, while continuing to do sprints and strength training. Both of us had our background/polygraph test in July 2004, but our grandpa, mom's dad, was hospitalized and our mom said he had cancer throughout his body.

KJ, the kids and I flew to NY to see our grandpa, say our goodbyes, and spend a couple days with friends and family before we flew back. Most people were shocked when they heard I was going through the process to become a cop recalling the trouble I got into during high school. Hazel was one of the few that continually supported me.

KJ and I came back to AZ and continued pushing ourselves physically. I took my polygraph and failed. The examiner was a jackass. The supervisor of the polygraph unit looked at the exams and asked him why I failed. He didn't have a good reason, other than he felt I wasn't truthful about my previous marriage and why I got divorced. I was set up for a second polygraph with a different examiner and passed.

In August, I was offered a job as a deputy sheriff trainee, beginning the academy the first part of October. My sister got her notification as well. She was also starting her academy in October, a week after mine. My academy was local, and I would be home every night, but my sister would be going to Quantico for her training.

We celebrated our birthdays together, she was 31 and I was 32, which always seemed old to us, but we were both starting a new and physically demanding career. We were ready. I put in my notice at dispatch, did pushups every hour at work and worked more OT to put money in savings.

Friends threw me a party, wishing me well and allowing me to thank all those that helped me get to that point. KM was able to fly home from Iraq for a few days and was there for the celebration. I loved that I could celebrate with my girls and the guys that helped push me physically and mentally. One of the best things was celebrating my friends, Kurt and Goldie, that started dating. This relationship bloomed after hanging out together at one of our ladies' nights.

They had been dating for a few months and learned they were pregnant. They were due right after I was supposed to graduate the deputy academy. They checked in on me regularly during the academy, which was easy considering he was one of the instructors at the academy.

I started the academy October 4th, 2004. Our uniform was black pants, white button-down shirt, black tie, and black boots, which had to be shiny for formation. We each had a nametag we wore on our shirt, and we were given a black pen, called the "sergeant's pen," that we had to carry in our shirt pocket daily. I had to wear my hair pulled back and off my collar, so I wore a ponytail that I braided then wrapped around the base, forming a bun.

I was the only female in our academy class, which wasn't bad, except I didn't have the camaraderie the guys shared in the locker room. The guys could talk, laugh, unwind, and commiserate before class, physical training or at the end of the day.

KJ was leaving that weekend and we had a small party for her, saying goodbye and good luck. According to our schedules, she was starting 1 week after me and would graduate 1 week before me. We were both scheduled to graduate in March 2005.

The first week was tough, getting used to the schedule, waking up at 3:30 A.M., showering and out of the house by 4:15 A.M. to meet my carpool partners at 4:30 A.M. We arrived at the academy at 5 A.M., giving us time to change into our uniform, whether for class or PT, take our notebooks into the classroom and put our lunches in the breakroom. We couldn't be in the classroom before 5:30 A.M., but we had to be in by 5:55 A.M., to be ready for class at 6 A.M. The day ended at 1600 (4 P.M.), and I was normally home by 5 P.M.

If we had PT first, then we would do the same thing except we would put our PT gear on, white t-shirt, black shorts, and tennis shoes, then line up outside, on the parade deck. The parade deck was the front part of the training center building with a large concrete area in front of the flagpole. Each deputy and detention officer academy class had specific areas to line up on for formation before 8 A.M.

Each class rotated through putting the flag up at 8 A.M. and the flag was taken back down at 4 P.M. The sergeants and RTOs lined up behind the formations. Once the flags were up, then they would do an inspection of their class.

Some days the inspections were more thorough than others. There were days we were dismissed quickly to get back to class and others were a kickoff to PT with pushups and sit-ups.

The first day of class, we were lined up on the side of the parade deck, to watch how the other classes lined up. Once we were done with flags, we got "smoked" on the parade deck for a multitude of reasons; boots not shined, not yelling loud enough, not being fast enough to recover from pushups to the position of attention.

Most of my class was prior military and we knew the first few days were going to be tough. The downfall of pushups on the parade deck was the scuffing it did to your nicely shined boots. The first day of class we lost one trainee. By the end of the week, we had lost 3 total, for personal reasons.

We were set up in the classroom by alphabetical order of our last names, which put me right in the middle of the class. Each instructor that knew me came into the classroom and asked where I was as they looked around the class. Because of my prior dispatch background, I was called on for certain examples and scenarios related to our class instruction.

We had to take notes for every class. All notes were to be printed in block lettering, with black ink and our notebooks were graded every week. We tested every Monday morning on the previous week's instruction. We made study groups. I typed up our notes and study guide each Thursday night, which helped me review the information again. We had a small study group that met on Friday mornings.

We had a bigger study group on Sunday afternoons. Time was limited during the academy, so I made sure I reviewed Thursday nights and typed the study guides, then met with the study group Friday morning. After study group, I did laundry, then Friday afternoon through Sunday morning was for me and the kids.

Sunday mornings, I ironed my uniforms for the week, packed my bag, reviewed notes, and rewrote them if they needed to be neater. I taught my kids how to shine my boots because they wanted to help me. They would compete to see who could make their boot the shiniest.

Sunday afternoon we would head to study group for a couple hours, then come home, pack lunches for the next day, get breakfast ready and make sure all homework was done, checked and school bags packed. When I came home after the academy, we would go over homework, pack bags for the next day, make lunches then have dinner and hang out for a couple hours before we went to bed by 8:30 P.M.

The initial weeks required essays be written. One was a long one about our personal life story and why we decided to become a deputy. It was the first time I shared I had cancer when I was 20, with someone outside of an American Cancer Society event and my testimony at church.

A lieutenant that was a supervisor, whom I didn't get along with when I was in dispatch, approached me and shared she was diagnosed with cancer. Our relationship changed after she opened up to me. She started checking in on me during the academy to make sure I was doing okay.

The days and weeks of the academy progressed. We sat in class, took notes, tried to absorb the basics of our job, the laws, constitutional rights, report writing and so on. Every Monday morning, we had a test. If we failed 3 or more tests, we were done.

We had to score at least 70 or above to pass and there were normally 3 tests to take each week. Some were harder than others, but the study groups helped. We didn't have anyone fail out with test scores.

We did PT almost daily. If someone got dinged during an inspection or during training, they had to do a trail run. The trail run was 1.5 miles long and you had to wear a weighted vest. There were many times the entire class had to do a trail run.

I didn't mind the trail runs. There were some obstacles that helped break up the run and it was helping me become stronger. During PT, we did stretcher carries with a 150-lb. dummy on it, ran the parking garage with strength training exercises in between, sprints racing against each other, and canal runs which were 3-5 miles long.

We had a sand volleyball court behind the training center that became our smoke pit. We lost a lot of sweat and skin in the pit. The first week of the academy ended with us doing a 1-minute boxing drill against someone similar in size. We had to do pushups for 1 minute before we started, with a weighted vest, then went to our knees and boxed for 1 minute.

The headgear didn't fit my head and ended up turning sideways so I couldn't see well, but I threw some punches and took some punches before we finished. The guy I boxed had been a boxer in Colorado, which helped boost my confidence because he didn't crush me. I'm pretty sure he used restraint and held back so he didn't hurt me.

Defensive tactics taught us holds, take-down methods, pressure points and how to fight off multiple attackers. DT was fun. It allowed us to let out some aggression on the bags and we tested our techniques on each other.

We started at the range the first part of December. We had to buy the gun we were going to carry on duty, our holster, along with our leather belt and gear for when we moved into the deputy uniforms. I bought a Glock 22, full-size 40-caliber. It was what most agencies carried at that time.

When I went to the range and started shooting, the range staff switched me out to a Glock 17, full-size 9mm, which helped my shooting immensely. We did movement drills, scenario-based shooting, night shoots and my favorite, the rifle.

One of the instructors told me with my rifle skills, I had potential after all. He asked if I had been in the military because I shot a perfect score each time with the rifle. We passed the first phase and were able to move from our black and whites into our deputy uniforms, minus the badge.

We had to wear our leather gear and once we qualified on the range, we carried our weapon, with no ammo, to get used to wearing the gear we would wear as a deputy. The amount of money I had to shell out for uniforms, supplies, and my weapon, left me little money for Christmas.

When Jack left for Chicago, he abandoned our Grand Am on the side of a street. It was towed and I eventually received a letter stating I could pay almost $1000 for storage fees to get it back. It was paid off and it would be nice to have the extra vehicle. I paid the fees.

In July 2004, while the kids were camping with my dad for the 4th of July weekend, I worked, knowing there would be a lot of OT available. Jack called to talk to the kids one afternoon and after telling him they weren't there, we talked for hours, working through some of the issues we'd had. He apologized for the way he treated me, and we were able to slowly move forward to becoming friends again.

Jack came down to visit the kids before I started the academy. I knew he wouldn't be able to make it down for the holidays or birthdays. LJ turned 8 right before Christmas. She wanted a party at the house with her friends and family, which helped my budget.

I asked Jack if he would pay half for a new Xbox system that the kids could share. They had a mini arcade game they loved, and the Xbox would give them more entertainment as well as a better DVD player. I thought the Xbox would be a good gift from both of us, for $300. I asked if he could help with even

$100. He told me yes, so I bought the system. It saddened me when he never helped to pay for it. It was the last time I ever asked him for help.

We had our Christmas caroling wagon ride Christmas Eve and it had become a bigger production, with a new trailer, pulled by the '39A John Deere that we helped restore. We had lights, bales of hay to sit on and a small sound system for music.

We planned a New Year's Eve party at our house with our friends and family. We had taser training, CS gas and OC spray training coming up soon and I was trying to bolster my courage for the OC spray.

Because of the holiday schedule, we had class for three 12-hour days with the last day Wednesday, the day before New Year's Eve. We were told we would be doing Taser training and certification on that Wednesday and the OC training would be pushed back due to all the rain we had.

We did all the training and testing for the taser and at the time, MCSO policy was that to carry a taser, you had to get tased for at least 5 seconds. We all lined up by the mock jail outside. There were mats on the ground and the never-ending video camera rolling. Kurt was there, to help with first aid. Several other employees came to watch.

I understood what the taser did to a person, but feeling it was an entirely different thing. As the line went through and people got tased, yelping out, it was my turn. As bad luck would have it, one probe hit me in the upper-left side of my back, near my shoulder blade and the other was lower, on the right side of my back.

As soon as the probes hit, my entire body stiffened. Not only did my body stiffen, but it stayed that way for 5 seconds. I could hear the brrrrrrrr sound of the taser.

We had our DT cargo pants on and our white class t-shirt. When they pulled the taser barbs out it was easy to see some of us bled more than others. Ironically, as soon as the taser was done, the pain and stiffness were gone. It was an odd experience.

Once everyone in the class had their "5-second ride," we finished the day and got ready to go home. None of us had a trail run that day and we didn't have PT. When they said dismissed, we were almost running for the locker rooms to change.

My carpool group met/parked at the Costco. I bought a case of beer. I wanted to dull my senses of the pain and the noise I felt/heard. The left shoulder where I had been hit with a probe had given me problems since 1993 when I landed on my left hand, breaking my elbow, and messing my shoulder up. The taser caused it to stiffen and tighten giving me a blinding headache.

I got home, drank a beer, took a shower, put a tank top and sweats on, drank another beer, then lay face down on the couch. My stepmom could see the small puncture wounds where the probes hit. The kids kept me supplied with beer.

The next night, New Year's Eve, I drank more than I had in years, margaritas, and beer, trying to chase the memory away. It didn't work, but I could laugh about it as I told the story.

January 2005 came in with weeks of rain and cold weather. We were halfway through the academy. We could finally see the light at the end of the tunnel. There had been several personnel and policy changes. They changed the Taser policy. We no longer had to get tased to carry.

We also found out the instructors knew they were changing that policy after the 1st of the year, which is why they changed our schedule so we could be tased. I'm glad we got tased because I was able to truly understand what a taser could do and how it could help in less than lethal situations. I also understood how it might not work.

We continued PT outside as long as there was no lightening. The end of February, we began all our final testing for PT. We had to do our Cooper PT test with the run, sit ups and pushups and we had to do the police officer physical agility test (POPAT), which included sprints, climbing 3 walls, a dummy drag and jumping over obstacles.

We completed the CS gas training, but still had OC training to do. On a Thursday, our last training day of the week, they told us we were doing OC after lunch. I was going to vomit. My heart was racing, I felt like I couldn't breathe.

Not only were we doing OC training, but we were also doing our POPAT test, first. I hadn't had any issues getting over the walls, but I couldn't get my head in the game. With the mud slick ground and damp painted concrete wall, I kept slipping until I finally swung my foot high and caught the top with my ankle.

I made my time for the course, but I was .03 seconds shy of the time needed to get over the first wall. I felt sick when we started doing the OC spray. I was one of the first to go. The RTO sprayed so much OC in my face, I stopped breathing.

We had to identify what kind of weapon the combatant was holding and give commands, while holding a training pistol. This was done to simulate we could work through the OC and continue our job, even when it hurt. It also demonstrated a suspect would be able to do the same and not to rely solely on the OC spray.

I successfully identified the weapon and gave proper commands, then went to the wash station. By this time, my eyes were burning, my nose had snot running out of it like a faucet and my body was on fire everywhere the OC had touched.

I stuck my entire head under the water, washing my eyes, rinsing my mouth, and letting the snot run freely. The rest of the class finished, and we were released for the weekend, but no one warned us not to shower when we got home, that the water would reactivate the OC.

There was a lot of OC in my hair and it was running down my face and body in the shower. It was cold outside, but I had the water as cold as I could handle. I was on fire. My entire body hurt from the POPAT testing and the obstacle course we did earlier in the week. I felt something pull in the side of my chest, under my right arm, where my scar was, during that obstacle course. Knowing I had to redo the POPAT with the pulled or torn muscle wasn't ideal, but I had to pass the POPAT to graduate from the academy.

I threw my clothes in the washer, grabbed my journal, and started writing. I had 2 weeks left. I hadn't come this far not to make it. I wrote, I prayed, wrote some more, and prayed more. Peace came over me, knowing whatever happened, I gave everything I had.

That weekend I stayed home with the kids, slept, and rested my sore body. We finished all the tests, except our final exam. I didn't have study group that weekend. Monday, we had outside instructors on radars, DUI equipment and other items we would use.

My sergeant said I could retest Tuesday afternoon. One of the deputies, Bob, reassigned from SWAT, said he would run with me and help motivate me during the POPAT. I had known him for years and we had the same last name, always joking he was my ex-husband. He was the fastest deputy in the agency.

I changed into my PTs, did some warm-up exercises, and stretched. "Let's do this," I said as my heart beat loudly. I ran one of my fastest times and cleared the walls with no problems, passing the POPAT with minutes left on my time.

I walked to the locker room, happy I didn't give up, tears running down my face. Some of the guys saw me as I went into the locker room and assumed I failed. I relayed they were tears of joy as well as frustration from failing the week prior.

All my requirements to graduate were complete, but we still had our final exam.

KJ was graduating that week. We talked every week, checking in with each other, sharing our frustrations, accomplishments, and fears. We both initially had trouble at the range, doubted ourselves physically at times because of our age and my health issues. Thankfully, we wound up having our child sexual abuse classes the same week and were able to talk to each other about it.

We talked for almost an hour, talking about how hard it was to get through it, trying to block out our own trauma and realizing we never wanted to investigate sexual crimes against children.

We were hoping she would make it home for my graduation because she was going to be assigned to the Las Vegas office, and our other sister, KM, had just gotten back from Iraq. KM went to Quantico for KJ's graduation and was in town for mine.

My class planned a graduation party at my family's house with bouncy houses, horseback riding, bonfire and my dad had access to a large grill. We ordered a keg, and everyone decided what they were bringing for sides during our last study group.

We had gotten to know each other's family, became a family ourselves and were ready to move forward in our careers. I was one of the few single people in our class. The guys joked about me getting married again and guys hitting on me daily, especially when I was in uniform. For 20 weeks, I said I was never getting married again. I wasn't picking up after a man, answering to a man or dealing with relationship issues.

On graduation day, my family, a few friends, and some coworkers came out. I was chosen as the recruit of the class by my peers, and I won the top report writing award for the class.

We did our final inspection and DJ pinned my badge on me. March 10, 2005, I was officially a deputy sheriff. I had accomplished something I never thought I'd be able to with the running and physical exertion, but I was in the top 5% of my class with physical fitness.

We had a small party at the house that night, then the big party on Saturday. My dad brought the grill home, we bought the meat and ice, picked up the keg, set up tables, chairs, tents and the bouncy houses, as others trickled in with their sides.

We had a great time celebrating. Everyone had a designated driver or were crashing at the house. We celebrated late into the night. I remember bits and pieces of the night, some memories restored with photos. I drank more beer than thought I would, and the release of stress kicked in, to fully unwind from the past year.

Everyone in our class that worked for our agency was assigned to the court-security division, initially, except for the top recruit, Stephen, who was assigned to a district. They had it set up that the new deputies would help with transporting inmates to/from their court hearings. As new classes graduated the academy, they sent deputies out to the districts for their field training.

Some guys from my academy were talking about celebrating St. Patrick's Day and drinking green beer. We went to the block party, a couple blocks north of where we worked, after we finished work on Thursday.

My allergies were always in overdrive around this time of year. We changed out of our uniforms into civvies (civilian clothes) and walked up to the block party. I wore a t-shirt, jean capris, flip-flops, and my hair was pulled into a ponytail. I was armed with a box of Puffs Plus to blow my Rudolph-looking nose.

We got our wristbands and made our way to the beer tent. There were Irish dancers and bands with people milling throughout the street. We knew people would ask us basic questions, names, what we did for a living. Our answer was going to be we worked in insurance. My pseudo name was Samantha.

We were used to calling each other by our last names. It was weird to use first names. Most everyone was intoxicated around us, and we settled in, to people watch. One of the guys was married and the other engaged so they felt they had to find a man for me.

9
You Had Me at Hello!

After an hour of mingling with strangers and people watching, I looked over my left shoulder and saw a group of guys at the entrance table. I fixated on one before I saw his face, checking him out from the work boots, up.

I made my visual tour up his body. Observing how he filled out the Levi's blue jeans, the well-muscled arms in a cut off t-shirt, his smile, and then his blue eyes. Those eyes were looking at me. He was grinning from ear to ear. I did a small wave and smiled, then turned back to the crowd.

My friends saw me flustered and asked what happened. I told them about the guy, and they immediately started looking around for him. He caught me checking him out, but it was worth the view.

After finishing the one beer I was nursing for an hour, I was ready to just go home, shower and go to bed. I was telling the guys I was going to head home when they saw him a few feet from us.

He was with a group of guys that all appeared to do some type of construction work. My buddies were egging me on to talk to him. If I approached him with all the other guys around, we wouldn't get very far, knowing the mob mentality of guys. They tend to act like they're in junior high or frat boys and I wasn't looking for that with my head hurting.

One of my buddies asked me if I wanted him to go over. I told him to find out if he's single and has any warrants. He walked up to the guy and said, "Hey, my buddy over there thinks you're hot." The guy looked confused thinking "my buddy" was referring to another guy.

My friend pointed me out and said I was the redhead with a ponytail. "Oh, yeah," he replied with a big grin on his face. I gave a small wave and went back to finishing my beer. His group slowly moved closer to where we were standing. The hot guy was in my line of sight.

We kept making eye contact, smiling at each other, and looking away over the course of 10-15 minutes. I decided to put up or shut up. I was ready to go home.

When he looked at me again, I tapped my watch and put my palms up, gesturing, "What are you going to do?" He surprised me by heading directly toward me. He put his hand out to shake mine, "Hi, my name's Branch, what's yours?"

I couldn't say anything, my mind wasn't working and when I looked into his eyes up close, with that smile, I was a goner. We continued holding each other's hand until I regained my senses and told him my name. My real name.

I debated using my "fake" name, but there was something different with him. He asked me what I did for work and after a quick mental debate, I told him I was a deputy, but whispered to keep it quiet.

He laughed. With my hand still in his, he replied, "That's cool, my dad was a deputy, too." I instantly relaxed and told him I was getting ready to leave because I had a headache from my allergies and needed plain food.

He hadn't eaten yet either and offered to buy me dinner if I drove because he carpooled with his work crew.

I told my guys I was leaving after introducing them to Branch. He was taking me to dinner somewhere close. They decided to head home too, and we walked down the street where their car was parked.

I had parked in the garage at work, which was further away. Branch and I started talking. He looked young and told me he was 24. I stopped on the sidewalk, letting go of his hand and told him I couldn't go out with him. I was 32.

He told me he was really 26 but lied thinking I was younger. I started laughing at the prospect of looking young enough that 26 was too old for me, then told him 26 wasn't much better.

We walked a couple more blocks when I felt a blister forming on my foot. The flip-flop was rubbing the top of my foot. I needed to stop to take them off, but Branch said he would carry me on his back, instead.

Branch was strong and solid, "What the hell, save a horse, ride a cowboy," and jumped on his back. He carried me another block until we made it to the parking garage and my car.

We couldn't decide where we wanted to eat that was close until I remembered there was an Applebee's. We talked the entire time we drove, finding out more we liked about each other and had in common.

We both had chicken salad at Applebee's and stayed for a couple hours, talking. I never experienced love at first sight and honestly never believed in it, until that night. I offered to take him home or drop him off at the festival.

He wanted to spend more time with me and drive him home. He was in town from Minnesota, working on the new convention center, 3 blocks from where I worked. He would be in town for several more months before the job was completed and wanted to know if we could go out again, soon.

While I was driving him home, Jack called, letting me know when his flight got in so he could pick the kids up. We talked a few minutes, then I told Jack I had to go because I was driving a guy home. He laughed, "Okay then, good luck and have fun."

Branch was surprised we got along well enough for him to respond like that. I provided a brief version of my marriage, separation, and divorce. We didn't run out of things to talk about. We had been talking since we met, at 5:20 P.M. It was now almost 10 P.M. when we got to the house he was staying at.

The house was empty when we arrived. The other guys he worked with hadn't left the bar yet and Branch tried talking me into staying the night. I couldn't. I wanted to see my kids before they left with their dad the following night, for a week.

I asked to use the restroom before I drove home. We went in the house; I used the restroom and he pulled me into a hug when I said I had to leave.

He didn't want me to go but understood. When I looked up at him, to say goodbye and confirm we could do something Saturday night, he bent down and kissed me gently, but firmly on the lips. That kiss sealed the deal. He had my heart.

I was floating with multiple currents of energy running through my body from that kiss. My heart skipped a beat, then started beating fast, as if I was running. I now believed in love at first site, chemistry and kisses that make you lift your foot.

After a couple more kisses, I pulled myself away. It was one of the hardest goodbyes, but we had a date for that Saturday, and it was now Thursday night.

I had to be up early for work the next morning, but I couldn't stop smiling driving home and when I went to bed. The next morning the guys at work noticed a difference and the razzing began, about me "getting laid," being in love, and so on. At lunch, the guys from our academy class circled me, asking nonstop questions about the "new guy."

He was an iron worker from Minnesota. We had a date for Saturday night. A group of us planned a fight night/date night with our families that Saturday. I figured I might as well jump into the deep end and introduce him to everyone Saturday.

After work Friday, I hurried home to spend time with the kids before they left with their dad. This would be the first time they would be with their dad for a week, without me or other family. I was nervous and the kids were apprehensive, Jack didn't have a great track record.

After the kids left, I went to the grocery store and bought stuff to make pasta Saturday morning. I was going to take lunch to Branch and surprise him before our date. We planned for me to pick him up from work, then he would shower, and we would hang out the rest of the night.

After I surprised him with lunch, I told him I would be back in a couple hours to get him. I drove to a local hotel, close to where we were going for fight night, got a room, then went home, packed a bag, and showered, before driving to pick Branch up from work.

I was going to surprise him when we drove the opposite direction of his house. When I pulled into the parking lot of the hotel, the grin on his face grew bigger than I thought possible.

It was fun getting to know each other more without people around and no distractions. Being able to freely explore this sexy man was a huge plus for the hotel room.

By the time we were ready to go to fight night, we were intimately familiar with each other. I was falling hard, which shocked me, but I let it happen. I was ready. This is what I prayed for in July 2004, what I journaled about. I was ready to love and be loved, scars and all. Up until this point, I didn't feel worthy of being loved and sabotaged every relationship.

When we arrived at the house hosting fight night, I introduced Branch to everyone. He immediately fit in, felt at ease. My work guys said we fit together and seemed like we'd been together forever.

We spent the night at the hotel, exploring each other and allowing myself to willingly and trustingly, fall asleep with a man. The next morning felt normal with no awkwardness. I took him to one of my favorite places for breakfast.

I had to stop at my house to get my softball stuff for my games that night before I took him home. He said he would love to watch me play ball and I should pack my work stuff to spend the night with him, then drive to work together the next morning. We worked near each other and started at the same time.

My parents were outside, loading a trailer, to take their first load of belongings to their new house/property, further away from the city. It would take a few weekends to move everything, with all the equipment, vehicles, horses, tools, and "treasures" acquired.

Branch jumped right in helping my dad and the neighbor, getting a telephone pole loaded. There was no hesitation and after they were done, I introduced him to my parents and the neighbor.

I packed my softball bag and another for work. Branch made me feel young, free, and open. I was attracted to him physically, but it was so much more than that. He broke through barriers that surrounded my heart and soul.

Branch sat through both of my softball games, which we won. He was impressed with my skills. I had 2 great games at bat and on the field, partly due to joy over going home with Branch afterward.

I was experiencing feelings I had never felt this strongly. I had no idea where we were headed, but I was willing to put in the work. The physical intimacy was a natural thing for us. We craved it. I fell asleep with my head on his chest and left bicep, snuggled up to his strong body.

He woke me at 3 A.M., touching me all over, fulfilling me in ways I'd never been fulfilled. He made me feel alive. I wanted to fully give myself to him, heart, soul, and body.

We had to be up at 5 A.M. to leave for work. Riding together, listening to the radio, and singing along to "nothing on but the radio." He wanted to make me dinner the next night and for me to stay the night with him.

The kids were with their dad, and I had nothing planned. We had only known each other 4 days, but I felt I had known him my entire life. As if I was waiting for him.

He stayed with me Monday night and we drove to work together Tuesday. On the way to his house Tuesday night, we stopped at the grocery store to shop for dinner. I was impressed he knew his way around the store. We bought fresh vegetables, herbs, and meat. He grabbed some wine, which surprised me. I had only seen him drink beer.

We drove to his place, showered, then he started dinner. We enjoyed wine and talking while he cooked, and I curled up in a chair. I felt like a princess. He wanted to make me dinner while I relaxed. I had fallen for him at hello, now, I was a goner.

After we finished dinner, he was cleaning up, when his roommates came home from the bar. One of the guys was his boss, the owner of the company. He sat down in the living room with me, introduced himself, and asked me questions, getting to know me.

He seemed impressed I was a single mom and a cop. He said I didn't look like any cop he had seen; I was the hottest cop he ever met. Branch came back in the room and sat in the chair, with me on his lap while we talked for a bit before everyone headed to bed.

We spent all our spare time together the next couple weeks, until he said he had to go back to Minnesota for a family emergency. I felt like part of me was gone.

We talked on the phone a few times. We didn't get to talk long, but he made the effort to call and check on me, let me know he missed me and was thinking of me.

The kids had met him and seemed to like him. LJ told him he had elf ears. We laughed and I knew she liked him. We had gone bowling and hung out watching movies after they came back from their dads. They asked when he was coming over again. They got used to him being around and we had fun together.

He returned about 10 days later. He surprised me Friday night, April 15th. We took the kids to the county fair. We watched them laughing and having a great time. The kids were on one of the rides and Branch was standing behind me, with his arms around me, pulling me against him. The kids waved each time they went by. Branch whispered he would love to have a baby with me, a part of each of us.

I smiled and told him I would love it, too, but my body wouldn't make it. He preferred having me healthy and whole, but he wanted me to know he could see us together in the future.

We stayed at the fair until the kids were tired, then went home and they crawled into bed, happy and exhausted. We felt like a family unit. They said good night to Branch and asked if he was going to be there in the morning when they woke up. He looked at me and I nodded yes, so he told them he would be, and we would go to breakfast.

That night while lying in bed, he said he loved me and I said it back, without freaking out. This was the first time, in a long time, I said it and meant it. We hung out with the kids and helped my parents move stuff out to the house and 20 acres they bought.

My dad sold the place we were staying at to a guy he knew from work, but he wasn't moving in until the following year, so he let me rent it, cheaper than an apartment.

Branch's phone kept ringing at random times, but he didn't answer it and then turned it off Saturday night. The next morning, Branch turned his phone on and listened to the voicemails. I could tell something was wrong by the look on his face. I heard a female voice on the messages and prepared myself for the worst.

He said he was so sorry, he had to go because his wife... yes, he was married, and I had no idea, was headed to AZ with his 3... yes... THREE kids, and his mom. I was sick, physically, and emotionally. Why would God play such a cruel joke on me? Was this some kind of karma? I asked him why he lied when I had asked him point blank if he was married. He said he didn't know; he really liked me and had come to AZ as a separation from his wife. I asked if that's why he really went to Minnesota and he said yes, to see his kids, but he realized he wanted to be with me and came back to AZ.

I was devastated. I took him home and told him he needed to take care of his mess and not to contact me. I was taking myself out of the equation. He could work out what he needed to. I told him I was done and not to consider me in his plans.

I looked at him with tears running down my face and told him I loved him, but not to touch me. He was off limits. I had to protect my heart from further damage. He apologized over and over. Unfortunately, sorry doesn't make the pain go away.

I drove home, wracking with sobs and crawled back into bed. I slept most of the day, worked Monday and listened to a voicemail Branch left. He said he was going to try to work things out with his wife. I was scheduled to work at the racetrack that Thursday through Saturday night which would hopefully distract me.

The kids knew something was wrong, but didn't ask, they did their homework and played on the Xbox. They kept looking at me, knowing I wasn't okay. Tuesday night, after I showered and got ready for bed, my phone rang. It was Branch. I was so mad he was calling so I answered the phone, "I told you not to call me anymore," then heard a female voice say, "This is his wife," then I heard yelling, a crash and nothing.

I was furious she called, but glad I answered the phone the way I did. Wednesday night the kids and I hung out. My parents hadn't fully moved out and were going to be at the house that weekend while I worked.

Thursday morning, I had to be at the racetrack by 6 A.M. and my alarm was set for 4:30 A.M. My phone rang at 4:20 A.M. I answered it out of habit. Branch's voice told me he knew not to call me, but he wanted me to know he was thinking of me and to have a good day.

I didn't cry, but I missed him, hearing his voice, and feeling him next to me. It was going to take a long time to heal from this. I went to work at the racetrack and worked with a cop, KR, from another agency. We talked and got to know each other. He was telling me about a woman he met, fell in love, and found out she was married.

I started laughing to keep from crying and told him I just went through the same thing. We told each other our stories and felt a kinship from broken hearts and souls. About noon, my phone rang. It was Branch. I debated answering it. KR told me to answer and find out what he had to say.

Branch knew I was working, and he wanted to tell me sorry for the other night when his wife called. She took his phone while he was in the shower and called me. When he heard what she said, he jumped out of the shower, took the phone, and threw it against the wall.

He sent his mom and kids home, but his wife wouldn't leave. He told her he wanted a divorce and she needed to leave. I told him okay, but I didn't want any part of his life. He knew that but asked me to wait and not give up on him. He told me to have a good day and he loved me.

The rest of the day was busy. I didn't get home until 8 that night. I showered and got my stuff ready for the next day, which I knew was going to be really long with a night race.

I worked the front gate all day Friday, from 6 A.M. until the race was finished. I fell into bed that night. Saturday morning, I worked the front gate again, and it was busier with NASCAR fans coming in for the big race that night. Another deputy showed up to help me at the gate. Soon nightshift showed up to help with traffic.

More deputies started showing up to set up cones for egress after the race was over, to keep traffic flowing at the exits. Once all the cones were set up, we had time for a quick dinner and break, then there was a rain delay.

When the race was over and we started the egress process, the wind was blowing hard, and the rain started again. The rain was pelting us and within minutes we were soaked.

My hat kept the rain out of my face, but my jacket, vest, uniform, and boots were soaked. Someone brought us big trash bags to put over our uniform and we put our safety vests over the bag.

My hands were numb holding my flashlight. Traffic was flowing out of the exit, but the rain caused huge puddles and there was nowhere to hide from the wind. When everyone was out of the park, we resumed normal traffic at the gates and on the roadways.

It was almost 10 P.M. when I got home, a soggy cold mess. I walked directly to the bathroom, took all my stuff off and took a hot shower. My daughter brought me sweats and a sweatshirt to put on, then we hung my gear up to dry. I threw my uniform and jacket in the washer and put newspaper inside my boots to help them dry out.

I snuggled on the couch with the kids, ate some food and finished watching the movie they had been watching. I threw my uniform in the dryer before crawling into bed, where my daughter snuggled with me, and we knocked out.

My phone started ringing a little before 6am. I thought I was dreaming, but it kept ringing. I answered and Branch asked me if I was up yet because he had something to tell me. I was up now, and he asked me to come outside.

I was confused. I looked out the window to see him sitting in a truck, next to my Jeep. I walked outside, stood a couple feet from him with my arms crossed tightly because there was too much temptation to reach out and touch him.

He was sorry for lying. He handed me papers and told me he filed for divorce. He was never as happy as he was with me, and he didn't want to lose that. I looked at the papers. He was waiting outside the house since about 3 A.M. because he drove directly there after he took his wife to the airport and told her to go home. She finally got out, told Branch she hated him, and was filing for divorce like she should have months ago.

As soon as she got out of the truck, he drove off, directly to my house but didn't want to wake me that early knowing I had a long night. He couldn't wait any longer to see me, hold me and kiss me.

I fell into his arms and cried, telling him I missed him so much, even though he lied to me about his family. I still felt we were meant to be. I invited him into the house, and we curled up on the couch, touching and whispering until the kids woke up.

We spent the day together. He went home that night while the kids and I went to my softball games. He hadn't slept much and didn't have clothes with him for work. The next day he sent me a text he was looking for another place to live. His boss, Greg, and him got into an argument. Branch's wife, Devlin, called Greg and told him Branch was leaving her and the kids for me, the "homewrecker."

Branch packed, planning to sleep in his truck until he figured things out. He didn't have much money because his entire check went into an account to pay for the house, truck, kids, his life in Minnesota. He lived on about $50 a week, although he made well over $2500 a week with his pay, overtime and out-of-town living costs.

I told him to meet me at the house after work, Monday, he could stay with me until he figured things out. My parents were moving out that weekend so it would be just me and the kids. There was plenty of room. I got home before he got there and sat the kids down, to let them know he was going to stay with us for a bit.

They shrugged their shoulders and said, "Okay," then went outside to play. It was a weird time for all of us and if Branch and I were going to be a serious thing, we were going to have some crazy and rough times ahead. I didn't know HOW tough or crazy.

While at work, I couldn't use my phone in the courtroom and there was no service in the basement. At lunch, I would check my voicemails.

One day, I wasn't paying much attention to my voicemails, when I heard a lady cussing at me, calling me names and telling me how awful I was. I wasn't sure who it was. When I called Branch at lunch, I told him about it and saved it so he could listen to it.

I regained my calm after I let my coworkers listen to the messages. They said I should kick someone's ass.

Branch listened to the messages on the way home, by then I had 2 from 1 lady and 1 from his wife, Devlin. Branch listened to the first, "Holy shit, that's my mom's voice." It bothered me his mom didn't call Branch; she immediately took Devlin's side.

We found out later, Devlin threatened everyone if they wanted to see the kids, they would support her and not Branch. My family was a little crazy and dysfunctional, but I couldn't imagine my parents or siblings choosing a spouse over blood.

In addition to the drama surrounding Branch's divorce, Jack was trying to convince me to let the kids live with him, in Chicago, for a year. Neither of the kids even wanted to visit Chicago for a week or two. Jack accused me of keeping the kids from him. When we were together, he said we had parented 50/50 and he did a lot to help me with the kids.

I couldn't contain my disbelief at his arrogance and the absurdity of his request. I asked the kids if they wanted to go. They both yelled, "No way!" The kids then told me every time their dad visited, he had a different girl with him, never just the 3 of them.

After Branch moved in, he told Greg he would finish the job, then he would be done with the company. A couple weeks later, early May, Branch and I drove separately to work as I had to be in early. He parked his truck in his normal parking place in the parking garage and went to work. When he finished work, he walked to his truck while talking to me on the phone. Something was wrong.

His truck was missing. Branch found out Greg helped Devlin fly down, use the extra set of keys, and take Branch's truck back to MN. Branch was furious. Things went from bad to worse. I asked if he was ready for the ugly battle. If he wasn't 100% committed to the divorce, then he needed to work it out without me.

He knew it would be ugly from her part, but didn't realize Greg, the guy he'd worked for, for years, would become part of the problem.

That weekend, we flew to MN, early Sunday morning, rented a car and drove to the house Branch was still paying for, so the kids had a place to stay. Branch had to be quick about getting into the truck and out of the driveway, otherwise there was going to be a confrontation. He didn't want that in front of the kids.

We drove by the house and Branch saw Devlin's parents were there. Everyone was in the front, as if they were waiting for him to show. No one knew we had flown up, except my parents and kids.

I parked down the street where we could see the driveway, but they couldn't see us. Branch planned to run to the truck, hop in, start it and back up as soon as the front was clear. I would follow him to the airport to drop off the rental car.

We sat for about 5 minutes, when we saw everyone walk into the house. It was about lunchtime, so the timing worked. Branch got out of the car silently closing the door, then took off at a full sprint when he saw them working their way inside. I slowly pulled closer to the driveway so he could just back up, without worrying about traffic.

He opened the door and hopped inside, putting the key in the ignition before the door was shut. He started the truck, put it in reverse, backed up quickly and put it in drive to take off. He was out of the driveway and in drive before Devlin and her dad came running out of the house, yelling, and cussing. I drove by nonchalantly.

We dropped the rental off and headed for AZ. Devlin called Branch's phone several times, cussing at him. He would hang up on her. If she had something to say, then they could talk civilly, but he wasn't going to listen to her spew profanities.

On the last phone call, she said she wasn't going to let him see the kids, he would be hearing from her lawyer and if he stayed with me, he would never see the kids. It was approximately 2 minutes before she lost her mind and started screaming and cussing again, so Branch hung up. Or thought he had hung up; she could still hear us.

We jokingly talked about driving to MN to "rescue" the kids from her. His phone rang again. As soon as it connected, Devlin was screaming, we weren't going to "kidnap" her kids and I was a homewrecker before Branch made sure the call was disconnected.

I asked if she was always that angry. He said she always talked to him like that. That's not a normal or healthy relationship, I said. "I know, that's why I chose you and will keep choosing you." He kissed me on the forehead and pulled me close to him.

No matter what was said or done, in her mind, I was always going to be the reason for the end of their marriage. I wanted to knock her on her ass, punch her in the mouth, and verbally respond to her ugly words, but that wouldn't help anything.

We tried to maintain as much normalcy as possible for DJ and LJ. We planned a trip to Rocky Point, Mexico, with a friend from work and her family.

We rented a huge, 3 story-house overlooking the water, within walking distance of the beach. There were 3 families, each with 2 kids and the aunt. There was a bedroom with attached bathroom for each couple and each kid, with a huge kitchen on the 2nd floor. There were 2 huge decks, with the 2nd-floor deck going all the way around the house and the top deck was almost 360 degrees with steps up to a rooftop deck. The downstairs was for the kids, with a pool table, small kitchen, TV, video game console, DVD player and other fun things.

We were there 5 days and 4 nights, eating, drinking, swimming, playing poker and enjoying the company. The room Branch and I were in opened right onto the terrace, overlooking the water. We watched the sunrise every morning, no matter how late it was when we went to bed.

Early one morning, Branch and I were walking across an area that was sandy then turned into rocks. We talked about the future. I thought about getting a dog for the kids. He loved dogs. We decided to name a female dog "RockSea."

One night the guys were playing poker, smoking cigars, and drinking while the girls chilled out watching the water, enjoying the kids having their own play area. I went to the restroom and heard Branch's phone. I took it out to him and sat back down.

The guys said they were starting a new game if any of us wanted in. We walked over to the table, and I asked where Branch was. They thought he had gone upstairs on the roof.

I walked upstairs to make sure everything was okay and heard him on the phone. I couldn't quite make out what he was saying, but it sounded intimate.

I turned around to walk back downstairs, when he must have heard me and said, "I have to go." He called my name, but I kept walking. He ran over to catch up with me. He was intoxicated, which hurt more because "a drunk tongue tells the truth." I knew he had been on the phone with Devlin.

He grabbed my arm, asking me to come back up so he could talk to me. I didn't want to. But I needed to face whatever was coming, head on.

He called to talk to the kids and Devlin got on the phone. He was trying to be nice so he could talk to the kids. Things weren't making sense. She left a voicemail, and he went upstairs to call the kids. He didn't want me to get upset, which was why he didn't tell me and went upstairs alone. I didn't believe him.

I didn't want to be the jealous person, but I needed the facts. I asked him to play the voicemail. He said he deleted it. It would be in his deleted history then, so again I asked him to play it for me, unless he was lying.

He played the voicemail. She said something about wanting to work things out and to call her back. I felt sick. I asked why he lied. The only thing I asked from him was honesty.

He kept apologizing, saying it was me he wanted, but he felt guilty and confused, which is why he called her. He had been with her for years and they had 3 kids together, which is why I didn't want to stay involved. He said it was over and wanted to be with me.

We sat up until the early morning, talking. I was doing a lot of crying. My heart was telling me to stay, but my head was fighting my heart. I didn't know if I wanted to continue the fight, knowing how hard it was going to be emotionally. I asked Branch what he would do if I asked him to move out and we broke up. He said his life was in AZ. He wasn't going back to MN or Devlin, even if we broke up.

I wanted to be with him, but it was going to be hard for me to trust him. He lied about being married and now this phone call, but he never lied about how he felt for me. He had never been as happy as he was when he met me. I brought light into his life. He'd never known that kind of happiness or that a relationship could be like ours. He loved me, but he also liked me. He loved that we were friends.

After a dinner cruise, Branch and I sat on his tailgate, outside the bar, where the dock was, smoking mini cigars I had bought earlier. There were 40 for $20 and I ended up getting 2 packs for $15. The passengers on the cruise could purchase beer at the bar, for $1 and we drank, smoked, talked, laughed until the bar closed, which was about 3 A.M.

It didn't matter how much my head was telling me I should end things, my heart was telling me love is love, and we can't stop it. I decided then I would take whatever time I was given with this man that stole my heart.

We were home for a couple days before we went camping up north, where my dad's friend owned a 160-acre cattle ranch. We stayed on the ranch, camping in tents, or campers, using an outhouse, and showering at the RV park, down the road.

I had to work M-W, then I was off for the 4th of July weekend. Branch worked Monday and Tuesday, then dropped me off Wednesday and picked me up that afternoon. I came out to the truck and opened the door to grab the long-sleeved shirt I wore to cover my uniform shirt, while driving to/from work.

When I picked the shirt up, I heard a noise and saw a little brown and white head poke out and these chocolate brown puppy dog eyes look at me. I looked at Branch with a questioning look and he said, "RockSea." I jumped in the truck to cuddle this cute little puppy with the long ears and big eyes.

We drove home and surprised the kids with RockSea. We would get to camp that night and the rest of the group would be up the next afternoon. Branch and I planned to sleep in the back of the truck and the kids were going to sleep in my dad's airstream trailer.

RockSea loved sleeping outside. We took her fishing; she liked the water. She would run toward the water until her paws got wet, then she felt the cold water and ran back out. We spent hours playing with her and watching her. She was part of the family.

The rest of the summer flew by. DJ was playing tackle football and school started. Branch was invited to a wedding in MN, to be a groomsman in a high school friend's wedding. The invitation said, "For Branch only." Branch planned to decline the invite because he wanted me to be with him.

I told him to go. I didn't want to cause a scene during their big day, knowing Devlin would be there because their son was the ring bearer. She had been sending letters, photos with guilt trips written on the back, there were regular phone calls and voicemails, and each time Branch tried talking to the kids on the phone, she would jump on at some point and start cussing at him. An in-person meeting would be ugly.

My birthday was a couple weeks before he left and we went to visit KJ in Vegas, to celebrate our birthdays. I would be 33 and I was grateful for every birthday I was given.

Branch and I decided to get matching tattoos, with a shamrock symbolizing when we met. I got mine on my lower back, by my left hip, with his initials above it. He got his on the inside of his right forearm, with my initials above it and the word "FATE" spelled out vertically. We knew it had been fate that we met.

Branch initially came to AZ in January. He was working at the yard across the street from my training center. He would see us running. He noticed there was only 1 girl in the class, and silently cheered me on. They worked in the yard until the end of February, getting materials ready for the upcoming job once it stopped raining. He saw me every day for 6 weeks, with neither of us realizing it, until we talked later.

Branch was served with official separation papers. He had to rescind his paperwork as the divorce had to be filed in MN and Devlin filed when she got home. Branch didn't contest anything because he just wanted it to be over.

Unfortunately, there was a large sum of money she would receive for alimony, as well as child support. The money wasn't an issue while he was still working with MN union wages, but once he finished and started work for AZ wages, there was a huge difference in pay. AZ is a right-to-work state and unions aren't as strong. Also, AZ doesn't require skilled trade labor to be part of unions, therefore a lot of trade jobs were being underbid.

I dropped Branch off at the airport Thursday afternoon for the wedding. I went to work Friday and spent Saturday with the kids and RockSea. We went to the lake and explored in the Jeep. I didn't know if/when I would talk to Branch, but I didn't want to bother him. It would be an awkward time. This was the first time he had been home since we started dating/living together.

I was trying to stay busy. I hadn't heard from Branch, but I knew the wedding was over. I sent him a quick text saying I missed him. I couldn't shake the feeling something was wrong.

My phone rang and I jumped on it. It was a guy I had talked to off and on for the past couple years. I hadn't heard from him since my graduation party and never thought about it, after meeting Branch. He asked how I was doing, what was going on, and I shared my distress about Branch.

He was shocked I was dating someone steady, and we were living together. We had been friends for years and he was a go to person for me to share "life" with when I needed more than a journal. He told me to call Branch's phone, see if it was on or went straight to voicemail, then I would know if he'd even seen the text.

We hung up. It was now 11 P.M. in MN. I called Branch and the phone rang, then went to his voicemail. I left a message saying hi and told him to call when he got a chance. The gut feeling intensified, and I felt sick.

I called my friend back and told him. I didn't want to be that person that called and text several times, but I felt ill. He kept me on the phone for almost 2 hours, talking and calming me, distracting me.

Branch called me Sunday, late morning, said he was sorry for not calling or responding, said yes, he had gotten drunk and passed out in a bathtub.

He was going to see his kids. Devlin relented after the kids saw him at the wedding. He would be at their house for a couple hours before he headed to his hotel for his early morning flight home. I still had the feeling something wasn't right, but I didn't want to mess up his time with the kids so I stayed quiet, told him to have fun with them and I would see him in the morning.

I picked him up from the airport. Instantly, I knew something was wrong by the way he was acting. Not meeting my eyes. We drove home and I told him not to lie to me, just tell me the truth. I would find out and I would rather find out from him. The kids were with my sisters, SE and KM, and the house was empty, except for RockSea, when we got home. I could barely stand because my gut was burning and I told him to tell me, now!!!

While he was at the house with the kids, he had gone to the downstairs bathroom to shower because he hadn't had time to shower at the hotel. He got out of the shower when Devlin came in the bathroom and started kissing him, saying she wanted sex one last time.

He responded out of habit. As they laid on the floor, he realized he didn't want to be with her in any way and he couldn't lose me because he was stupid and weak. He got up and told her to leave. She started cussing at him and told him to get out of the house.

He dressed and said goodbye to the kids as they were crying and hanging on him, not wanting him to leave. I told him to get out. I couldn't look at his face. I heard him say he was so sorry for being stupid and he loved me so much. He was crying but I didn't care. I let the emotions bottled up inside me out. It was going to be ugly.

The sliding door shut, and I curled on the bed to let the heart-wrenching, full-body cry come out. I had no control over it. I never cried like that before. My head, heart, body, and soul were crying, screaming in pain, agony, and fury. I don't know how long I cried, but suddenly Branch was wrapping his arms around me, pulling me onto his lap, whispering how much he loved me, how much he needed me and how much our family meant to him.

I couldn't talk. My throat was raw. I had nothing left inside me. I couldn't summon a thought or feeling. No words could express how gutted I was, but as time passed, I felt safe in his arms. I didn't understand. Slowly, my thoughts came back, and I thought, how could I be mad, when I was the "other" woman. They were technically still married until October 12th.

It didn't make me feel better, but it allowed me to process the emotions, anger, betrayal and hurt. He asked what he could do to fix things. We sat together, him holding me tightly on his lap, my head against his chest while he rocked me. I started to feel a calmness come over me.

I asked him if he had ever been saved. He grew up going to church, but I told him that didn't mean he was saved. Unless he had asked Jesus to come into his heart, cleanse him of his sins and ask for forgiveness, then he wasn't saved. He said he wasn't. He knew scriptures and memorized readings when he was younger, but he never asked for forgiveness.

The only way we could try to move forward was him asking for forgiveness, not from me, but from God. He sinned in his marriage with me, among other sins. I could work on forgiving him, but it would be hard to forget. I didn't want to hold that against him. I also needed to pray and ask for forgiveness.

Branch said he wanted to do it, for himself and for me. He asked if I would pray with him and help him with the words. I told him about Gramma B and how she prayed with me when I was 12.

We got on our knees, on the floor, beside the bed and I started praying, out loud. I prayed for each of us, our family, his ex, and the kids. I prayed to help soften my heart, for patience, wisdom, healing, and comfort. I asked Branch if he was ready, and he said yes. He repeated the words I said, then continued asking for help in his daily walk, guidance to be a good father and protector.

He asked for many things, and we stayed on the floor praying for approximately 30 minutes, then we climbed on the bed, falling asleep in each other's arms, exhausted, but filled with hope.

I felt lighter. I had been carrying my own burdens, being involved with a married man.

Branch started making our lunches, leaving notes in my lunchbox. He didn't smother me, but he let me know, daily, how much he cared. He slowly became a father figure.

He showed up for all the games and practices. He helped with homework and around the house. He developed his own relationship with the kids. He kept showing up, every day, because he wanted to be there and we started to regain our center, as a couple.

I was asked to be the survivor speaker for the local Relay For Life event. I said yes, I was finally ready to share my story. It had been almost 13 years since I was diagnosed with cancer, and I would be speaking the day of DJ's 13th birthday. He had been my hope and it was time for me to share hope with others.

As I scanned the crowd, I saw Branch, holding LJ's hand, DJ standing next to them, surrounded by friends and family. This was the first time the kids had heard my story and how much of a difference they made in my recovery. My wish to fully live and cherish every day.

As I walked the survivor lap, with my friend, Rick's wife, Evelyn, she told me she had just gone in for another scan in her breast, but I had given her hope, even if she was diagnosed again. We walked the lap, hand in hand and then our families joined us for the caregiver lap.

The next weekend we celebrated Branch's birthday and a couple days later, October 12th, 2005, the divorce was official. We celebrated. We could officially start our journey. We spent time with friends, singing karaoke and enjoying family time, outside of work.

Evelyn told us the lump was cancer, she would be starting treatment and she was ready to fight. She had a great support team and she expected us to keep her laughing. Rick and I were scheduled to work the week together at the racetrack, in early November, so we planned our snacks, meals, drinks and entertainment.

Branch joked he was the only (cop) spouse of the group that was male, but he was in for coupon poker or whatever, with the other spouses while the deputies worked. We grew as a couple. Our community of friends grew, and friendships strengthened.

Branch and I went to Vegas the end of October. I was going to be the best (wo)man at Goldie and Kurt's wedding. We had gone from coworkers, to friends, softball teammates, ladies' night partners. I was so happy for them, even if Kurt told me I had to wear a dress for the wedding.

After the week working at the racetrack, we had gone shopping for Thanksgiving dinner, and I stopped by to talk to our neighbors, Doug and Rosie, for a minute while Branch and the kids went home to start dinner and put groceries away. I came in the house, showered, and came out for dinner.

Branch asked me to get the cups out. I was talking about my conversation with the neighbors, not really paying attention when I got the cups down. Branch laughed, "OMG, shut up." I stopped, with my hand midair, confused. Branch came over and lifted me up, so I was eye level with the shelf. I yelled for him to put me down.

The kids were laughing and telling me to just look at the shelf. I was thoroughly confused and looked at the shelf. I saw a velvet box on the shelf and fell speechless. Branch set me down, grabbed the box and asked me if I would be his wife. I felt the tears and looked at each kid, as they nodded their heads yes, with huge grins on their faces.

I looked back at Branch, "Yes, absolutely," and jumped into his arms, wrapping my legs around his hips, kissing him, and laughing through my tears. He asked the kids first and they both said yes, but they had to keep the secret. He put the ring on my finger. It fit perfectly.

I couldn't stop looking at the ring. It had a square-cut diamond on the top, with 2 smaller diamonds on each side. Branch told me he wanted something signifying me and the kids, because he knew I was a package deal. Soon we were all in a group hug.

He was going to talk to my dad that weekend, when we took our stuff out for Thanksgiving dinner. I was nervous, but Dad liked Branch, and this would be the first time he would be asked for a daughter's hand in marriage.

I told Branch I wanted a small, intimate wedding. We discussed a date and wanted to wait until after Christmas, but I didn't want a long engagement. We chose a holiday weekend; it would be easier for out-of-town friends and family to make it. He was ready and asked if January 14th would be long enough to plan everything.

I laughed, that would work. We would be pressed for time, but I figured we'd have better luck with venues and rentals before the wedding season started.

Branch and my dad walked to the barn after we arrived. They were gone longer than I expected. It made me uncomfortable. My dad liked Branch, but he was also concerned about Branch just getting out of a marriage, my independence, job, and the kids. Apparently, Branch passed the test because my dad gave him his blessing and said, "Once you say, 'I do,' there's no return to sender."

That became their mantra leading up to the wedding, but it also solidified this was it for both of us. There was no "out" once we said, "I do." Divorce would not be an option.

Branch wanted to ask his friends from MN to be in the wedding, the one that recently got married would be the best man. Branch wanted me to meet them before the wedding to avoid drama at the wedding. We drove to MN so I could meet them and see the kids.

We stayed with the couple recently married, which was awkward, but if they were going to be part of our wedding, I had to let bygones be bygones.

Branch's best man and I got along, but his wife was standoffish until we had a deep conversation about how everything started. She said it was hard to accept, but she could tell I made Branch happy. She'd never seen him like this before.

That night I met Branch's brother, who was an ass and the other friends that would be part of the wedding party. We had a fun night, laughing and getting to know each other. Branch said he never really got along with his brother, but they had all wrestled together.

The next day, Branch called Devlin, asking if he could see the kids. She refused, then started cussing at him. He hung up. I told him to try again later, see if she calmed down. I asked him to let me talk to her. I would apologize and be civil and see if he could see the kids if I didn't come in with him. Initially, she didn't want to talk to me, called me names and screamed at me. I listened and let her get it out, then I calmly talked to her, apologized and we had a decent conversation.

She agreed Branch could see the kids in an hour. I told Branch I would feel better if he had a deputy do a civil stand by because she was extremely volatile. I didn't want him to get in trouble if she attacked him.

The kids jumped at Branch, and he scooped all 3 up at the same time. The deputy stood in the front door, where he could see everything, but gave Branch some privacy with the kids. As I sat in the vehicle in the dark, I noticed a light turn on upstairs. Devlin was standing in the window flipping me off. I laughed and shook my head. We would never get along, but I would be civil.

She flipped me off again before Branch got ready to leave. He was saying goodbye to the kids, when she came down the stairs and attacked Branch, in front of the kids. The deputy intervened, separating them. He told Branch to finish his goodbyes and leave. He told Devlin to calm down because he didn't want to arrest her for assault.

I watched it happen because the doorway was lit up, but I wasn't surprised. She seemed unstable. She was used to getting her way. The kids were crying, yelling, "Bye, Daddy, we love you," as he walked to the truck.

He was upset and I held his hand when he got in. He was glad the deputy was there, but angry she acted like that in front of the kids.

We stopped for beer before going to our hosts and Devlin called his phone. He listened to the voicemail when we got in the truck but didn't call back.

We got to the house and his phone rang again. He was done dealing with her and wasn't going to let her ruin our weekend. She said the kids weren't coming down to be part of the wedding. As I came out of the restroom, following a couple beers, I heard Branch's phone buzzing again.

It was her again. I answered the phone. At this point, it wasn't going to hurt anything. She seemed stunned at first, then asked to speak to Branch. I told her he didn't want to talk to her. He was no longer her husband, and she wasn't going to verbally abuse him anymore.

I didn't yell at her, but I told her she had been ungrateful. Branch was an amazing man, but she never realized it. If she really saw him, she would see how generous, kind, smart and talented he was. I told her I was sick of her calling him names and saying he "abandoned his kids." He didn't abandon them, he "left" her and her abuse.

Regardless of what she said and did, Branch would always be a great father. She could keep the kids from Branch and fill their heads with lies, but as they got older and away from her, they would learn the truth. I told her I was sorry for how things worked out.

The conversation was going okay for a while, then she completely lost it again. I told her that was the last chance, goodbye. I wasn't the kind of person to be mean and I felt bad for the way things went down, but I would never be sorry I met Branch.

Branch and I left the next day and stopped outside of Albuquerque, NM, on a deserted exit, to sleep while the snowstorm passed through. We snuggled, made love during the snowstorm, and fell asleep with smiles.

By the time we got home, my allergies were out of control, and I had a bad headache. Different from my normal headache caused from my neck and shoulders. I went to work that morning. 15 minutes later, I got dizzy and grabbed the wall to steady myself.

One of the guys, Milk, grabbed my arm, and set me in a chair. He felt my head and said I had a fever. He was calling Branch. I needed to see the doctor, likely a sinus infection.

Branch had dropped me off because he was going to register with the AZ union. He picked me up and took me to urgent care. I had a severe sinus infection and they put me on antibiotics. They told me to take a couple days off until the dizziness passed.

I went home and crashed on the couch. I slept most of the next 2 days and took the rest of the week off because we had LJ's party that weekend and I wanted to be rested for it.

Branch and I had our bridal attendants set. We chose our colors and theme and looked at venues. We saw a couple we really liked, but I didn't want to pay that much money for something simple and intimate. Rick, from work, was gifting us his DJ services and Evelyn was making our wedding and groom cake. Rosie was helping me make my dress.

Before we could decide on venues, we did the Christmas wagon ride. We hosted the ride at the neighbors. Improvements were made to the wagon that year. There was a railing around the sides and a frame over the top. Benches were added, with a walkway up the middle, and handrails in the back for the elves to hang onto.

Rick brought his karaoke machine and sound system out so we could sing carols and have louder Christmas music while we went through the neighborhoods. We had baked goods, hot cocoa and marshmallows, snack plates and chili. There was a fire in the backyard where people could hang out between wagon rides.

We needed a venue fast, so we could get invites sent out. We asked the neighbors if we could use their place. They had a long concrete driveway where we could do the ceremony and a backyard big enough, we could put a tent, dance floor and tables.

They said yes and we moved forward. It was a western theme. My dress was a creamy ivory with vines embossed into the fabric. The guys would be in tuxes, with DJ and Branch wearing cowboy hats and Branch wearing his boots.

I was going to wear cowboy boots with my dress, my bridesmaids were wearing emerald green and carrying ivory tulips. We found a place that gave us a great deal on the tent, chairs, tables, dance floor, heaters, and lighting. They delivered, set up, tore down and took away, which was perfect for us.

We did photos on New Year's Eve at KM's house, in front of her fireplace, before our NYE party. Goldie and Kurt were doing our wedding invites and get them in the mail. The hardest part of the photo was getting us to stop laughing for a good picture.

SE helped with sewing my dress, the tablecloths and finding theme-related items for decorations. The tablecloth fabric was a black and white cow print.

She found western bowls, cowboy boot photo holders and other random fun decorations.

I found a huge wine glass that she engraved with our names and date on it. We put green and shimmery clear stones inside it for the main table centerpiece. Branch and I wanted something to symbolize the joining of not just us, but our families. We found a heart-shaped jar that we would each pour a different color of sand into, during the ceremony.

We found tuxes to rent for all the guys. LJ wanted to wear my high school prom dress which we altered to fit her. We now had everything we needed for the wedding, except someone to officiate. The commissioner I worked for heard I was getting married and said he could do the ceremony for us. I looked around at the guys I worked with and the court staff, grateful for the family I gained.

Berryhead and her husband would be staying at the house with us, along with Branch's dad. The other out of town guests were staying in a hotel, arriving the day before, in time for the rehearsal dinner. We started decorating Thursday, putting the trellis and decorations up on the gate of the driveway, which would be the backdrop for the ceremony.

We decorated an arch with tulle, ivy, and fake tulips. The tent and rental items were delivered and set up Friday morning, which allowed us to get the lights hung in the tent. Branch, his dad and the kids built a wishing well to sit on the gift table, for cards.

We had barbeque chicken, chili, and cornbread. We had a keg of beer, keeping it simple. The cake was 3 separate tiers, with a clear topper of a man and woman dancing.

We had the rehearsal dinner Friday night at an all-you-can-eat seafood buffet, giving us all time to relax. Berryhead and I hadn't seen each other in 6 years and had so much to catch up on. Her and Branch got along great.

The only family Branch would have was his dad, but we were grateful for that. I would be doing my hair and makeup. Clara helped the bridesmaids with their hair and makeup. SE helped me dress and coordinated everyone walking out the door for the ceremony. She took most of the stress off me that day.

The morning of the wedding Branch got a phone call from Devlin. She was cussing at him, asking how he could just abandon his family and he still had time to walk away from me. I was upset with her for calling and his friends who seemed to be waiting for us to call it off.

Branch and I argued about it. He told me nothing was changing his mind. He had no doubts, we would be husband and wife before 3:30 P.M. He turned his phone off, left it in the truck and pulled me into his arms, holding me tightly. We stayed embraced for 5 or 10 minutes, letting our hearts speak to each other. We had written our own vows and would be speaking from our hearts.

The photographer started getting pictures of the guys while the girls finished getting ready. The ceremony would start promptly at 3 P.M. and I was ready to go at 2:30 so I sat in my button-down shirt and shorts, waiting to put my dress on. I looked around at my bridesmaids, comprised of blood sisters and sisters of choice and my baby girl.

I couldn't believe how blessed I was to have this tribe of women sharing my day with me. LJ was 9 but looked so grown up. She was wearing her first pair of heels and I wanted to squeeze her tight. We had a quick toast of champagne, then they all helped me get dressed. It was time to go.

My dress had a halter top, with a button holding the two pieces together around my neck. It had an open back, all the way down to my hips, dropping to the dip in my back, where the zipper started. This was the first time I was publicly showing the scar on my side, near my right breast. It is not a pretty scar, but my scars have a story and represent strength, hope and determination. I wore it proudly.

The bodice of my dress dropped into the waist, lightly flaring out at the hips, down to the ground. The front just skimmed the ground and flared out into a train in the back. We had sewn buttons onto the side of my dress so I could pin the train up while we danced. I didn't want a veil and wore my hair pulled back lightly from my face, clipped in the back, with curls cascading down my back.

Branch and I picked my wedding march song, but he didn't know it would change to "You Had Me from Hello" before I started down the aisle. The girls started walking out, 1 at a time and my dad and I were ready to go. He looked handsome in his suit and cowboy hat and asked if I was ready. Absolutely. SE gave us the signal to come out the door.

Branch wore a smile that lifted my heart, higher than it had ever been. This man was about to be my husband and I couldn't wait. When the song changed, his face lit up even more. He was fighting back tears.

I didn't see anything else, other than his eyes as I walked down the aisle. There were friends from work in the seats, most were like family. They were shocked when they heard the "ice princess" was getting married. I felt surrounded by love and saw the smile on DJ's face as he stood with Branch and the smile on LJ's face as she stood with KJ, my maid of honor.

My dad gave me away. Branch and I said our vows, did our unity ceremony with the sand, had Doug and Rosie read some scripture, then the commissioner was saying, "I now pronounce you husband and wife, you may kiss your bride." Branch's grin grew bigger as he stepped in to kiss me, wrapping his arm tightly around me, then dipping me, pressing into a deeper kiss.

I heard the cheering. We turned to face our family and friends as the commissioner said, "I would like to introduce you to Mr. and Mrs." We walked down the aisle together with our attendants following behind. We walked to an open area for a receiving line.

What we didn't expect was my mom to plant a kiss on my husband's lips when he bent to hug her. I don't know who was more shocked by the display, but I couldn't help laughing at Branch's face as he scrunched his face and lips, pulling away from her. A "WTF just happened" look was on his face. It remains a source of amusement for us.

We finished the receiving line, friends started moving chairs to the back to put them around the tables, while the wedding party did pictures. When Branch and I signed the marriage license, my dad looked over Branch's shoulder and reminded him there was no return to sender.

After the pictures, and wagon ride for the wedding party, we started the reception. We had a champagne toast, KJ's was the best. She told me to put my hand out and then for Branch to put his hand over mine. Then she said that was the last time he would have the upper hand. We all laughed and that set the mood for the rest of the night. Everyone was eating, drinking and it was time for our first dance.

We did the waltz to "Can I Have This Dance, for the Rest of My Life" by Anne Murray. It was an older country song, but one we loved. My dad and I danced to "Forever, Amen" by George Straight because it was the song he sang when I was deployed.

It was a fantastic night. Dancing and holding hands with my "husband," seeing my kids enjoy themselves and knowing we had a community of love and support surrounding us.

We did the garter event. I surprised Branch because I had a regular garter and another that had a small holster holding a small gun. He laughed and the guys I worked with laughed. They were taking bets on whether I was carrying.

We danced the night away, laughed and enjoyed every minute of our reception. As the night wore on, the temperature dipped and by midnight, the chill was setting in. Exhaustion was catching up. I wanted to go home to "consummate" our marriage.

We said our goodbyes and walked to the house. Branch carried me over the threshold, into the bedroom, where he kissed me solidly. We lit candles and he helped me out of my dress.

He took my dress off and tossed it to the side. Things really heated up because it caught the candle, causing it to spill over onto the nightstand and my dress. We got the candle under control and peeled the wax off my dress. Thankfully, it was on the train part.

The rest of the weekend we hung out with out-of-town friends before they left. We drank beer, ate leftovers, watched football, and opened gifts.

I didn't want to let go of Berryhead at the airport. I missed her and knew she wasn't happy in her marriage.

Branch and I decided to wait on a honeymoon. He was in a new job and his paycheck was basically going straight to the ex, for alimony and child support. He was already behind because his checks were so much smaller. We were also moving in a couple weeks into an apartment close by, so the kids wouldn't have to change schools.

I started working off-duty on Sundays, with Rick. It gave us a couple extra hundred dollars a week, which helped cover the loss of Branch's income.

Branch called the kids every Sunday, as this was the time Devlin initially said worked best. It wasn't often she answered, and the kids never returned the calls. Branch started writing letters and sending cards to the kids, hoping they would get those.

We moved into the apartment. It was a tight fit. The kids shared a room with bunkbeds. They had their own bathroom and we had ours. We made it work, knowing it wasn't forever. Branch and I started talking about moving closer to my dad. It was a rural area, which I was used to and wanted to be in again.

Branch was almost finished with the job at the arena and there wasn't anything lined up when he was done. My dad was starting a job in Utah. I told Branch he should work with my dad; it paid more and would help him catch up on back support/alimony.

We didn't want to be apart, but knew we needed to do something. We didn't realize Devlin stopped making payments on the truck, so when we missed a payment, it was repossessed. We didn't have the funds to get it out.

Branch's son needed another surgery for his heart. Surprisingly, Devlin kept me updated with text messages for Branch.

I was having more issues with my neck/shoulder and the headaches. I was living on 800 mg of ibuprofen, every 4 hours. One morning I got up for work. After using the restroom, I walked into the bedroom, bent down to grab clothes out of my dresser and blacked out when I stood up.

I was still lightheaded when I woke up and Branch was sitting next to me, making sure I was okay. He told me I should see a chiropractor for an adjustment, because massages weren't helping and wearing my vest was making it worse. He got me in to the chiro he had been seeing and we found out the ribcage protecting my spine, was out of alignment.

When I landed on my hand in '93, the force pushed things out of alignment and over the years, with the overuse from doing hair, typing, the taser and wearing a vest, caused it to start pressing on the nerves, which caused the headaches and pain. He adjusted me and I had immediate relief. He set me up for 3 visits a week.

Branch bought a used truck before we went camping for the 4th of July. It was a diesel; it would run forever, and the payments were low. We explored the area and LJ found elk antlers. She asked Branch if we could put them on the grill of the truck. He loved the idea and drilled little holes in the antlers and mounted them to the grill. We had a great couple weeks before he went back to work, and DJ started football.

I enrolled the kids in school near my parents and we would stay with my stepmom during the week, coming back to the apartment on weekends. It wasn't a great setup, but the apartment was leased through October. I hadn't found a place to rent near my parents yet and I wasn't ready to buy a house.

Branch came home for my birthday, surprising me with the Pussy Cat Dolls CD and a hoodie sweatshirt, that had "Dontcha wish your girlfriend was hot like me" embroidered around the edge of the hoodie. One of the new guys I worked with, Clay, had a birthday the day after mine and we celebrated together. I brought him a princess cake, purple and pink tiara and a purple shag pillow with princess embroidered on it.

He loved it and loved showing it off. Only a few of us knew he was gay. We became fast friends, working together, hanging out on the weekends. My kids and sisters loved him. When Branch met him, they got along great.

DJ was playing football so we would drive home after his games on Friday night. LJ and I went to most of the games, then we would do laundry on Saturday, hang out, then head back to my parents, Sunday night, after dinner.

Branch came home Labor Day weekend. We floated the river with my sisters and Clay. It was a fun end to the summer and bonding time for us. After my off-duty job, Branch picked me up and we hung out for a bit before we drove to my parents. He would head back to Utah with my dad. He hated leaving. I hated it, too. We laid in our bed talking about the things he wanted to do. He loved being a volunteer firefighter and always wanted to go in the military, but he had asthma when he was younger and was denied.

I didn't want him to do the military because I had just started my career and we would have to move if he went active duty. I told him we should check the fire department where we were moving to and see what they had because they were a full-time department.

That week I looked at a couple places to rent and chose one that was a couple miles from my parents. It wasn't that big, but it had 3 bedrooms, 2 bathrooms and a huge backyard for RockSea. We moved right before Halloween. The kids had their own rooms again.

I got DJ a cell phone and LJ a phone that only called me, Branch, DJ, my stepmom or 911. I didn't want her home without being able to call. She had to call when she got off the bus and into the house. She had the dog and I taught her to shoot. If anyone tried getting in the house, other than me, Branch, DJ, or her grandparents, she needed to grab the gun, call 911 and be ready to shoot.

We talked about what people might want to do by breaking in and though I didn't want to traumatize her, she needed to know there were bad people that did bad things. I wanted her prepared.

Branch received a call that his grandpa passed away. I found out I would be starting my FTO program after we got back from MN. We flew up the day before the funeral, rented a car and stayed in a hotel close by.

Branch's mom and Devlin listed Devlin as Branch's spouse, not me, under the survived by portion of the obituary. It was ridiculous, but Branch was pissed and called his mom out on it. I was in the lobby when some of the ladies Branch's mom worked with, came up to me, hugged me and told me they knew Branch since before he got married to Devlin and they've never seen him as happy as he was with me.

They loved his mom, but they didn't agree with how she was treating us. They said Devlin was wrong for not allowing Branch to see or talk to the kids and his mom was wrong for encouraging it. I thanked them for their kindness and smiled.

The night before we flew home, Devlin told Branch he could see the kids and I could meet them. We did a civil stand-by, just in case. I didn't want to jeopardize my career. We bought the kids' books; one was a sticker storybook. We let Devlin know we were outside, once the deputy got there, and after we went in. Devlin was calm, told us the kids were in the bedroom and she would stay in the living room.

The deputy left when they realized she was calm. She had moved into an apartment after selling the house and living with Branch's mom for a short period. The kids warmed to me and the youngest was climbing into my lap, asking me to read to her, while she put stickers all over the book, me, and Branch.

We spent an hour with the kids. Devlin took a picture with us and the kids before we said goodbye. We left with hope for the future. Branch and I flew home the next morning and I had 1 day to get ready for FTO.

I was assigned to the Special Assignment Unit, SAU because I knew the districts, radio codes and other basics from dispatching.

We worked swing shift, from 1 P.M.-11 P.M. Sundays we were in District 3, Mondays, District 4, Tuesdays, District 1 and Wednesdays, District 2. We had Thursday, Friday, and Saturday off. I loved the schedule, except not seeing the kids, M-W afternoons.

The more Branch and I were apart, the more we fought. My dad could tell how miserable Branch was and told him to go home. Branch did and found a job working in town, welding, and fabricating. He was done by 3 P.M. which worked great because he was home in the evenings with the kids.

He found out that there was going to be a fire academy starting in January, with classes every weekend. If he worked for the local fire department as a reserve, he could take one of their free slots, so he signed up.

I worked the racetrack again, with the SAU squad. The week before Thanksgiving, SAU was assigned to go through a 1-week SWAT training. This wouldn't count as part of my FTO training, but once we were trained, we would be doing search warrants with SWAT, which would help me with OT and extra pay.

The training was tough, but fun. We did building clearing in the shoot house, shot from different positions with our rifles and handguns. Shot with our gas masks on, learned different tactics for clearing buildings, hostage situations, working with the bomb squad and more.

By the end of the week, I was physically and mentally exhausted, but exhilarated. I began my days at 4 A.M., falling into bed at 9 P.M., after a shower and dinner. Branch made my lunches, packed snacks, and made sure I had breakfast for the road.

They told us we should be done about 3 P.M., Friday, if we passed the tests. We ran several scenarios in the shoot house, each of us running point and switching positions. One of the sergeants told me if he ever got command of the SWAT team, he wanted an all-female team and he wanted me on it because of my rifle skills.

We successfully completed our training. DJ's football season was over, and we would all be home for dinner. Branch helped unload my gear from the truck and told me to go relax before dinner.

I laid down on the floor, in front of the TV, sprawled out and closed my eyes. RockSea was sniffing me, and Branch said he had a surprise. I opened my eyes and saw a little golden ball of fur. Branch got me a golden retriever puppy; I had always loved them.

The puppy walked over to me, sniffed me, licked me, and curled up next to my chest while I laid on my side. He was so soft and snuggly I didn't want to let him go. I eventually got up to shower. We had dinner, then I snuggled with the puppy. Branch had been studying Russian and we named the puppy "Sabaka" which meant dog in Russian. His nickname became Saba.

I continued my FTO training, moving along quickly and my supervisor told me that I was on track to finish and go solo sooner than scheduled. I would still be on FTO, but I would be by myself, going to calls on my own, taking reports, doing traffic stops and other normal duties.

Our team was busy all December. We would work our district and get called for search warrants. Some search warrants were preplanned because they were high risk, others were not. I started taking extra clothes, snacks, pillow, and blanket so I could sleep in my vehicle in between shift and search warrants.

The extra money from OT helped us, but it was exhausting. I hardly saw the kids. By January, I met all my FTO requirements, and they signed off for me to go solo. They transferred me to a district, close to my house.

I was now working Wed-Sat, graveyards. I enjoyed this time better because I could see my family and I was off during the week. I also enjoyed not driving so many miles to the different districts.

I went through extra DUI training and horizontal gaze nystagmus, HGN, certification, finding I enjoyed DUIs. I could spot a drunk driver quickly and finish the stop within 20-30 minutes, depending on if it was a regular or aggravated DUI.

Fridays and Saturdays were the busiest with DUIs. I worked the area most people drove coming from the clubs and bars. Part of my beat was a retirement community. They were normally quiet after 7 P.M., which allowed me time to find DUIs.

Branch started the fire academy the middle of January 2007. After the initial weeks, I told him to switch to part time at work because the academy would be part of his future career which was more important than trying to keep up with alimony. I would help pick up the slack by working more off duty once I finished FTO, to help take the pressure off him.

I officially finished FTO. On my way to work, I got a call from Lt. Strong. I answered and he told me to hang up so he could call back and listen to my ringtone, which was the Pussy Cat Dolls, "Doncha." I called him back. When he answered, he was still singing. He called me Suzy, one of the few that got away with it. He was excited as I was transferring to his district, the following week. He told me what time to report and where.

I was confused. Why was I being transferred? I got to work and saw Lt. Shanley, newly promoted from Sgt. The Lt. at my current district. He was sitting with my Sgt. I said, "Let me guess, I'm being transferred to ElMo?" He cocked his head to the side, with an expression of disbelief, wondering how I already knew.

He said that there were 3 slots to be filled over there. It was a contract city, they took priority. I was the first one chosen by their command staff, once they found out I was done with FTO. I was honored to be chosen, but I was irritated he didn't tell me first. He said that's why he was there now. He didn't realize my new Lt. would call me. Apparently, Lt. Strong was excited and wanted to tell me.

I reported to my new district Monday at 1 P.M. I walked in and saw many familiar faces. I was wholeheartedly welcomed. As I rode around with Gage, he showed me where the bad areas were, who to watch out for, where gangs hung out and shortcuts around town.

The first week I was on my own; a call kicked out for shots fired and it was in the known gang area. Everybody started that way. We knew it could be an ambush or an actual gang fight. Normally, I only went to my calls, unless it was a domestic violence call or other active assault.

After the call kicked out, we couldn't get the info because so many people were responding. Finally, the dispatcher told everyone to hold traffic for the info. I was less than a minute out, when she said there were multiple shots, multiple people in the streets fighting and multiple callers.

I was going 23, which means on scene. She held the station until there was a code 4. I saw one of the other guys coming the opposite way towards my vehicle. We slowly walked in with weapons drawn, heads on a swivel, looking for an ambush.

We saw a huge crowd ahead, in the intersection and heard more of our guys arriving. We told units to cover the exit points in case people started running or trying to leave. Soon it seemed like there were 100 of us, in reality, there may have been 15 or 20 to the 100-150 in the streets.

We moved people back, for their safety and ours, as we worked our way to the fight. There were a couple guys with bats. We found the ones that had guns out and held them at gunpoint until they dropped their weapons and were in custody. It took 10-15 minutes to clear everyone out, get suspects in custody, then move to witness statements and medical attention.

I was the first on-scene, and it was in my beat, so I took the report. I got everyone's info that were taking statements, involved in any way, then approximately 30 minutes later, my supervisor, Sgt. Painter, told me the human smuggling unit, HSU, guys would be taking the report and transporting subjects because they were in the country illegally.

I turned all my info over to Gage before he left. 15 people were taken into custody and transported. A couple of us stayed in the area in case of any backlash, but it stayed quiet.

I adjusted to my new schedule, was able to be home on the weekends and most nights with the family. DJ was starting baseball, Branch was doing well in the academy, and I was working off duty every Monday before work, every Tuesday before work, then Fridays, after work. Sometimes I worked Saturday nights at a club that paid cash at the end of the night.

As we all got used to the schedules, the kids helped Branch study and practice for his timed tests. We were able to watch a couple of the trainings, with the live burns, fire tower and car fires. This was what Branch was meant to do. His previous training would serve him well with structure fires. He had no fear of heights, heat or getting his hands dirty. I loved watching him in action. Although it was tough with all the hours I was working; it was going to be worth the struggles and sacrifices.

I found myself slowly gaining weight. I became out of sync with my body. I could tell it wasn't just weight gain, my hormones were affected too. I hadn't changed my diet; I was still taking PB&J sandwiches to work to make sure my IBS didn't act up while on duty.

I wasn't sleeping as much, but I hadn't slept much when I was on SAU either and I ate more junk then. I didn't want to bother Branch with how I was feeling. He was close to graduating and had a lot of testing.

I set up a doctor appointment. I was helping in LJ's classroom a couple hours a week and found myself losing patience quicker than normal. I went to the dr., had my labs drawn and they did a chest x-ray, where I'd had my tumor removed.

All my tests came back fine, but I should watch what I was eating and exercise more. I wanted to punch the guy in the face. I made the same lunch but ate less of it while working and drank more water. This made me use the restroom more, which we didn't get much time to do at work.

I was still seeing the chiro, once a week, likely a lifelong endeavor, from wearing a bullet proof vest, 40 lbs. of tools on my belt and getting in and out of patrol cars.

We were in the middle of briefing on a Monday, when a call kicked out for a domestic violence fight, with weapons. My partner and I answered because our cars were loaded and ready to go. We were less than a mile from the substation, driving lights and sirens, but not going faster than 35 mph. We were in the residential area.

I was always watchful for kids and dogs. They tended to dart into the road. I saw a dog on a chain, but he broke the chain. I hit the brakes when the chain broke, grabbed the steering wheel tightly and braced myself for impact. I hit him dead center. He went under my car and out the back side. He was dead.

It was a German shepherd mix and my heart hurt. My partner stopped to make sure I was okay, told the guy to get the dog out of the road and we would be back after the call. I checked my car and didn't see any damage and we took off again.

We ran call to call all night, so Sgt. Painter went to the guy's house to get the info and apologized for the accident. The guy said it was his fault, he only had the dog on a thin, swing set chain. He inquired if I was okay.

It was almost time for shift change when we got a call for a burglary in progress. I was less than a ½-mile from the building and said I was enroute. When I stopped at the stop sign to make sure the intersection was clear, before I turned left, I saw steam coming from my hood. I looked at my temperature gage and it went into the red.

I limped my car to the call. Afterward, I limped it back to the substation, a couple miles away. When I hit the dog, he must have hit something on the radiator and over the course of the shift, running nonstop, my radiator busted. We already had the accident report info for risk management, but I knew the Lt. in charge of the fleet and property was not going to be happy.

I finished my shift, drove home, and had the day off from off-duty, so I slept longer. I went to work, but I could tell my shoulders were tight. I took some ibuprofen. When I got up the next day, I had to run to the school before I got ready for work.

I was sitting at a stop sign, looked to the left to make sure the intersection was clear, and my neck locked up. I called my chiro to see if he could get me in, but he couldn't until the next morning. I called Sgt. Painter and told him what happened. He told me to stay home and go to the chiro the next day.

Branch took me to the chiro, then dropped me off at work and picked me up Friday morning. He came to my off-duty job and studied. We spent some time together and he kept me awake.

The adjustment made a difference, but the chiro told me I needed to come in a couple times a week for the next month to make sure nothing slipped again. I would be sore, and I probably had whiplash from hitting the dog.

DJ had been wanting to do a ride along with me because he was 14. We set it up for a Monday when he was out of school. We would be busy, and I prepared him for it. I packed us lunches and we headed to work.

The first call was an ATL, attempt to locate, for a vehicle driving erratically with 4 teenagers smoking pot. We headed out. I had an open road, so I hit the gas.

We found the car and I did the traffic stop. They were in the next city's jurisdiction. They took the call over to use as training for their trainee. The next call came in for shots fired. The lady said her 5-year-old daughter had been jumping on the bed and a bullet came through the side of the house, about 6 inches above the daughter's head.

The next call came in from a neighbor of the shooter. They said the "gangbanger kids" were out back shooting rifles. The map showed the shooter was less than a mile from the house that was hit, with an open park between the two locations. Sgt. Painter told me to head to his location with the shooters and be prepared to make entry.

I had a patrol rifle and Sgt. Painter had one. I drove quickly, but safely through the residential area while briefing DJ on what was going to happen when we got there.

I was going to pull up, and as soon as I put the car in park, he needed to crawl into the driver's seat as I got my rifle out, then climb out to squat beside the front, driver's side tire. I told him if shots started flying, the engine block would protect him. I told him not to move from there until me or my Sgt. came out.

As we were getting ready to turn into the neighborhood, I asked him if he was ready, he was. I said I loved him, and I would stay safe. On my command, we pulled up, I put the car in park, then grabbed my rifle as he climbed to the driver's seat and out the door to squat by the tire.

Sgt. Painter and I heard shots and ran to the front door, keeping cover, knocked and entered the house, yelling, "Sheriff's office!" The shots stopped. We encountered an older Hispanic male who said everything was okay. We asked where the shooters were, and he showed us their room.

We opened the door quickly and both teens were holding their hands up. We didn't see a rifle but after talking to the kids, they told us they hid it when they heard us at the front door. The older male asked why we were there. We explained they were shooting in city limits, too close to structures and one of their bullets almost hit a kid in the head when it entered the house.

My Sgt. took the boys to the station while I went to the house the bullet hit. While we were driving, I asked DJ if he was okay. He said yeah, but it was kind of scary when he heard us running and yelling, then kicking in the door. It was worse because he couldn't see what was going on, but it was also cool to see what I did at work and how quickly the calls could change.

We finished out the shift in relative calmness. While driving home, DJ said he wanted to ride with me again and I laughed. My kid was going to be an adrenaline junkie.

Branch graduated the academy, earning top recruit of the class and highest-grade point average. He talked me into doing the Emergency Medical Technician, EMT, class with him, which started in June. It would give us a chance to spend more time together.

Towards the end of May, we were in class for the new system we were getting at work, when I couldn't get comfortable. Sgt. Painter asked me if I was okay and I told him my back was bothering me, but it was different than when I needed the chiro. Because we had class during the day, Branch had dropped me off, and planned to pick me up later.

We hadn't gotten 20 minutes into the class, when I broke out in a sweat and couldn't sit up because I hurt. Sgt. Painter could feel the heat radiating off me. He knew Branch had dropped me off and told me to call him to come get me. I had a kidney infection.

Branch picked me up and took me to our dr., who was able to get me in right away. He did bloodwork and urine test; told me it was a severe kidney infection and gave me a shot of antibiotics in the office, then put in a prescription for antibiotics and something to help with the pain.

I had to be careful because wearing the duty belt, waiting so long to pee, and then not fully emptying my bladder was causing the infection. I called Sgt. Painter and let him know I had to take the rest of the week off. If I still looked like death when I came back, he said, then take more time off. He had never seen me that white before and didn't want to see it again.

A couple days later, I got a call from some high school friends. One of our mutual friends had been killed in a helicopter accident, while checking power lines. This was the kid that lived up the road from me, picked me up almost daily my senior year and taught me the meaning of "get out and lock the hubs."

I spent hours talking to him, to and from school, on the weekends playing cards, getting into trouble. It was the guy that almost got me in trouble the night before I left for basic training. He was 34, a veteran and father. There were so many memories.

Branch and I started our EMT class, which was every Saturday, from 8-5. He came to my off-duty job every Friday so we could study for our test the following day and we were competing against each other for the highest grade.

EMT class, the other students and our instructors were fun. Branch and I got to spend the day together, sitting side by side, having lunch and our commute together. The kids became our patients when we had to practice listening to breathing sounds, heartbeat, checking blood pressure and pulse. Then they were bandaged, triaged, and splinted.

We were in class when I got a call from the Lt. that oversaw the ballpark. He needed a dispatcher that night because we were playing the Dodgers. I was the only other person he knew that could handle the traffic. I told him where I was, and he said he would have our helicopter pick me up if I could get a ride to the helipad, a couple miles away.

I also had to work the off-duty job at the club that night and didn't have my uniform. Branch dropped me off at the helipad, then went home, got my uniform and duty belt, and picked me up after the game. He then drove me to my off-duty job. It was crazy, but we got out of class earlier than expected, so it worked perfectly.

The Lt. picked me up and drove me to the ballpark. The game started and I monitored radio traffic. My headset cord was long enough I could hear the traffic and use the restroom, so I didn't miss anything. About 8 P.M., the feeling of a urinary tract infection came over me. I felt like I had to pee, and it hurt when I went.

The Lt. brought me cranberry juice and I kept drinking water to try to flush it out. I was going to be miserable during my off-duty job. I text Branch and asked him to get me more cranberry juice. I didn't want to cancel my off-duty assignment. It was a $600 cash job, for a few hours, standing outside the club.

I finished the baseball game and met Branch. I got dressed while we were driving to the club. The guys knew I was going to be late.

Branch parked so he could sit on the tailgate and talk to us. I checked all my tools on my belt, pulled my taser out to do a test fire, like I did at the beginning of every shift or off-duty job. I was working with a new guy, and Clay. I pointed my taser at the ground for the dry fire and heard the barbs hit the ground. I forgot to remove the taser cartridge.

Clay jumped and squealed, making us laugh. The new guy looked at me, then the taser and said, "Well, damn, now it's a party." He had a heavy southern accent which added to the humor. Branch looked at me, shook his head, then said I should have gone home.

I was starting to run a fever, but we only had 30 minutes left and that's when there was a fight in the club and security escorted them out to us. Most of the club goers were professional athletes and at least a ½-foot taller than me.

I grabbed one guy and told him not to struggle or fight because I could easily end his career having to take him down. He might be bigger, but I could take him down faster than he would blink. He started laughing and said, "I believe you and I just want to leave." I told him I would escort him to his car and made sure he was okay to drive. He did a quick PBT, portable breathalyzer test to make sure he wouldn't get a DUI.

He blew all 0s. He was good to drive. He thanked me for being cool, making sure he was good to go and keeping them safe. He appreciated what we did and told me to be safe.

When I got back to the truck, the club had mostly cleared out, we had no more issues and after we got paid, Clay told me to go home because I looked like hell. It was the end of June, and it was warm, but he said I was sweating like a whore in church. I logged off the radio and climbed in the truck.

Branch brought me an extra shirt and bra to change into for the drive home which I was so grateful for. I had spandex on under my pants and took everything off down to my spandex. My vest was soaked, and I was running a fever. I put my other shirt and bra on, and laid down on the seat, with my head in Branch's lap.

The next day he took me to urgent care, where I was given more antibiotics. I went home and slept all day Sunday and most of Monday morning. It was almost the 4th of July.

I was ready for some time off from work and off duty. I hadn't taken time off since before I started FTO. My body had enough. The first couple days, I didn't do anything but read, color, and hang out. Branch's dad came out that summer but wound up in the hospital the day before the 4th. He couldn't breathe with the elevation and his COPD.

Branch took him to the hospital and found out he was supposed to be on medicine but wasn't taking it. I was aggravated, which was exacerbated because I was so tired, and my hormones still didn't feel right.

We left a couple days after the 4th. The SAU Sgt. called, asking me if I wanted to come back to SAU. They had an opening and all the guys had me as their #1 pick. I wanted to go back but I was in an EMT class every Saturday. He said we would work around it if we had a call out. After conferring with Branch, I accepted the position.

I loved Sgt. Painter, the command staff, and my squad, but I hated working for a city and dealing with the city managers. I wasn't cut out for politics or the "favors" and who knew who games. I learned much in the 7 months I was there. I felt I had the experience of a deputy that had been on for years.

The last few days I worked there, I had a call where a guy walked in front of a semi, killing him instantly and seeing what priapism looked like up closely. We had just learned about it in EMT class, and Sgt. Painter looked at me like I was crazy when I told him what it was.

Right before I transferred to SAU, the acting commander pulled me aside and asked me if I wanted to go to SAU or am I being pushed into it. He said he would keep me there, working for him if I didn't want to go. I appreciated him looking out for me, but I wanted to go. I missed the search warrants, working with SWAT and being able to sleep every night.

It was a crazy and busy summer, DJ was watching my sisters 3 kids and LJ, in a house that was only 1200 square feet. I was still working a lot, with OT and off duty. Branch and I were gearing up for our final EMT testing so we could take our national test. The closer it got, the more nervous I was. DJ started football again.

Soon school started, SE had met a guy and they were getting serious. He lived out near us and our dad. Over time, she ended up moving in with him and enrolling her kids in the same school as LJ.

Branch and I were busy on Thursday nights, working with a group of parents to provide spaghetti dinner each week to the football team before their game on Friday. A lot of kids weren't getting enough nourishment and Branch said it was something the booster club had done for his team when he was in school.

Branch and I passed our EMT class and set up our national test. We got our results before I left for work. Branch could now work as a paid reserve for the fire district he did the academy with, and he was also working at the local fire department to get experience. I went to work that day and had just stopped to get a drink when a call kicked out for a dog mauling a kid.

I arrived on scene with another deputy and in the backyard was an English bulldog, with blood on its mouth, from where he had bit the little girl's scalp. The deputy shot the dog and ran to get the girl. I called for a helo and started CPR on her. She was only 18 months old, and she bled out in our hands, in the front of their house.

I felt my training failed me. Realistically, we did everything we could. I had to interview the nanny/housekeeper, then break the news to the parents, who had been at work.

After the interviews, I was able to piece together that the girl and dog were outside playing. The girl had a barrette in her hair and when she moved, the sun must have caught it, catching the dog's attention and he started licking it, then bit it, thinking it was a toy for him.

When he bit down, he must have bitten through skin, drawing blood, causing animal instincts to kick in and he kept trying to get the barrette. I don't remember much of the shift after that, I responded to calls on autopilot.

The drive home, I couldn't get her face out of my head and cried the entire 90-minute drive home. Branch knew something was wrong, but I couldn't talk about it yet. He pulled me close and held me tight.

We were told we were getting a new Sgt. The new sergeant, Scrum, had been part of SAU when he was a deputy. He was part of the "good old boys" mentality, and he started recruiting the old guys that used to be on the squad with him. I stayed out of his line of sight, doing my job. I got a letter of commendation from a local business owner after I defused a bad situation with a drunk customer.

In November, I was getting ready for work on a Sunday, but wasn't feeling great. My sinuses were bothering me. I took a hot shower, trying to clear them before I got dressed for work. I put my uniform on and bent over to tie my boots when I must have fallen because I woke up on the floor and Branch was kneeling next to me.

He triaged me, took my temperature and I told him my head, neck and shoulders hurt. I could barely move and felt like I was going to throw up. He called the on-call nurse for our insurance, and she told him to get me to the ER, ASAP, because I had symptoms for meningitis. He called my supervisor to let him know I wouldn't be in, and we were headed for the ER.

I had an MRI, CT scan, blood drawn, urinalysis, spinal tap, blood cultures and more blood drawn before they finally told me I didn't have meningitis, but I had a severe sinus infection, urinary tract infection, bladder infection and kidney infection. They were afraid of me becoming dehydrated and admitted me to the hospital.

Every part of my body hurt. I could barely move. They started me on antibiotics in my IV and gave me pain medication. Branch had to work at the racetrack the next day, helping to get the fire and rescue vehicles ready for the following week. I told him to take the kids home and to go to work.

The next day he came to visit after work. They weren't releasing me yet. The doctor had come in and after pressing under my eyes, me seeing stars and almost punching her, she told me she wanted to make sure my sinuses cleared up and to make sure I didn't get any other infections.

He laid with me for a while. I told him to let Sgt. Scrum know I wouldn't be in rest of the week. The next morning, the doctor said if I improved more, I could go home that afternoon. I told Branch to plan on getting me because I was sick of the hospital after 3 days.

He took me home, got me settled into bed and I went back to sleep. He sent a text to Scrum and let him know I was home but would be off Wednesday.

DJ's football season was over, so our spaghetti dinner nights were also done, but the group wanted to do more for the kids and sports throughout the year.

I was still working off duty but pulled back from working as much now that Branch was working more shifts with the fire department. I worked PIR again and had a couple standing off-duty jobs, but I stopped working at the club on Saturday nights. I picked up a Tuesday night club job, which was after my shift as I was already in uniform, and they closed at midnight. I made the same money, but it was much easier.

I was still running after work, when we didn't have a call out or search warrant scheduled. I worked well with most of my squad mates and looked for traffic if I wasn't on a call. Branch rode with me a couple times, one night after a crazy traffic stop and my partner saying what a bad ass I was, Branch said I was kind of scary, but he loved it.

I was called into the Scrum's office one day, after briefing. He told me someone said I was unprofessional on a call earlier that week. I asked him what he was talking about. He said I was heard cussing loudly about having to go to courts, in front of a new trainee and officers from other agencies.

As soon as he said that, I knew who was trying to start shit. I had been on a call in the retirement community when a deputy, Jethro showed up on scene with his trainee and said they were going to take the call for training purposes.

A couple officers from another agency were there as back up and they were two I worked with several times when I was in ElMo. I hadn't seen them in months.

We were outside talking, reminiscing about one of the calls we had all responded to. We were laughing at the memory, and I yelled out what the officer had been saying on the radio when she had left her mic keyed up, yelling at kids. Apparently, this was construed to my Scrum as me being "unprofessional" and acting crazy, yelling loudly. I was furious and told the Scrum to get all the facts before he started accusing people of bullshit.

He said the trainee had written a statement about what he heard. Of course, he did, he doesn't want to fail and knows Jethro is that much of an asshole to do just that. I told him I was going to work and walked out of his office.

I was done with dealing with Scrum, who played favoritism, and obviously had no idea how to supervise. One of the guys that had been part of our karaoke group and worked in courts with me, Milk, had been wanting to come to SAU, in order to go to SWAT.

I called Branch, told him what had happened and that I was going to call Milk to see if he wanted to do a 1-for-1 swap. I couldn't work in that environment anymore. Branch agreed. I called the chief and asked him if I found someone to do a 1-for-1 swap with me, would he approve it. I briefly told him what was going on. I wanted to do my job without all the stress.

My chief asked who I had in mind. He told me he would approve it if the guy agreed. I called Milk and asked him if he would do the trade, told him why, and the chief was aware of what was going on.

He said he would switch and thanked me for calling him. I was going to see if I could make it happen with that being my last night on SAU. I called the chief back, told him the trade was good and asked if he could make it happen so that would be my last night with SAU. I could start fresh Sunday night, Monday morning with the new district without missing any work hours.

About 30 minutes before my shift ended, chief text and said the transfer was done, thanked me for my hard work and to enjoy my new assignment. I text Milk, told him we were good, and he would get an email about his new assignment and hours.

I text a couple of the guys and told them what I was doing. When I got back to the district, a bunch of the guys surrounded me, asking me what the hell had happened after briefing. I told them to watch their backs for the snakes in the squad and I would see them down the road. We all hugged. I finished unpacking my vehicle, walked in the district and hung my keys on the board.

Scrum called my name. I told him, I wasn't his problem any longer, he could talk to the chief if he had questions. On the way out, I saw the trainee and Jethro in the report writing room and said, "You know that lying is a lack of integrity and it's sad that a trainee is starting out his career on the wrong foot." The trainee's eyes were super wide. Jethro's face turned red. I threw up the peace sign and walked out relieved and with my head held high.

Branch and I celebrated our 2nd wedding anniversary quietly with the kids as 2008 started to unfold in front of us. DJ was a sophomore, getting ready to finish basketball and begin baseball. With my new work schedule, I was working Saturday night through Tuesday night. This opened my entire week up and the high school softball coach asked me if I would help him coach the team.

I contacted Goldie. She had been a pitcher in college and asked if she would help work with the pitchers and catchers a couple days a week. She was happy to be back on the field.

Branch helped when he was off work, working with the outfielders and I worked with base running and infield work. The head coach worked with batting and some infield/outfield plays when we brought the team together. LJ came over to the field every day after school and helped shag balls, running, and learning more of the game. She traveled with us, helping with equipment.

My schedule allowed me to travel to all the games and if we had a game on Monday, my early day at work, I would take a couple hours off and come in later. Our longer away games were later in the week, which worked, and I didn't take much time off work.

I loved the squad I was on. I was back at District 2, squad 4, the squad I worked with when I dispatched.

Branch and I ended up running calls together when he was working. We saw each other on accidents, fires, flooded washes, water rescues and other random calls. It was amusing watching people put together he was my husband when we were on calls together.

DJ rode with me a couple more shifts now that I worked weekends. One call was dealing with a juvenile that had been beating his brother and mother then destroyed his bedroom. We had been to the house before. I had a record for making the juvies break and cry.

We got the kid under control and took him to my squad car. We shut the door, knowing the mom didn't want to press charges. She just wanted help calming him down. We were going to try to scare some sense into him. My partner, Nevo, asked me if I was going to beat my time in making this kid cry. We would see. Nevo told DJ, "Watch this." I said go, opening the back door of the squad car.

I got down in the kid's face, yelling at him, calling him out for being a crappy big brother and son. Telling him he was selfish, cruel, and other things. He broke within less than 30 seconds, beating my previous record. After shutting the door, to let him "think about his actions and consequences" and let him think he was going to juvie, Nevo said good job. DJ looked at me and said, "Mom, you're really scary sometimes." I laughed, "You're damn right and that's why you're a good kid."

Following another crazy shift where DJ accompanied me, we were headed home in the truck. I got pulled over by DPS. DJ was wearing my sheriff's office windbreaker because it was cold. I had a long shirt covering my uniform for the drive home.

When the officer got to my window, he peeked inside the cab and saw my windbreaker, asked if I was just getting off work. I said I was headed home from D2. He pulled me over because I was "snowing" all over the roadway. I was confused and then realized the guys had poured the bag of paper shreddings into the back of my truck. I didn't see it because I put all my gear in the back seat of the truck, and I was not tall enough to see into the bottom of the bed.

I told the officer it was the guys I worked with, their stupid pranks. He started smiling, trying to keep from laughing, told me to have a safe drive home and walked back to his patrol car. I could tell he was laughing when I looked in my mirror to pull onto the highway.

I called my other partner and told him I got pulled over for "snowing." He and the other guys at the district started laughing. I would get them all back, in due time.

We had a great squad. I enjoyed going to work again. Branch got hired full time with the fire department and was working overtime when he could. He was behind on child support and alimony. We didn't know how we would catch up. They were taking 75% of his check for child support and putting the rest towards back support.

He didn't have much left to contribute to the household after fuel and food for work. I picked up more off-duty when I could, during the day, before softball.

While working an off-duty job, I got a call from Lt. Strong. I answered and he told me I was on speaker phone. I laughed and asked if that was a good idea.

He said he was with Sgt. Painter, and the acting Sgt., Baker, that had been my beat partner in ElMo. They wanted to ask if I would be willing to transfer to their unit to work as a detective in the criminal employment squad. I would report on Monday morning if I said yes.

I called Branch and told him about the transfer. He was glad I was working for good supervisors again. As much as I loved working patrol, I wanted to be a detective. We had a game that night and I told the team that my hours would change some, but I was going to finish out the season.

I met my new squad, already knew most of them, was assigned my take home car, given my desk, and briefed on my assignment. One of the guys showed me the systems we used to research, how we got information from other agencies and how it tied into our cases.

He explained how our cases tied in with the human smuggling cases. I didn't speak Spanish well enough to do interviews with Spanish-speaking suspects, but I did most of the typing to help the guys that did the interviews.

I started taking the rest of my classes needed for my detective certification and found there were a lot of distractions with 4 people in our small office. The guys stopping by needed help on a case or suspect, other employees stopping by to say hi when they saw me and then, breakfast and lunch breaks.

We finished the softball season, the kids finished school and we decided to buy an aboveground pool for the house, instead of buying season tickets to the waterpark. The kids loved the idea. We were watching SE's kids again during the summer, so it kept them all busy.

We had our normal camping trip, participating in the 4th of July parade. We drove up to the top of some of the mountains, exploring dirt roads, "goat" paths, and the local culture/history. I fell in love with the town. It was 8500 feet above sea level, snowed in the winter, rained in the summer, but the pines surrounding the town and the small community, drew me in.

We got home and bought the pool, putting it up right away. Branch and I enjoyed some quiet afternoons every now and then, but the kids' spent hours in it. In August, I had to attend a 4-week training, to get my 287g certification through Immigration and Custom Enforcement.

The days were long, the material was dry, but it helped me understand the difference between visas, lawful permanent residents (green cards), EWI (entry without inspection) and multiple other abbreviations. Each afternoon after I got home, when Branch was home, we grabbed beer and relaxed in the pool. It was the only way I was going to get through the class. At the time, we had to be 287g certified to investigate our cases.

We bought a phone, like LJ's, for Branch's kids at Christmas. He wanted them to be able to call him. He programmed their mom's number, her mom's number, his number, and his mom's number, hoping that would help establish and encourage communication. By the end of the summer, the phone still hadn't been turned on and Branch hadn't been allowed to talk to the kids in months.

According to Devlin, she wanted Branch to be part of the kids' lives. When Branch tried to contact the children, Devlin would say, if he really cared, he would take care of the back alimony he owed. It didn't matter what he said or did, it always came back to the money. The divorce decree stated he had to pay almost $1000 a month in child support, and he had to pay HER $1200 a month for 5 years. Devlin had a college degree in education and constantly threw it in Branch's face, yet never sought employment.

He was paying Devlin more money in alimony than he had to pay for child support for 3 kids. It baffles me that Devlin and the court deemed a verbally abusive wife had more value than three children.

Now that Branch had a full-time job, they were taking the support directly out of his check. They were also taking a portion to apply toward the back support. The alimony wasn't getting paid and continued adding up. Our daily lives were affected by his miniscule paycheck, and it was a negative on his credit report.

After I got my 287g certification, I started working my own tips and cases. It wasn't unusual to have several cases going at one time. As one of us got a case ready, we planned the search warrant, set up the operations plans, met with SWAT and then had to personally brief the sheriff beforehand.

We started getting more detectives and we were given a couple more offices. Mine was through the breakroom, away from all the others, except one who was around the corner from me. We kept up a steady stream of chatter and messing with each other through the days, but it was nice having my own office. There were less distractions, less gossip, and more productivity.

We helped HSU with human trafficking search warrants, assisted the undercover drug unit with search warrants and took custody of suspects in the country illegally or "undocumented."

We were talking with Branch's dad, but his mom was still not talking to Branch. I wrote her a heartfelt letter and told her about my part in the story, what I knew and didn't know as our relationship progressed and how much family meant to me.

We didn't get a response. We had family pictures taken with me, Branch, DJ, and LJ. I sent a framed photo to her to show I was going to keep reaching out.

That fall of 2008, my cousin was diagnosed with brain cancer. She was 32 and a mother of 2 young girls. I had never sewn a quilt before, but I wanted to make something for her so she could wrap herself in hugs and prayers from family.

I asked family members to send fabric with quotes, prayers, or handwritten messages to her. Once I got all the fabric, I started piecing things together. It was a work of love, filled with frustrations. There were many ripped seams that were sewn back together. Finally, I finished it. Working from our living room floor, I had to pick the project up when I left for work and set it back up when I had time to work on it again.

She and her daughters loved the quilt. Facebook had taken off and I was able to connect regularly with my cousin and other family members. Facebook would become a time suck down the road. It was hard not to get sucked in, especially when people you had gone to school with, served in the Army with, met while doing hair, Relay For Life, dispatching and becoming a deputy, were all on it.

DJ started his junior year of high school. I was at every football game and Branch was at every one when not on shift. We made friends with other parents over the years. I worked with the school district to get our deputies to work off-duty at the football games after kids were found selling drugs under the bleachers during a game.

Our agency got the contract for off duty through one of the guys I worked with on SAU. He had his own off duty company and hired deputies to work several events and jobs. I was selling hot and iced coffees in the concession stand at halftime during football season. Branch and I worked full time in the concession stand for basketball season.

Branch and I worked at the racetrack in November. While dropping stuff off at the guy's house that Branch worked with, I met and fell in love with a chunky German shepherd they rescued. They named him Truman and said he was skittish. He had been abused when they rescued him and were looking for a home for him.

I sat on the floor with my hand out and he slowly crawled over to me then put his head in my lap. We had 2 dogs and RockSea had 2 litters of puppies already. We just finished finding homes for the last litter, but my heart went out to this big guy and when I looked at Branch, he shook his head and said, "See if you can get him to get in the car."

I put a leash on him, and he followed me outside while I talked to him. I opened the car door slowly and climbed inside, moving over, to see if he would climb inside with me. He did and put his head in my lap again. We said good-bye. They thanked us for adopting him and we drove home.

It was only a few miles, and the kids were dog lovers. We knew he was afraid of guys, so Branch went in the house first and stayed in DJ's room until I got him inside. I had named him Tankker. He was a tank.

LJ saw him from where she was sitting on the couch and her face lit up. She sat on the floor and let Tankker work his way over to her. The other dogs sniffed him, then went back to their spots to lie down. I took him off the leash and let him roam around. DJ and Branch sat on the floor, but Tankker wouldn't go to them yet.

He became a fixture in our room, lying on my side of the bed. I think he felt safe with the wall to lean on. If someone came in the room, they couldn't see him unless they walked around the end of the bed. Slowly he would sniff around the guys, if there were no sudden movements, but he would run right up to me and LJ.

There was plenty of room in the backyard for all the dogs to run, roam, sniff and do their thing.

In 2009, for mine and Branch's 3rd anniversary, we planned a trip to Napa Valley. KJ was transferred to Oakland and we would stop and see her before we flew home. I found us a great deal at a resort, set up a couples' spa day for us and mapped out the wineries we wanted to go to.

DJ and LJ were old enough to stay home by themselves and my parents were down the road to check on them. Branch and I departed early Wednesday morning and we stayed there until Saturday afternoon. We would spend the night at KJs, before we flew home. My aunt and cousin would be there Saturday also because they were there for a wedding in San Jose.

We drove through the hills and rolling vineyards, found fun hikes, and explored offbeat paths. We found a couple wineries to visit, but the main one I wanted to go to was the castle. We toured the castle, the basements, vineyard and finished in the tasting room, where we learned specifics about the wines, grapes and how to pair them.

We chose the wines we liked. Shipped a case home and bought others for our anniversary dinner. We found carrot cake, our wedding cake, bought fresh calzones from a little Italian place and some snacks for our dinner.

We drank wine, got in the hot tub, right off our room, had more wine, then went to the room for dinner. We ate dinner and cake then we drank the dessert wine, called "il pasita" the pass-out wine. It was a smaller bottle and they had warned us that the alcohol content was higher because the grapes had stayed on the vine longer and had more sugar alcohol.

I don't remember finishing the bottle or the rest of the night. When I woke up the next morning, bathed in sunshine, snuggled in the down comforter with Branch, I laughed and asked what happened. He laughed, "Il pasita." We left early for our spa day to enjoy the hot springs and other amenities before our appointments.

I scheduled us for massages, mud treatments, scrubs, and a seaweed wrap. They had wine, water and snacks set out for us. Soft, fluffy, oversized robes enveloped us. We had our own sitting and relaxing area. We enjoyed the springs. We were both ready for this pampering.

The last morning, we drove to my sister's. It would be the first time, since 2000, that I had seen my aunt and cousin, after seeing them almost daily and weekly, for years. We had a simple dinner, played some games and KJ showed us her condo. It was a 1-bedroom, 1-bath, but it was huge.

She said we could come back and visit so she had time to get a honey-do list together for Branch. We planned to visit over spring break, then we all went to bed because we had an early flight in the morning.

That spring was extra busy. Branch and I were working lots of OT and coaching softball. DJ got his permit and Branch tested to be an engineer. We rented a car and drove to KJ's.

When we arrived, she had her Home Depot list ready. She wanted part of the kitchen wall taken down between the living room and kitchen, so it seemed more open. We were redoing her counters, sink, faucet, and she wanted a back-splash behind the stove.

We spent most of our time in Home Depot while she kept lying tiles out in the pattern with colors she wanted. She told the employee not to touch it when she walked away to get more tiles. He looked afraid. We also changed out the lights to make it brighter before Branch moved on to his "smaller honey do's."

The projects were finished, and she got me hooked on Zuma, a video game on Xbox. I wanted to knock her out for getting me hooked.

We had 3 events coming up for the Relay. We were going to do a survivor celebration by having survivors ride the wagon, decorated in purple, in the annual local parade, before the rodeo. The Remembrance ceremony was going to be at our high school, with a local mom sharing her story of losing her daughter to cancer, when she was in 1st grade. She had gone to school with my nephew and the community had rallied around "Sissy" and her family. The fight back was going to be in the community where the main event would be held, with booths set up for fundraising, awareness, education, advocacy, and the programs offered because of the fundraising we did.

KJ called me a couple weeks after we got home. Her doctor felt a lump in her neck and wanted to get an ultrasound. The ultrasound showed a couple lumps in her thyroid, and the subsequent biopsy proved it was cancer. She scheduled the surgery. I would fly out to be with her.

I requested a week off for her surgery, bought my tickets and flew out. I made her a quilt with all her stuff that I was hanging on to for her. I had a couple of her softball jackets, the dress she wore in our mom's wedding and a couple t-shirts from when she was in the academy. I was going to surprise her with the quilt.

KJ picked me up and surgery was scheduled for the next morning. We knew she would spend at least 1 night in the hospital. Surgery went well and she was resting when her throat started swelling up. She was having trouble breathing and it scared me. I was supposed to go home that night and pick her up in the morning. I didn't know if I would be able to.

They got the swelling taken care of and she told me to go home and sleep because she was going to be a demanding patient when she got home. I went to the grocery store to stock up on soft foods, soups and of course, ice cream. I didn't sleep, but she text and said she was doing good.

We came home. She was a demanding patient, extremely demanding! She loved her quilt. I had spread it out on her bed before she got home. She grabbed it, wrapped it around her and curled up on the couch, asking for ice cream.

We watched *Pride and Prejudice* and other movies throughout the day. I made sure she ate, drank, and rested. I read, wrote, prayed, and cleaned. The doctor said she would have to do a round of I-131 radiation treatment in a couple months. I would come back out to help her again.

When I got home, I was feeling even more off than normal. I was bleeding heavy and cramping. I kept bleeding through tampons, pads and it lasted longer than a week. I gained weight, my face was puffy, and I had to buy bigger pants.

I went to the doctor. They thought I miscarried from a pregnancy, where an egg fertilized in the tubes. There's no place for the fertilized egg to go and is often deadly for women. My thyroid levels were checked again. I gained over 20 lbs. in 1 month.

We went camping for the 4th of July. I was miserable, moody, antsy and couldn't stand being around myself. I couldn't get along with anyone and found a spot to sit, color, read and be alone. I was tired of my own attitude.

A couple days after we got there, I got an email from the event chair for Relay, telling me I was no longer needed to help with the Relay event. How could you get fired from being a volunteer? I was glad. They didn't care about the mission, only the status and recognition they got.

The staff partner said that would give me more time to help with the Southwest Valley RFL event, which would be held October 2009. It was a new event chair, looking for lots of help and guidance. I went and SE, who had been helping with media, came with me.

KM was deployed again and wanted to do a mom/sister cruise for mine and KJ's birthdays, when she returned in August. She paid for the cruise and airplane tickets for everyone to fly into Florida, cruise to the Bahamas and back to Florida. It was a 4-day/3-night cruise, with a stop for snorkeling and shopping in Nassau.

KJ was scheduled for her treatment in September. She was miserable. She had been off her meds for 2 weeks for the treatment. She finished a week of specialized training and was exhausted. We went for a run that afternoon before her treatment the next day. She knew she wouldn't be able to leave the condo after the treatment.

We were almost done with our run, when I felt something snap in the heel of my left foot. It was a searing pain. I had no idea what it was. I couldn't put pressure on it and limped up the hill to her condo.

The next morning, she got her treatment and was confined to her bedroom for a couple days. I tried icing and massaging my foot, but the pain was still there. I wouldn't know until years later, I had plantar fasciitis from standing for hours at a time in boots on concrete, compounded by the quick weight gain.

I got home and made DJ a quilt for his birthday. He was now a senior; LJ was in 8th grade and DJ had shot up several inches over the summer. He had thinned out a lot, was running and riding his bike daily so he could play tight end, as well as tackle.

We were still doing the Thursday night dinners for the student athletes. Before I left for the school, I completed DJ's quilt. We were going to have a party for him that weekend. My grandma was admitted into the hospital for lower back pain. They released her to home hospice. She had cancer. It had started in her liver and metastasized to her spine. They only gave her a couple weeks to live.

Plans changed dramatically. We had cake and ice cream for DJ's birthday and prepared for the final week before the Relay. We realized we needed a new stove after I tried baking a cake and it didn't bake. Branch checked the wires and opened the top of the stove to find a nest of baby mice that I killed when I turned the oven on to preheat.

A hospice nurse stopped by a couple times a week to assist my grandma, but my stepmom was doing most of the work during the day, until I could get there to help. Family started coming in to say their goodbyes. A couple days before the Relay event, Branch got a call from his mom, letting him know she was diagnosed with multiple cell myeloma. We knew there was nothing to cure it, treatment would delay it and a transfusion would postpone it, but her marrow would start attacking again.

Branch and I were devastated. We tried to absorb and deal with everything. We told her we would plan to come up for Christmas and we would stay with her, help her get to her treatments and spend time with her. He told her we would light luminarias in her honor that weekend at the Relay event. The bright side, they talked for over an hour, and she apologized for being stubborn and not standing up for him.

I took time off work to sit, read and pray with my grandma. We had never been close, but she was always a part of my life. DJ had senior night for football. Branch and I walked with him onto the field and there was family there to see him play his last home game. He topped the night off with a TD catch after some great runs.

After showering and eating, we visited Grandma before we went home. Her time was close. We all needed a good night's sleep, and we were back over in the morning. I helped my stepmom bathe and change my grandma, then my dad brought his stud horse, Buster, up and stood outside her window.

I had been reading verses to my grandma throughout the past weeks and was sitting next to her bed, talking with my aunt, cousin, and dad, when she reached out, grabbed my hand, and said, "VERSE," as loud as she could. I was dumbfounded. She looked at me again, pulling me closer to her and said, "VERSE," again.

I grabbed my Bible and opened to the 23rd Psalm, which begins with "Though I walk through the valley of death" and kept reading. My grandma was still grasping my hand. Others started quietly coming into the room. Slowly her grip loosened on my hand. I placed both our hands on the bed, still holding hers.

I kept reading, but it was getting harder to see. I lifted my head. The entire family was in her room. The only noise was my grandma's breathing, "death breathing," and me reading. I felt the tears on my face. It was a matter of hours before she was physically gone, but I felt honored to have fulfilled her last wish of reading verses to her.

I set my Bible down and stood up from my chair, walking silently out of the room. I walked out onto the patio for fresh air. I had read for a couple hours. Branch, the kids and my cousin came out to sit with me. The rest of the night consisted of people moving in and out of my grandma's room.

Branch and the kids said goodbye, I kissed her on the forehead and her hand, said I love you, then we went to lie down on the pull-out sofa. At about 3 A.M., I heard my stepmom and my dad as my grandma took her last breath. Even though we knew the end was near for that final moment, you're never fully prepared.

The decision was made to have her cremated, have a small celebration of life in AZ, then have one in NY, the following weekend, which would give everyone time to get there. I went back to work for a couple days, then Branch and I flew to NY, taking the redeye and getting there the morning of the celebration.

My back had been bothering me for months and on the plane I couldn't get comfortable. My lower back felt like it was on fire, so I didn't sleep on the plane. My aunt picked us up at the airport and drove us to the fire hall where we were having the celebration.

SE rode to NY with my dad and stepmom and we were going to ride back home with them. The trip was a whirlwind of people, memories, and it was the first time all 5 of us girls had been together since 2000. After the celebration, we went to the local bar next to the firehall to dance, drink, shoot pool and let loose.

The next morning, we met at the corner diner for breakfast before everyone headed out. I had to be back to work by Wednesday. I was scheduled for a 2-day class to finish my detective certification. My dad was starting a new job and Branch didn't have any more PTO to take.

We got home Tuesday, spent time with the kids, then crashed. I had to be out of the house by 5 because of traffic and class started at 7. I finished class Thursday and was back to work Friday.

When I got to work Friday, my supervisor, Brock called me into his office. He tried acting concerned about my grandma dying but called me in to tell me I needed to get my priorities straight.

I had taken time off for my grandma, went out of town for bereavement, then came back and had a 2-day training. My priorities were right where they needed to be, family would always come first. He was the one that told me to take the class, no matter what. I still got my work done and had been able to keep up with my caseload while helping others, even with time off.

I was furious. I threw his office door open, which echoed throughout the building when it slammed the wall. I headed to Lt. Strong's office. As soon as he saw my face, he told me to come in and shut the door. I told him what happened. He was pissed. He just talked to him about not saying anything to me. Lt said he would talk to Brock again.

I walked back to my office. Everyone started coming by to find out what happened. I was sick of being treated like crap and being disrespected. My squad took me to lunch to get me out of the office and told me I couldn't transfer because they would be lost with everything I did behind the scenes.

I said I would sleep on it and decide after the first of the year. We did my search warrant the following week, working 50 hours straight from briefing, to SW, interviews, and bookings. It was a long couple of days and most of us were working the racetrack that weekend.

The last night of the races, we had cones set up for traffic egress and we stood by the cones with flashlights, directing traffic into the lanes. We were almost done when a big vehicle was hauling ass towards me and my partner. I had nowhere to go. I kept flickering my flashlight towards the driver, trying to get his attention. The closer he got, the harder I prayed and at the last minute he swerved to the left, missing me, but close enough that I hit his back taillight with my flashlight.

I called it out over the radio, described the vehicle and my partner said, "You can't miss it, it's flying over the dirt berms dividing the parking lots and has a broken right taillight." The deputies on 4-wheelers raced towards the vehicle and got it stopped. The driver was intoxicated and didn't see me but saw a light flickering which caused him to turn.

The deputies told him he narrowly missed hitting a deputy that was directing traffic. Once they said the guy was in custody, a couple of the guys came over to get my statement for the report. I felt the adrenaline dump coming. One of the deputies had been my RTO in the academy and sat me down, knowing what was coming.

I called Branch on my way home and said I was done working PIR. Once I got home and showered, I told him what happened and let the emotions out. I could see the guy's face clearly as he barreled toward me in what ended up being a Chevy Tahoe. I wouldn't have stood a chance.

The next month passed with basketball games for DJ, lots of work, Branch's firefighter union Christmas party and getting ready for our trip to MN. Some of the union guys had contacted me for some pics of Branch during training. He was being awarded "Union Member of the Year" and "Booter of the Year."

This year we had to go because Branch was getting the awards. I wore a dress, my knee-high black boots, and my new red "Jenna Jameson" robe or as the guys I worked with dubbed it, my "Hugh Hefner" robe and had a great time. I got to know some of the guys he worked with better, as well as their spouses.

We decided to rent a car and drive to MN, in case Devlin let us have the kids. We promised the kids sledding and playing in the snow, hot cocoa, and cookies. This was the first Christmas Eve wagon ride we would be missing, but the kids just wanted to play in the snow for Christmas. We took Branch's mom to her first chemo appointments, sitting with her and getting to know the nurses.

Branch left a message for Devlin. We took DJ and LJ out to play in the snow at the park behind the house. That night Branch's mom, Caryn, and his brother, apologized for the way they acted towards Branch and me. She appreciated that I took the time to sit and write her a letter. She still had it and was thankful to be able to spend time with us and get to know me and the kids.

We went to see Branch's dad. They were calling for a blizzard later that night and the next day. We still hadn't heard from Devlin. We were 10-15 minutes from his dad's house when she called and said we could pick the kids up in 2 hours. Initially, I was elated because we would get to see them and they were going to be able to spend the night with us, but I was irritated she waited until she knew the forecast called for a blizzard, putting all of us at risk.

We told Branch's dad we couldn't stay long because Devlin was letting us have the kids, but we now had over a 2-hour drive to get them, then another 45-minute drive back to his mom's. It was already snowing by the time we got the kids. Devlin went off about her money, but we got the kids loaded and headed to his mom's.

By the time we got off the freeway, visibility was almost zero, there was freezing rain and the windshield wipers kept freezing up. The 45-minute drive took twice as long because of the weather. Branch was trying to get a conversation started with the kids. At one point his son, EM, told us his mom said I was older than dirt and asked what it meant.

She was ridiculous. It's sad that dads get such a bad rap when there are many toxic and narcissistic moms raising kids. I calmly asked, "If I was older than dirt, what did that make grandmas and his grandpa?" I asked him if it would be nice to say that about them. He said no, then I asked if it was nice to say things like that about anyone. After thinking about it for a minute, he said no.

We arrived at the house and got ready for bed. The kids were sleeping in the living room and wanted Branch to sleep with them. When I started saying goodnight, the girls yelled, "No, Suzy, you have to sleep with us, too," and Branch said, "Yeah, Suzy."

The next morning, we had breakfast then took the kids out to play in the snow before their mom picked them up. I noticed HM, the oldest, didn't have any winter boots or pants. I asked her where her boots were, and she said she didn't have any. I knew the kids had been walking to and from school, and from the daycare house which was at least a half-mile.

We went and played in the park for an hour, then the kids were cold and ready to go back. We needed to take HM to get boots and pants. It was negligent she would be walking in this weather without the proper clothing.

We went to Ross. I found a pair of snow pants and boots that fit HM. We would keep them at her grandma's in the event they were allowed to visit again before we left. If not, they would be available when she next visited her grandma. Devlin arrived to pick the kids up. There was a physical change that came over them. They looked upset and scared.

Hopefully, we would see them again before we had to go home. Branch brought his first fire helmet to give to EM for Christmas and I was making pillows for the girls out of his old work shirts. I was making little hearts to stick in the pocket, so they knew they always had his heart.

We wrapped the presents, whether we saw them before we left or they came over to visit Branch's mom, they would be there. We took DJ and LJ out sledding at the big hill and as much as I hate snow, I had fun, too. We stayed out for hours, sliding down the hill and climbing back up. We tried our surf sledding skills, falling several times, and rolling down the hills.

We were exhausted, ready for food and cocoa. When we got to the house, his mom said HM called and wanted Branch to call her back. He called back and she said their mom would drop them off the next day and they could spend the night with us again, then she would pick them up Christmas Eve, after dinner.

We were shocked. Branch told them to bring their snow clothes so we could go sledding on the big hill.

Devlin dropped the kids off the next day and I stayed in the house while the kids got their stuff out of the car. Branch went out on the front steps to help them carry their bags in. We got everyone in and settled, made sure everyone was fed, then bundled everyone up to go to the big hill. It had started snowing again, sledding would be great.

We played in the snow for hours. We built snowmen, made snow angels, had snowball fights, and raced in the snow. Our hearts were full to create these precious memories with all the kids, as a family. DJ and LJ were loved on. KM wouldn't leave LJ's side. She climbed on her lap, held her hand and wanted LJ to always sit and lay beside her.

The next day we had pancakes and went out in the yard to play in the snow again. It was cold. We didn't get too far from the house. After lunch and cocoa, we had the kids open their presents. EM asked DJ and LJ where their presents were. They said their present was coming to play in the snow and meet them. He thought about it, said, "Oh," and went back to his present.

We watched a movie and read books before their mom came, savoring the little moments. We were leaving the 27th and Devlin said we could pick the kids up the following night and bring them home the 26th.

After dropping the kids off on the 26th, we worked it out with Devlin to allow us to bring the kids to AZ in June and bring them back in July. She agreed to it, and we prayed she didn't change her mind.

The day before we left, I got an email saying I was preapproved for a house loan and the realtor said we could start looking at houses when we got back. I was so excited, I started crying. We would have our new house when Branch's kids came down for the summer.

The realtor sent me houses and I narrowed down the ones I wanted to look at. We set an appointment for a few days after New Year's Day. New Year's Eve we had our final celebration in our current house.

I was preapproved for a large amount, but I didn't want to spend that much money and be house poor. The first day, we looked at a 2100-square-foot, 3-bedroom, 2½-bathroom on over 2 acres, with a 2-car garage. The house was just over a year old, and the owner was just trying to get rid of it. The kids chose which rooms would be theirs then sat in the living room, saying where the TV and couch would be.

The 2nd house was 3600 square feet, 4 bedrooms, 3 bathrooms, 2.5 acres and 2-car garage. The house was gorgeous. The only downfall was the kitchen, there wasn't much counter space.

The next house was the biggest, also the most expensive. It didn't have the cozy feel. We looked at a couple more homes and none appealed to us.

I was done looking at houses. I found 3 we all liked and wanted to narrow those down so we could move. We sat down and listed pros and cons of each house. We narrowed it down to the first 2 we had seen.

The remaining two option were 2 miles from each other, on the same street. We all agreed we wanted the first house we looked at. It was cheap, DJ would be graduating that spring and going to college, so we didn't need a big house.

I called the realtor and told her the house we wanted. She said she would get started with the paperwork. I was getting the loan in my name only. I had the credit and the long-standing job. Also, Devlin couldn't try to take it in the future.

Everything moved forward quickly. On our 4th anniversary, we celebrated buying our first house together. We got all the inspections done and the other paperwork that goes with buying a house. We would close the end of February and could start moving in.

We started packing and downsizing, storing boxes in the shed, rented a U-Haul and planned to load everything Friday, after we signed. We would clean the house before we started moving in. Branch and I planned to sleep at the new house Friday night, then finish moving Saturday.

A few nights before we moved, I got a call from my mom. Her youngest sister died after they tried removing a tumor from her kidney. This was the aunt that came to live with us for a few weeks after leaving an abusive relationship. Her and my mom were close. My aunt was a light to so many and would be missed.

The rest of the week passed in a blur of working, packing, and grieving. We figured out how to move my "clubhouse" that we got in 2009. It was formerly a "crow's nest" for rodeo announcers. It sat off the ground, was 8x12 with windows across the front of it. There were steel stairs welded to the entire steel pipe frame and it stood about 8 feet off the ground.

Getting it from the rodeo grounds to our house originally took a lot of ingenuity, 2 trucks, a winch, tow straps and 12 people guiding it down to the trailer. Branch said he would cut the steel pipes, just under the floor, transport the top, then transport the frame. When we put it back up, he would weld the frame back on, but he would cut the frame down, so it was only 6 feet off the ground.

The first order of business was putting a fence up. RockSea had become an explorer, taking off as soon as she found an opening. We also had to keep Saba and Tankker separated because they had started fighting.

We couldn't figure out why there was a sudden change in them until a neighbor said another neighbor, whom we didn't like, was aggravating and agitating the dogs when we were gone.

We had gotten into a fight with the problem neighbor over the water bill in the spring because we were on a shared well. The bill came to them, and they were supposed to give us a copy of the bill, then we paid what we owed. We paid the bill every time we got it, but the wife hadn't given us a bill in months. I asked her about it, and she said it wasn't fair we were paying the same amount when they used more water daily for their cows and horses.

Our portion of the bill was less than $40 for 6 months for the past few years. When I asked for it, she said not to worry about it. One day we were out front of our house, planting flowers when the neighbors were leaving. The neighbor yelled something out the window and Branch asked him if he had a problem.

The neighbor backed up and said, "Yeah, I have a problem, you're spending money on flowers and trees, but you can't seem to pay the water bill." I snapped my head up and looked directly at his wife and said I had been asking for the bill for months. She was in the passenger seat shaking her head, looking scared to death. If I said anything more, he would probably hit her or something. I didn't say anything further.

Branch told him if he had a problem, then talk like a man and stop acting like a pussy, hiding in the truck with his wife and kids. The boys were in the back seat, hiding their heads from embarrassment. I felt bad for them. The neighbor said something else about me. Branch was fired up. He dropped the pick and told the neighbor to get out of the truck and say that shit to our face.

I put my hand on Branch's arm and told him he wasn't worth our time or energy; he was just a miserable bully. I told him to get the water bill to me that night and he would get his money, but he'd better not say shit to us again.

When I got the bill, it was $36.71. I wrote a check, so we had proof, then I put it in a big envelope, with a copy of the water bill, with a big piece of posterboard that said, "Here's your damn money for the $36.71 water bill and I added extra so we're covered for the next year." I had written the check for $100 and made it out to his wife.

When we moved, it was the best feeling in the world.

Branch was finishing the fence when RockSea escaped. Saba decided to join her and followed. Branch went out looking for them and couldn't find her. We waited to see if we would get a call. They both had their collars on. Branch finished putting the fence up and Tankker was exploring his new home.

While we were painting LJ's room and Branch was outside grilling dinner, we heard shouting. Branch came in and said there was a domestic dispute at the neighbor's, 1 house west of us. The yelling got louder, and I went running out back to check. It must have been going on for some time inside the house because we saw 3 sheriff cars fly down the road.

When they finished and were leaving, they saw us outside and asked if we'd seen or heard anything. When they got closer, they realized it was me and asked me why I hadn't taken the call. I told them we just moved in that day, but I remember responding to that house a couple years prior for a domestic violence call.

I asked if the female was Brazilian. They said yeah and I told them it was the same couple, describing the bedroom. They were booking both. She said she just wanted to go back to Brazil, but he wouldn't let her leave.

We never heard or saw them again and a year later we had new neighbors. Thankfully, it has been a quiet neighborhood since.

The U-Haul and trailer were unloaded, and the guys would put my shed up the next day. When we woke up the next morning, RockSea was lying on the front porch, in front of the door, as if that was her spot. While we were eating breakfast, I got a call from a lady, a couple miles north of us saying Saba was on their front porch.

I had to take furlough time because all the agencies were experiencing budget issues. I took my 9 days all at once so we could paint and unpack.

We talked about what they were learning in school and LJ said she was learning about the reproductive system. She drew a picture of the female reproductive system. It was in her bag and could show us.

I told her to paint it on the wall. We could paint over it. Before we finished painting, we had ovaries, a vagina and a penis painted in wine red on our dining room wall, which was still mostly white. We made the house ours.

By the end of the weekend, we had all the boxes unpacked and everything put away. We did our first grocery shopping trip to fill the fridge, freezer, and pantry. The house was officially our "home."

Branch and I were busy coaching and I was playing softball with our local bar and grill. We were mentally and emotionally preparing for Senior Night for DJ. We watched and cheered him over the years, it was hard, we were in the last days of his high school sports.

My dad had a growth removed from his face. It was skin cancer. The growth was under his eye, and it was bigger than they initially thought. They also removed skin cancer from his ears. Thankfully, they got it all and he had to make sure he covered his ears when in the sun.

We participated in another Relay event. KM was the event chair, and we were in the planning stages for our fall RFL event for the southwest valley. I was now the official event chair for that event and Branch was my logistics specialist.

We were in full preparation for DJ's graduation and party. We were having it at the house, with tables, chairs and tents set up in the driveway and garage.

We had a small dinner after graduation and the party was going to be Saturday. The party was a lot of fun, with people in and out all day throughout the evening.

DJ and Branch were going to leave in a couple weeks to drive and pick up the kids from MN. After the party we got everything cleaned up and prepared for 3 extra kids.

I had gone for a mammogram after feeling something different in my breast and they wanted to send me for an ultrasound. I had started doing "functional fitness" aka CrossFit without the licensed name because I had continued to gain weight. I gained over 80 lbs. since 2006. I was now 240 lbs. I had to do something different.

I started seeing a new doctor. He was worse than the previous. When I told him that I could feel something was off inside and I hated being around myself, he told me I needed to reduce my stress, work out more and stop eating as much. He said what I was feeling was in my head because my thyroid levels were stable.

The day after DJ and Branch got back with the kids, I had my ultrasound. I had done one of my first workouts with my squad, which included hundreds of squats. When we got to the doctor's office, I had to use the handicap handrail to help lower myself and to stand back up while going to the bathroom. The ultrasound showed what I felt was a cyst.

We took all the kids camping and they loved it. We went fishing, they participated in the parade, we went horseback riding and exploring. Branch flew to MN with the kids, then flew back to AZ after Devlin picked the kids up at the airport.

DJ would be moving in the middle of August to start college and LJ was starting high school. I wasn't ready for any of it.

Branch told me about one of the guys at work doing a diet with HCG and he lost 20 lbs. We tried it to see if it would help. It was a low-calorie diet, eating no sugar, oils, or fats, while giving myself a shot of HCG daily. I had to try something, and I did well with it. I lost almost 30 lbs. and was down to 210 lbs.

We were in final planning mode for our RFL event. DJ was going to come home for the weekend, which would be his first weekend home since he left for college. LJ and one of her friends were in front of the local store fundraising and selling luminaria bags for the RFL event, when I met one of the local vets.

He was in a wheelchair and was currently fighting cancer. He found out I was also a vet and told me I should join the local American Legion, which they just moved to our town. I got his info; told him I was going to purchase a luminaria in his honor and invited him to the event for the survivor's lap.

DJ called while we were there. He normally didn't call so it was important. I answered and he said, "Mom, don't be mad, I'm okay, but I was arrested for underage drinking last night at a party," then he told me I had to show up for his court appearance because he wasn't 18 yet.

I was in disbelief. He'd been arrested after staying out of trouble his entire high school years. I asked for the specifics. He told me what he remembered, but it wasn't much.

I sat down on the bench, with my head down. Branch saw me sit and came over to find out what was wrong. He was as shocked as me. I was ready to pack up and go home. I needed to think and let it all sink in, then call DJ back.

Branch and I drove the 2 ½ hours to DJ's college, picked him and another girl up that were arrested and took them to court. The girl was 18 and didn't need her parents, but she was glad we were there. There were 8 kids total that were cited at the party. DJ was the only one under 18.

The judge read the police report and the charges. We found out someone called in a noise complaint. When the cops got to the apartment, DJ and another kid had been playing beer pong. The cops told them not to move. DJ was going to be sick and ran to the bathroom.

The female cop thought he was trying to attack her. She felt threatened when he pushed her arm down so he could get to the toilet. He was sick, but the female officer said she felt threatened, which was why all the kids got cited.

When it came to DJ's turn to stand, the judge looked at his information, then looked at DJ and asked, "Are you 18 yet?" DJ said, "No, my birthday is the following weekend, but my parents are there with me." We stood up and the judge shook his head saying DJ shouldn't be in his court because he was a juvie, according to the law. After looking at the charges and the kids, he said all of them would be on unsupervised probation for 6 months.

He told DJ he would also be on unsupervised probation and as long as he finished probation without getting into trouble, nothing would be on his record. We thanked the judge and were grateful for the outcome. All the kids would still have clean records if they stayed out of trouble the next 6 months.

DJ said he wasn't drinking anymore. He didn't want to risk his chance of being able to go in the military. We took the kids to lunch and were able to joke about everything. I asked DJ if he remembered anything that was in the report, and he said he didn't. He vaguely remembered he was going to be sick, but that was all.

We dropped the kids off and headed back home. We would see DJ the following weekend. We planned a small party at the house for Friday night, then we were going to the SWV RFL the next morning. Branch's mom and uncle flew in that morning so she could do the survivor lap with me and my dad.

One of the deputies I worked with, who had been part of the "Women of Maricopa County" show, was going to come out for pictures and sign autographs. We had Rick as the DJ, and Evelyn would walk beside me during the survivor lap.

We had a full track, filled with teams from local schools, businesses, families, and friends. I walked the survivor lap with my dad and Branch's mom, friends and strangers that became friends. There were events and activities for everyone leading up to the luminaria ceremony.

There wasn't a dry eye in the house as we shared of love, loss, grief, courage, strength, and hope, remembering our loved ones no longer with us and honoring those that had fought or were still fighting. Each bag had a name with a candle inside, reminding us that every candle has a name.

The mood slowly shifted from melancholy to one of determination, a reminder of why we were all there, staying up all night, raising money and walking, we were fighting back against cancer.

LJ started playing basketball, she was playing JV and varsity. I loved watching her grow into her talent and confidence. She had never been interested in playing basketball, but the coach told LJ she'd better be at practice and LJ went. She fell in love with the game.

The coach was taking over the softball program and asked Branch and I if we would help coach again. She said we could start working with the girls before basketball ended, then she would help after basketball.

My chiro referred me to a spinal specialist for my neck/shoulder/scapula and she had given me some injections to help with the pain. I had to go back after Christmas for more.

The beginning of November, my mom called to let me know that my uncle had been diagnosed with cancer and they'd only given him a few weeks to live. My uncle had refused treatment, instead choosing to spend his remaining days lucid, sharing memories with all the American Legion guys he'd been members with since coming home from Vietnam, and spending time with his family.

My mom called to let me know he passed peacefully in his sleep, after spending hours with his old buddies and family. He was at peace. He had been a huge part of my childhood. He was married to my mom's oldest sister, and we used to go there Friday or Saturday nights so they could play cards, drink, and catch up.

He gave me one of the greatest hugs before I left for basic training, then again when I came home from Desert Storm. I could see how proud he was and knew he talked about me with the legion guys.

Branch's grandma passed away the end of November and his mom asked us if we would stay with her when we came up. We flew up for the funeral and I told Branch I wanted to make a quilt for his mom. We could buy fabric, cut it into squares and have people write messages for her at the funeral.

We found a few different fabrics that would work, I cut them into 7x7 squares, bought fabric pens and sharpies, then put them in a Ziploc bag to have at the funeral.

The kids sat with us during the funeral. I told them what we were doing for their grandma's quilt and asked if they would help us secretly get people to write messages for her. They were excited to be part of the secret mission and by the end of the funeral and gathering, we had all the squares signed by family, friends, and coworkers.

The kids each did a square and I kept a couple out for DJ and LJ.

LJ was having a small party with friends for her 14th birthday, after their basketball game. I brought cake to the game so the girls could sing happy birthday after the game and have some cake.

Branch, my sisters and I were invited to the private Christmas party at the local bar and grill. Drinks were free and everyone was asked to bring a dish or dessert. KM was going with us and staying the night so she could drink and not worry about driving home. DJ was home from college for winter break, so he was our DD that night.

KM had gotten married a couple years prior, but he didn't come out with us. We went to the party, talking with people we had gotten to know in the community. As the night went on, someone said something about dancing on the bar, like coyote ugly and my sister said she was in. I was wearing a dress and passed.

I could see things going south after a couple songs and noticed KM flirting with some of the guys. I told Branch I was going to get her off the bar and we would go home. KM wouldn't come down and I laughed, trying to keep it peaceful.

It took me 10 minutes to get her off the bar and when I looked at Branch, I could tell he was mad about something. I asked him if he'd text DJ to pick us up and he just said, yeah. He was short with me.

We got home and started getting ready for bed. Branch was slamming things around. After I put my robe on, I came out to ask him what was wrong. He had another drink. He'd had more to drink than I realized. He wouldn't talk to me. I started to follow him into the room when he slammed the door in my face.

I put my hand up to stop the door and got angry. I yelled at him to tell me what was wrong instead of acting stupid. He pushed back against the door to shut it and I had my arm up to stop it. I still had no idea what was wrong. He was cussing at me. I was finally able to push my way into the room.

He was grabbing for my purse. I ran over and grabbed my purse, sliding my hand and wrist through it. I was scared. I had never seen him like this and still had no idea what was wrong.

He was yelling at me, but nothing was making sense. KM was on the couch, trying to stay out of it. DJ was in his room, but left his door open, making sure everything was okay. Branch started saying if I didn't want him there, then he would leave, and I wouldn't have to worry about him again.

We had similar arguments like this over the years as our family adjusted to being a blended family. He was used to being verbally and psychologically abused by Devlin. I kept reinforcing I wasn't her and the kids and I wanted him to be part of our family.

When he started getting more aggressive at taking my purse, I yelled at him to stop acting like an ass and a fucking child. He yanked on my purse again, breaking the strap off my arm and opened it on the bed to grab my car keys. I wrestled with him to get the keys, not sure what he was going to do. He was in no condition to drive, and my gun was locked in the car.

We had been fighting for 30 minutes. Tensions were high, adrenaline was pumping and both of us were angry, but for different reasons. I was crying and begging him to stop acting like this when he got my keys out of my hands. He started running out of the house to the garage and opened the garage door.

I yelled, "Noooooo!" really loud and yelled for DJ to help me. I ran out the door and Branch was in my car. I saw him searching for something, then DJ ran out of the house, pushing past me to the car. He started talking loudly, but calmly to Branch while he wrestled with him to restrain him.

DJ had the advantage because he was sober. DJ got the keys from him and got him out of the car. I was on my knees, bawling, scared, and lost at what to do. I felt hopeless and devastated.

KM came outside and told Branch to come in the house with her. She took him in the room and talked to him, calming him down while I sat on the kitchen floor sobbing. DJ asked if anything happened at the party and I said no, we were fine till KM started dancing on the bar and flirting with guys, then things changed.

He asked me if I had danced on the bar. I tried discouraging KM from doing it. I was holding my arm, without realizing it and DJ asked if I was okay. He asked to look at my arm. There was a large knot on the outside of my forearm, with a big bruise forming. My arm looked deformed, but I knew it wasn't broke. I could still use it and put pressure on it.

DJ calmed me down, got me a box of tissues, then KM came out and said Branch was okay. He just wanted me to listen to him and was asking for me. I hugged DJ and thanked him for being there to help, thanked KM, then went in the room. Branch put his hand out to me, but I sat on the side of the bed.

He scared me and I was afraid he was trying to hurt himself. I told him I wouldn't have survived something happening to him, especially if it was because of me. He was sorry, he didn't know what he was doing or was going to do, but he was glad DJ was there to stop him from doing something stupid or harmful.

I grabbed my purse off the bed. The strap was broken in the middle and at the buckle. It was my favorite purse. He put his hand over mine, saying he was sorry. I was crying again, and he asked me to look at him, but I told him it was hard because I hadn't recognized him during those moments.

He sat up, pulling me into his arms, kissing my head, telling me how sorry he was, and it would never happen again. I was fighting exhaustion and he helped me into bed, then snuggled behind me.

I still had tears falling when I fell asleep, but my husband was back. When we woke in the morning, I rolled over to look at him and he apologized again, while he softly tucked my hair out of my face, behind my ear. I needed to know what set him off because I was at a complete loss.

The alcohol was part of it, but he said when my sister was dancing on the bar and he saw me shaking my head, but chuckling, he thought it was something I was condoning, a married woman dancing on the bar, flirting with guys. The more he thought about it, he wondered if this was the kind of behavior I was okay with doing when he wasn't with me. The whiskey fueled his anger.

When I went to get her off the bar and laughed, that tipped him, and he wasn't rationale. He didn't know what he wanted from me, but he wanted to do something to get my attention and as we argued, he couldn't stop the spiraling thoughts.

When DJ got the keys and got him out of the car, he saw me kneeling, crying, he was able to think straight again. He knew he could never forgive himself for causing me that much pain and talking to my sister was more about him just wanting to talk to me.

When I got up to use the bathroom, he saw my arm. He jumped out of bed and asked to see my arm. He tenderly touched it and looked at me with such sadness in his eyes. He asked if he had done that. It must have happened when I tried pushing through the door, but he hadn't physically harmed me in any way.

I went to the bathroom. He waited, then wrapped his arms around me when I was done. He would never physically hurt me and never meant to hurt me emotionally. We needed to learn to communicate better, and he needed to work out his demons from his first marriage so we could grow together.

Branch contacted a therapist through our insurance and set up ongoing phone appointments.

It was the last year we would be doing the Christmas Eve Wagon ride in our old neighborhood. I had leftover toys that were donated, to distribute on our last stop, a small trailer park with families living in poverty. It was one of the best rides. Watching the kids' faces light up as Santa came by, then his helpers give them a toy.

We would continue this tradition, but we were going to do it closer to where we lived. Branch had to work Christmas Day and we planned to make dinner for the crew and spend the day with them. He was still bothered by his behavior, but he was getting help and we were working through things together.

I went back to the spinal specialist for more shots. She wanted me to get an MRI of my neck before she moved further with spinal and neck manipulations. She scheduled the MRI, and my follow-up appointment would be January 14th, our 5th anniversary.

Branch and I decided to have dinner at home, to celebrate with our family. We chose to do crab legs, shrimp, and steak. I went for my MRI, then we went back for my follow-up. As soon as we walked in, I could tell by her face that things weren't good.

She brought my MRI up and showed me the images. She asked if I saw the lumps. Those were possibly goiters, which grow out of the thyroid, but it could also be Thyroid cancer. She referred me to my primary care physician, PCP, to get them checked out.

There were at least 15 different spots on the scans. One of them was large and close to my windpipe. I asked her if that's why I was having trouble breathing while I worked out. She said it was most likely the large goiter was pressing on my windpipe, especially when my neck was extended.

I looked at Branch, with tears in my eyes and said, "I'm sorry. This isn't how we planned to celebrate our 5-year anniversary." He grabbed my hand, wrapped his arm around my shoulders, pulling me close to his side, with his head on mine and told me we were still together which is what counted. He was by my side, no matter what and we would meet whatever was coming, as a team.

We left to do the shopping for dinner and pick up the special carrot cake that I ordered as a surprise for Branch. I called my PCP to set up an appointment, then tried to push the thoughts out of my head.

After we got home, we sat down with LJ and texted DJ saying we wanted to FaceTime him before the party. We told them both what was going on, so they weren't surprised when we shared with the family at dinner. They each had questions, but said we were going to fight it like a family. DJ wanted to know as soon as we heard anything.

We broke the news to the family that night. I was helping train team captains around AZ the next few weekends and shared my story as things unfolded with the doctor appointments. It kept me busy, along with work, instead of thinking about what it could be.

By now, my squad had taken over a large room. We kicked the HSU guys out, so our entire squad was together for better efficiency. We were always in each other's offices anyhow so we figured this would be the best solution for us to spend the day bull shitting and messing with each other while also being productive.

I saw my PCP who referred me to a thyroid specialist. He looked at my MRI and set up an appointment for an ultrasound-guided needle biopsy on the nodes. My stepmom and Branch came with me to the ultrasound. The doctor said there were 7 nodes he was going to test.

He warned me I would feel the pricks and pressure as he drew the fluid out. He allowed Branch and my stepmom in during the procedure. He would have the results in the next couple weeks, but I would need surgery. One of the goiters was pressing on my windpipe and another was almost at my carotid artery.

If there was any cancer, or chance of it, he wanted to remove everything before it grew into my carotid. He told me to find a surgeon and recommended a couple he worked with.

The next day, I told Lt. Strong what was going on, after he asked me what had happened to my neck. He referred me to a surgeon that he worked with when he was in the Air Force. He said the guy was an ENT, ears, nose, throat doctor, but also cross trained in plastic surgery so he left almost no scarring.

I contacted the ENT and they set me up to come in the end of February. He had access to my records and tests and told me one of the biopsies showed cancer. They weren't 100% accurate, but plan for that frame of mind, just in case.

I loved the doctor and his nurse. He talked to Branch and me about the procedure, what to expect before, during and after surgery. He showed me where he would cut, then he would remove the entire thyroid with all the goiters and depending on how the parathyroid glands looked, he would remove those too.

He would contact me once they had a date and time for surgery. I asked if we could push the surgery toward the end of March so I could clear up some of my open cases and give my sister time to request leave for 2 weeks.

Branch and I were still helping with softball. LJ was now playing for us, continually amazing us with her athletic ability. We had started planning for the SWV RFL that would be in October, coordinating team captains, vendors, and new team recruitment. I told the committee I would be having surgery, March 29, 2011, and Branch would keep everyone updated via my Facebook page.

Branch and I celebrated our "You had me at hello" anniversary on St. Patrick's Day. We took LJ and my oldest niece with us while they were on spring break. We went downtown to the place we met like we had the previous years, but soon left. The atmosphere seemed different that year and we wanted the girls to have fun, too. Normally, there were Irish dancers, bands, and other fun activities, but this year was more subdued.

We decided to drive back to our local bar and grill for some green beer and to meet my sisters. We got the huge booth so we could all fit in and enjoyed the rest of the night with family and friends.

I asked SE if she would help with coaching while we were gone and make sure LJ got home after the game. It was a 3-hour ride, 1 way and we knew it would be a late night for them. My other 2 sisters, KJ and KM, were going to be at the hospital waiting with Branch. A couple guys he worked with were also going to wait with him, along with my dad and stepmom.

I kissed him as they rolled me to the operating room. They had given me a sedative to help me relax. I remember being in the OR, going from the hospital bed to the surgical table. I remember how cold it was and asked for more blankets. My surgeon came in and made sure he looked in my eyes, then said, ready to do this? They told me to count back from 100. I only remember 99.

Surgery went well. He took out my entire thyroid. There were 19 goiters growing out of my thyroid and he removed some lymph nodes in my upper chest, to make sure there was nothing that spread. The initial biopsy showed there was no cancer, but the doctor said though it was good news, we needed the full biopsy for results.

I woke up in my room. I saw my dad, Branch, and my dad's ranch friend. I always called him a grumpy old goat and that's the first thing I said when I woke up. Everyone laughed and said I must be feeling better. They told me the initial info the doctors had told them, Branch said he had text, SE, and he called LJ then text DJ, who was in class.

I had visitors all day. My squad was doing a detail in the area, so they showed up in their tactical vests and gear to say hi. It was hard to talk because of the swelling, but they had me laughing before they left.

Branch and KJ spent the night with me, taking shifts sitting with me, while the other tried to get some sleep in the front seat of the truck. I didn't sleep well. I had an awful headache and the morphine made me nauseous. I asked if I could just take ibuprofen and they added some into my IV, which helped the headache.

The doctor came in the next morning to check my incision, said it looked good, explained the drainage tubes he'd put on both ends of the incision and told Branch what to look for in case of infection. He told me that if my vitals were good, he would let me go that day because no one got rest in hospitals.

I had to keep the bandage on until I saw him April 7th. I was leaving the hospital by 1 P.M. in the afternoon. Branch and KJ got me home, settled in the bed and let me sleep. I told Branch to go to practice, KJ had the watch.

He went and brought LJ home after. They had a home game the next day and I told Branch that I wanted to go, just to watch. He asked me if I could really "just" watch, without yelling and cheering. I grinned and said as much as my neck hurt, I would behave myself.

He went up early, set up our canopy to give me shade, put chairs for me and KJ, right next to the dugout, by home plate where we could see the entire action, then came home and picked us up. All the girls were excited to see me at the game and said, "We're gonna win this game for you, Coach," and got ready to play. KJ was awed by how much I meant to the kids when the coach handed me a huge envelope filled with cards and drawings from the girls, parents, and staff.

April 7th, we planned a dinner with Kurt and Goldie, and a couple other friends, after my doctor's appointment. Branch and I sat in the waiting room, holding hands tightly, waiting for the doctor to call us in.

10
You Have Cancer...Again

The doctor sat me down, grabbed my hand and said, "Honey, you have cancer, again."

I didn't cry when he told me, I nodded and said okay. I wore a vest, carried a gun, and risked my life in a job, knowing I may possibly take a bullet. I wasn't going to cry over cancer. I beat it once and cancer doesn't mean an automatic death sentence.

He said I was one of the toughest and bad-ass people he ever met, as well as the most inspiring. Then I teared up and laughed. He chuckled, and said my weak spot was taking a compliment. Branch laughed, "You have no idea, Doc."

He took the bandage off and handed me a mirror. I could see the drainage tubes and an ugly incision but knew it would heal. It was a badge of honor to show his work.

There were stitches inside that would dissolve. In a week he would take the outer ones out. If Branch was comfortable taking them out, then we didn't have to come back. Branch shrugged his shoulders, grinned, and said, sure.

We stopped at Walmart before meeting Kurt and Goldie for lunch. As we walked around, I saw a crayon tower and stopped to look at it. It had a handle in the middle that pulled up into a tower of crayons. Branch grabbed it off the shelf and told me it was for being good at the doctor's.

Lunch was emotional, but I showed off my crayon tower. We had drinks and laughs before we went home. In the quiet, the emotions overcame me. I appreciated Branch being by my side every step. I told him how alone I felt the first time, even when I was surrounded by people.

We were a team, united in the fight. The next day we got a letter in the mail. Devlin was taking Branch back to court. We had to fill out a bunch of papers for financials, household expenses and a list of assets. We had to send the paperwork back by the end of April, then we were notified that the judge had set a hearing for the end of June if we didn't resolve with mediation.

We couldn't fight this on our own. As the case was in MN, we had to get an attorney that practiced in MN. We found a couple attorneys, but the one we wanted was the most expensive and we needed a $5000 retainer for their firm to begin. My medical bills were piling up. We had insurance, but insurance covered 90%. We had to pay 10% in coinsurance.

I was paying DJ's tuition and meal plan, until I could only pay the meal plan so he could eat. He wanted to drop out of college when we called him to tell him I had cancer, but we told him to at least finish the year and we would go from there. He hated being so far away, but it was just a few more weeks.

I was sitting in my work vehicle after lunch, talking to the mortgage company trying to work something out so we didn't lose our house, after talking to the insurance company about my costs for my upcoming treatment.

We were bleeding financially. Hemorrhaging with no relief in sight. I hadn't been cleared for full duty by the doctor and I couldn't work off-duty, either.

One of the guys I worked with was walking by my car. He could tell I was crying. He knocked on my window. I was far from okay.

I was struggling to maintain all our expenses with the medical bills and now we needed $5000 for an attorney by June. I was juggling between paying medical bills and keeping food on the table.

He asked me if I had deferred comp. I did. He told me I could apply for an unforeseeable emergency to have funds released to me, with no penalty. He gave me the number to contact.

I walked into my office and my squad started asking what happened, if I was okay, whose ass did they have to kick. I laughed, telling them I had to make a phone call to see if I could get some of my retirement money out, to help catch up on financials. I hated feeling weak.

I sent the paperwork for the funds. The unforeseeable emergency funds were approved for release. I felt relief, I cried. I was so grateful. I went into Jacob's office and gave him a huge hug, thanking him.

The mortgage company called me back saying they could do a forbearance, which would push my past due payments to the end of my loan, without any late charges. My day had taken a drastic turn, filled with hope and thankfulness.

Branch was home, working in the garage. He was dirty, but I didn't care. I parked, jumped out of my car, and ran up to him, hugging him.

He came in, showered and I poured him a glass of wine. I told him about the retirement funds and the mortgage company. When we got the money, I wanted him to retain the attorney. We weren't getting hosed again. It was time to fight back.

Branch contacted the attorney, and we did a promise to pay, with our account information and would let him know when the money was in the account.

Mediation didn't work. Devlin fought for us to cover the cost of her attorney, several other things, then tried to put a claim on the house. Branch was not on the house loan, and we had a document he signed stating he had no rights to the house. I was grateful the United States Department of Agriculture, USDA, loan required that.

We prepared for court. The attorney said we had a good case. We arrived in MN a couple days early, to make sure everything was set for court. Branch asked Devlin if we could see the kids before court, she said no. We knew where the kids went to daycare after school and we decided to see the kids at lunch, in school.

We drove a faded 1999 Expedition that was abandoned on my dad's property when he moved there in 2005. We acquired it, by doing a VIN check with MVD. We fixed it up with parts mainly purchased from the junkyard.

In MN, we drove to the attorney's office before they closed. He looked at the original divorce decree, the judgments filed since then and we went through each request, then added our own requests/changes. He had copies of voicemails, text messages, letters, and other things Devlin sent to us.

He had the phone records, the receipt for the phone we sent for the kids, and the documented trips we made to see the kids. There was something called parental alienation, which the courts were now looking at with all the custody battles. What she was doing fit the criteria.

We drove by the kids' daycare when we were done. Branch saw the kids outside playing. He went up to the fence and the oldest came running over.

The younger 2 ran over when they saw him, then the daycare lady came out and told him he couldn't be there. He was paying the childcare bill every week, so he had every right to see his kids. There was nothing stating he couldn't see them, and he wasn't taking them from daycare.

He wanted to say hi to his children. The daycare lady must have called Devlin because his phone started ringing right after we left. He let it go to voicemail. We didn't want an argument and if it was a nasty voicemail, we could add it to the others for court.

Later that night, Nicole called Branch on his mom's house phone, telling him we could pick them up the next day at the daycare. They were done with school, and they could spend the night.

We were waiting to hear what the call was about, when he turned around, grinned at us, and said we could pick the kids up in the morning at daycare to spend the night. We were able to keep them for the weekend.

I needed something to wear to court so we went shopping with the kids. I bought them each a couple pair of shorts and shirts. They only had 1 set of clothes packed. I found a dress and Eric found me shoes to go with the dress. When I tried everything on, Eric came up to me, put his arms around my waist and told me I looked pretty.

We got pizza and each kid picked out a movie to watch. We went to Caryn's and settled in for an evening of movies, pizza, snuggles and laughter. The next day we walked to the park. I took pictures of the kids playing. We had to take the kids home that night. They didn't want to leave.

We dropped them off, then drove quietly back to his mom's. Court was the next morning. We met early, with our attorney. He was going to ask for a set amount of time for us to have the kids during the summer and we agreed to 5 weeks.

Branch and the attorney would be at the table, while LJ and I would be in the viewing section, behind them. I was nervous, but excited to have our day in court. Things couldn't get worse. They were already taking most of his paycheck.

The judge read everything, asked some questions to clarify the requests, then made his ruling. He lowered the amount Branch had to pay in child support, considerably. Devlin had to carry insurance on the kids through her work because it was cheaper than what Branch had to pay. That alone freed up almost $400 a month. He then divided the amount of childcare costs between her and Branch, cutting our portion down to $250.

Branch would still be responsible for paying the back pay but awarded us 5 weeks during the summer, starting June 16th through July 21st, every year. As Branch had continued trying to be part of the kids' life, and he would be parenting full time for 5 weeks, the average time most non-custodial parents had their kids was why he lowered the amount of child support and backdated it to April when Devlin filed for the change.

Devlin started working full time since the original divorce decree, therefore she was bringing home just as much as Branch. Each party would be responsible for their own attorney fees and Branch would be responsible for travel arrangements for the kids.

We were already at the end of June, Eric was in summer school, so we would get the kids for 3 weeks in August, then June 16th every year, following. LJ and I sat holding hands, grateful for the ruling, while Devlin's mom sat across the aisle glaring at us.

When court was over, Devlin and her mom walked out of court, calling me a bitch as they walked by. The attorney asked what happened. I told him, but I was used to it. If it continued, let him know and he would file a harassment order against her.

We thanked him and paid his final payment. He had set us up on a payment arrangement, which totaled over $14,000 by the time we were done. It sucked, but it was worth it. Branch had a chance to catch up and pay off the back pay judgment, but he also got to have the kids 5 weeks a year.

The deferred comp rep said to fax her the new information reference the attorney, the medical bills, and any power bills then she would release emergency funds. She had my bank information and said if I sent it in that day, she would process it that afternoon.

We stopped at a local print shop, and I faxed the information. I took Branch to lunch to celebrate. He deserved it. We were planning on leaving Thursday so we could get home and pack to leave for camping Saturday.

While we were eating lunch, Branch's phone rang. He was hesitant to answer it. She would be a fool to start in already. He answered. It was the kids, they asked to spend the night with us before we left. The rest of the summer flew by.

The doctor set my treatment up for the end of September. I would have to be off my thyroid meds for 6 weeks and eat a low-iodine diet. That meant I would be off my meds while the kids were there. We had planned a trip to the beach while they visited, which was going to suck because I wouldn't be able to eat seafood.

DJ and Branch looked for and applied for jobs at places near DJ's college but couldn't find anything. The apartments and rentals were full, so he decided to drop out of college and work construction with my dad.

We flew the kids down with Branch's mom. Branch would fly home with the kids at the end of their stay. We departed for the beach after I finished work. We stopped an hour outside of San Diego, to sleep, after cramming all 8 of us into the expedition then 1 motel room, because DJ's girlfriend came with us.

We drove rest of the way in the morning, stopping for breakfast, grabbing subs and snacks for lunch by the beach. We couldn't check into our rooms until after 3 but were staying 2 nights next to the beach.

We played in the water, walked up and down the shore, watched the seals and sealions, then went up to the park, in the cove for lunch.

Everyone was getting cranky from lack of sleep, too much sun and exhaustion from playing in the water. We checked in at the hotel.

We went for a couple long walks along the beach, with the normal commentary, "I'm tired, I'm hungry, I have to go to the bathroom, stop touching me, I want to hold Dad's hand." I could feel my patience slipping, along with my energy.

I needed a few minutes by myself when we got to the beach club. Branch was getting irritated too and we got snippy with each other. We reached our destination, clear stretches of beach and ocean for miles with no rocks.

Branch got me a beach chair and the kids got in the water. DJ and his girlfriend set chairs up next to mine and chilled out. This was the ultimate birth control, I said, and they laughed.

We stayed at the beach until almost 5, before walking back to shower and clean up for dinner. We were going to a seafood restaurant overlooking the ocean. Each kid was given 5 minutes in the bathroom, if they didn't take care of business, then they would miss out. That was 30 minutes for all the kids and 10 more for Branch and me, giving us 20 minutes to walk to the restaurant.

To say it was chaotic was to undervalue the comedy circus of 2 girls, 1 boy, 2 teenage females and 1 teenage male, getting undressed, showered, and dressed, within 5 minutes. I had a timer set on my phone and I would start notifying with 2 ½ minutes left, 1 minute, 30 seconds until done.

The next to shower had to be lined up and ready to go, at the 2-minute mark, in case someone finished early. We set our bedroom up as a place the girls could get dressed and do their hair to free up the bathroom. I had cut my hair super short, the end of July, preparing for treatment, so all I had to do was run my fingers through it.

By the time we were all done, wet towels and swim clothes hung up to dry, we were headed out of the door, making it to the restaurant, 5 minutes early.

When we left for home, we drove up the coast and stopped to eat dinner at "Ruby's on the Pier." We watched the sun lower over the ocean. It was going to be 8:30/9 P.M. by the time we got home. I had to work the next day.

The following weekend, we had a surprise 25th Wedding Anniversary for my dad and stepmom. I loved celebrating my parents' 2nd-chance love story.

Caryn flew down a couple days before the kids left so she could fly home with them, instead of Branch. She met my parents and we showed her around.

LJ started her sophomore year of high school. DJ was working and spending time with his girlfriend. Branch and I were preparing for the RFL event, which was the same day as his birthday and 2 weeks after my treatment. I had much to do with dwindling energy and focus.

At work, I had a search warrant coming up, with hours of surveillance that needed to be done. I set up schedules for everyone to help and had the SW typed up with everything except the surveillance.

I was going to be isolated after treatment, so we set our bedroom up for me. Branch couldn't sleep with me or use the same restroom. Friends and family bought me books, magazines, coloring books, activity books and Branch had hooked up the old Xbox in our room, so I could watch movies and play Zuma.

One of our softball girls, Lina, called me Momma, hand-painted an ivy trim around the top of our bedroom walls and over our door. Branch hung up some of the photos and we had my bland food set up for my liquid diet during treatment.

I had a water cooler filled with ice and water, as well as disposable dishes that I would bag up before setting outside the door. He set up a card table that looked out one of our windows, where we had planted bougainvillea and I could have fresh air.

We were ready. He drove me to the treatment center. Once I took the radioactive pill and they confirmed I didn't have any adverse reaction, they let me go home. The radioactive pill was in a container. When the nurse opened it, she would empty the container into a cup I held, then everyone would leave the room and shut the door until I took the pill.

She went out the door, put a suit on, opened a vault, then returned with a heavy, thick egg-shaped container. She told me to hold the cup out, tipped the container then quickly opened it, allowing the capsule to fall into the cup. I was expecting some kind of green or yellow glow coming from it and was mildly disappointed.

After taking the pill with no adverse reactions, I had to leave via the back exit where Branch would have the expo waiting. I had to sit in the back and Branch was to drive with all the windows open, straight home, where I would begin my isolation. KJs wasn't like this, but the nurse told me the dose I was getting was the highest dose someone could be given, outside a hospital setting.

I received a dose most people got half of. Branch was given a card I had to carry with me for 45 days after treatment. If I required any medical attention or got pulled over, I had to show the card, so they knew I was giving off radiation.

Branch and I had the same expression, the "What the hell are we about to do?" look.

After the nurse closed the container and backed out of the room, shutting the door, I gave Branch a thumbs-up as he was watching me through the window. The nurse opened the back door and showed him where to park. She had him open the back door of the expo and put the middle seat down so I could get in quickly.

Branch was given a packet of information to read when we got home. He was told to stay in the vehicle. The nurse came back, checked to make sure everything was okay with me, then opened the back door. I walked out and climbed into the vehicle.

As we headed home, Branch asked me if I felt different. I didn't, but in the event of a zombie apocalypse, Branch could shake me like a glow stick.

I couldn't have anything but liquids for the first 5 days. I was already hungry. It was a good thing I was going to be isolated. I became hangry, hungry, and angry. We got home and I stayed in the driveway, so Branch could put the dogs outside. I couldn't be around them either.

He yelled out the front door I could come in. I went into my room, shutting the doors behind me. I looked forward to the quiet time by myself, but now that it was there, I felt imprisoned.

I took a shower and put a nightgown on, then I lay down and watched a movie. I slept more than I thought I would over the next couple days. I still couldn't take my thyroid meds and I hadn't had anything but broth for the last 3 days. I could hear my hair crunching when I laid on the pillow.

I played Zuma, colored, wrote, typed, read, watched movies, slept, showered, and peed what felt like every 30 minutes. I was drinking water constantly. My mouth always dry. If I wasn't drinking water, I sucked on Lemonheads to keep my mouth from drying out.

LJ would sit outside my doors when she got home to tell me about her day and DJ would say hi, when he was home. The 5th day, I told Branch to go to work. He read all the information in the packets and said if my scans were good on Monday, I could be in the living room, if I stayed 6 feet from everyone.

I posted updates on Facebook. One night, some of the girls that were part of the Relay committee came to visit me outside of my window. They brought chairs, some wine, and the big "cock" one of my friends won in a raffle. Before the night was over, a couple more friends and my sisters came by.

LJ told us we were crazy, but she loved hearing us laughing. After all the Relay events we had done together, they had watched LJ grow up. They made sure she had everything she needed, then said goodbye. I gave them air hugs and felt the fullness in my spirit. I was blessed.

By the end of the week, I felt like I was coming out of my skin. I felt like crap, but I had to get out of the house for fresh air and nature.

I went for a run. It had been a few years since I had run more than a mile at one time. Functional fitness was more cardio, with strength training, and some running thrown in.

Branch opened the front door for me, and I was off. I told him my planned route. He would follow on his bike, in case I needed something, with a 10-minute head start.

I started walking, then added in running, slowly, feeling the sun on my face, shoulders, and arms. I kept a pace that didn't get me overheated and felt comfortable without spiking my heart rate. For some, it could have been a fast walk, but at that moment I felt I was winning the Olympics or Boston Marathon.

Branch never said anything when he got behind me. He stayed back enough that I didn't notice him. He gave me space to work things out. I had no destination in mind or distance. I felt like Forrest Gump and "just kept running." I went further than expected. I didn't have water with me. I needed to turn around.

I got back to the main intersection by our house, and all my energy was sapped. I was hot, tired, thirsty, frustrated, angry and a host of other emotions. I prayed out loud and asked God to give me the strength to continue fighting. Suddenly, I felt like a gust of wind was blowing at my back, gently lifting, and pushing me forward.

I sprinted the ¼-mile to our house, feeling like a new person. Branch asked me what happened because I was crying but couldn't explain they were tears of joy and gratitude. I wanted to hug Branch so bad at that moment, to thank him for being my rock, my soft place to land.

I drank some water and left the doors open to the bedroom so I could talk to him. It was going to be a long, tough journey and I was thankful he was by my side. I needed to find my new Zen and after talking to KJ, we started running together. Most was virtually, but we did a 10k together near my house when she was next in town. We tried to keep each other motivated. Somedays were brutal, just trying to get out the door.

I had my scans and could return to work the end of the following week. I could be in the same room as my family again but maintain 6 feet of space between us. At the end of that week, Branch could start sleeping in our bed again and I could eat real food.

I was nominated to attend the Making Strides Against Breast cancer NFL game, as well as a small dinner with some of the Cardinal's players and their spouses. We had practice for the pink ribbon display during the halftime show while the

Cardinals finished up their Thursday night practice. We met a couple of the players. I had my shirt signed by "The" Larry Fitzgerald and Darnell Dockett.

Our dinner was scheduled for the next night at a steakhouse, then the game was Sunday at the stadium. I was able to take DJ and LJ to the game with me. Branch was working. I was able to take my camera on the field and got some great shots of the players before the game started.

The halftime show was amazing to be part of, surrounded by so many amazing cancer warriors. The American Cancer Society recognized more than just breast cancer survivors during the halftime show, we all represented hope.

Before I went back to work, Branch had to pick something up from the fire station and I went with him. There had been a joke there was a ghost in the new station. I wrote on the board that I had walked through the station to radiate the ghosts away and it was all clear.

I went to work, finalized my paperwork for the search warrant, got everything signed, briefed the teams, and prepared for the next morning, which would be early.

We executed the search warrant, took several suspects into custody, and went back to the office to start interviews and processing. It would be a long night, but we had done a lot of prepping beforehand, so everything was labeled, the probable cause statement was typed for the booking sheets, and we were out of the office by 11:30 P.M. We had started at 3:30 A.M., but 11:30 P.M. was a good turnaround with so many suspects interviewed and booked.

The next morning, we were going to be in by 8 A.M., to finish making copies, return the search warrant and get everything into property and evidence. When I got up the following morning to take my daily medications, I went to pull my blanket up over my pillow and I saw a chunk of my hair on my pillowcase.

I ran into the bathroom, looking in the mirror and could see where my hair was breaking off. The chunk on my pillow broke from where I had my bangs pulled back the day before. I mentally prepared for it, but it was still shocking to see. I told Branch if my hair broke off or fell out, I was shaving it. He said he would do it for me.

When he got up, he saw me looking in the bathroom mirror, touching my almost bald spot. He grabbed a chair, my clippers and cape and told me to sit down. As he gently ran the clippers over my head, I felt my power coming back. I was choosing how I looked, cancer and treatment wasn't.

When Branch finished, he stepped back and grinned, then told me he liked it. After wearing my hair in a ponytail for so many years, tight to my head, it was a similar look, except now it was just scalp.

I showered while Branch made me breakfast to go. I had to be out of the house before 7 A.M. to be at work by 8. Branch gave me a hug and kiss, then kissed the top of my head, before I walked out the door. I felt like Wonder Woman and Supergirl combined.

I walked into work and went directly to my office to finish typing my report for the charging documents. By the time the other guys came in, I was completely immersed in my report. I forgot I was bald. The four guys I shared the office with, Harry, Marty, Gage and Schmall, came in together. It took them about 5 minutes to realize I was bald, then they were all touching my head.

If I hadn't been so immersed in my report, I probably would have found it more comical. They said if I went bald or had to shave my head, they would, too. We had a debriefing on the search warrant and after several minutes of the guys commenting on my bald head, Lt. Strong said he would shave his head, to show support.

I was touched by the support. These guys were like family. My crew made plans to shave their heads over the weekend. Lt. Strong said if everyone did it, he would take us to Buffalo Wild Wings for lunch.

Monday morning everyone showed up with bald heads and huge grins. We took a few photos before we headed out to lunch. I had the SWV Relay event coming up that weekend and most of the guys would be there or were fundraising to help. We finalized plans at lunch before finishing our work week.

DJ was helping Branch with logistics, my sisters were helping with several committee tasks, including luminary and opening ceremony. LJ was helping with the youth and survivor reception. Branch wanted to shave his head into a mohawk and dye it dark purple to show his support.

After we set everything up Friday afternoon, we stopped to get the hair color. It was Branch's birthday. We sang him happy birthday, and everyone loved his hair. My sisters made a sign that said "Bald is beautiful" to hold during opening ceremony.

The entire event was emotional, filled with love, hope, inspiration, as well as sadness and grief. I had been part of many Relay events, trainings, and other events, but there was something about this event that stood out. We raised more money that year, than the event had raised in previous years, and it seemed like we hadn't even tried that hard.

I had talked with the staff partner about starting an event in the community where me and many of our committee members lived in. At the end of the event, the ACS staff told me we would be able to plan and host our own event in our community. It was going to be hard with no businesses to get sponsorships, but there were too many people affected by cancer, not to try.

A few weeks later, we participated in the Buckeye Relay. There were new committee members and a new location we wanted to support. There were storm warnings that night, so they decided to move the event into the gym, which made it more personal.

I walked the survivor lap and was met halfway by both event chairs. They walked arm in arm with me during the caregiver lap. We had worked together for years on different events, trainings, and fundraisers. We were all an extended event family.

I sat with one of the ladies from my community, she was also a cancer survivor. Our husbands worked at the fire department together, our kids were in school together and she worked with me in the concession stands. She had invited her son's girlfriend and family because the youngest daughter, Mags, was recently diagnosed with cancer.

She had just turned 13, was conscientious of her bald head, but told her mom when she saw my bald head, she felt comfortable being bald. Through the course of the dinner, the girl and I became friends. They only lived a couple miles from us, and I gave them my number.

For Christmas, I adopted their family through our work toy drive and was able to take the kids shopping. They each got $100 to spend, which most kids spend on themselves. Not this Junior Warrior Princess of Hope, she bought gifts for her parents, brother and sister then bought something small for herself.

On the ride home, I took them to dinner and found out she and I shared a birthday. As we started planning for our community Relay event, I asked her if she would be willing to publicly share her story, in front of the community. I would be right next to her.

She didn't think about it for long and said she would do it. Our event continued shaping up, the community and schools were excited for the event, along with local organizations.

Branch went to MN between Christmas and New Year's to see the kids. LJ had a basketball tournament and DJ was working. We were in bed when I got a call at almost midnight. I didn't recognize the number but picked up.

The male voice said, "Yes, I'm just calling to let you know there's going to be a murder tonight, goodbye," and they hung up. My heart started racing, I felt the adrenaline kick in then I leaped out of bed, looked at the number and ran to DJ's room to see if he recognized the number. It sounded like my cousin who DJ had worked with earlier that day.

I called the number back and when they said hello, I asked who it was. He said, "This is your cousin," then repeated there was going to be a murder and hung up again. I was completely freaked and told DJ to come into the hallway area with me, where there were no doors or windows.

We made sure all the doors and windows were locked. I called Patrick, who was working the area. I told him what was said, gave him the number and the description of his truck. Then I called my cousins to see if they'd heard from him and they said they received similar calls. He was probably drunk from the way he sounded on the phone, but no one knew where he was.

I turned my work radio on and had my gun between DJ and me. I had him walk me back through the day, the ride home and the conversation. Patrick called. They just received a call of someone trying to get into a house, threatening to kill someone.

The lady said it was her ex-boyfriend, then as the dispatcher gave the description of the vehicle to the deputies over the radio, I said it had to be my cousin. I didn't know who the lady was, but he was seeing someone that hung out at a place he went dancing.

I called Branch, letting him know what was going on and to hear his voice. It was December 29th, 2011, 9 years after I took the call from the dad who shot his wife and daughters. Patrick was the same one I talked to in 2002.

It was my cousin trying to get into the lady's house. We're not sure of specifics, but they were at the bar, something happened, and another guy was in the picture. My cousin must have called his brothers and I, while he was driving to her house. None of us heard from him until the next morning. Nothing happened, he passed out in his truck somewhere in the desert.

On January 8, 2012, I got a phone call from Rick, early in the morning. One of the guys we had worked with, 2005-2006, was shot and killed, in the line of duty. He told me which hospital he was at. Branch was at work. I let him know where I was going, and he told me to stop by to pick him up.

I couldn't believe "Wild Bill" was dead. He was supposed to retire the next day. That night was supposed to have been his last shift and he was dead. He left behind 2 older children, 2 younger kids and a wife. We were working together when his youngest was born. He had been excited about having another little girl.

The hospital was filled with patrol cars from all over AZ, firetrucks and so many people. Some of the guys on his squad filled us in on what had happened. They had a call for a suspicious vehicle at a local business. When the patrol guys got on scene, they found a minivan. When they approached it, the guy inside opened fire with a rifle, striking Bill in the head, killing him instantly.

The other guys got into a shoot-out with the guy, contained the scene and had the ambulance on scene for medical attention to Bill. The guy in the van had been on the run for weeks, a suspect in several AZ murders. Bill never had a chance to fight back. There were bullet holes in his windshield and vehicle before he made contact.

Our office was in shock, mourning and disbelief. It had been years since a deputy had been shot and killed in the line of duty. Bill was a true cowboy, loved his job, his family and was a loyal friend. His death was a heavy hit to all of us.

They set up a schedule for the "Honor watch" so Bill would never be alone at the hospital, coroner's office, or funeral home, until he was buried. We signed up for 4-hour shifts and I was able to take a couple day shifts, along with the last shift, before the funeral service.

The morning of the funeral, I was supposed to start at 4 A.M. until 8 A.M. when the Honor Guard would arrive. The guy working before me had worked all day and asked me to come in earlier so he could go home, get some sleep and his dress uniform before the service. I sent a message to some of the female deputies that had worked with Bill, asking if they wanted to hang out with me.

By 3:30 A.M., the girls started rolling in. We sat around Bill, sharing stories of working with him, some of his more infamous calls and traffic stops. It was the time each of us needed to grieve and personally say our goodbyes to Bill. We started getting into our Class-A dress uniforms about 6 A.M., while sharing some of Bill's more comical stories.

I went to the restroom after the honor guard took over. We had been drinking coffee and water all morning and this would be the last chance to empty our bladders.

We started laughing again at another story. I couldn't stop to get my duty belt buckled. The leather has no give, and I told the girls they would have to help me get buckled up. It took us 5 more minutes because we were laughing again, trying to stay quiet, knowing people were showing up, which made us giggle more.

Even though we said our goodbyes, the service still had us all in tears. Seeing his wife and little kids broke my heart. While we had the honor watch for Bill, his close friends from work also set up a watch for Bill's family, making sure someone was always with his wife. They helped with funeral arrangements, making sure the family had food, rides to appointments, the funeral and gravesite. Although Bill was gone physically, his family would always be part of ours.

I had gone back to doing functional fitness with my squad and running when I could. I went for my 6-month follow-up for scans and bloodwork in early 2012. Instead of hearing everything looks clear, he said I had "shoddy images."

I went back to work and couldn't focus on our weekly briefing. I was at my desk and started researching cancer treatment centers of America. We had used their conference rooms for Relay meetings, and I decided to reach out.

I went to the online chat and after I sent him my follow up scan report, he said he would have someone contact me for more information. My phone rang that night from an odd number. It was someone from CTCA calling to get my information and set me up for appointments.

He sent me forms to fill out for release of medical records and he could get me in that Friday. He explained it would be a couple days of meeting doctors, doing lab work, scans, meeting with mental health therapist, spiritualist, nutritionist, pain management and physical therapy, if needed.

I couldn't do Friday but could start Monday the next week. I was nervous when Branch and I first got there, but there was a calmness of hope that settled over me once I stepped inside. We checked in at the front desk.

They called us back, took my bloodwork, weight, vitals and made sure we were comfortable. A medical oncologist came in, with a nurse, Jewel, that would be my care team nurse. The doctor asked questions about my background, treatments, and looked at my scans. He was referring me to one of the oncologists for follow-up.

Jewel stayed with us, explained what would happen next, that she would be my point of contact for questions, concerns, or any other problems. She explained that CTCA didn't just treat the cancer, they treated the entire person, including their family. They had people caregivers could talk to make sure the family was taken care of.

The doctor would do a full physical run-down, making sure I talked about any pain, side-effects and things I didn't think were related to the cancer.

We enjoyed breakfast and lunch at the CTCA cafeteria, which was more like a 5-star restaurant, in between my appointments. There was a nail and hair salon, coffee shop, smoothie counter, gift shop/bookstore, library, resource center, chapel, gym, rooftop garden and comfortable furniture throughout the hospital.

After a full day at CTCA, Branch and I headed home. Branch was relaxed knowing I was being fully looked after.

Our community RFL event was approaching quickly. I was busy with work, Relay event planning, CTCA appointments and coaching. I had started running in the desert by our house, at least once a week, and continued doing workouts with my squad before work.

Branch ran power to my shed, the one we had gotten in 2009. He added insulation, drywall, sealed the floor, added new floorboards, tile leftover from Evelyn and wood flooring from KJ. I painted while Branch and LJ worked on shelves and storage. Lina painted one of the walls with a tree, Relay For Life logo and an owl sitting in the tree.

My first project was to reupholster the free chair I had gotten the same day we got the shed. I found some dark purple fabric to use. The plan was to put it in my shed, but it took up most of the space. Once I finished it, we moved it into our bedroom.

I had my first tattoo session for the design on my upper-right arm. It would be parrot tulips, with a banner running through it, "Hope Blooms in a Garden of Faith." It took three appointments to finish, and it was gorgeous.

I made a quilt for the Relay event for survivors and caregivers to put their handprints on, with fingerpaint. I made a purple satin cape to wear at a previous event that said "Warrior Princess of HOPE" on the back. This had become my name over the course of events. One of the staff partners called me princess after I started calling her precious.

Our event was on a Friday night through Saturday morning. One of the ladies I met at a training asked me to speak at her event, which wound up being the same weekend as ours, but started Saturday night. Branch was okay with going if we got some sleep in between.

Our event kicked off at noon because there was no school that Friday. The opening ceremony would be at 3 P.M., with the survivor ceremony at 6 P.M.

Mags, my Junior Warrior Princess of Hope, spoke from the heart, about being a kid with cancer, a cancer that most kids died from. If there was a dry eye in the stands, I didn't see them. Mags stood there proud, fierce, and courageous, wearing the cape I made. Her story brought more awareness to the fact that kids get cancer and needed a voice in the fight against cancer.

We had local first responders, and other local VIPs on hand to put the survivor medal around the neck of survivors before the lap started. Each survivor was called to the track by name, and soon the area was filled with men, women, and children, of all ages, ethnicities, and backgrounds, wearing dark purple shirts with the word "SURVIVOR" across the back.

There were fun laps, crazy laps, sentimental laps, and regular laps, tucked between ceremonies. We had the luminaria ceremony, followed by the silent lap, and slowly worked into the glow lap.

There was dancing, singing, Misster Relay, food, drinks, and hope swirling the track. We had pizza brought out for a midnight pizza party, pajama party, luau and closed the morning out with a pancake breakfast made by the owner of one of the local construction companies. We met through the American Legion, and he volunteered his pancake making talents.

We were cleaned up, off site by 8 A.M., home, unloaded and showered by 8:45 A.M. Branch and I slept from 9 A.M.-1 P.M., before we had to leave. Opening ceremony was at 6 P.M., but we wanted to be there earlier to see a guy I worked with, Robbie. He had been diagnosed with the same type of cancer I originally had in '93. I invited him to walk the survivor lap with me. I also had an official Miami Dolphins football helmet for him. He was such a big fan. (I'm still trying not to hold that against him.)

I found the lady that asked me to speak. We learned later that she was the mom of DJ's roommate in college. We had that in common as well as being birthday twins.

Robbie and I did our first survivor lap together, joined by our spouses during the caregiver lap and enjoyed a beautiful survivor reception and celebration.

Eventually, Branch and I went to the expedition to take a nap, before I spoke at the closing ceremony, at 6 A.M.

We left soon after closing ceremony. We spent time with the new puppy we got a couple weeks prior, Syren. The puppy was a Belgian Malinois. Her mom and father were both working police dogs and she was the runt of the litter.

We fell in love with her big ears and playful self. She got along great with all the dogs, but we were still having to keep Tankker, and Saba separated so they didn't fight.

Branch and I were both stressed. With work, finances, everything we had going on and we were not communicating effectively. The closer it got to June and time for the kids to come down from MN, the more we fought. I wasn't sleeping well. My scans weren't completely clear. They were going to do another round of treatment in October.

I was seeing the chiro at the CTCA, getting massages and acupuncture, after the pain management doctor did nerve block injections. I was spending nights with Mags at the hospital when she was getting her chemo, which left me more exhausted. Then we got a notice from the IRS, Internal Revenue Service, that said we were being audited for our 2007 taxes.

The stress load made me feel I was buckling under the pressure. When I looked at our taxes, I didn't make a mistake. The company I had worked off-duty for sent me a 1099 with a different amount listed than what they sent the IRS. After talking to others, several of us had the same issue and were being audited.

I started pulling our tax stuff out of storage. I needed a break. I couldn't catch my breath before another shitstorm landed in our laps.

I was grateful to be invited to a night out for a Mother's Day event, honoring moms that were cancer survivors. The lady that put the event together was the GM for Victoria's Secret. We were given gift bags, gift cards, flowers, then taken to dinner. I had my first official bra fitting and wound up buying 2, using my gift card.

I always had issues finding bras that didn't rub on my scar, roll up at the bottom, or bunch up under the armpit with the underwire. When I tried the first one on, it felt like a soothing balm, securely holding my breasts. It had just enough lace over the front cups to add a touch of sexy, without directly touching my skin.

The second one was more of a t-shirt bra. It was sleek black, with a small piping of leopard print around the top. The first one felt good, but this one was like magic. My boobs got a great lift, where they were supposed to be, without looking like they were squished under my chin.

After breastfeeding 2 kids, surgery that numbed my right breast, thyroid cancer surgery and all my scars, I needed something close to my skin, reminding me that I was still a powerful warrior. Some might wear armor; I wore feminine bras that reminded me of my power as a woman.

June came fast. This was our first official 5 weeks with 3 more kids in the house. DJ was working for my dad in NM, so his bedroom was open for the kids. We set the girls up in his bed and Eric wanted to sleep on a cot. He was always up early. We put him in the living room, so he didn't wake the girls.

We were leaving for our annual camping trip a few days after they arrived. This added more stress as they each only brought a carryon, which meant we had to go shopping to get them warmer clothes. We found windbreakers and some warm clothes at Goodwill. We bought more shorts, shirts, socks, and underwear, to get them through at least a week of camping. We had to buy another tent, more sleeping bags, and other necessities for the trip.

The first day we were set up, ready to explore, we got the news that my cousin, the one that had called me in December about a murder, was found dead from an overdose. There was no evidence that it was suicide, but he had mixed some hard liquor with strong pain medications.

It was tough for our entire family as we came together that year. My sisters and I grew up with him and his brothers, including traveling on cross-country road trips.

We took my camera and spent the first few days exploring, taking photos, fishing, horseback riding and trying to stay dry from the daily rain. I was praying daily and writing in my prayer journal. The girls and I got along well, but Eric was a different story.

His grandma and mom told him I would beat him or taze him if he didn't behave. We had to work through that. When he was home with LJ in charge, he didn't listen to anyone and hit his sisters.

Branch and I argued a lot at night and snipped at each other through the day. Right before we'd left for camping, the audit showed the off-duty company I worked for in 2007 had sent a 1099 with a $7,000 difference of what I earned. That started a domino effect of audits through 2012.

I set up payment arrangements but could only afford $125 a month. We hadn't fully recovered from my medical bills.

After camping, I worked for 2 weeks before we left to drive the kids back to MN. We were going to the 4 corners of AZ, CO, UT, and NM before driving up through backroads of CO. From there we were going to Mount Rushmore before going back to MN.

I made each kid their own activity book, to help with reading, math, geography, comprehension, and history.

They had maps to show where we were going, interesting points and facts along the route, mile markers, distances, and history of the local areas. The expedition was big enough for Branch and me to sit in the front, 2 kids in the middle and 2 kids in the back. We had a cooler of drinks and a bag of snacks, with Syren sitting between the kids in the middle seat.

We planned to stop every 2-3 hours to stretch legs, see sights and use the restroom, advising the kids to watch their fluid intake.

There were some stops that were 30-40 minutes after we started because Eric had a small bladder. He threw a fit to sit all the way in the back, so we had to upend everyone just to let him out of the vehicle. After the 3rd time, I made him switch because he was making everyone angry.

I was irritated all the time. I could not explain it. It was affecting my marriage, and everything was spiraling. Branch and I still cared for each other, but there were many times we didn't seem to want to be around each other.

We were rarely intimate and at one point he told me to find someone to satisfy my sexual needs. How did we get to this point? I had no idea how to fix it, or if I wanted to. We were both miserable and so busy, we didn't take time to work on us.

I spent more nights at the children's hospital with Mags, going over after I finished work, staying until the next morning, then going back to work, to work out, shower and change. While Mags and I were walking the empty hallways at 3 A.M., we planned our birthday celebration, 40 going on 14, or 14 going on 40. Mags and I called ourselves the PCH (Phoenix Children's Hospital) zombie hunting team.

After the IRS audit and money owed, I started getting bills for DJ's student loan. We were always strapped for cash. We sold the truck; Branch drove the Expo and DJ bought a car for better gas mileage.

In August 2012, LJ started her junior year of high school. DJ was working construction with my dad in NM, and we stopped to see him on our way back from MN. My dad ended up in the hospital in AZ for A-Fib. He couldn't control his heart rate or blood pressure. They shocked his heart back into rhythm.

DJ, LJ, Branch, and I participated in a Climb To Conquer cancer event in Flagstaff, along with some coworkers. It was a tough climb. I was back up to 240 lbs., even with staying active. We made it to the top and chilled out the rest of the day before we drove home. That climb cemented how much we loved being in the pine trees.

I was turning 40 the end of August and planned a 3-day celebration. DJ was going to be home. We started Friday night. While sitting outside, eating, drinking, and laughing, my mom and stepdad surprised me. They flew in from NY and my sister picked them up. It was awkward. We didn't really know each other, and my kids didn't really know them. I was thankful they came out and we had a good time.

Saturday, we kicked off the celebration at 1 P.M. We were on the patio, with swamp coolers which helped some with the desert heat, but until the sun went down, it was warm. Lots of people showed and we stayed there until 1 A.M. I rocked my cowboy boots, jean shorts, tank top and purple tiara. I kicked 40 off fabulously.

My mom asked me to join her for the "Dirty Girl" mud run obstacle course she signed up for. The event was in NY, at the ski resort close to where I grew up. My friend Mandy was going to participate with me. She had moved back to NY to go to cosmetology school.

I hadn't seen her since I graduated high school. Mandy worked on planning another party to celebrate me and my 40th birthday when I got to NY. She got friends and family involved with the planning. It would be a potluck with a couple friends grilling. I flew in Thursday night, the party was Saturday, and our mud run was Sunday, then I would fly home on Monday, Labor Day.

I was staying at my mom and stepdad's so we could all ride together the morning of the event. When I got to the house, I went in and peed, but I didn't know which room I was sleeping in and didn't want to wake anyone. I could smell the cats; it gave me a headache. I slept in the backseat of the car until I heard my parents get up.

After saying hellos and hugs, I took my bag up to my old room I had until my senior year of high school. The green carpet had been replaced, the walls repainted with all new furniture and bedding. It felt so foreign, but familiar. There were so many memories tied to the room, but I wasn't ready to let the memories wash over me. I was too tired and felt vulnerable. I hadn't stayed at the house since 2004.

Mandy and I were meeting up to finish some of the details and she planned lunch for us at one of my favorite places, Texas Hot, with a "surprise."

Texas Hot has been a favorite in the community since it opened. They make their own "Texas Hot" sauce. It's a combination of spices, ground beef and magic. They put it on their hotdogs, burgers, and fries. Their old-fashioned thick milkshakes and the booths with the high privacy walls are my favorites. Each table has its own jukebox and when you're sitting in the booth, you felt like you were in your own private little world of nostalgia and deliciousness.

We ordered, then Mandy said, "Oh, here he is." I turned around and saw a dark-haired male who looked familiar, but I couldn't place him right away. He said hello to me, and I probably didn't remember him, but he photographed and wrote the sports section when I was in high school. At that moment, it all clicked together, but I still had no idea how he was my surprise.

Mandy told him I was coming home to do the mud run, told him about me being a 2-time cancer survivor, and was now a deputy sheriff in AZ. The more they talked, he had an idea to do an article on me. I was flabbergasted, humbled and nervous. This was one of the biggest papers in the area and all the people who lived there read it. The good news, the story wouldn't run until after I left. He wanted to get pictures of us doing the mud run.

He asked me some questions while we were eating. He always knew I was kick ass after watching me play sports all those years. I laughed but had tears in my eyes at the compliment. I hadn't been home in years other than to see family quick. To hear the pride from someone during my high school years was humbling.

After we finished, he asked if we could do some photos outside, to capture some of the town. As he asked more questions, my story started tumbling out. He was putting my story on the front page of the paper.

He said I needed to put my in-depth story on paper to share with others, in a book. People kept telling me that, but I had no idea where to start or what to share. He told me to start at the beginning and share everything. Different parts of my story would inspire and provide hope to different people.

Not many people overcame even one of the hurdles that I had, let alone several. I had a melancholy feeling from what he said. This thanks is for John for inspiring me!

We finished our errands and I wanted to go say hi to my aunt while we were in the area. We met 3 of my aunts at the Legion for an early dinner, talking about my party the next day and they said we should have a family dinner before I left.

After dinner, I took the backroads showing Mandy where I used to live, but the house had been torn down. We headed back to where we were staying that night.

It was still early, we decided to go to the local bar where she was a bartender.

The bar was mostly for older people when I was growing up. Now, it was a fun hangout. Mandy and I were staying in town, so we didn't have to drive after drinking. We were shooting pool, catching up with friends I hadn't seen in years and avoiding people I had no desire to reconnect with.

I had walked out of the restroom, headed back to the bar when I felt someone grab my arm. I turned around and looked directly at Tom's brother. My adrenaline spiked. I still wanted to punch him. He didn't say hi or make small talk, he asked me directly if my son, DJ, was his nephew.

I covered my surprise, knowing there would be a day like this. My son would never be his nephew and I tried to turn away. He grabbed my arm again, "I've seen the Facebook photos and he looks just like my brother. You guys were together during that time, then stopped talking."

I told him again, DJ was my son, period. His brother had no part in my son. Instead of turning around, I pushed past him to walk outside. I couldn't breathe and didn't want to show weakness in front of him. I ran across the street, out of the streetlights, so I could catch my breath and calm down.

Mandy called me on my phone asking me where I'd gone to. I told her I had to get out of the crowd for a bit and I was across the street. She asked if I was ready to leave and we left.

The next day was filled with hugs, seeing, and talking to family that I hadn't seen since my sisters graduated and some friends I hadn't seen since I was in high school. Teachers, coaches, friends, and family kept showing up throughout the day.

I felt out of place at times. Some acted like I did amazing things. I only saw myself as that farm girl with skinned knees and a bad attitude. As the evening rolled on, the cops showed up for a noise complaint. I told them to invite the person that complained. He didn't find humor with my comment.

Mandy knew the other officer and talked to him, explaining what the party was for and we would be done by 11 P.M. I didn't recognize him, but he said he remembered me from school. He went to the neighboring school and was a few years younger than me. I thanked them for their service and told the new guy to relax before he burnt himself out. I had a couple MCSO challenge coins with me. I ran to my car to get them, then provided each officer with one.

The officer who knew me couldn't believe I worked for MCSO with "The Sheriff Joe Arpaio." I told him if he was ever in Phoenix to let me know and he could do a ride-along with us.

They left. If we shut down by 11, they wouldn't come back to bother us.

It was after 12 A.M. when Mandy and I headed to my parents' house. We fell into bed exhausted. We wound down about 1 A.M. and settled into sleep when I heard the stupid rooster crowing at 2 A.M.00

I yelled, "Shut up, you damn rooster!" then laid back down. As I fell asleep, he started again. I tried putting the pillow over my head and Mandy was laughing. I hated that rooster and on almost 100 acres of land, he chooses to sit near the porch, under my window.

We got up to get ready. My stepdad saw my face and asked, "Didn't you sleep well last night, sunshine?" and Mandy laughed. I walked into the bathroom and slammed the door while she told them about the "fucking rooster" outside the window.

Mandy and I were driving separately. We were there with plenty of time to put our "Muddy Mounds" shirts on that mom had made. Mine said "survivor" on the back.

Our heat was starting 45 minutes after we arrived. They started each team and heat separately to avoid congestion at the obstacles. We were ready to go, and it started with a straight uphill climb to get to the first obstacle.

I told the team to conserve their energy going up the hill. It wasn't about winning, it was about having fun and finishing as a team. The gun went off for us to start. While others started running to get up the muddy hill, we moved to the side to walk up the hill, at a quick pace.

The first obstacle, we had to crawl through a huge puddle of mud, through a long water pipe, ending in another huge puddle of muddy water. I slid on my stomach most of the way. I was fully covered in muddy water, but ready to go.

The event was women only. Opposing teams helped each other over obstacles, it was beautiful to watch. There was a huge net we had to climb up, over and down the other side. There were many women scared of heights. I sat at the top for a few minutes coaching on how to start, sliding over the top, and start down the other side.

People hugged me and thanked me the rest of the run. I was proud that my team, none of them runners or workout people, except me and Mandy, had made it through every obstacle.

The last obstacle was a large wooden structure we had to climb over. The wood was covered with slimy mud water and there wasn't any place to get a good hold. I told Mandy to step on my thigh, like we did during cheer, I would boost her up then she could help the others down the other side.

I helped boost the entire team over and my mom was last, so she sat on the top of the wall and reached down to help me up. Once I got my hand in a place to pull myself up, she went down so I could come up and over. We were so happy, we had finished all the obstacles, no one was injured, and we were all muddy messes.

As we came toward the finish line, down the hill and around the corner, we saw all the spectators standing at the fence, waving, cheering, and taking photos of their teams. We held hands as we ran towards the finish together, ranging in age from almost 60 to early 20s. We were all handed a free beer when we finished along with our finisher's medal.

We took our tennis shoes off to drop at the donation tent then got pictures. A photo of Mandy and I, completely covered in mud, with huge grins on our faces, made the front page of the newspaper for the article. We left for wings and football. The next day I drove around saying hi to friends and family before dinner.

We met everyone there, Mandy had also been invited, so we showed up together. It was an older house turned into a family-style, Irish pub restaurant. We talked about the mud run, my party and I felt my normal uneasiness around my mom.

She took little sarcastic jabs at me. She had always done it, but now, I jabbed back. She said something about the snow and why I didn't like it. I responded the real reason I didn't like the snow was freezing in it while I was left outside the school, waiting for her to pick me up.

She said that wasn't her fault, blamed it on me and the neighbor I was supposed to ride with. We obviously remembered my childhood differently, which was a big reason I didn't come home often. My aunt said something about family. If family was so important, then how come no one really knew who I was, why I hated being home or what was going on with my life other than what I shared on Facebook.

My stepdad, ever the peacemaker, stepped in asking how work was. He said all the guys he had worked with couldn't believe I was working for the most famous sheriff in America.

We had dessert and said our goodbyes. I had an early flight the next morning.

The weekend after I was home, we went up north to help the old goat with his cattle. He was diagnosed with stomach cancer in the spring and didn't have the energy to work the cattle. We had to tag, vaccinate, and load the cattle to bring down to Phoenix during the winter months.

Several guys showed up with horses to help round the cattle up. I grabbed my camera to get photos of the cowboys, roping and riding, rounding up the cows. It was such a cool thing to watch, not as a rodeo event or practice, but real life, using their skills. We got the cattle loaded just before the snow started and we left the next morning.

The end of September, I had my 2nd round of I-131 treatment, having done the low iodine diet, no thyroid meds and liquid diet after getting the pill. Branch and I had bought a Vitamix at the local home and garden show which helped liquify more fruits and veggies for my liquid diet.

The 2nd dose wasn't as high as the original in 2011, but I still had to be isolated for 5 days. I went for my first scan, and they still saw some thyroid uptake, so they sent me home to continue my liquid diet. By the time I went in the 3rd time, my scans were finally clear, and I could eat real food. Branch had started buying me baby food to make sure I had the nutrients I needed. I needed to add foods back slowly otherwise I would be running to the bathroom with my IBS.

I was burnt out at work. I hated getting out of bed to go to work. I started volunteering to do more surveillance for the other guys to stay out of the office. I was running in the afternoons at the school, waiting for LJ to finish basketball practice and to help manage my stress.

In November, after hinting around, DJ asked me if I would be okay with him joining the Army instead of finishing college. I was fine with that if he at least finished his associate's degree at some point. He went to the recruiter with Branch.

DJ signed up for active duty. He would leave March 2013 for Basic training, then to AIT. His basic and AIT locations were the same places I went. It felt like we were coming full circle. He had stopped working construction with my dad and started working at Lowe's near the house. It allowed him to be home more, make the same amount of money and get an employee discount at "Disneyland for Guys."

But it wasn't just DJ signing up. Branch signed up for reserves, after they told him all the waivers he would need, but as a reservist he could still work his fire job. I wasn't shocked he was going to go through the process. It was something he'd always wanted to do.

We had a big Thanksgiving dinner at the house, knowing it would probably be one of DJ's last for a few years.

LJ and I came back from her practice, where I had been running the bleachers. When we got to the house, we were switching the dogs out, while talking to each other. I had the door open, letting Tankker out when Saba and Tankker started fighting. It was bad the way they were both growling, and the other dogs were acting crazy.

LJ and I tried the hose on the dogs, tried hitting them with the broom, but they wouldn't let go of each other. I was afraid one of them was going to kill the other. I went behind one of the dogs, grabbing him by the neck and LJ grabbed the other.

We had them separated. LJ was taking one into the house, but the other 2 dogs were still amped up, setting Saba and Tankker off, again. The one LJ had broken loose and jumped at the dog I was holding back, but I jerked the one I had away, and the attacking dog ended up biting my left hand.

It was dark and it happened quickly. I had no idea which one I was holding, or which one bit me. I felt the bite go through my hand, yelled out and screamed. They must have realized it was me and let go.

We got the dogs separated and I ran in the house to run my hand under hot water. I watched the water run through my hand. The bite had gone all the way through. It was my left hand.

My hand was bruised and swelling, but I needed to stay calm for LJ. I told her to call Branch. He sent one of the rescues out to drive me in, make sure my hand stayed clean and would meet me at the hospital.

LJ stayed at the house with the dogs. The rescue picked me up a few minutes later and drove me to the hospital. Branch got there just as they were taking me in the ER. I was given Percocet to help with the pain and they said they had to do an irrigation flush, to make sure there was nothing inside the wound.

They did an x-ray to make sure nothing was broken after cleaning the wound. They had to cut my wedding band and engagement ring off with 2 separate cuts because my fingers were so swollen. That was when I felt the tears come. There had been so much adrenaline when it happened, then shock on the ride in, but reality hit when they cut my rings.

They irrigated the wound several times and told me they couldn't do stitches because it was an animal bite. Because it was our dog, I didn't have to get rabies shots, but my left hand was out of commission for some time.

They gave me another Percocet before we left the hospital and a prescription for Percocet and Tylenol with codeine. I knew Percocet could cause hallucinations but wasn't prepared for things jumping at me in the dark, while Branch was driving us home.

It must have been midnight or 1am when we left the hospital. As I would doze off, something would jump out at me in the dark. I would yell, scare the bejeezus out of Branch, while grabbing onto the roof and door.

At home, Branch helped me shower and put me to bed. He sent a message to my supervisor as soon as he got to the hospital, letting them know I wouldn't be in the next day. I declined more Percocet. I hated the hallucinations.

We had to decide what to do with the dogs. They had gotten into a fight over the summer while Branch and the kids were walking them, and Branch had gotten some bruises from breaking them up. Then with this fight. We couldn't risk LJ dealing with it by herself, let alone when the kids came down again that summer.

We didn't know how to choose which dog to take to the no-kill shelter, but as a family we decided Tankker would do better with being an only dog, with an older person or couple with no young kids. I didn't want to leave Branch with the task of taking Tankker by himself, but I couldn't handle it. I was the one that brought him into our family.

Branch took him when I was at work and LJ was at school. They couldn't tell us where they went when they were adopted out, but an older lady was looking for a dog just like Tankker. I prayed for a happy, loving, and safe home for him.

After Branch dropped him off, he stopped by my office because he wasn't that far away and took me to lunch. We were both teary eyed, but knew it was for the best. I told him that because I couldn't do the training with my squad, they gave me the open slot for the FBI Crisis and Hostage negotiator course, which started Monday.

I always wanted to be a negotiator and drove the negotiator van a few times during call outs. I was excited for the training. It was an intense training, with lots of classwork, scenarios, and practicals, with simulated situations. We finished right before LJ's birthday.

2013 brought many changes, good, bad, and ugly. Mags had been declared cancer free. She had stayed caught up on her schoolwork and was excited to go back to school. January 8, 2013, a lighted flagpole, and memorial was erected, dedicated to Deputy Coleman. I kept my emotions hidden behind my camera but caught up with people I hadn't seen in a year.

Coleman's wife and kids were still grieving, but his wife was a beacon of strength and light. She was grateful for the love and support shown to her, through the support of her husband.

Branch and I celebrated our 7th wedding anniversary without much fanfare. He commented he needed to get me a new wedding band after my hand was bit. I told him not to worry about it because we couldn't afford it. My finger felt naked, so I started wearing my tanzanite diamond ring.

January rolled into February. We had our Relay meetings and Mag's mom told me at one of the meetings that Mag's scans showed her cancer had come back. They were starting chemo again, and radiation. I dropped into the chair, as if someone had sucker punched me. I looked at her mom, who was not a hugger and decided we both needed a hug.

We hugged for several minutes, not saying a word. She said her husband was going to be home for Valentine's Day and wanted to go to dinner. She said Mags had asked if I would stay with her on Valentine's Day, through the night. Mags wanted me specifically. I said yes, absolutely, while I smiled through my tears.

Branch came back in after walking some committee members out and saw me teary eyed. I told him that Mag's had asked me to spend Valentine's Day with her while her parents went out. We set up time to shop for Valentine's treats for Mags.

The guys I worked with made her cards and bought her fun zombie hunter gifts. I had all the gifts ready to go, finished work at 3 and drove to the hospital. I settled in while Mags said goodbye to her mom, then asked what was first on our agenda.

She wanted to take a quick nap and they would start her chemo at 11 P.M. I changed into my pajama pants, slippers, and comfy shirt, finished my work on the computer, then started reading. Mags woke up a couple hours later. I ordered her dinner, then told her I had all kinds of Valentine's gifts for her.

She had met a couple of the guys I worked with, Marty, Gage and Harry, during Relay events and our Shop with the Sheriff event. She opened the cards and gifts, then I gave her my bag with candy, a new fuzzy blanket and "Fuck Cancer" rubber wrist bracelet, lime green colored.

She ate dinner but complained of a headache. I rang for the nurse. She gave Mags something to help with the pain and I told Mags to try to nap before chemo to see if it helped. She asked if we were going zombie hunting after chemo started, and I said absolutely. They normally made her wait 2 hours before she could get up and walk around so 1 A.M. would be our hunting time.

We both napped briefly, but she kept tossing and turning saying her head hurt. They added more pain meds with her chemo dose. She was pain free when we grabbed her zombie hunting pole (IV pole) and headed into the abyss of zombie land.

Nevo's daughter was admitted, and I wanted to stop to see her mom. She was okay with that, and we headed to their floor. The baby was sleeping, but Mags had a beautifully serene smile on her face as she looked at the baby. She had tubes running out of her arms, legs, and stomach, but Mags said she was beautiful.

I talked with the mom for a few minutes and told her we might stop by after our "hunt" depending on how Mags felt. We left that floor, went to the main floor, got a snack from the cafeteria and she showed me the new kids' activity room. There were video games, reading areas, and activities for older kids, too. We walked in to check it out, but she wanted to go to the garden.

We went to the rooftop garden. She talked about her dreams. She wanted to be remembered as my junior warrior princess of hope. She put her head on my shoulder as we talked about what we would do with the garden. She loved butterflies. She felt like she had been a caterpillar and the cancer morphed her into a butterfly. Then she looked at me and said sadly, "Butterflies bring beauty to the world, but butterflies don't live for long." I wrapped my arm around her and squeezed her tightly against me, then she said we needed to take a selfie together.

I laughed. She hated taking pictures, but she meant it. She had a serene look in her eyes. I grabbed my phone and took a picture, tagging it on Facebook as the PCH zombie hunters. We sat quietly with our own thoughts for a few minutes, then talked quietly about us being birthday twins, cancer twins and zombie hunter twins. I told her she brought so much joy and inspiration to me, as I watched her courageously slay the beast.

She put her cold hand into mine, looked at me, smiled a small smile and said she was tired. I helped her up, grabbed her pole and we shuffled to the elevator. By the time we got off the elevator, she was gripped with a headache and could barely stand. I half carried her to her room, calling for the nurse as I went.

The nurse came running. I told her what happened, and she gave Mags more pain meds. Mags curled up on the bed, crying with pain. I was scared we overdid it, but the nurse said it was possibly pain from the tumor growing on her pituitary gland. She was getting scans and radiation that morning at 6 A.M., but the pain wasn't going away.

Mags put her hand out, reaching for me. I grabbed it and sat in a chair near the bed where she was curled up. Her dad was going to be there between 5 and 5:30 A.M. to go to radiation with her, but I was afraid to leave her. She kept holding her head, moaning in pain, while holding my hand with the other. As her grip loosened, I hoped it was the pain meds working.

When her dad arrived, they still didn't have the pain under control. It had been 2 hours since they started trying to ease the headache, but nothing was helping. They prepped her for the ambulance ride to radiation, shocked at how quickly she had gone downhill.

Her dad hugged me and thanked me, saying they would update me after the scans. I grabbed my stuff and walked to the elevator with them, then headed to the garage to go to work. I couldn't concentrate at all. I tried clearing my head by going for a run, but it didn't help. I left work after lunch to get some sleep and I wasn't doing anyone any good.

On the way home, I received a text from Mag's mom. The scans showed the tumors on her pituitary gland grew significantly, in 5 days, even with chemo. They did radiation before the scans were back but didn't know if radiation would help shrink it. I was going to start a quilt for Mags, with love, prayers, positive thoughts, and good vibes from everyone. Her mom thanked me for everything and said she would let me know how things went over the weekend.

I got home, showered, and went to my sewing shed. I found fabric and colors that Mags loved. I started embroidering sayings and quotes on some of the fabric before sewing it together. The middle was a larger square of fabric with "Mags' Angel" embroidered on it. That was what her dad called her.

I embroidered PCH zombie hunters, Jr. Warrior Princess of Hope, and several other things. I wanted to finish quickly in case they decided not to do more treatment.

I worked and sewed all weekend, crying, praying, writing, sewing, begging, and pleading, before falling into exhausted slumber. I finished the quilt and gave it to her mom Monday. The doctors said there was nothing else they could do. The chemo and radiation weren't working. Surgery wasn't an option.

The family moved Mags to a hospice-type facility for kids, so they could spend time with her, away from a hospital environment. Mags wasn't opening her eyes because the pain hurt so bad, but when her mom gave Mags the quilt, said it was from me, Mags reached out, grabbed it, and snuggled with it.

I never got to see Mags again. It was family only at the hospice house. I never stopped praying and her mom sent me a message telling me Mags was gone. It was February 26, 2013, the anniversary of her parents' wedding when she left her body. The family did a celebration of life, with a balloon release and glow sticks in the colors Mags loved, purple and lime green.

My family planned to go to the beach for our last family weekend together before DJ left for basic training. I did my own ceremony at the ocean the first night, with purple and green lights, glowing in the water, spelling out "Mags."

I would always carry Mags with me, bonded by cancer, separated by age, but connected. Branch made a huge wood frame with sliding glass windows so the family could hang the quilt up. He made a large square case with a glass front, to put the Care Bear holding her ashes inside.

Branch acquired the waivers he needed for the Army. His official join date was in February 2013. We met up with my cousin living in CA and toured the *USS Midway* Museum.

LJ and Branch played in the ocean while DJ and I sat on the beach huddled up in towels and sweatshirts. LJ had gotten her permit, so we let her drive to the beach.

We had a going-away party for DJ before he left in March. LJ finished basketball and now we were on the softball field. LJ was playing while Branch and I helped coach. I had put in transfer requests at work, but the chief told me not to bother. I wasn't going anywhere. I was doing too good of a job, but when I was asked to help with the new computer system in dispatch, he allowed me to do it.

I helped with the CAD, computer-aided dispatch system, during the spring, then after that was finished, I was assigned temporarily to the new group working on the computer systems for deputies in their vehicles.

It was a relief to leave my office. I had moved to my own office again, but I couldn't stay focused on any tasks. My head was all over the place. I couldn't concentrate, I couldn't remember things and I couldn't sit still. I was up and down in my chair all day.

I saw an ad on Groupon for B12 shots and started doing those, then the doctor's office did a 6-week weight/inches lost challenge. I tried the HCG diet again, this time with more information and support, to try to lose weight. I was running more on my own but doing less functional fitness because of the bite on my hand.

I lost over 50 lbs., over the course of 6 weeks. I stayed very strict with my diet, while doing the HCG shots, then maintained the diet for 3 weeks, after finishing the shots. I ended up winning the contest and won several weeks' worth of B12 injections or Botox. I chose the B12.

I got a call from Rosa. We were in the Army together stationed at Ft. Gordon, GA. We kept in touch off and on over the years. She went to school and started work as a nurse. She was living in Flagstaff, working as a travel nurse, and asked when we could meet up.

She traveled between Flagstaff, LA, and San Diego for work. We had years of catching up to do. I hadn't seen her since before LJ was born in 1996 and it was now 2013. She came down for a weekend and went to one of the Relay events with us, after we had gone to a wedding for one of Branch's coworkers.

I was invited to share my story at NAU, Northern Arizona University after college kids heard my story during a training event. Branch and LJ went with me. There was still snow on the ground. I fell in love with the college Relay atmosphere, watching so many young kids hanging out an event that was alcohol and tobacco free, fighting back against cancer, instead of partying.

My daughter took a photo of me, posting it on Facebook with this status, April 19, 2013:

"Today is my mom's 20th birthday since she was first diagnosed with cancer. This woman has taught me that no matter what life gives you, you can overcome anything. She has also taught me the true meaning of strength. She is the strongest person I know, mentally and physically. Both me and my brother are extremely blessed to have her as not only a mother, but a 20-year cancer survivor. I love you, Momma."

I cried reading her post. How did I get so lucky to be the mother of such amazing kids? I was thankful.

The next night we went to the RFL in Cave Creek, where Robbie was part of the committee. I saw one of the guys I had worked with in dispatch. He was one of our posse members that worked with Lake Patrol and shared his time in radio to help when we needed it.

I hadn't seen him since I had left dispatch and I couldn't wait to get one of his amazing bear hugs. He was a great guy, full of life experience, wisdom, and knowledge, but humble, with a smile and hug always at the ready. I introduced him to my husband, and he squeezed me again, telling me how proud he was of me. I told him to stop talking and just hug me; otherwise he would make me cry.

We were all exhausted and only stayed until after the luminaria ceremony. Our local Relay event was the following weekend. We had shirts to sort, programs to make, confirmation calls and last-minute things to take care of.

Branch sent me a text while he was at work, of a wooden sign cut out in the shape of an awareness ribbon, painted purple with purple lights around the border. One of the guys he worked with made it for me so we could attach it to the stage. I teared up again from all the love, then Branch sent me more photos of wooden "HOPE" and "CURE" signs with rope lighting outlining the words.

Branch said he would take them to the school, then get the rest of the stuff on the trailer when we went up Friday afternoon. He knew how hard this event was going to be for me and Mags' family, as well as the entire community. She had been such a lively presence the year prior and now we were remembering her with a large Chinese lantern we would light and send into the sky after the luminaria ceremony.

There were a lot of amazing moments from that event, but the grief was overwhelming at times. I shut most of it way, trying to get through the event, without a full breakdown. People from Relay events all over AZ joined us for our event, knowing how hard it was going to be.

LJ finished school right before DJ graduated basic training in May. We flew out for his graduation. After graduation, we went to my aunt and uncle's for a BBQ celebration and spent the night. We took DJ to Georgia the next morning to sign into his AIT and get a weekend, then we drove to Charleston.

Jack called me a couple weeks before graduation, asking if it was okay for him to bring his new girlfriend to the graduation. I told him it wasn't up to me, then LJ told him to do what he wanted, he didn't spend time with them anyhow. We had a great couple days at the beach with just Branch, DJ, LJ, and me.

Branch and I were still snippy and short with each other. I had no energy and he had energy in abundance. If he came home from work to anything on the counters or sitting out, his mood changed soured. It got to the point that if I wasn't working when he came home from shift, I stayed in my shed sewing until he chilled out.

There were days I purposely left an item on the counter or table to aggravate him. I couldn't help wanting to push his buttons. We argued about many stupid things. I had no idea how to stop. One minute we would be laughing and having a great time, then suddenly the mood would completely change. Sometimes it was me, sometimes it was him, but we argued in the vehicle, on the phone, at home, sometimes just bickering, other times full-blown yelling.

When you're amid the swirling pit of mire, overcome with physical, financial, spiritual, social, mental, and emotional stress, it's hard to see past it to what is right in front of you. Neither of us seemed to be able to get out of the rut of taking our stress, tension, and work issues out on each other. I was miserable and he was too, but we still loved each other. We lost our way on being able to show each other love.

We went camping again. It was my dad's 60th birthday celebration and there were family and friends coming in from all over. They rented the cabins down the road from where we stayed, but us regulars stayed at the ranch. Branch's girls kept talking about moving to AZ to live with us. They fought with Eric all the time and said their mom always took his side.

We learned Eric had pulled a knife on the girls, but instead of putting him in counseling, Devlin made him stay with her parents for a couple weeks. The girls said Eric was aggressive and never got into trouble. I told Branch to spend more 1-on-1 time with Eric and I would keep the girls occupied.

DJ called so we could FaceTime. He showed me his new tattoo on his arm/back. It was the Grim Reaper, with chains, going up his arm, to the shoulder. The Grim Reaper continued over the shoulder towards his back, where a female warrior stood, with a shield and sword, fighting the Grim Reaper. The shield was my badge and there were 3 tombstones around the warrior. The tombstones had my first cancer date, 2nd cancer date and last treatment date.

I teared up when I saw it and when he said what it represented. He got it in honor of me and to symbolize he was starting a career in the Army, to continue the career I had given up for him.

I was so touched by his words and the tattoo. DJ had never been overly affectionate as he got older, but he always checked on me to make sure I was okay. He shared memories of things from when he was younger, what I did for him and LJ and how it shaped who he was. He would share stories about me with other guys and tell them what a bad ass I was. He was proud of me, too.

Branch and I still bickered while camping. I was in a vortex of anger, frustration, irritation and had no control over my emotions toward Branch, then I realized I was also acting like that with my family.

I was a hot mess. I kept adding more things to my busy life to keep me distracted. I wish I had known then you can be depressed and suffer from PTSD, without thoughts of suicide or homicide. There are so many other symptoms that go unnoticed.

I couldn't stop to appreciate all the family and friends in town for my dad's birthday. I didn't appreciate everything my husband did for me that I took for granted. I didn't appreciate the stress and worry he lived with as a caregiver and spouse of a cop. I went through the motions, smiled when needed, but didn't feel it.

I couldn't see how far off track my marriage and life was.

Branch started drinking a lot more. Before he left for Basic Training, our sex life was nonexistent and there was no intimacy. We went through the motions, said "I love you," but there was nothing behind the words or hugs.

We had a going-away party for Branch before his kids left. His mom flew down to spend a couple days with him, then flew home with the kids. We were in town after dropping his mom and kids at the airport when something happened to the expo. It ran enough to get us back home, but it was making a loud noise.

We used DJ's car while he was gone. We had another smaller party 2 days before Branch left. I went to bed. It felt like he was sliding little snide attacks at me while he was drinking.

Branch finished getting his stuff together, so he was ready to leave the next morning. I dropped him off at his recruiters.

Before he left, we sat down and talked about where we were, where our marriage was and decided we would wait until LJ graduated the following spring, then we would get a separation. It wasn't what either of us really wanted, but we were so far apart from each other.

We said our goodbyes. LJ had summer workouts at the school, and I was working a couple days at the training center with the new system. The other days I drove around to the remotest parts of the county, testing the radio/GPS signal in the computers.

I continued running and KJ asked if I wanted to do a half-marathon with her in October. It would go through Scottsdale and Tempe, ending by the Tempe Beach Park. I signed up and had a goal. To think I would finish 13.1 miles at one time seemed crazy.

I was sewing new quilts daily for kids with cancer and soon friends with cancer. It felt like I was living in my sewing shed when I wasn't working. I put a post on FB and said I needed a girls' night out, where I would be and what time. LJ was my DD, she hung out with me until 10, then said she would be back to get me. She left to hang out with friends down the road while I drank, laughed, sang, and let my hair down with my girls.

LJ and I got matching mother/daughter tattoos for my birthday. We did a design of a mother and daughter holding hands with their feet connecting to form a double heart outline. Hers says "Like Mother" and mine says "Like Daughter." They are on our inner forearms as a daily reminder of how much alike we are. As she says now, she is me and I am her.

Branch sent me his address. He was writing to me daily. As I responded, we found we were both able to express ourselves better on paper, while we were apart from each other, with time to think and process.

He went to Sunday service and felt like the preacher was talking directly to him. Branch apologized for his actions and reactions, as well as how he treated me. We shared our deepest feelings, our fears about our relationship and not being together. 7 ½ years after we got married, we were both finally able to share about our personal fears, hopes, dreams and future.

Neither of us was ready to give up but we weren't sure how to move forward. The letters were bringing us close again, sharing intimacies that we hadn't shared with each other in years. He went into caregiver mode after I was diagnosed with cancer, which scared the shit out of him. He told me he couldn't let go of that role, which is why he kept treating me like an invalid.

He always loved how independent I was, but he also realized he wanted me to need him. I may not need him in the "honey-do chores" like most, but I needed him in a way that allowed me to be me.

We slowly worked through some of our communication issues. He kept going to church and I started the power of a praying wife, again. This time focusing on MY change, while praying for my husband. I continued staying busy, sewing, working out, running, hiking, and paying attention to my nutrition.

LJ was a senior, playing volleyball, driving, and hanging out with friends. She hiked with me, we shopped and made dinner together, meal prepped, and I was at every one of her games, home and away.

LJ and I drove to MO for Branch's graduation, while his mom, uncle, brother, and sister-in-law flew in from MN. I was nervous, excited, apprehensive, and somewhat scared to see him again.

It had been over 8 weeks since we said goodbye, with a possible separation hanging over our heads. I knew both of us had grown through the letters we wrote and thoughts we shared, but in person "us," what was that going to be?

We met his family on post and walked to Branch's barracks. After formation, they were released for family day. We could go anywhere on post, but he couldn't drink.

I had packed stuff for sandwiches, chips, snacks, cookies, and drinks so we could drive to a little pond he'd seen on one of their ruck marches. It was quiet and away from the drill sergeants. While we ate, he shared stories of basic with his family, while I feasted my eyes on him.

He would be turning 35 in a couple days, but he looked younger than before he left. He had lost a lot of weight and looked so different, yet the same. The same man I had fallen in love with at hello, the same man I had been willing to get a tubal reversal for so we could try having a baby. He was also the same man I treated critically, taking him for granted and being afraid to share with him, because I didn't want him to think I was weak.

This man was my husband, my lover, my heart, my soul and now, my soldier. He truly was my blessing and I needed to figure out a way to remember that when we went back to daily life, together.

His family was driving back to St. Louis before flying back to MN after he graduated and LJ and I were scheduled to leave, after graduation.

We proudly watched him graduate the next morning. It felt like the ceremony would never end before I could hug and kiss him again. I was selfish in not wanting to share what little time we had together with his family, but knew he was happy they were there.

We went to breakfast after the graduation. My dad called during breakfast to congratulate him, then DJ called while he was on lunch. We left, said our goodbyes then went to the hotel so he could change into his other uniform, out of his dress blues.

We spent the few precious minutes we had, joining together as a couple before he had to shower and get back to post. We were hoping he would get to his barracks, then be able to sign out for a weekend pass.

LJ and I waited in the car. We had gotten food for lunch, while waiting for word from Branch. They weren't getting a pass for the weekend, and he wasn't able to leave the barracks. We were both upset because the plans we had changed drastically.

I didn't want to stay if we couldn't see him, so we went back to the rooms, packed our bags, and departed. I was sad the first couple hours driving but held onto that feeling so I wouldn't take him for granted when he came home. He was scheduled to graduate AIT the first part of December and would fly home.

LJ and I spent the weekend watching movies and eating our emotions. We had changed my bedroom around and I could use my cozy reupholstered chair.

Over the summer, I started working out 2x a day, running in the mornings and weights at lunch. One of the girls I worked, Heather, with was working out with me. We were eating shredded chicken breast, mixed with Pico de Gallo, and chopped avocado.

We were both losing weight, inches and overall felt better. After we finished teaching for 6 weeks, we started only meeting at the training center once a week on Wednesdays. The rest of the work week, 3 of us were testing the computer and the new report writing system.

I was working from home, which allowed me more time to run and write to Branch. I bought him a personalized leather-bound Bible for his birthday. I sent him a devotional book for couples. We would both do it during the week and write a letter at the end of the week about our thoughts.

When my sister and I ran our ½-marathon, I told Branch I would call him so he could run the final .1 miles with me as I crossed the finish line. My sister and I finished just over 2 hours and 15 minutes and I crossed the line, holding my husband's face in my hand, on Facetime video.

I was exhausted but felt elated. I had accomplished something I never thought I'd be able to do again. I needed to keep up with it and asked LJ if she wanted to run one with me in San Diego, by the ocean. She hesitantly agreed. We started doing long runs together on the weekends.

She was running regularly for basketball. I ran the bleachers and sprints during the week while focusing on my nutrition. I was down to 180 lbs., fit with more endurance, and I was holding steady for 6 months.

The first part of November, after my ½-marathon, I went in for my mammogram and ultrasound. I met with the breast cancer surgeon, and he told me I was high risk for breast cancer after receiving such a high dosage of mantle radiation to my chest. He wanted to do a biopsy on the lump found in my breast and they would put a surgical clip in to mark it for reference. It took me 3 days to fully process what they'd said. I was going in the following week for the biopsy, but I was blown away that I was at the same risk for breast cancer as someone with the BRCA gene, breast cancer gene.

Branch and I moved on to another devotion called the Resolution, his was for men and mine for women. The idea came from the movie *Courageous*. I had just started the book when I learned I was high risk for breast cancer.

How was I going to tell Branch while he was still in training? I prayed for peace and calmness as I delved into my devotions. I briefly told Branch about my upcoming appointments but didn't go into much detail. He was on duty that weekend and couldn't talk much.

We couldn't talk at all during the week, so I would have answers before I talked to him again. I went in for the biopsy. I also contacted someone about applying for veteran's disability for my thyroid issues.

The lady helping with my veteran's disability sent me a huge packet to print and fill out, then I had to take pictures of my surgical scars, wounds, and tattoos. I had to take photos of the bruise down the entire right side of my right breast. She told me to get pictures of that and note that I had a marking clip in my breast.

LJ had a basketball tournament in the Grand Canyon, and I went to help chaperone. I filled out the information while we rode the bus, going deep into memories for details, dates, and information. I didn't realize I was crying until LJ sat next to me in the seat to ask a question.

I was okay, I was just reliving a lot of unpleasant memories. She told me no one would have ever known how bad things were because I always had a smile on my face.

I finished my forms, then tucked everything away until we got home. We were going to visit the Grand Canyon, after the tournament. I don't remember the tournament, but I remember looking into nature's beautiful crevices with awe as I held my daughter's hand. We'd seen it before, but it never failed to take my breath away.

I sent my packet in the mail the next morning. I didn't have to go into work that week and school was cancelled for LJ due to roads flooding. We snuggled in to read, write, watch movies, talk, and work. I worked through the second chapter of my book, I had to set it aside. The chapter was on submission.

I'd heard many guys explain their version of submission and submissive wives. I had never been agreeable to their version. I decided to read through my journals. The first one I picked up was from 2003-2005. I read about my sense of limbo, my loneliness, and my thoughts about being ready to be loved, for all my faults.

As I read further into 2004, I came upon the entry I wrote, July 2nd, 2004, where I specifically asked God to bring me someone that would love me unconditionally, through life's ups and downs, the beautiful and ugliness of life, my moods and everything about me. I had love in my heart, and finally felt worthy of love, ready to share, but it had to be the right person.

I stopped reading. I specifically prayed for my husband to come into my life. He was everything I prayed for. I had to finish the chapter on submission. It wasn't saying I didn't get to have my own thoughts and opinions. I had to be respectful and loving of my husband and his.

I sent Branch a message, "I'm ready to be your submissive wife." He got his phone that night and called me asking what I'd meant. I told him about the chapter I was working on, then read him exactly what I'd written in my journal.

He asked me what date it was again. I said July 2nd, 2004. He made the decision to take the job in AZ on July 3rd, 2004, knowing he would be away from his family at least a year. After he found out Devlin was pregnant the 3rd time, he couldn't continue living with the psychological abuse, never being good enough for her, making enough money and always being called stupid.

He was done trying to make her happy and had to take care of himself before he lost himself. He started drinking every night after work with the guys.

He was drunk every time he was home, then he stopped going home on the weekends because he was tired of fighting.

I knew he'd been in a bad situation, but I never realized how bad the verbal, emotional, mental, and psychological abuse had been from Devlin. Some people call it narcissistic behavior.

LJ and I spent the next day watching the rain, watching old movies and I continued working on my devotions. I felt so much lighter knowing Branch was my gift from above.

We were trying to decide on dinner while we were in my room, watching a movie. It was quiet except for the movie on low and the rain in the background. We heard the garage door opening and both jumped up, grabbing a gun, standing around the corner, to see the garage door. We both realized that if it was the garage door, it had to be someone we knew and set the guns down.

We were peeking around the corner when the door opened into the house and in walked my sexy husband. I stopped breathing from surprise, then tears were falling. None of the dogs had barked until they heard my husband say hi.

Syren ran directly to Branch, then LJ and I swarmed him with hugs. We had questions, but also didn't care because he was home. He had known from the day we left that he would be home that weekend but told us December so he could surprise us. He set it up with his friend and they kept it a surprise, too.

I couldn't believe he was home. They told us how they had kept it quiet, how the rain slowed them down, making the flight and drive to the house crazy. His friends left and we tackled him onto the bed.

We had to go shopping the next day. None of his clothes fit, he'd lost so much weight. He'd gone from a 36-38 waist to a 30-32. While we were shopping, he squeezed me and told me I needed new jeans because I had lost weight, too.

The following week was Thanksgiving. Branch wanted to look at vehicles for Black Friday and we went to the Chevy dealer. We found a 2014 Chevy Equinox with 21 miles, they took the Expedition as a trade-in, giving us $3,000 for it.

They said as long as we could get it there, they would take it. They let us drive the new car home and Branch loaded the expo on my dad's trailer the next morning. We had our first brand-new car.

We spent the days and nights getting reacquainted with each other, finding a new and healthy routine, while learning how to express our love for each other. We continued doing devotionals, learning each other's love languages, exploring our childhoods and how we show/accept emotions or love. It was an eye-opening experience for both of us.

LJ and I had signed up to do the Iron Girls 10K, which was right before LJ's 17th birthday. Branch was proud of us doing the run and amazed at our run time.

DJ was home for LJ's birthday and Jack flew in to surprise her. She had a basketball game, 45 minutes from the house and we planned for DJ to pick Jack up. We decided to have Jack come into the game without LJ seeing him, so he could watch her play and didn't mess with her game.

We had dinner that night, then LJ and DJ spent a couple days with Jack at a hotel, before he flew home again. We were happy to have DJ home for Christmas, before he left for Germany. We drove to Alpine, to find and cut our own Christmas tree. As we played in the snow, I got to know my kids as the adults they were becoming. I enjoyed hanging out with my kids and husband, loving the depths of our relationships.

I was grateful to see how much DJ and LJ loved and respected Branch, thanking him for stepping into the father figure role, when he didn't have to. I watched us become a true family as our friendships blossomed.

As we rolled into 2014, we said goodbye to DJ. LJ was finishing her senior year. We were running every Sunday morning, enjoying the peacefulness that stretched over the miles.

Branch and I celebrated our 8th wedding anniversary. Our planning for the Relay event ramped up and Branch was busy with work. We made sure we took the time for each other as a couple to connect regularly and honestly.

Old goat, my dad's friend, was quickly deteriorating from cancer. I made him a quilt with western, ranch and John Deere themes. I embroidered his ranch brand onto the quilt and my dad gave it to him while we stood around his bed. We knew he wouldn't be with us much longer and wanted to show him how much we loved him.

February brought us closer to our half-marathon and Jack asked if he could come with us, to spend time with LJ and watch her run. We set it up for him to fly into Phoenix, spend the night at the house with us, then leave early the next morning.

Our race was Saturday morning, so we got settled into our rooms Friday, picked up our bibs and found the best place for Branch and Jack to hang out during our run.

LJ and I set our pace, about a 9-minute mile, to conserve energy for the entire race. As we ran, we felt the cool salt air from the bay. When we ran around one of the islands, before heading to the road to run to the next island, we saw Branch and Jack on the corner.

LJ and I were feeling good, enjoying ourselves, taking in the scenery, acting goofy for the race photographers, and excited for breakfast once we finished. We had less than a mile left to the finish line when I felt my lower back and left hip tighten up. I immediately started falling behind LJ, running with a limp. I told her to finish on her own and I would meet her there.

Branch knew something was wrong when he saw me slow up so quickly, but he was still ¼-mile down the street from me. By the time I reached him, I told him I was going to limp to the finish and meet them there. We had to go up over the bridge, down a trail under the bridge to the main walkway that took us to the finish line.

Going up the hill was painful, but I was almost done and kept telling myself not to quit. After I passed Branch and Jack, they took a shortcut to the finish line to watch LJ finish, then Branch walked down to the .1 marker, near the finish line, to cheer me on.

My hip and back were so tight, it was hard to lengthen my stride, but once I saw Branch standing there, I pushed through the physical and mental wall, opened my stride, pushing myself hard to the finish line. It's crazy what we can do when we truly allow our mind to push us further than what our body physically tries to limit us to.

Even with me slowing down, LJ and I finished just over 2 hours. Putting in the work and miles had paid off, but I was ready to see the chiropractor when we got home.

We grabbed some bagels, bananas, and water before we decided to drive to the beach. It was still early, and we wanted to put our feet in the water before we went to shower. It was gorgeous. The ocean was cold but felt great on our feet after running.

We toured the area and the shops, enjoying each other. After dinner, Branch and I headed back to the hotel while LJ hung out with Jack, for the first time, by herself.

We left the next morning. I opened Facebook to devastating news. One of the guys I had been in the Army with was diagnosed with cancer and passed away. He was married with 2 younger kids. A great guy that always sent me encouraging messages.

One of the guys I had played softball with for years and ran karaoke at the bar was killed in a motorcycle accident the night before. He was only a few miles from home, after doing a charity poker run earlier, when he ran the stop sign, crashing into the field across the road.

We had talked a few weeks earlier about all the things we were going to do to help the community, putting both of our forces and skills to work. My heart hurt the rest of the drive home. It felt like someone I loved was always dying or being diagnosed with cancer.

The neighbor's daughter reached out to me, asking me to make a quilt for her friend that had been diagnosed with the same type of cancer I had when I was 20. I made a quilt with her favorite colors of lime green, pink and peace signs.

When I met her at CTCA, I found out we had the same care manager and doctor. When they came in the room and saw me, they did a double take, then ooohhed and aahhhed over the quilt. It was officially her last day of treatment and the quilt was her gift. We became instant friends.

Branch, LJ, several nurses from CTCA and I were all running the Kiss Me, I'm Irish 17k for St. Patrick's Day. The nurses were running their first ½-marathon the following month and wanted to make sure they were ready. My care manager, Jewel, always called me her inspiration and I called her my hope.

I decided to make personalized running bibs for our team. I used shamrock fabric as the border for the bibs, with green embroidery on white fabric, with our team's name on them.

Branch, LJ, and I finished, and stood at the finish line to cheer the others on. I saw one of the nurses with her sister come around the corner and ran out to meet them. We crossed the line together and a few months later, she became my primary care manager when Jewel moved to Oregon. That was the first of many finish lines we would all cross together.

I had been telling Branch that I needed to sit and write my story because so many people kept encouraging me to help inspire others. He agreed and we talked about some of the stories to share. This was when I began this book.

I told Sgt. Towns and Heather I finally put my outline on paper and started typing. He told me to go home after our morning meeting to sleep.

March 26, 2014, after a PET scan, bone scan, and bloodwork, I was deemed "cancer free." I was leaving a couple days later to fly to MN and help Branch's mom. She was strong enough for a stem cell transplant, using her own bone marrow and cells. She had finished all the chemo. After the transplant, I was going to stay at the recovery house with her. She ended up being released the afternoon I got there.

Her bloodwork looked good, and her levels were stable, so the doctor said we could go home. We had to follow up 3x a week with her local office for bloodwork, only if she rested at home, we could leave.

I got her home, settled in with her "favorite blanket," a quilt I made her, then went to the grocery store. There were certain things she couldn't eat and others that would help significantly.

She started slowly with soup and lighter bland foods until she got her appetite back. She napped in her recliner during the day. I kept her fed with smaller meals and snacks, then she would go to bed early.

I slept in the room next to her, making sure if she had to use the restroom or needed anything during the night, I was there. After she felt better, I moved upstairs because Branch would be coming back with me. I was there for 2 weeks, flew home on a Thursday to get LJ ready for her senior prom, then Branch and I drove back to MN for 2 more weeks.

Our Relay was the end of April and the doctor approved her to visit AZ, if she still got bloodwork done 2x a week. She was excited to get out of the cold weather and to be part of our Relay event again. We met my stepmom in North Dakota so she could ride home with us, stayed a night in SD, then headed to Colorado.

We were staying a night or two at Hazel and Liam's house, then a final night at KJ's before driving home. We knew it would take us some time but wanted to make sure the ride wasn't rough on Caryn.

The day after I got home, LJ and I did the final leg run of the Law Enforcement Torch Run for Special Olympics. I did okay the first few miles, but the heat hit me harder than I expected. After running in cold weather for a month, the 90-degree temps make quite a difference.

I got on the bus that was following to pick up stragglers. Some of my old squad was running with me and we all circled up by the university stadium where the games were being held and ran in formation, into the stadium, holding the torch. We ran a lap around the track as everyone stood and clapped, then we got to meet some of the athletes. It was such an honor to meet these athletes with different abilities, overcoming the "dis" abilities labeled by society.

They had competitive spirit, teamwork, drive and determination, but the biggest thing they had, was heart. I thanked them for sharing their talents with the world and inspiring us all.

LJ finished her senior year of sports, passed all her finals and was ready to graduate. We were having a graduation party at the house. Jack and his fiancé were coming in the night before she graduated so they could help us set up for the party.

We asked our neighbor if Jack and his family could stay in their house while they were gone. Our neighbors were snowbirds. Other family was staying with my sisters.

LJ was sad DJ wasn't going to make it for her graduation. We told her we would put him on FaceTime so he would still be a part of it. She left for school Thursday morning for senior pictures, graduation walkthrough, then to get ready for graduation. We told her we would be up there before 6. I was wearing a bright yellow dress so she could spot us in the crowd.

After Branch dropped LJ at school, he drove to the airport to pick up DJ. We had set it up to surprise LJ at the school after graduation. Branch and I were the only 2 that knew until Jack came to the house and saw him.

I went to the school to save our seats for family, then Branch brought DJ up right before the graduates walked out of the school. Branch brought him by the softball field and snuck up under the bleachers. Once we had him in the stands, we had him sit behind Branch, so he was mostly hidden. DJ had worn his Army uniform so we knew he wouldn't stick out as the graduation was outside at dusk.

DJ worked his way to the bottom of the bleachers right before the ceremony was over, then when the graduates threw their hats up and started looking for their families, DJ was almost in front of LJ. She didn't see him at first because she was looking for me. I had my camera up to record when she saw DJ.

I saw that forever bond when LJ turned her head, saw the uniform, and realized DJ made it to her graduation. Her lips trembled from emotion, then my babies hugged.

I couldn't contain the emotions. Tears ran down my face, the pride at seeing LJ graduate and the 2 of them hugging. Branch and I were going to be empty nesters but knowing God had granted me this time to see my kids grow up, made my heart smile. I was glad we were doing a smaller family dinner after graduation. I was an emotional mess.

The weekend went by too quickly. Branch's mom, all my parents, and Jack's family was there. We had a fantastic day and night, taking pictures, playing games, and loving on each other.

Branch's mom was flying home Monday, DJ was home a few more days, and Jack's family was leaving Tuesday.

Jack, his family, DJ and LJ went to Vegas Sunday night, which gave Branch and I some time to catch our breath, get his mom ready to fly home and the house back in order.

I came home and Branch asked me to dance with him in the garage to a new song, "Who I Am with You," by Chris Young. He was the calm to my storms.

The girls were coming down, but only staying until after the 4th of July. This was the first year our family wouldn't be spending the 4th of July on the ranch.

None of us knew what to do with each other without our annual camping trip. Eric had football and summer school, so he didn't come down. Branch took the girls and dogs camping. He went with a couple guys he worked with and their girls. They hiked, fished, and enjoyed the outdoors for a couple days.

One of the girls I worked with, Bab, had been trying to get me on a road bike for years, to compete in triathlons with her. I went over on a Saturday morning to try one of her bikes. I had bought a pair of padded cycling shorts and a helmet. She had the bike and gloves for me. I could wear my tennis shoes for the test ride.

One of our football parents' friends, Ed, also knew Bab, and he came out to ride with us, too. We left her house, rode the back roads to the main road going into one of the county parks, before we turned around. When we came down the hill from the park, I felt the freedom of riding a bike again, reminding myself how much I loved riding.

When we got back to the house, Branch saw my face and knew I had loved it. Branch and I headed home. We talked about biking the entire way home, and the next day I got a text from a friend that helped put athletic events together. He had been contacted for a fundraising event that would be a bike race and he wanted my input.

They were looking for input from a cancer survivor/patient at CTCA for the event and he immediately thought of me. He said it would be a 3-mile fun ride event, 25-, 50- and 100-mile events. I had an idea a couple years prior for ACS, but they didn't have a way of putting the money specifically towards pediatric cancer research at the time.

I sent him my ideas and logo before we met with the entire event planning committee. CTCA had done some fundraising events prior but wanted to rebrand and have it specifically go to pediatric cancer research. The group we would be raising money for did clinical trials as well as advanced research, not just for CTCA.

We came up with Trails for Trials, using the logo me and my squad mate, Marty, helped design and began getting the community involved. There was a kid in the community that was fighting cancer and the entire community rallied around him.

They knew his cancer would never go away and he made a bucket list of things he wanted to do. I followed his story for months, having met him at another event. His story went viral, and he had support from local sports organizations, nonprofit groups, businesses, as well as people from around the world. Everyone wanted to help him reach all his bucket list items. I recommended he be our VIP for the fun ride.

Everything was set in motion for the event. We had a day selected, the other members started working on logistics for the rides, traffic control, sponsors and the after party. I found a photographer who was a veteran and married to a cancer survivor.

Before Branch left for his Army training, we went to the local sports shop for a few things he needed, then looked at bikes. The guy we talked to was a huge military and first responder supporter and his wife was battling stage 4 ovarian cancer. After hearing my brief story, what we were doing and why I was looking for a bike, he said he would give us a great deal.

I laughed, what kind of great deal, the bike is over $1500, on sale. He said if I was serious, he would get me fitted for the bike, with shoes, gloves, water bottle holders, bike tool and repair kit, along with a jersey, for less than $1000. I stood there with my mouth hanging open and before I could respond, Branch said, do it.

I walked out with a brand-new Diamondback road bike, split saddle seat, the gator tube/tires, gloves, shoes, water bottles and everything I needed to hit the road. He made sure the bike was custom fitted to me before I left and said to bring it in after 50 miles for a free tune-up, then again before the Trails for Trials ride.

Branch and I walked out, after paying less than $1000 for everything, still in awe. I was initially going to sign up for the fun ride, but Branch said, "Well, now we need to sign up for at least the 50 miles. You've already done 14 miles for your first time on someone else's bike, and we have 8 weeks to prepare." I laughed; we would be out of town for 2 of those weeks.

We signed up for the ride. Our friend, Ed, had an extra bike Branch could ride and train with. He said he would get it ready to go while Branch was gone for Army. We spent a couple quiet days at home, with the girls, before Branch left. LJ and I were leaving the day after, to drive the girls home.

We had the car packed to take the girls home. I gave the girls a map, flashlight, and pencil so they could choose our route. I told them I wanted to stay off the interstate as much as possible so we could enjoy nature. The youngest, Ann, was the main navigator, she kept track of where we should turn, how many miles until we hit our next road and when we should stop for food/gas.

We saw some old houses, ghost towns, lots of pasture and animals during the day. We were a few miles from turning onto one of the state highways and I had slowed down, giving the girls time to find where we had to turn. Suddenly, there were deer along the shoulder of the road, right next to the car.

The girls squealed because the deer had scared them. We were all laughing when Branch called to let us know they had made it to CA for their training. He asked how the drive was going and we laughed sharing the deer story.

Ann continued navigating until we had to get on the freeway, taking us into Iowa and north to MN. There was no other direct route to get there. We drove until we were about 6 hours from MN, then I pulled into a parking lot for a quick nap. LJ could have drove, but we weren't in a hurry.

All of us took a nap, then we had breakfast, washed our faces, replenished snacks, and fueled up. Branch called as we were entering MN. The girls loved talking to him over the car speaker.

After we dropped the girls off at Caryn's house, LJ and I hit the road. I was dropping LJ off in Chicago with her dad, then I was driving to NY. In Chicago, we met up with Jack and his family a pizza place we all loved. I got to catch up with his aunt, cousins, and their families.

My friend Mandy had gotten sick, was on a feeding tube and J tube, in and out of the hospital, with no true answer as to what was wrong with her. I made a lap quilt for her, with Steelers fabric and bright colors.

I told her I was driving to NY. She was staying at a friend's house, near my parents. I didn't know where I was going to stay, but I was going to see her first thing.

I left after 9 P.M. for NY. I was going to drive as far as I could before I needed to stop for sleep.

Branch called and we talked for a couple hours while I was driving. Having the Bluetooth speaker in the car was great.

I made it into Ohio, outside of Columbus, when I decided to stop. There was a truck stop, in the middle of nowhere, and I needed fuel. I was on the phone with Branch, told him where I was stopping, and I was going to nap for a few hours. I was 5 hours from my final stop and didn't need to push it.

I parked in a spot close to the store front, but out of the main traffic area. I rolled the windows down enough to let fresh air in, hung sweatshirts in the windows for privacy, a towel in the front window to block out the light, grabbed my pillow and light blanket, then I knocked out.

It was after 3 A.M. when I stopped. I didn't have a set time to wake up. I slept until after 6 A.M., feeling refreshed, knowing I had enough sleep to get me to NY. I was in familiar territory now, having traveled these roads for years.

As I entered NY, I drove along the highway my dad had helped build, when I would go to work with him. No one knew I was coming except Mandy and the friends she was staying with.

I made it to see Mandy by early afternoon, surprising her that I had gotten there so quickly. I was shocked when I saw her, lying in the hospital bed with tubes coming out of her stomach, her gorgeous thick hair lying limp and the look of defeat on her face. There were bottles of medicine for pain, to feed her, to clean her tubes and to help her digest food.

It was less than 2 years since I'd seen her for the mud run. She looked completely different. I sat with her, talking about my drive, filling her in on the crazy of my life, while we waited for her friend, Kassie, to get home. I knew her friend's husband, Ryan, but I didn't know the wife. She must have a big heart to open her home to Mandy and take care of her daily.

I had been there for almost an hour when Kassie came home with the kids. She had 2 boys and was in the process of adopting an older girl. The quiet was suddenly filled with noise, activity, and life. Mandy introduced me to Kassie, who seemed very short with both of us, as if she didn't want me there. I told Mandy I would come back later.

Mandy asked me to stay. Kassie was just busy. She was working, taking care of the kids, house, Mandy and was coaching the youngest's soccer team. I went out to see if there was anything I could do to help and brought some groceries in.

Kassie had to leave in an hour to get to the field for the youngest's soccer game and asked Mandy if she wanted to go. Mandy said she was going to stay home, but I could tell the kids wanted her to go. I told Mandy I could drive her. The wheelchair would fit in the car, and I could get some photos of the kids playing soccer.

Kassie helped me load the wheelchair after we loaded Mandy into my car. I told her I would stop for some snacks before we got to the field.

We got to the field, unloaded the wheelchair, and got Mandy a spot close to the field, under a shade tree. Mandy had been a photographer. She missed the feel of the camera in her hands.

I asked if she wanted to take some photos, but she was too tired. I heard the depression in her words but didn't want to push. I wanted to talk to Kassie, hear what the doctors said, and hear how things were really going and if I could help.

Kassie invited me to the ice cream place they went to after the game. While we were standing in line for ice cream, she told me that was the first time Mandy left the house in weeks, other than going to the doctor's office.

She asked where I was staying. I wasn't sure yet. She offered her home, there was an extra bed in the boys' room because her youngest normally slept with her. I started to decline when she put a hand on my arm and said I would be helping her.

We got pizza for dinner then went back to their house and I saw her husband, Ryan. He had gotten home from work and was excited to hear I was staying with them.

I found out Ryan did all the cooking. Kassie didn't know how to cook and didn't want to learn. I offered to cook dinner a couple nights.

I made parmesan chicken and broccoli casserole the first night. I bought some of my favorite items for the house: salt rising bread, cheese curd, heavenly hash ice cream and Genesee Cream Ale beer. These had been staples of my childhood.

Mandy had a doctor's appointment the next morning and asked me to come along. We discussed what was physically wrong with Mandy, but what the doctors said, what Mandy said and what her signs/symptoms were all differed.

Mandy wouldn't let anyone go into see the doctor with her, which was why Kassie was skeptical of what was going on. The dosage for pain meds continued to get higher. Some of the things Mandy said contradicted what Kassie knew. Kassie suspected Mandy was lying about things.

The next morning, we went to the doctor's, where Mandy told us to wait in the waiting room until she was finished. We sat there and when the door opened, I asked the doctor if I could talk to him quickly because I had some questions. I told him I had just gotten into town and wanted to understand some of the medications, what to expect short term and how I could help.

I had told Kassie I was going to do it, so she was prepared with Mandy. Mandy tried to stop me, saying she didn't feel well and wanted to go home to rest. I told her I would only be a couple minutes and would be done by the time Kassie finished loading her into the vehicle. Kassie took her outside while she protested. I walked directly into the doctor's office.

Mandy was never officially diagnosed with gastritis, but she presented as if that's what it was. I asked what some of the things were that could cause a similar situation. There were entirely too many strong pain medications for it not to be something major.

After a few seconds of thought and silence, he told me one of the main causes of what someone like Mandy was dealing with, was long-term addiction to pain medications.

I asked if that's why there was a consistent increase in her pain medications. He told me that was a dependency issue. Her body was used to the larger doses, but constantly craved more. I knew she was killing herself slowly.

I thanked him for his time. I would be able to make peace with the situation now, understanding what we were truly dealing with. I walked out to the truck. Mandy wouldn't look at me or speak to me. I didn't talk about the visit at all and asked Kassie about the kids' soccer schedule.

The oldest boy had a game the next night, in a town nearby and the girl had one two days later.

We stopped at Walmart on the way home. I told Mandy she needed to get out of the truck and come in with me so we could spend time together after I'd driven all that way. I was guilt tripping her, but I wanted to see how far I could push her, knowing she wasn't sick the way we thought she was.

I bought some random items. As I was leaving the craft section, I saw my mom. She was working and I could see the surprise on her face. I gave her a hug; told her I was there to see Mandy and invited them to dinner for lasagna in a couple nights. Kassie said they would love the company and we made plans for 6 P.M., Thursday night.

My mom talked to Mandy briefly, gave her a hug while Mandy milked the attention. Kassie and I made eye contact, rolling our eyes in unison, then smiling, knowing we were on the same page. We loved Mandy, but we weren't going to be manipulated.

We went to the house, got Mandy settled in for a nap. I ran to the store for a few more items while I waited for Mandy's new prescription to be ready.

Kassie and I laid on her bed in the room with Mandy, after she woke up. We shared memories and some of the crazy things we had done. I put stuff together for dinner, then went back in the room. We were talking about how the 3 of us would always be intertwined now.

Mandy wanted to do something with just the 3 of us. She talked about skydiving. I immediately shot that idea down. We talked about other things, then she asked, what about a tattoo, representing the 3 of us, intertwined. I liked that idea. We came up with the Celtic trinity symbol representing, mothers, sisters, daughters. The 3 rings would be intertwined, in purple, teal and pink representing each of us as a mother, sister and daughter.

Mandy contacted her friend that owned a tattoo shop. He could get us in that night. He said he would have something drawn up for us to see when we arrived.

Mandy went first. If she got tired, hers would be done. We loved the sketch. We decided to have it placed on the nape of our necks. All of us had longer hair so we could cover it if needed. We got the matching tattoos as a symbol of our individual relationships with each other.

Mandy was still upset with me after a comment I made. She said she wasn't coming because she didn't feel good. Kassie said she was going to hear about it after the game that night but thanked me for being upfront about things.

We got to the game, set up our chairs on the sideline when the referee came to Kassie and told her the other ref wasn't going to make it. Kassie looked at me and said, "You know soccer, go out and ref for me." I looked down at my flip-flops and said, "I can't run in these." She kicked off her tennis shoes, which she had just put on before we left, gave me her socks, and said, "Get your ass out there," while the other parents cheered for me to go.

I was shaking my head and laughing, then ran onto the field after I got the shoes tied. We wore the same size, which worked out perfectly. She gave me her extra whistle and the other guy kept time. I just had to watch for out of bounds, off-sides, penalty shots and high kicks.

We finished the game, our team won. I dubbed her son playing "Big Booty Rudy" because he was fast but had the trunk behind him. We stopped for ice cream before driving back to the house. Ryan was laughing and telling stories of when we played soccer in high school. He told the kids about how aggressive I was on the field, some of the plays I made as goalie and that the guys were afraid to play against me.

I put the casserole in the oven after we got home, giving everyone enough time to shower and get ready for dinner. The kids were excited to try something different and Kassie said it smelled amazing. I said hi to Mandy, but we purposely stayed in the kitchen so she would want to come out, instead of everyone coming to her.

The boys weren't sure what was going on, but they were used to their mom jumping up when Mandy called. Kassie waited a minute before going in and Mandy called her again. Kassie went in, made sure all the lines were clear, and Mandy asked for more pain meds. Kassie told her no, it wasn't time for the next dose and the doctor had made it clear.

Mandy started yelling at Kassie, saying she was being mean, she was purposely being hateful since I got there, and Mandy would find someplace else to go. Kassie told her to do what she needed, but she wasn't going against the doctor's orders.

I sat down to talk to Mandy. There were so many stories, but the one thing that kept sticking out to me was the money. Most drug addicts never have enough money when they need a fix, especially when a daily habit begins to cost more. I started asking Mandy questions, in a non-threatening way to get her to tell me a story, noting the inconsistencies.

I searched public information and court records where she used to live, as well as the places she had "stayed" in between. She had been pulled over, found with prescription drugs in the car and her system, while she was driving her kids.

I don't know why or when she started using the pain meds, but it had progressed to the point she was always over medicated. She had burnt her bridges with several people in other states and went to NY where her brother lived. She enrolled in school, worked at the bar and I think she tried to start over.

After I had seen her in 2012, she met a guy from NJ that was visiting NY for the summer. They got married after dating for a couple months and it went downhill fast. He made a lot of money and she had started using again. She worked her way in, pushed for marriage, then less than a couple months later, the problems started.

Her husband had spent time in the hospital with her, taking her to and from specialists all over, NY, PA, and NJ until he realized she was searching for prescriptions for pain medications from the visits. Friends that knew both sent me messages about her lying to everyone, how she had been borrowing money and no one knew the truth.

After I dug further, the puzzle started coming together. She wound up divorced, less than 6 months of marriage. She lived with friends, then got the gastro diagnosis. She had a strained relationship with her mom, but I figured there were more underlying issues from her childhood.

My mom and stepdad were coming for dinner, so I pushed my thoughts aside while I put the lasagna together. I had put the lasagna in the oven, turned to the sink to wash my hands, then took a step towards the fridge when I stepped in water, felt myself falling, but somehow stayed upright.

Kassie and the kids were at the kitchen table eating a snack, laughing after watching my ungraceful dance to stay up. When the kids were putting dishes away, one of the bowls must have had water in it, dripping onto the floor. Kassie said I was like Wonder Woman and Supergirl combined after that display.

I laughed, but I tweaked my shoulder and lower back. I limped to the refrigerator to get my snack, then limped back to the table.

My parents got to the house just as I was pulling the lasagna and garlic bread out of the oven. I set the salad, bread, and lasagna on the table.

It was a lively meal, but also strained. My mom kept making comments about not knowing I was home, me not staying at the house, and other comments about being kept out of the loop. I didn't try to defend myself, just changed the subject. The kids talked about my superhero moment earlier, how I refereed the soccer game and took the boys down during a wrestling match the day before. It was after 10 P.M. when we got up from the table, said our goodbyes to my parents and put everything away.

The next morning, I laid down on Kassie's bed to read, while Mandy slept. After she woke up, I asked how she was feeling, if she needed anything and how she'd slept. She was still drowsy while we talked, I didn't confront her about the lies she'd told, but asked her if she'd really been diagnosed with gastroparesis and she said no. They just thought that's what it was originally.

I told her what was going on in my life. I was asked to go to Washington, D.C., in September as an Area Congressional Team lead for ACS CAN. I explained we would be talking with our senators and representatives directly, pushing for specific bills to be passed and sharing how our cancer stories tied into the ask.

I had been asked to share my story for the palliative care ask because I'd had such a different experience fighting cancer after going to CTCA, where they took care of the whole person. How I was going to write a letter to my mom, explaining things from my view and perspective growing up. I wanted her to know the reasons it was hard to connect with her and have a real relationship. We talked until Branch called.

I was doing a 5k cancer charity run that Saturday with my cousin's daughters. The youngest asked me if I would run with her and she wanted to beat her older sister.

It had been almost 5 years since my cousin had passed from brain cancer and I was honored to run with her daughters in her memory. The youngest was 8, but she was determined to beat her older sister. I told her we would go at her pace, if she wanted to run, we would, if she wanted to walk, we would do that, too.

We ran through familiar neighborhoods, past houses with people sitting on their porches, cheering us on. There were encouraging signs in the front yards, along the road, on trees and light poles. We kept the older sister in our sights until we were close to the finish line, and I said it was time to sprint.

We sprinted to the end, passing her sister. She crossed the finish line with a huge smile on her face. She was just like her mom, quiet but full of determination and competitiveness.

I went to my niece and nephew's soccer game and planned a night out at the Legion before I left.

Monday, after I got up, I was talking to Branch when I heard arguing. It was Kassie and Mandy. I didn't know what started it, but it was getting heated. I talked to Branch a few more minutes while he was on a break, then went into the living room.

Mandy accused Kassie and I of conspiring against her. She didn't need to put up with friends like this and she would go to another friend's house. If she did, she would go downhill quicker.

When I heard Mandy bad mouthing me, I got pissed, after trying to keep my emotions in check for almost a week. I stormed into the room, saw Mandy's face was red, full of rage and hate. I didn't recognize her at that moment and let go of my anger. She needed an intervention. It wouldn't do any good, but I would have it off my chest.

I fell to the bed with tears running down my face. I already said things to Mandy that we wouldn't recover from. She wasn't the person I knew. That person was lost to addiction.

I told her to do what she was going to do, but I couldn't listen to any more of her lies. I knew she was an addict. It was causing her to wither away and made me sad that my friend died to the addiction. I would always love the Mandy I knew, but I wasn't going to add more stress to my life, fighting her when she didn't want to fight for herself.

I walked out of the room, sat in the recliner in the living room and let the tears come. It was time for me to let her go, let the mourning begin and start to heal. She and Kassie continued to fight, but I put my headphones in.

Kassie came out of the room, slamming the door shut and sat on the couch. Mandy had called another friend and she was coming to pick Mandy up. Approximately 15 minutes later, we heard a vehicle pull up and a knock on the door. She didn't know what had happened but started helping Mandy move her stuff to the truck.

Kassie went in the room to pack Mandy's meds, medical equipment, clothes, and personal items. 30 minutes later, Mandy was dressed, with her hair styled, and she walked out the door.

No one said goodbye, waved or acknowledged she was walking out forever. I watched her go, as she clutched the pillow and quilt, I made her. Tears were running down my face. Kassie and I sat there in silence for several minutes feeling the loss.

I finished the letter to my mom, sharing my heart, hurt and feelings on 12 sheets of paper. I dropped it off Tuesday morning before I went exploring with my camera. I traveled back roads, hiked old paths, trying to restore my balance.

Thursday night my mom dropped a letter off at the house while I was at the kids' soccer game. I was saddened by my mom's responses. Instead of reading what I wrote or trying to understand, she told me I was ungrateful for all the things she had done for me. I didn't bother replying. Our relationship was what it was, I had to let go of the "be grateful you still have your mom" guilt.

The rest of the week passed with soccer games, swimming, BBQ and Saturday we went to the cemetery to my grandparents' and cousins' graves before I left.

I told my mom I would meet for breakfast the next morning before I left and packed my bags. It was hard saying goodbye to this family that had taken me in for 2 weeks, becoming more than friends. Being in NY for 2 weeks, my childhood memories had stirred some things up and I was able to remember that I had some good parts to my childhood.

I spent Sunday night in Chicago with LJ, before we left the next morning. Branch and I had talked for 6 hours straight while I drove through Ohio and Indiana. He didn't have anything to do and wanted to keep me awake for my drive. We had some of the best conversations, since he'd come home from training the year before.

We had connected on a new level, with a better understanding of each other, ourselves, and our relationship. I loved talking to him as my best friend, my partner in crime, my confidante, and my lover. Our conversations had more depth, meaning and directions. We weren't afraid of saying what we felt or thought, for fear of making the other mad.

We learned to crush the eggshells instead of walking on them. We were learning to listen to understand, not just to reply, and to think about something from the other's perspective. We had to stay strong together, instead of fighting each other.

LJ and I left just before a storm moved into Chicago. We stopped at KJ's house in NM before we continued to AZ the next morning.

It was an 8-hour drive from her house to ours and we knew Branch wouldn't be home until late Tuesday night. We made it to my sister's before midnight. She had cookies for us and gave us her bed, as she says, she must have felt exceptionally gracious. She slept in the guest room that night. We ate breakfast the next morning, showered and hit the road again.

LJ was recruited to play basketball at a junior college and started college in August. Branch and I started riding bikes a couple times during the week and did a longer ride every weekend with Ed, who was signed up to do the 50 with us.

Branch, LJ, my stepmom, and I went to San Diego to celebrate mine and my stepmom's birthdays. I found a great deal on Coronado Island, at the Loews Resort. We stayed for 3 nights and 4 days, invited Rosa down for a birthday bonfire. My cousin and his girlfriend came by, too, they were getting ready to move to Hawaii, so we were glad to see them.

We went sailing one day, enjoying the ocean air and views. We spent a couple hours at the beach that night to watch the sunset and the last day we stayed the entire day at the beach.

The morning of my birthday, my daughter posted a photo of us with this post: "Happy birthday to the greatest woman in the entire world! Mother, you are just so cool. I can't imagine if someone else was my mom. Thank you for all that you do for our family. You are greatly appreciated, and I love you to the moon and a little more. If I wasn't distracted by watching Sophie the first you could have seen this about 20 minutes ago... but anyways I'm gonna get you that Viper for your birthday one day, I promise.

Love yours truly"

My kids were always bringing me to happy tears with their words. Branch had been making me personalized cards for years, starting when he couldn't afford a real card. I loved the personal and customized touch, knowing he put a lot of time and thought into each card. His squishy mushy side came out when he gave me my cards and I've cherished them all.

Branch and I discussed me learning how to swim correctly, learning how to breathe as I swam underwater, for competitive swimming. Our friend said he could teach me if we had access to a pool. We asked the principal at the school because they had a pool that wasn't used after school started.

The principal gave us access to the school pool and warned us it wasn't heated. The first couple months, it wasn't bad. I practiced turning my face out of the water to breathe, while keeping my head in the water, moving forward.

I went to the ACS CAN event in D.C. I got to the hotel for the dinner/reception, 30 minutes after it started. I was able to get checked into my room, dropped my bag, and headed to the dinner. The AZ team was sitting together, and they saved me a plate/seat.

I loved the energy of the room, cancer fighters from all over the country, including Guam and Puerto Rico. We were given our packet and agenda for the next couple days before we were excused from dinner. We had to meet for breakfast the next morning at 8 A.M., to start the day of training.

We would be "Storming the Capitol" the next morning, with all of us in our light blue polo shirts, AKA "Smurf" shirts. Each of the 3 asks was explained in detail, along with how to tie the personal stories into the ask.

Our entire team would go to both senators' offices, then we would split up and go to each of our representatives' offices, with at least 3 people teaming up for each representative, to cover them all.

I was chosen to share my story during the palliative care ask at Senator McCain's office to tie in my diagnosis during the Army. I would share the difference in treatment, and recovery with and without palliative care.

We went to Senator Flake's office first; I sat by the window to watch the interaction and listen to the transitions between asks and stories. I was nervous about sharing my story with McCain, but he avoided us, and we spoke with one of his staff. As we introduced ourselves, what district we were from and town we lived, I was the last to share my info so I could transition into my ask/story.

I knew I had a limited amount of time to share and went right to the meat of it, with being in the military, mother of a 6-month-old when I was diagnosed with cancer. I shared the loneliness, the fear and uncertainty and tied in the ask. When I finished, the staffer had tears. I looked around the table to see that everyone had tears in their eyes. I saw up close and personal how much 1 piece of my story impacted others.

We headed back to our rooms to change for the Lights of HOPE ceremony at the capitol. Each person had sold luminaria bags as fundraisers, giving people the chance to share the name and photo of their loved one touched by cancer. We had over 10,000 bags surrounding the reflecting pool outside of the capitol, each bag representing a loved one, each candle had a name.

We finished out the event on Wednesday, hearing how many senators and representatives had voted yes on the asks we made. Individually our voice was effective but combining our voices from all over the country was saving lives and changing legislation that affected cancer patients. My voice had to be loud enough for all the voices in my district, because more voices made a bigger impact.

I got home late Wednesday. My team had one more long training ride to get in before our event, the Trails for Trials 50-mile bike ride. We had a large group for the fun ride to support our VIP.

We had been hit with a huge storm that dumped a lot of rain and the logistics people had to ride the route, changing it a bit to avoid flooded washes.

I was at the front of the pack, mostly for photo ops, but told my team I would move to the left as the real racers took off. My team let me set the pace and I felt great. The sky was scary with storm clouds ready to burst. We had ridden about 3 miles before we started turning and we rode directly into a head wind blowing at us.

I kept my energy output the same, even though it slowed me down. I needed to conserve energy for the entire ride and a huge hill was coming up. I didn't fully understand when I should shift, which gear I should shift into, if I should be on the big shifter or the smaller one.

Branch was trying to coach me with shifting while I was just trying to stay focused going up the hill. He was trying to help me, but he didn't understand how I had to stay in my zone, with no distractions, to finish my small goals. I snapped at him a couple times on the course instead of doing what he said, to make it easier.

He got in front of me so our team could draft off each other. I would do what he said without him seeing. I am not a team person when it comes to running, bike riding, etc. If I am doing all the work on my own, then I am in my own mental zone. I tried explaining that to Branch, but he was used to helping people when they needed it. I was un-coachable in that moment.

There must be other people with this mentality, I can't be the only one. I have tried to be more coachable because my husband is full of knowledge, but I can still be an ass during coaching moments. There's a pattern since childhood of my stubbornness.

We were rolling along at a good pace during the ride, everyone was staying hydrated, we had 35 miles under our tires and came to the detour. I hadn't been this way and didn't know what to expect so we kept pedaling. We came around the curve to a huge hill, steeper than the first, but not as long.

I kept pedaling, using the knowledge on shifting and made it over halfway up the hill before I physically and mentally couldn't pedal any further. I looked up and most of the bikers were off their bikes, walking up the hill with their bike.

I didn't want to be that person, but I was going to crash because you can only balance so long on a bike not moving. I unclipped from my pedals, worked my way to the far side to dismount. I drank some water while I huffed and puffed the rest of the way up the hill.

I heard seasoned riders talking about the hill, they hadn't expected it and it took the wind out of their sails, too. I was grateful that other than a couple slighter inclines, we would be going downhill before hitting the last few miles of the ride, which was a flat ride.

I kept a steady pace when I got back on the bike, made it up the inclines and had prepared myself for the long downhill. I feared going too fast and losing control. I kept myself at a fast pace I was comfortable with, using the downhill momentum to practice my bigger gears to get more distance out of each downward push.

We flew out of the hill, across the bridge, through the intersection, over the railroad tracks, past the spring training facility, then we were turning onto the final stretch. It was just over 3 miles to the finish line. We kept pedaling and the wind came back strong, making us all work against it.

I was gassed but I wasn't going to quit. Branch and the team said they weren't finishing without me. I told Branch I would be behind him but needed to find my zone for the final push. He would stay in my line of sight and understood what I was asking for.

I switched gears and set my mind to just keep pedaling. Each downward push I used my upward pull to use different muscle groups in my legs. I kept a repetitive mantra in my head, keeping a steady pace, turning onto the main road then onto the last part to the finish line.

I could hear the music, the cheers and pushed with everything I had, pulling from places deep within me that I hadn't pulled from in years. My team waited for me at the final corner to cross the finish line together. I wanted to cry because I finished, but I didn't have the energy.

We rode our bikes down the road to cool our legs down into the parking lot where we had parked the trucks. Branch was off his bike when I pulled up so he could help me dismount. He didn't say anything, but he knew I had nothing left.

I had already unclipped from my pedals and was coasting to a stop when Branch put his hand on the back of my seat to keep me steady when I came to a full stop. I was grateful for his support because he kept me from falling when I put my foot on the ground. My quads were shaking from muscle failure and Branch was the only thing holding me up.

I leaned against the front seat to change my shoes, while they loaded the bikes. I drank more water before we headed back to the finish line tent. We were doing a surprise for the VIP, presenting him with his own scooter so he could get around easier.

The tent was filled with people and spilling out into open spaces. We grabbed some after race snacks, got some photos, presented Nick with his scooter, just as the rain started. Everyone had crossed the finish line and there were no bikers left on the course.

The logistics people quickly disassembled the tents, start/finish line, and barricades so we could all get out of the rain. 30 minutes after crossing the finish line, Branch and I were driving home, in pouring rain.

It rained the rest of Saturday, all day Sunday and Monday morning. By rush hour Monday, the I-10 had flooded, stranding motorists as water came up over their vehicles. The news showed people running up the side of the hills of the highway to get to higher ground.

LJ had stayed in town that weekend, but they cancelled school and Phoenix shut down. No one could get anywhere, and the rain was still coming. Branch and I stayed at home; he didn't have to work until Wednesday. Sgt. Towns told us all to stay home, and we did a meeting via conference call.

The rain started again Thursday night, causing more flooding. People's houses were washing out with the water coming down the mountains. Other houses, schools, and businesses were flooding, up to the 2nd floor. It was a complete mess and took months to clean up.

Kiki flew into Phoenix for a work conference and asked to meet us for lunch. I hadn't seen her since moving to AZ. I bought Branch a GoPro for his birthday, so he was videotaping us while driving. We had lunch with LJ before her practice, then dropped Kiki off at her hotel.

I was asked to speak at the Relay event that weekend, in the town next to ours, then I was asked to be the keynote speaker at the Making Strides Against Breast Cancer kickoff. It was the first time I was publicly speaking about my high risk for breast cancer, the nodes found, the clip and being monitored every 3 months. I told them what the doctor had said, "It's not a matter of if you get breast cancer, it's a matter of when."

I shared my continued hope with the funds raised for research through the American Cancer Society, such as MSABC and Relay For Life events. One of the event photographers captured a photo of me, my face reflecting raw emotion. It was a powerful image. I still tear up when I look at it.

Branch and I continued swimming at the local school. We were doing burpees before we got into the water, to help warm up. I was finishing up my burpees when I felt something in my left wrist pop. I went to get x-rays and asked if he would x-ray both wrists at the same time.

After the results came back, my left wrist was a ganglion cyst, which they put a shot of cortisone or something in, but my right wrist showed it was broken and had been for over 20 years. The doctor asked me how I had done the police academy and continued to hold my gun to shoot with a broken scaphoid bone.

I told him I thought I just needed to toughen up and work through the pain. He said I was a tough cookie to work through that pain with the arthritis. Every time I held my gun, the weight pulled on the broken part of the scaphoid bone, which overtime built up arthritis.

We scheduled surgery for Veterans Day, 11/11/2014, with a follow-up, 6 weeks later. The next afternoon, I went to the office for a meeting with Chief Franks and other employees to start planning for our own MCSO Relay For Life event.

I had met with Chief Franks right after I flew back from D.C. He wanted to do a big cancer event for the office. He explained what he was looking for, an event to bring the employees and families together, while raising money for the community.

I explained to him what a Relay event was like, how we could shorten it to fit into our schedules and different ways to fundraise. He asked me to take the lead on it as I had the most experience. He opened the meeting and introduced me to the group. I was so excited to see so many employees wanting to help.

While we were setting up before hand, Brad, a deputy I knew, asked me where I was assigned. I told him that I had been TDY to help with the computer stuff, but they disassembled our group, and I was in limbo. Brad was at training and there was an open cubicle. He wanted help with the court-ordered training.

We set up our next meeting and chose a date for the event. I gave everyone a copy of each committee position with bullet points of duties so they could decide what they wanted to help with when we met in 2 weeks. After the meeting, I asked if there were any questions and Brad raised his hand, asked where I was assigned now and told the chief he needed help.

The chief asked me later if I wanted to go to training and I said it would be easier to work there while planning for the Relay. He said he would put the transfer in, and I would be assigned to training, helping write policies for court mandated trainings, while also working community outreach. Chief Franks would be my supervisor, with one of my old squad mates, Harry, as my immediate supervisor/sergeant.

I jumped into planning mode for our first Relay For Life event. I set up our meetings and agendas, trained the committee and team captains, and helped advertise for the event. Fundraisers started happening at the districts, jails, and administration buildings. I was hindered with typing for a few weeks because of my surgery, but I was able to organize the Relay event and get things prepared for the policies and court-mandated training.

Branch's unit was slotted for possible deployment to Afghanistan, and we had to attend an event in San Diego, called the yellow ribbon. The event was set up to help soldiers, spouses and families prepare for and manage deployment. Most of the classes were redundant for me, after already being deployed to a war zone, but we met several couples that became lifelong friends.

Branch and I enjoyed some quiet time together, walking along the ocean, sipping whiskey, and smoking cigars, knowing that we had overcome so many things already, we were ready for a deployment, if it happened. The last night we were there, I received a phone call from LJ, she was crying, and I couldn't understand what she was saying.

Her teammate got on the phone and said that LJ had suffered another concussion during the basketball game. LJ was going up for a layup, on a steal and fast break, when the opposing team tried to stop her. She was hit in the head and her feet were knocked out from under her. When she came down hard and hit her head again.

She was healing from having her 4 wisdom teeth removed and the concussion took her completely out. Branch and I left the event early to get home and make sure she was okay. She was going to struggle. She was stubborn and she wanted to continue playing.

She went to practice a couple days later so the trainer could check her out, but she wasn't cleared to play. Instead of the coach letting her stay home, sleep and rest, she required LJ to be at practice, at 6 A.M. and 4 P.M. She had no time to heal.

We made the decision for her to quit basketball and college. She needed to heal. She had a headache daily and it was hard for her to focus.

11
Blessings

I started 2015 off with long work hours and the decision to train for a marathon. I started getting to work at 4 A.M. to type for a couple hours, go for a run at 6 A.M., shower quickly and be back at my desk by 7 A.M. I was drinking a lot of coffee, running to the bathroom every hour, to pee, then back to my cubicle.

During the day, as others started coming into the office, there were many distractions, it was hard to stay focused. I started working on the Relay stuff during the noisy times and went back to typing after people started leaving.

I was asked to speak in Flagstaff at the American Cancer Society Gala event, in February. They wanted me to do a call for action for the Cancer Action Network. The event was "Denim and Diamonds" and I had to find a formal gown. Branch was going to wear his custom suit and cowboy boots.

Branch, LJ, and I headed to the mall, looking for a dress. I tried on several dresses at different stores, settling on a red off the shoulder dress. It draped from my left shoulder, with my right shoulder/arm, bare, to the floor. There were pearls and rhinestones around the left shoulder and collar. As soon as I tried it on, I knew it was the dress.

We left the mall with my dress to find shoes. We were at Kohl's when my back was really bothering me. Within 30 minutes the pain increased, and I could barely stand. I was pretty sure it was a kidney infection and Branch drove me to the urgent care.

They confirmed the kidney infection, gave me antibiotics, and sent me home. The next day I went to work but instead of running, I walked the track due to the pain. Tuesday, the doctor called to say the kidney infection needed to be treated with a stronger antibiotic.

That Friday, Branch and I left for Flagstaff. I still had some pain from the infection and ran a fever before it was time to take my meds again. I timed my meds with the event, so I didn't run a fever during the gala.

The event was amazing. The decorations were breathtaking. I felt I was in a fairytale with the twinkling lights around the ballroom. We met a couple that were there as a showing for CTCA all four of us became fast friends.

We had dinner and the auction began shortly after. Towards the end of the bidding, before the high-dollar items came up, was when I spoke. I had done this many times, but I was nervous, my hands were shaking, and my voice cracked when I began. Soon, I settled into sharing my story, bringing the audience to tears, before I closed with a call to action.

By the end of the evening every person had signed up to become part of ACS CAN (American Cancer Society Cancer Action Network), with a minimum $10 fee. There were some that gave more, with one person giving an extra $100 to cover 10 students from NAU that were volunteering to help with the event. My call to action raised over $2500.

I had shared that I was there, 5 days after being diagnosed with kidney stones and a kidney infection. Before the bidding began again, the band played a couple songs. They dedicated their song "Warrior" to me. Branch escorted me to the dance floor, where he held me tightly while I let the tears flow.

He kept telling me how proud he was of me, for my strength, my voice, and my passion to find a cure for cancer. As we came off the dance floor, we were bombarded with hugs, including hugs from a couple girls that went to school with LJ.

The evening ended, raising over $100,000 from the auction and I was exhausted. Branch and I went back to our room, where I showered and fell asleep.

I was in final countdown mode for the MCSO Relay event. Every day was busy the last 2 weeks before our event. The event was from 6 P.M.-10 P.M. at our training center track. We started setting things up Thursday.

Branch, LJ, and I sorted all the team shirts, finished the programs and the event script. Branch had his monthly Army drill that weekend. It was going to be tough without him there.

Teams started coming in to set up their sites at 3 P.M. and I found myself with extra time on my hands. I sat down in the shade with Chief Franks. We made a fundraising bet of who could raise the most money by the beginning of the event.

We opened the event with the MCSO Explorers lined up for the honor guard to post the colors. One of my supervisors from dispatch sang the national anthem before I began the welcome. As I looked at all the people in the bleachers, sitting and standing around the stage, the emotions welled up inside me, grateful to be able to give back to our own MCSO family.

Sheriff Joe and the Deputy Chief handed out the survivor medals before the survivors made their way to the track, for the survivor lap. Both hugged me and thanked me for allowing them to be part of the event.

I joined friends and coworkers on the track, so many more than I knew were survivors. Robbie and I walked that first lap, hand in hand, showing the world we had so much more fight left inside us.

As the evening continued, I saw my husband when we did the caregiver lap. He surprised me. He had gotten out of drill that day to be with me. He knew how much this event meant to me and our office. I walked hand in hand with Branch and LJ around the track for the caregiver's lap.

We had dinner, provided by Carrabba's, for the survivors and caregivers. We had several themed and fun laps but the funniest was the MISSter Relay contest. We had deputies, detention officers, family members and friends dressed for the part. Robbie won the contest.

We had a moving luminaria ceremony where a friend and her dad shared about losing her mom to breast cancer. Her mom had been an employee of MCSO at the time of her passing.

There were many stories to share, hugs to give and hope to provide. At the end of the event, we had raised over $50,000 for a first-time event, made up of deputies, detention officers, civilians, dispatchers, family, and friends. I won the bet against my chief, so he had to buy me lunch.

I finished my last pill of antibiotics the day before our Relay event. By the following Wednesday, I was back at urgent care. I was running a fever again and could feel pain creeping into my back.

I was given more antibiotics, this time for 14 days. I started feeling better by the weekend and started running again, taking it slow. I finished my antibiotics right before St. Patrick's Day, so I could celebrate with Branch, by drinking green beer.

Branch and I celebrated our "You had me from hello" day, St. Patrick's Day, with my stepmom at our local bar and grill. Branch and I had been together for 10 years, so we celebrated more than usual. LJ was our DD and picked us up after closing the bar down.

The next week, I had my CTCA appointments. I knew I had another infection. When I saw my doctor, she asked what was going on because I looked awful. I told her about the infections, antibiotics, and continued pain. My vitals showed I was running a fever, too. She sent me for an x-ray of my kidneys, so she could see what was going on inside.

The x-ray showed I had several kidney stones in each kidney. A couple were quite large, and she referred me to the urologist for follow-up. My bloodwork was somewhat stable, but the x-ray showed one of my ovaries was enlarged, and a spot on my lungs, which began a round of ultrasounds.

I was given more antibiotics, then the urologist said I needed surgery, to break up the stones because they were too large for me to pass. The first surgery was scheduled for the middle of April, on a Friday. I was scheduled to speak at the ASU Relay that night.

They prepped me for surgery, scheduled for 10 A.M., but had to move me back to 2 P.M. I came out of surgery and was released at 5 P.M. We had an hour to get to Tempe for the event. I walked slowly and I did the survivor lap. Branch could feel how hot and swollen my back was when he put his hand on my lower back. My right side was red, and the pain medicine was wearing off.

I told the committee I wasn't going to be able to stay until 9 P.M. to speak. The event chair asked if she could share my story for me, explaining why I couldn't be there. I was honored she shared my story for me.

Branch took me home, gave me some of my pain meds and put me to bed. My next surgery was scheduled the end of April. I had to pee in a bowl to see if I passed any stones or crystals. 2 weeks later, I still hadn't passed anything.

I went through the next procedure. Knowing the toll it would take on me, I didn't schedule anything that weekend. I went through the same procedure, peeing in the bowl, antibiotics, and pain meds. 2 weeks later, the end of May, I had my follow-up. The x-rays and ultrasound showed the stones were still there.

The urologist scheduled more surgeries, this time doing the laser inside my kidneys. He would do the right one, then place a urethra catheter to help the stones move out of my kidneys. The surgery was scheduled for June.

I had been helping Sgt. Towns, the deputy recruit training class sergeant, with his class, taking action photos, mentoring, and teaching. They had their class hike scheduled for June, a couple days after my surgery. I asked the doctor if I could still do my daily activities, including running. He said I might have some pain, but I should be fine.

I took a couple days off after the procedure, then went to work, starting with my morning regimen of running. I was doing my track work of sprints and some of the recruits were walking into the training center. They stopped and asked, "Didn't you just have kidney surgery?" I laughed and said the doctor said I could still run.

I finished my workout, cooled off, then went in for my shower. There was blood on my spandex. I called the doctor. It was normal with activity because of the catheter.

Having the catheter was completely miserable because I wasn't comfortable, no matter what I did. I also noticed my hair was breaking and brittle from all the medications I was taking so I decided to cut it off. My hair was down to the middle of my back and auburn red when I cut it. I kept cutting more, until I had cut it close to my head, in a short pixie cut.

Not only did I cut it all off, but I bleached it blonde. When I went to work that Monday, no one recognized me. They were looking for a long-haired redhead. I loved the freedom of having my hair short again, it wasn't in my face. I could wash and let it air dry, saving me time in the morning after my run.

My mom and stepdad were in town for my niece's graduation. My niece had moved out of her mom's house in January, after she turned 18. She started dating a guy that was in his early 30s, which had my sisters upset.

I went to the graduation and the graduation party was the next night. I knew it would be awkward, but LJ and I went early and helped decorate.

I spent some time with my mom, we talked about cameras, she was showing me her new one. I met my niece's boyfriend and felt the tension in the room when he was there.

Branch's kids were scheduled to arrive a couple days before my next procedure. We took them to a Diamondbacks baseball game for Father's Day. I didn't feel great, hadn't been sleeping well and it always took a few days for the kids to decompress from their mother's programming.

I wasn't looking forward to 2 more weeks of another catheter or antibiotics. My procedure was on a Wednesday, and I was scheduled to hike with the recruit class the following morning.

Branch was off so he brought the kids with us, not knowing how I was going to fare during the hike. We started hiking at 6 A.M. I could tell this procedure was worse on my body than the first. It hurt to walk, let alone hike up the mountain. After I climbed a quarter of the way, I stopped by the bench to rest. The heat, procedure and catheter were taking its toll.

Branch kept trying to get me to stop before I got to the bench, but I told him I would rest while they went the rest of the way. I would wait until they came by the bench on their return trip down and go down the trail with them. Branch relented, but he was mad at my stubbornness and worried. I told Sgt. Towns that Branch would take the pics for me, and I would get some of them coming down.

I sat on the bench, in complete pain, feeling like the catheter was pushing through my bladder. I drank water and tried to relax, but I couldn't get comfortable. Branch's youngest daughter, Ann, sat with me on the bench, but it was hard to conversate without wincing. As the class headed down, I took photos and they all high-fived me.

Once I saw Branch, I got up to slowly make my way down. I thought going up was the worst, but the jostling of my body coming down the mountain had me in tears. It took me longer to get down than it did to hike up. By the time I got down, I was out of water, tears were running down my face and my spandex were bloody.

I called Sgt. Harry and told him I wasn't coming in, then Branch took me home. I took the next day off too and went back to work Monday. I didn't know how I was going to make it until the following week when they took my catheter out.

I had scheduled family pictures and they were set for the day after my last surgery.

LJ came to pick me up from work, after dropping me off in the morning. We were taking the kids shopping for the family portrait. Harry let her in, and they found me in my cubicle, lying down on the floor. I could tell they were worried and told them I was just trying to get comfortable. Harry told me to go home and take the next day off.

We found our outfits for pictures, then I went home and tried to sleep. I didn't get out of bed the next day and went to work that Thursday. I had to finish some typing before we got final approval. I finished my typing, sent everything to Harry, then went to lunch. When I came back, I waited for Harry to come back from the meeting to see if everything was approved.

I shut all my stuff down and got ready to go, then Harry walked me down to the car. Branch had come to pick me up, so I didn't have to drive, which I was thankful for.

When we got home, my dad called and asked us if we could go up to Alpine to get his airstream trailer. He didn't want it sitting there now that his friend had passed. It would probably need tires for it, before bringing it back down the hill.

Branch asked me if I was up for the drive, and I told him I wanted to go if we stayed overnight at the lodge before heading back. We got a 2-bedroom suite at the lodge, I took my crayons and coloring books, as well as a notebook. I knew I wouldn't be able to help with the trailer and wanted to stay occupied.

When we got to the room, I was miserable, and Eric was upset about something. I couldn't take it anymore and told Branch he needed to take the kids and go get the trailer or do something before I lost my shit. The girls could tell I was upset, but Eric wouldn't let it go. I finally walked out of the room with my notebook and walked to the little park area. I sat on a stump, enjoying the silence, when an idea for a book started forming in my head.

I started writing and before I knew it, I had an outline written for a book. As I looked around, I knew I could make a series out of the book and started writing my ideas. Branch came out and said he was going to get the trailer then drive into Show Low to get the new tires.

He had an appointment then would be back so we could have dinner. As he walked over to give me a hug and kiss, he saw my notes and asked what I was writing. I told him I had written an outline for my first "smut" book. He laughed and said at least something good came out of the afternoon. He knew I hadn't been able to write any of my personal book, this story, because of writer's block. Although, I know now it was the trauma locked inside that was blocking me.

By the time they got back, dinner was ready, but I could tell something was wrong. We ate dinner, Branch showered, and I cleaned the kitchen. Branch sat on our bed, and I asked him what was wrong.

He told me of the conversation he had with the kids. Devlin poisoned their minds, and he didn't think he would be able to have a relationship with them. He was upset. I sat next to him with my arms around him.

Nicole came out after she showered and asked what was wrong. I told her, "Her dad was upset because he was trying to be your dad, but it was hard when there were so many negative things said about him." She started crying and hugged her dad, then Ann came out and she was crying.

I told her to come over and put her on my lap so Branch could put an arm around her. Eric came out, seemingly oblivious to everything and turned the TV on. The girls were upset with Eric and eventually everyone was crying. We all sat on the bed, talked through some things, tried making peace with the situation and had a family hug before we settled in to watch a movie.

The next morning, we headed home with the airstream. My dad said we could have it because we put the money into the tires. I wanted to pay him at least $500 for it. He said to count the tires towards the $500 and it would be square.

The rest of the weekend passed with the kids playing in the pool. Branch had to work, and I relaxed on the couch before my next surgery. The kids wanted their hair cut and the girls asked for highlights before pictures. They asked their mom and she said it was fine. I spent Sunday and Monday doing hair, getting clothes ironed and preparing for my surgery.

Surgery was Tuesday and our pictures were Wednesday. Everyone came to the hospital for my last procedure. We were scheduled for 8 A.M., but my doctor was called in for emergency surgery. I was pushed back until 11 A.M., but still couldn't eat. The nurse told me I was pushed back until 3 P.M. and I started crying. I was so miserable and just wanted things to be over.

I couldn't sit in the waiting room with the kids, not being able to eat. She told me she would get me a room so I could lie down and apologized again. I said thank you and told her it wasn't her fault; I was emotional. She took us up to a room, about 10 minutes later, and said she would come get me when the doctor was ready.

The room was huge. There was a sofa, 2 chairs and the bed. Branch told me to lie down and turned the TV on, but I told him to take the kids for lunch and a movie instead of waiting there and all of us being miserable. He didn't want to leave me, but the kids would start fighting and fussing, which would be worse.

Right before they left, one of the staff came into the room with an envelope. They said there were movie tickets and coupons for dinner, to apologize for the delay in my procedure. I thanked them again and told Branch that was his sign.

I woke up in the recovery room and my doctor told me I was bad for his ego because none of the procedures had removed the kidney stones. After looking at the images, the stones were imbedded into my kidneys. He gave me a plan of treatment and tests.

The nurse let Branch in to see me and I could tell the doctor had already talked to him, by the look on his face. I started crying again because I was frustrated. I had gone through so much pain, for absolutely nothing. I was back to square 1.

I was drained, emotionally, physically, mentally, and spiritually. The thread of hope was unraveling.

The next day we got dressed for our pictures. I was still in pain, standing up or sitting down, but I pushed through. Thankfully it was one of my friends taking the pictures. She was quick, efficient and was able to capture some great photos.

I don't remember much of the rest of that time the kids were with us, before they left. I was starting to spiral into depression. I continued running, trying to outrun the frustrations of my physical issues. I saw a urology specialist and did a 24-hour urine collection.

The collection would be tested for urine output, calcium, kidney functions and several other things. The specialist put me on meds to help the urine output and cut down on my calcium.

Still no answer as to why I kept having so many issues and infections. I was now on Cipro, trying to keep the infections at bay, not realizing how Cipro can harm your body.

Branch started the medic academy, which we knew was going to be tough with the studying and hours. I was transferred full time to our HQ building, downtown, to do Community Outreach. Relay was going to be my major event, but I would be going to schools to read, talk to kids and other community events.

Before we went to D.C. again for the Cancer Action Network, I was asked to be the State Lead Ambassador for AZ, ACS CAN.

When we went to D.C. that year, we had several new ACT leads from AZ. We had a solid and passionate team.

The next day we were at the Capitol, talking to our local and state representatives, asking them to vote yes to more funding for cancer research, saying yes to palliative care, for all patients with chronic/long-term illness and closing the loophole in Medicare for those getting colonoscopy and needing polyps removed.

It was a busy day, but we made a lot of progress. That night we had our lights of hope ceremony. There was a brief reception where we would load the busses to go to the ceremony and it started sprinkling.

By the time we loaded busses, they were handing us umbrellas because it was pouring. The ground was completely soaked, and the rain soaked all the luminaria bags. They closed the ceremony early due to lightning, but as we walked by the stage, we could see the glow of all the lights around the reflecting pool. Those lights made a statement. No matter what was thrown at them, each light represented a name that had never given up hope.

The rest of the event passed quickly. We were scheduled to leave Wednesday afternoon. I was asked to speak and have a tent for ACS CAN at the SWV Relay event that weekend in AZ. It was weird going back to the event where I had been the event chair but was grateful.

I helped with the Making Strides Against Breast Cancer event in October and spoke at other events for ACS CAN, American Cancer Society Cancer Action Network. One of the events was the AZ cancer summit, talking about the need for palliative care for all cancer patients. Palliative care is treating the whole person, not just the illness and I was able to share the differences between my two treatments, in the Army and at CTCA. Treatment with palliative care, was such a relief for me and my family.

The first part of November, I flew to NY because another friend died, suddenly. We had cheered together, played soccer and softball together, and double dated several times. I had seen her every time I went to NY because she lived down the road from my mom with her boys.

By this time, my school had lost 4 people, within 6 months, including Mandy. I knew each of them well, 3 were on the cheer team, the guy was our mascot, and the other was the one that bought (racy) pictures of me from my sister, when they were juniors. The racy pictures were a result of KJ taking unauthorized photos of me while I took a bath.

Several of us got together for the viewing and stayed at a friend's house. Most of us stayed in their basement, so we could be together. After the funeral, we had a bonfire and several more friends came by. There were lots of tears, but we also shared laughter as we strolled down memory lane.

The group dwindled to the few of us that were always close, and the conversation turned to relationships. Sam was there. We snickered because no one else had known about us our senior year. When something was said about our senior year, I laughed and told them about all our "sexcapades."

It was funny to see the jaws drop, and eyes widen at the announcement. The main question was how we were able to keep it a secret. Soon the conversation moved to what we were all up to now, with the consensus of the guys saying they couldn't believe I was a cop.

I headed to the airport around 3 A.M. after the bonfire. As soon as I landed in AZ, I had to speak at the Buckeye RFL event, near our house. Chief Franks, Marty, and Branch were also there. We had a helicopter coming in for the event and it was bigger than normal.

I changed in the parking lot at the school, went to speak, cried more because of the grief I allowed myself to feel over the loss of so many friends.

We were invited to participate in several Veteran's Day events, but I chose to participate at my KM's school. I knew several vets that would be there, from other organizations, my sister SE, and I knew a lot of the kids. Our dad's friend drove his old Army truck to the event, and we took pictures with him in front of it.

The next morning, I went out for one of my tempo training runs. I was 6 weeks from my scheduled marathon, and I had dropped my pace from a 13-minute mile down to a high 7 to low 8-minute.

I had an appointment at CTCA later so it would be a quick run. I was about a mile into my run, when I felt the ground give way and my toe fell in. There was a pull in my shin bone area. I didn't fall, but I wasn't able to put weight on my leg. I found it harder to walk than limp/run, so I limped back to the house, showered, and went to the urgent care portion of CTCA before my scheduled appointment.

After x-rays and an exam, the doctor said I pulled the tendon. She looked at my medication list and said that Cipro causes the tendons to be more vulnerable to pulls and tears. She would not recommend any running until the end of December.

I text my friend to say I wouldn't be able to run the marathon, trying to keep the tears of frustration from falling. Branch was just as upset as I was because he knew how much work I had put in.

Branch was going to the Chevy dealer where we bought the Equinox and see what they had for Black Friday deals. He went by himself when he got off work.

Branch came home a couple hours later with a brand-new Chevy Silverado. He had traded in the equinox and gave him a discount for first responders. He was happy. This was his first new truck, in years, and he had earned it.

I stopped running, but there was a run benefitting the American Cancer Society, in December, so the girls from CTCA and I made a team, had shirts made and ran together. It felt good to run again, but I kept it slow to avoid re-injuring myself.

That Christmas, DJ came home. We all enjoyed participating in the family Christmas Eve Wagon ride. DJ drove, as Rudolph, while LJ and I were Santa's helpers, again. I had set up for us to get family photos while DJ was home. We were going to each wear our uniform, with LJ wearing a nice dress, for some photos.

We rang 2016 in with style. Branch worked and DJ went to Vegas with our neighbor and her friend, to a concert. LJ worked until closing then came home ready for bed. New Year's Eve was a relaxed night at home for me.

It had been years since I worked an off-duty job, but I was asked to work the Cactus Bowl because they needed a lot of deputies. I had a cushy job of sitting outside the money room. I read, talked to people that went by, and watched some of the game.

It wasn't hard, but it wasn't comfortable wearing my uniform, especially my belt, with the pressure on my kidneys. By the time I got home, I was miserable and took some pain meds.

We had a blast doing photos, helping my friend with the creativity of some of the shots. They were going to be great, and I couldn't wait to see them. We went to dinner after our pictures then home so DJ could start packing to return to Germany.

Branch and I went to Alpine for our anniversary. We stayed at the lodge. We had a full kitchen, so I made some chicken pot pie and we snuggled in the room, watching the snow. We played in it a couple times and enjoyed the down time.

LJ quit her job and flew to Chicago to help her dad and his family pack and drive to AZ. They were moving to AZ and LJ was going to live with them, so she was closer to work for her new job. She started working at Nike, the premiere store.

Branch and I helped them move in. We took LJ's stuff over to help set up her bedroom. Branch and I turned her old room into our office.

We painted, tore up the carpet and painted the floor. We set it up, so our desks faced each other, and we each decorated our respective wall space.

The beginning of February, I was a speaker at the ACS CAN lobby day at the AZ capitol. We had a huge turnout, talked to our representatives, and sat in on a hearing. We were scheduled to be at another hearing later, on tanning bed age limits. I was also being filmed sharing my story for ACS CAN, to use for recruiting members.

One night I was at home in the office, with Branch, when I got a text from my friend, Rosa. We had seen each other several times since she'd moved to San Diego, including in December when I flew out to surprise a mutual friend of ours.

The text said, "Hey, I went to this meeting to do a hike on the JMT. There's a group but I want someone that I know and trust with me if I do this." She called, explained the JMT was the John Muir Trail, part of the Pacific Crest trail. The trail is 211 miles, we would need backpacks, hiking shoes, bear canisters, tent, etc.

I didn't think it all the way through and said yes. The rest of the details would be worked out. In the meantime, I needed hiking boots, break them in and get used to wearing a pack. I was already training to do the Honolulu marathon in December 2016, so I figured this would help me with training.

I started taking the stairs everywhere I went, carrying my backpack, with at least 25 pounds in it. I slowly bought the rest of the things I needed. I wanted to keep my gear as light as possible because I would be carrying it, every day, for miles.

I started using my elevation training mask, beginning at 9000 feet, and working my way up to 11,000. I wore it hiking, running, biking and strength training. I bought books on the JMT, joined some FB groups, and set up my hiking and running plan.

I went to the chiropractor for my regular visit and told him what I was doing. He encouraged me and told me about the new triathlon that was being held at the YMCA, in May. He said it was called "MomsTri," for women of all levels of fitness, even if you couldn't swim, you could use a flotation device.

He gave me the info and I signed up for it. Branch and I had been swimming every week at the gym, we were riding a couple times a week and I was running. It was a sprint tri, 400-yard swim, 12-mile bike ride and 3.1-mile run. I was officially doing my first triathlon, which was exciting and scary.

I had signed up to be a brand ambassador for Esprit de She and found out the next week I was accepted. There was a 5k run scheduled for Mother's Day, the day after my triathlon. I couldn't miss it and talked my daughter into running with me.

I went for my checkup and I was given the green light to train for the hike, marathon, and triathlon. I told the doctor I wasn't having regular bowel movements, and I felt sicker than I did from my kidney infections. She put me on medication to help me have regular bowel movements because she said I could become sepsis from being "backed up."

I hadn't been training as much because I hadn't felt good, but Branch and I ran the St. Patty's Kiss Me I'm Irish run. My friend, Liz, asked if I would run with her son in the "Let Me Run" event for his school. I did the run, but still didn't feel any better. I didn't know if I was overtraining, if it was the meds or a combination, but I could barely get out of bed to go to work.

I stopped training to give my body a rest. We were busy with our community outreach stuff at work. I was bringing a new event, "Wills For Heroes," to our office, in April, which I had to get people signed up and scheduled for. The MCSO Relay event planned for a separate "MISSter Relay" pageant fundraiser, and we were organizing a new summer camp for kids, "Camp Summer STARS."

On top of my workload, I had to fly to Salt Lake City, Utah, the end of April for my first State Lead Ambassador training conference. Branch and I were driving to several Relay events so I could speak for ACS CAN, and I was invited to be the MC for the Flagstaff Gala, in June.

Saturday, April 23rd, 2016, I was finishing up the Wills For Heroes event, when I got a call from Liz. She said our friend "SherBear" was in ICU. She had surgery on Wednesday but kept getting sicker. She had sepsis.

I finished with all my appointments, then drove to the hospital. She hadn't woken up since that morning. There was a huge group of friends, family, co-workers, and American Legion riders. The mood was somber waiting for the doctor to update us.

I text my chief to let him know how the day had gone, that I was at the hospital, and I would keep him updated on the situation. He told me to take what time I needed and to work from the hospital so I could be there.

I stayed most of the night, went home, showered, slept a couple hours, grabbed my laptop, and went back to the hospital. I stayed Sunday night, through Monday, along with a core group, hoping to hear good news.

I went to the office Tuesday, then sat at the hospital Wednesday and Thursday morning. I had to go home and pack for my conference before I flew out early the next morning. The nurses had let a couple of us go into her room Wednesday night to see if hearing our voices helped. She didn't stir at all.

Her entire body was swollen from the fluids, and I did everything I could not to let the tears fall as I watched her, breathing from a tube, hooked up to all kinds of monitors. The doctor told us the longer she didn't wake up, the less chance there was of her waking up.

I left for SLC with a heavy heart. I met the other SLAs and by lunch, I had them sending prayers upwards. The training was great, the passion in the room was like a living, breathing thing. We trained all day Friday, Saturday, and Sunday morning before we flew out.

While we were sitting in training Sunday morning, I got a text that SherBear died. It was May 1st, her 50th birthday. I couldn't hold the tears back any longer. Thankfully, training was wrapping up early so I left for the airport after saying goodbye.

They planned SherBears celebration of life for Saturday. I had my triathlon, and I told her family I would be swimming, biking, and running in her honor. I cried in the pool during my laps, I cried during my bike ride, and I cried during my run, knowing my beautiful and kindhearted friend was gone.

I crossed the finish line, hugged Branch, saw some friends, took pictures, then went home. My body didn't feel physically drained, but emotionally I was done. I went to bed early and got up early to drive to Tempe, Sunday morning. LJ met us in the parking garage before our run.

We lined up with the rest of the women, waiting for the gun to go off. We took a leisurely pace the first half to make sure I had gas left in my legs for the finish. As we hit the 3-mile mark, with .10 mile left, I told LJ to go. She took off, which fueled my drive to pick up the speed and finish strong. I did it. I completed a sprint triathlon and a 5k, in the same weekend.

After the event, one of the organizers told me about the triathlon in San Diego, in October. I looked at Branch and he said I should do it.

I got home, signed up for the triathlon and text Rosa that I would be staying with her in October. Branch was close to finishing medic school and we were excited to have more free time together.

He had put in for his test slot and studied for his final. He was trying to get ahold of his dad and finally asked someone to do a welfare check. They found his dad, between the wall and kitchen chair, deceased. It looked like he had been at the table and slid out of the chair against the wall when he died.

We knew his dad wanted to be buried in the cemetery in Minnesota, where the rest of the family was buried. The funeral home said he had been in that position so long they couldn't do a funeral. We asked about cremation and having the ashes sent to MN for his burial. There was so much red tape to cut through because he was living in SD, and we wanted him buried in MN. It was going to cost several thousand dollars to get everything done.

Branch had enough on his plate with medic school and we didn't have enough on credit cards to pay for everything. I text KJ and told her we had a financial favor to ask. She called and I let her talk to Branch to get the numbers needed. She sent us several thousand dollars and I set up a repayment plan.

Branch finished school, passed his final and was ready for his national test. We planned on leaving after his test. We had a funeral, the VA paid for the military burial, then had a get-together at Branch's mom's house.

We took the kids for walks to spend time alone with them and Nicole said she wanted to do a half-marathon with me that summer. She had been running track and we had gone to a couple of her meets while we were in MN. The training would be different, but she would have enough time between track season and our run, to get some distance runs in. We took her to get fitted for running shoes for her training, found a race for July, and set up a training plan.

We left MN, Branch found out he passed medic school and all his tests. He started studying more for the captain's test and another agency's test.

We hadn't been home long when I had another infection. I drove to the urgent care and began the testing process. The doctor gave me some pain meds and my friend, Liz, came to wait with me. She said I shouldn't drive home with the pain meds, but Branch was working so I would wait it out. She said, no, we will get you home. I asked her who "we" was, and she said she was going to call SherBear's husband to see if he would follow us out to give her a ride back. We called each other "sister wife" and SherBear's husband was our "brother husband."

He agreed to follow us out. I took the next day off because Branch was leaving for his 2-week Army training. I was driving with a friend to Flagstaff the next day for the Gala event.

I packed all my "changes" of clothes. I had ordered 3 outfits from Amazon to go with the theme. The first was an olive green military dress with red stripes and stars, with a matching hat. The next was a "Rosie" the riveter outfit. It was a jumper with shorts, button-down top and belt. I bought the wig that went with it, also.

The last was a blue dress from the 40s pinup style. I bought a blonde wig with pin curls in it and wore my black Mary Jane pumps. I had my script ready, bags packed, said goodbye to my hubby then left to pick up my friend.

I had to be at the site by 4 P.M. the next day. I wore shorts and button-down shirt then changed into my "Army Dress" for the first outfit, so we could mingle.

After the event started and we were getting ready to start showcasing items up for bid, I went and changed into my Rosie costume. When I went back to speak again, it took several people a while to figure out it was me.

There was a gorgeous diamond and pearl necklace up for bid and the audience wanted a closer look. The owner asked if I would wear it so they could see it. The bidding kept going higher for the necklace and the owner said I would have to model his jewelry more often for those prices.

As the auction started winding down to the band and dancing, I did my last change into the dress and wig. The look on the audience faces was priceless and I was glad I had thought to make the outfit changes fun. I was done with my speaking roles by 9 P.M. and the event would go until 10 or 11 P.M. with the dancing. I was wiped from my medication and the fever I was running.

The next couple weeks after the Gala were busy with last minute details for the Camp Summer STARS.

Branch's kids arrived from MN on Thursday afternoon, and I brought them to work with me so they could help put binders and material together. They all asked if they could participate as a student in the camp. My chief said it was okay because they would be with me anyhow.

Registration started at 8 A.M. with class starting at 9 A.M. The kids had to change out of their "street" clothes into the "juvie" uniforms. We did this so the clothes status symbol was not interfering with learning and the class.

We had it set up for the kids to have lunch, dinner and breakfast the next morning from our food factory. They would eat the same thing that was served to the inmates in our jails. We would have all our classes in the auditorium, with class for 50 minutes then a 10-minute break before the next class.

We had girls on one side, boys on the other, with 2-3 seats between each kid. A lot of the kids were good kids, but some kids were already on the path to ending up in our jails. As the day went on, the normal cliques started so we would break them up by changing groups around. The kids were from different backgrounds, cultures, and ethnicity.

At night the kids stayed outside in our tents, on bunks. The bad thing about it was the chaperones, me, had to stay out there, too. We had some large air conditioning units, but they didn't cover the entire tent area. I was lucky if I slept 60 minutes total.

The next morning, everyone had to be up by 6 A.M., they were given hygiene items, a place to wash up, then lined up to walk back to the training center for breakfast. Some of them didn't eat much for lunch or dinner so by breakfast time, they were starving.

We started Saturday with fun things. They wore the alcohol goggles, to show how certain levels of alcohol affected your system and judgment. We played a game of dodgeball in the mat room and finished the day out with a speaker, after lunch. The first meal that wasn't from the food factory. The kids changed back into their street clothes at 3 P.M. for their "graduation" when the parents came.

Most of the kids showed significant change, apologized to their parents and to this day have stayed on the right side of the law. A few didn't care, had no support system at home and found "family" in jail.

After the graduation, staff, kids, and parents were treated to dinner and dessert by a local famous chef. The training made an impact on Branch's kids, especially Nicole. She said the domestic violence portion made her realize her mom was psychologically abusive and controlling. Branch had come to graduation to surprise the kids. They thought he was coming home the next day, so they loved seeing him when they got their certificate.

I took a couple days off work to spend with Branch and the kids before our next round of camp summer stars. LJ and her dad hadn't been getting along, for many reasons. There were times she would come home to "dinner" finding out someone had eaten her food or there was no food in the house to make something.

She decided to spend the 4th of July with us. We had been playing in the pool, having a great day when LJ and I received a text from her dad. The text asked us to keep our trash talking off social media and something about our attitudes. I had no idea what he was talking about, and LJ said it was probably something she put on Twitter. Her dad's stepdaughter probably saw it and thought LJ was talking about them.

I initially ignored it, then sent back, "I'm a grown-ass woman that can say what she wants, when she wants and where she wants. If you don't like it, that's too damn bad because you're not my daddy or my husband. As for LJ, she is grown too."

After that, LJ started spending more time at the house with us and slowly moved her stuff back in. She stayed at the house to watch the dogs when Branch and I took the kids to Bryce Canyon for our ½-marathon.

It was a gorgeous drive up, but Eric was sitting in the middle of the girls. He wouldn't stop talking and kept asking questions. I wanted silence because I was tired, still on medication for my kidneys and it was a 6-hour drive.

I got out of the car quickly when we arrived and checked us into the hotel. We walked to the park to get our race packets, then found a place for dinner.

Nicole and I took a bus up to the starting point at 5 A.M. We were starting at approximately 9000-feet elevation, running downhill the entire way, to about 3000-feet elevation. We bought cheap sweatshirts at Walmart. If it got too warm, we could take them off and if we lost them, it was no big deal.

We started our run at 7 A.M., before the sun was up. It was chilly, so we started slow, to warm our muscles up. Running downhill would be tough to keep proper form so we would take it slow and steady until the last stretch where it flattened out.

She was struggling to find her pace. She was used to sprinting and not distance. She would fall behind so I would stop until she caught up. After the first couple miles, she found her rhythm and we ran in sync. As the sun came up and the heat descended, she started to struggle again.

We stopped for water, and I had her take some electrolytes before we started again. She would keep up then slow down again so I told her I would be in front of her and if she didn't see me, she needed to yell.

She stayed close behind me for a few miles and we had about 2 left when she started walking. She was okay to finish, just needed a break. She was getting side cramps because she wasn't used to long distance, heat or downhill for so long. We walked the next mile and she committed herself to running the last 1.1 mile.

We walked, talked, checked out the scenery and let her catch her breath. As we rounded the last corner, we could see the town. I saw the 12-mile marker and asked if she was ready. She said yeah. She would be behind me even if we were further apart.

We stayed together for most of the last mile until we hit the flat surface. We had less than a half-mile to go and she told me to keep going, she would see me at the finish line. I took off, wanting to finish, shower and eat. I was using different leg muscles because I was now on flat surface and lengthened my stride. I turned the corner for the final push to the finish line and pushed.

I finished and told Branch that Nicole was close behind me. I hadn't been there for long when I saw her and went to finish with her. Ann ran out with me too, so we all crossed together.

After a quick breakfast/brunch provided for the runners and families, benefitting one of the local organizations we left for home.

I wasn't as agitated on the way home, but Branch asked Eric to stop talking for a while. Eric was surprised his dad said something, but the girls were relieved. We stopped at a couple tourist attractions and historical markers to get out and stretch our legs.

I had a follow-up with the urologist that week and she thought the stones imbedded in the kidneys were the cause of the infections. It was the only thing that made sense of why I couldn't overcome the infection. She put me on another antibiotic and set me up for another 24-hour urine test.

I had just over a month before I left for my hike and no answers for my kidney issues. I didn't know how much more I could take. I wasn't sleeping more than 4-5 hours and I had zero patience. I was tired from my health, work, volunteering, the kids fighting us, and the stress at home.

After the second summer camp, Branch and I drove to Flagstaff to test my hiking equipment and do a shakedown.

The next day we hiked the back side of Humphrey's. We took our time, and I adjusted as needed. We planned for lunch on the trail and enjoyed the scenery. We saw a couple other hikers otherwise it was just him and I for miles.

That night, I put up my tent, blew up my sleeping pad, set my stuff out, then made room for Branch to lie in the tent. I couldn't stop laughing because we were almost on top of each other in the tiny tent.

Neither of us slept much because when one moved, the other felt it. It rained some through the night and we stayed dry. Knowing my tent would keep me dry was a good thing. We left our site to go to the one we wanted originally, after the people left. Branch and I would be the only campers that night which was perfect.

We set up our tarps to help if it rained. Got dry wood for the fire and set our site up, to sleep on our cots. We explored the area until we noticed the rain getting heavier. We got back to the site and saw rivers of water. We looked at the radar and the storm was going to get worse.

We packed up, then went to town for a hotel and Chinese food. When we left the next day, it was still raining, with flooding in some areas.

LJ had moved a lot of her clothes back in with us, staying in DJ's old room now that the kids were gone. She said it took about the same amount of time to get to work from our house as it did from her dad's because of traffic. By the end of July, the only thing she had at their apartment was her bed, dresser, and TV.

The beginning of August, I saw the urologist and she said I needed to do a vegetarian/vegan diet, to see if it helped. I went shopping for my resupply bucket that needed to be mailed Wednesday. My bear canister would have my first half of food supply for the trip, then I would get the bucket at the JMT ranch.

LJ and I stayed up all night packing my bucket, after making sure it would fit into my bear canister at the resupply point. I had packets of peanut butter, trail mix, tortillas, and a mix of other things. I mailed it off, with my trail name, "Greene Goddess," and my return address.

2 days later, on Friday, I saw my urologist again and she said I needed to do a low oxalate diet, instead of vegan. She said no nuts, chocolate and basically my entire resupply bucket. I was flying to Bend, Oregon, the following week to see my care team lead nurse, Jewel, and to do the Relay with her, before I left the following Tuesday for my hike.

I had to go shopping for my new diet of food for the trail and had no idea what I would be able to eat. I found Lenny and Larry cookies, which were my saving grace for food. I found a few other things I could eat that weren't too heavy then relied on my running sport beans and Hot Tamales candy for my daytime snacking and energy.

Thursday night, LJ told me she was thinking of going to IL, to go to college and play basketball. I told her I would support her, regardless of her decision. Friday, she did all the placement testing, sent her transcripts, and applied for financial aid.

I flew into Bend, OR, late Friday night. Jewel and I stayed up talking for a few hours before we finally went to bed. I was the opening ceremony speaker and as I looked into the crowd, locking eyes with Jewel, the emotions of gratitude overwhelmed me, knowing she was a huge part of the hope I carried.

I met the event committee and the ACS staff person. I had made a quilt for her which Jewel surprised her with at a RFL meeting. I felt like I was meeting old friends as we made our way around the track.

We left the event about 10 P.M. Sunday, we wandered around downtown Bend. Jewel and Mack took me to Deschutes brewery for some beer tasting. Mack told the manager that I was doing the JMT beginning Wednesday night. While Jewel and I were sitting at the high-top table, the manager approached with several Deschutes gifts for my trip.

They gave me a patch to put on my pack, sunglasses, stickers, keychain beer opener and a beer on the house. I liked their beer but fell in love with the hospitality.

After we toured more places, we headed back to the house. I had an early flight the next morning.

Branch and I were leaving Tuesday, staying at a hotel in LA until it was time to meet Rosa and the group at the train station. Monday night we had dinner with LJ and my parents. LJ told us that she was accepted and would be playing college basketball for her coach from high school.

LJ was going to leave Thursday morning at 6 A.M., to drive to IL. Branch got her a hotel at the halfway mark so she could get some sleep instead of driving straight through. Branch would meet LJ early Thursday, at her dad's, so Branch could get all her personal stuff and furniture before she left.

Tuesday morning, Branch and I left for LA and LJ went to work for her last day at Nike. She was planning on telling her dad when she got home from work. Branch and I got checked into our hotel, got some stuff for an early dinner, and overlooked all my gear again. My phone started ringing and I saw it was Jack.

I answered. He asked if I knew what LJ was doing, driving to IL to go to college. I told him I knew. She told me the night before, knowing I would be out of cell range when she left. He asked how I could be okay with her traveling across the country by herself to go to a school we knew nothing about.

I laughed; she was the same age we had been when we were driving all over the place. I told him Branch paid for a hotel room for her Thursday night, and she would arrive in IL, Friday night. I knew and trusted her coach, so she wouldn't be alone.

He sputtered more, and I told him I had to go, then I hung up. I called LJ and made sure she was okay after talking to her dad, told her I was proud of her, and I loved her. Branch said he would make sure she was okay and not to worry about anything.

I met Rosa Wednesday morning at the train station. She introduced me to the rest of the group that came from San Diego. I didn't like the organizer of the group because of things he said and the way he acted leading up to the hike. Rosa and I already made plans to hike on our own once we arrived.

We got on the train that would take us as close to the trailhead, but we still needed to take a shuttle to the trailhead. We were on the train for a couple hours, then went to find our shuttle. After walking around, not finding it, we ended up getting another ride.

With all our gear, the van was packed to capacity. Our permit had us scheduled to start in Cottonwood, south of Whitney, hiking NB to Yosemite. Due to the wildfires in the area, the cottonwood trailhead was closed.

We had to go to the permit issuing building to learn the new route. They told us to enter from Whitney Portal and continue NB, to steer clear of the fires. There was a shuttle that would pick us up in town to take us up to the trailhead that evening so we all went to get our last real meal.

I text everyone before we got to the trailhead, to say that I'd made it and would talk to them when I came off the trail. It was after 6 P.M. when we got to the trailhead, but we made the decision to hike up a few miles to camp at Mirror Lake. It would help us slowly acclimate to the elevation and we'd be closer to hiking into Whitney's base camp the next day.

The organizer of the group, a misogynist jerk, took oxygen tanks with him, after telling Rosa and I to make sure we could keep up. Rosa and I weighed our packs before we started up the trail and I was shocked to see my pack was 75 lbs.

I knew it was heavy with the food, tent, sleeping bag, woobie and bear canister but I didn't want to run out of water, at all, I carried an extra 3 liters of water. I had 2 changes of spandex, 6 pairs of wool socks, 2 sports bras, 2 long-sleeved and short-sleeved hiking shirts.

I wore a running skirt for ease when going to the bathroom. I used my "She Wee" to pee, without showing my entire back side.

I had several carabiners hanging from my pack so I could let my clothes dry in the sun while hiking after I washed them. You don't realize how much all the little things add up for total weight until you start carrying it on your back, for several miles. The good thing was that it would lighten up as the days went on because I would be eating the food.

We all started up the trail to mirror lake, with Rosa and I in the back. Rosa and I took our time, enjoying the sounds of nature as the front of the group took off.

I figured it would take us a couple of hours to get to mirror lake, which would be about 9 P.M. There were some really steep switchbacks as we climbed but I kept telling myself it would help me get stronger, faster. We walked on wooden logs to cross streams and dodged other obstacles as it got darker.

Rosa and I had our headlamps on, which only lit a few feet in front of us. I was sweating from the climb. Once we were at the lake and setting up, the temps had dropped. The wind was blowing enough to give me a chill.

Rosa and I set up our tents away from the others, with some logs for privacy when we used the bathroom. I was so amped up it took me a long time to get to sleep and I didn't sleep well. The next morning, I refilled water that I filtered from the lake, washed my "pits and bits," and packed up.

I was ready to go by 6 A.M. but the others were still sleeping or lounging around. Rosa got up about 8 and at 9 A.M., we were ready to hike. The organizer said he was staying another day to acclimate because he had a headache from the altitude. I whispered to Rosa, I guess we don't have to worry about "keeping up" with the group.

We started hiking, taking in the changing scenery as we went. The climb was tough, we were going from 9000 feet to 12,000 at the base camp. Some areas we had nice shade, others we were in the sun, as we scrambled around rocks. We had hiked almost 4 miles, about halfway to base camp, when we were stopped by a ranger.

We showed him the permits on our phone, and he said we had to have a "wag bag" if we were hiking Whitney. We told him the ranger district office told us we had to enter here because of the fires and didn't give us anything. He said we needed to turn around because we had to have the bags. We were told that we could face a fine if we didn't have the bags.

I was pissed. I was hot, tired, and now I had to hike back down. The ranger headed down before us and I felt so many emotions rising inside me. The hike was meant to give me time to work things out in my head and help me heal my soul with the quiet, but I didn't expect everything inside me to start opening just then.

By the time we got back down to the lake, the ranger was talking to our group and apologized to us, saying we didn't need the wag bags because the office changed our entry point. I dropped down to a stump and angrily asked, "So we DIDN'T need to hike all the way back down?"

The ranger put his head down, shook his head and apologized again. I was more pissed than before, but I was too tired to let it out. Rosa and I set up camp again. I was grateful we didn't have to hike all the way to the trailhead to be shuttled to another trailhead, but I was upset because we'd lost an entire day and we hiked miles that we had to repeat.

The next morning, we headed out about 9 A.M. The group organizer said he was going to hike back down to the trailhead and get a shuttle to the next trailhead, to give him more time to acclimate. I don't think he planned to go any further because we never saw him again.

The other 4 of us left. We started the hike again with plans to meet at the base camp if we separated. For the most part, we stayed together as a group. We helped each other scramble up and over rocks that were part of the trail, crossing streams and pointing out wildlife as we hiked along. The hike up didn't seem as long as it did the day before. I knew when the switchbacks ended and took us straight up.

The green from the trees, leaves, meadow, and grass was beautiful. I took pictures as we went but wanted to enjoy most of it by being in the moment. We stopped for lunch at a small pond, going to the bathroom where we could find semi-private spots.

We were about 2 miles from base camp when we were walking along a river and decided to stop. Rosa felt lightheaded, then nauseous. I gave her some Hot Tamales candy to see if it helped. We drank some water, and I finished my Lenny and Larry cookie that I was snacking on since breakfast.

I had no appetite, but I needed to eat to keep my strength up. After resting for about 30 minutes, we started slowly climbing again. There were now people passing us heading down the trail and some that were going north-bound.

We made it to basecamp, and it looked like a zoo. Unfortunately, it smelled like one too. We found a couple spots to put up our tents, got our stuff out for dinner and refilled our water. We saw the other 2 that were part of our group, not far from us. We talked about getting an early start climbing Whitney because there were 99 switchbacks, climbing from 12,000 to almost 14,000 feet.

Rosa and I had talked some during the hike that day. I told her I felt unsettled in my soul and in my mind. I didn't sleep well that night. The next morning, I got my spot cleaned up and everything packed before I ate some cookie.

There were people up and hiking before dawn. They wanted to watch the sun rise from the peak, but I had no interest. Thinking I would be the slowest, I told the group I was heading out to get started.

I worked my way up the switchbacks, one at a time. As I climbed, I started singing "I'm a Little Bit Stronger" by Sara Evans. I didn't know all the words, but the chorus stuck with me and became my mantra.

There were people passing me that were only hiking to the summit, then heading back down. They didn't have heavy packs. My group caught up with me and we hiked in a single-file line, for a couple miles.

Soon we were on the side of this mountain with what seemed like a small goat trail. The wind was blowing and there was nothing but a steep drop down the mountain if you strayed off the trail. I don't know what happened, but I stopped because I had tears running down my face.

Rosa told me it was my trauma trying to escape and I needed to let it happen. I slowly made my way along the mountain, scared, knowing I had to keep putting one foot in front of the other. I was crying and singing at the same time. Passersby probably thought I was a basket case.

We made it out of the crazy switchbacks and there was about 1 mile left before we got to the summit. I told Rosa to keep going and I would be along. I felt more emotions trying to escape. I sat on a rock, just off the trail and let the tears come. I didn't realize how much I was holding inside, just trying to make it through each day.

I started feeling lighter, so I started walking again. I made it to the summit area with the others and took a break to eat more of my Lenny and Larry cookie. We were going to hike down the back side of Whitney before we stopped for the night at Guitar Lake.

Once we started down the switchbacks, I was glad I had worn hiking boots with ankle support to keep my feet from sliding all over. Rosa was wearing Merrill trail shoes, but because the gravel kept giving way, her feet were sliding in her shoes. By the time we got to the bottom, she had blisters on her feet, and she was miserable.

We found a large area by guitar lake for the night. The other girl with us said she would jump in the lake if I did. It was going to be cold, but a cool dip would clean the trail dust off.

I stripped down to my spandex and sports bra, put my water shoes on and ran straight for the water without stopping. The water was cold enough to rob me of my breath. The other girl jumped in, and we were treading water, as the others dipped their feet in.

I put on my clean sleep shorts and tank top, washed my shirts and shorts, letting them air dry from my tent poles. I tried eating some of my rice, but I didn't have an appetite. I snacked on salty dried broccoli.

Before we went to bed, it started sprinkling. I hung my clothes up inside my tent to finish drying. The other girl, Abby, didn't have a tent because she was using her hammock. I let her lie under my outer door in her sleeping bag.

She was in the Marines and was used to sleeping on the ground and in crazy places, but she appreciated having a dry spot to sleep. The next morning, we refilled water, repacked, and headed out.

Rosa and I slowed down from the others, they wanted to put miles under them while we wanted to enjoy the scenery, nature, and journey. That day we walked along a gorgeous stream, saw wildlife, walked through forests of trees, across streams and up hills until it started raining.

We put our rain gear on, covered our packs with rain covers and kept going. We climbed another hill and came to an open meadow. The rain had let up, but it was disgustingly humid.

We knew the area we wanted to get to before we stopped for the night, but the change in weather was crazy. We saw the sign for the area we were going to stay. The 2 miles to get there were across a cold and windy plateau, down a winding dirt path through trees and brush, across a stream and up another hill. Once there, we set up camp.

I changed out of my wet clothes, hung up what I could to dry, and fell into my sleeping bag. We'd hiked 12 miles and I felt every one of them. The next morning, I woke to sunshine and blue skies. I walked to the stream not far from my tent. I was now 44 years old, and my body felt every bit of 44. I sounded like "Rice Krispies" cereal with all the Snap! Crackle! Pop!

Rosa got up and we set out for the day. Our goal was to get over Forrester Pass, the highest pass we would be climbing during the hike. We had about 6 miles before we climbed the pass, so we set out at a steady pace.

Once we turned from the stream, we walked through the woods until everything opened to rolling hills and meadows. At one point it felt like it was about 80 degrees, then across one of the meadows, the wind and rain started again. We put our raincoats on but didn't want to stop to put our pants on.

We kept hiking with our heads down to the blowing wind, trudging one step at a time. Our hands were freezing from holding our hiking poles, even with gloves on. Soon the rain started changing to hail and we were about a half mile from starting up Forrester Pass.

We had no idea what the weather was like on the other side of the pass, and we didn't want to get stuck on the side of the mountain with harsh weather. We found a couple spots we could set up tents, warm up and start out after the storm passed.

We saw hikers coming down from the pass, trying to find shelter. The temps dropped rapidly, and the hail soon turned to snow. We found a place that gave us a little protection from the wind, set up our tents and climbed inside.

I read for a while, then took a nap, waking up about 3 P.M. We had set up camp about 1 and when I looked out my door, there were a couple inches of snow around my tent. I couldn't believe it snowed on my birthday, for the first time in 44 years. I had brought a small bottle of wine that I was going to drink on my birthday, but I wasn't in the mood.

Rosa said we should camp there for the night and set out in the morning. I went to the bathroom, grabbed some food from my bear canister and climbed back into my tent. I ate, wrote in my small journal, and read some before I went to bed.

The next morning the wind stopped, there was evidence of the storm on the ground, but it was a gorgeous day. We started hiking to get over the pass before we stopped to refill our water.

8/23/16, we climbed the pass and took photos at the top. I climbed the tallest pass that I was dreading during the planning stages. It was an exhilarating moment. We took in the views of both sides, looking at the lakes we couldn't see from the trail, hidden in the hills.

We started down the hill, taking it slow because of Rosa's blisters, seeing more lakes as we walked along the higher ridges. We crossed another stream via a wooden bridge, through a forest where we saw deer, then stopped for lunch along a busy section of a river.

We had to climb a crazy set of rocks to keep on the trail. The rocks were damp and covered with moss, which made them slicker than normal. A few times, I didn't know if I was going to make it. The climb was tough, and we had just refilled our water at lunch. We kept going, following the twists and turns of the trail until we found a place we wanted to camp. We were on the side of a mountain, overlooking a river, surrounded by trees. It was a gorgeous spot, completely alone.

8/24, the next morning, we had to climb another pass, before we came down through Rae Lakes. We were making really good time, until we got to a sign that wasn't marked correctly and took us several miles out of our way. Once we figured it out, we turned around to go back.

We ended up camping in Rae Lakes, setting up about 11 P.M. I decided to drink my wine that night instead of carrying it. It didn't taste good, so I poured it into the cat hole I made to go to the bathroom.

I had finally fallen asleep when I heard noises outside my tent. The bear canisters were being knocked around on the rocks away from the tents, then something rubbed up against my tent. I didn't know if it was Rosa messing with me, or something else.

I didn't move a muscle or sleep another wink, getting out of my tent at 4:30 A.M. Rosa came out, asking if I had messed with her tent. I told her I thought she was messing with mine. Our bear canisters were in the same spot, but we saw others on the ground. When we started packing up, we saw bear prints in the dirt between our tents. We looked at each other, laughed and said we had almost been bear burritos.

8/25, we set out earlier, knowing it was going to be a long day. We hiked through a lot of trees, across wide open spaces of rock, along streams, up and down hills. We came out of the trees and saw a clearing with several people hanging out. As we walked closer, I saw a huge bridge we had to cross to get across the gorge. It was a suspended bridge that hung by steel wire, with wooden planks spaced apart, swaying in the breeze.

I felt sick to my stomach looking at the bridge. We were eating lunch and resting, deciding we wanted to cross the bridge and start on the other side before it got dark. Only one of us could be on the bridge at a time. I needed to go first, or I was going to overthink it.

I set across the bridge, white knuckling the wire rail the entire time. I didn't want to look down, but I had to make sure my feet were on the wooden planks. I was so damn scared.

After we both made it across, we found the trail and set off again. We hiked through more rocky areas, climbing the entire time. We came across a bigger stream and we decided to refill our water then keep going until we found a spot for the night.

There was a small waterfall in the stream, so I took my boots off and put my feet in the water while I was filtering my water. It felt good to have the cold water flowing over my tired feet. I double checked for blisters and hot spots but didn't find any, thankfully.

We hiked a couple more miles until we found a shaded spot along the river gorge. Listening to the water rushing down and over the rocks put me to sleep and I slept better than any other night on the trail.

8/26, we continued climbing along the river gorge until we came into a forest. It felt like a magical forest, with water bubbling along the rocks, leaves and trees all over, creating a cover from the elements. We hiked to another open meadow, leading to another pass.

After a break for lunch, before climbing the pass due to the heat, we started the climb up the switchbacks. Rosa told me to keep going, she slowed down because of her blisters.

I got to the top and sat on a rock to wait. I could see smoke and smelled it but didn't know where it was coming from. A lady hiking up from the other side said a fire started but it hadn't closed any of the trail.

Rosa made it to the top. She was hating life. She wanted to stop when we got down the other side so she could check her bandages on her blisters. I was fine with that because I was sick of seeing dirt and rock. I expected to see more greenery along the trails.

We made it down the pass, with me slipping and almost busting my ass on some slick rocks. We were close to the lake and had to walk through heavy shale stone, making the hike harder with the packs. It looked like it was going to rain again, and I wanted to set up as soon as possible. I went ahead and found a spot for us to camp for the night. We were right on the edge of the water, surrounded by some trees and shrubs, with sand as our floor.

I put my stuff down then went back for Rosa and took her pack. We made it back to our spot and set up our camp. We both took our socks and shoes off, put our water shoes on and sat by the water with our feet cooling off. Rosa took her bandages off and I saw blisters on top of blisters, on top of blisters.

I have no idea how she was hiking with those blisters. We needed to find a place she could clean them and make sure nothing got infected. She was thinking the same thing. She was a nurse and needed her feet to be in good shape.

We looked at our map and decided to head out the next pass which would have us off the trail by the next evening. We ate like kings that night. Eating macaroni and cheese with tuna fish mixed in. We laughed at how we thought that hot meal was the best thing ever.

We talked about what we were going to eat first when we got off the trail. I was eating barley and hops, in the liquid form, a beer. I wanted an ice-cold beer in a frosty mug.

We decided we would go to Mammoth for a couple days to clean her feet and let them heal, then get back on the trail from there. The next morning, we both got up early, excited to be leaving the trail for a bit.

8/27, we hiked along a river before crossing it, then we saw the sign for Taboose pass, the pass to exit. We started hiking across a meadow that slowly turned into a forest. The forest opened to a meadow, which turned to rocks. The rocks became bigger when we descended, hiking down nothing but rocks. The rocks ranged from huge boulders to watermelon sized stones.

They weren't easy to hike down on, especially with the weight we were carrying and Rosa's blisters. When it didn't seem like the rocks were going to end, Rosa said this is where rocks come to die. We hadn't passed another person since we crossed the stream and had no idea how close we were to exiting.

We kept going and about 8:30 P.M. we saw campers. We asked them how far to the trailhead. It was a couple miles. One of the campers said he saw a bear by the river about 20 minutes prior. We probably should have stopped there for the night, get some sleep, and start out fresh the next day.

We were both stubborn and pig headed. We kept going without discussion. We were ready for a hot shower and a soft bed. We came to the river, it was deeper than others we crossed, but we had to cross it.

As we stepped in, Rosa was in front. I saw something out of the corner of my eye and slowly turned my head to the left, to see a bear, in the water, about 5 feet from us. He looked at me and I stopped. Quietly, I told Rosa to go slowly because there was a bear. We couldn't go to our right or we would plummet over 200 feet down the waterfall.

The bear put his head back down and started eating the fish he had in his paws. Hoping that satisfied his appetite, we made our way to the other side. We didn't run, but we walked quickly to put more distance between us and the bear. We had no idea where we were, and it was completely dark now.

Our head lamps barely lit the way for us, but we kept going. Fortunately, we were on dirt and going downhill. We turned a corner of the switchback, which went along the side of the river, with a 200-foot drop, when my foot slipped on a large rock. I fell down, backwards, from the weight of my pack.

One foot was straight out in front of me, the other was tucked underneath me and one of my poles had gone all the way into the ground. I couldn't roll to the side. On one side was a rock wall and the other side, a cliff. If I died falling off a cliff, Branch was going to be pissed. Rosa laughed at my sentiment and reached back with her pole for me to grab onto.

I felt like a turtle flipped onto its shell, with no way to get up. After multiple attempts, I was able to grab her pole and slowly pull myself to a sitting position. I pulled my pole out of the ground then used it for leverage to help me get up. I was thankful I didn't mess my ankle up because it's the one I'd twisted and rolled, several times.

Once on my feet, we were trucking again. It was after 10 P.M. and I felt like we'd walked miles. I had just enough charge on my cell phone to check for signal. With no service, I turned it off again.

We made it off the switchbacks and walked across a flatter meadow. By the time we made it to the trailhead, it was almost midnight. I called a local hotel to see if they had anyone that could pick us up. After more persuading and pleading, the hotel owner agreed to come get us.

We had no idea how far the trail head was from the road. We had very little water left. About 1 A.M., I saw lights and started walking towards them. I was on the dirt road to the trail head but couldn't tell how close the lights were.

Defeat overwhelmed me when I saw the lights turn around. My phone was dead, it was 2 A.M. and had no idea how far it was to the main road. We walked a little further until I told Rosa we should stop and rest our feet for a couple hours until we could see.

We stopped on the side of the trailhead road, in a small dirt patch. We put our pack covers on the ground and covered ourselves with our rain gear while our feet were elevated on our packs. I slept a few minutes at a time, but it was hard to stay warm with just a raincoat.

8/28, at 6 A.M., the sun started breaking above the mountains and I could see better. I was hoping someone would drive down, that we could bum a ride from. Unfortunately, no one came and the longer we waited the hotter it got. We needed to move. We needed water and soon it would be too hot for us to be in the open desert.

I started walking faster, knowing if I could find a ride, we could come back and pick Rosa up. If I walked with her, we would be out there even longer. Finally, I came to a turn and saw the main road. Our thought was to get to the road and hitchhike. As I kept walking, I saw a small campground and my thoughts turned to water. There was a stream we could filter from.

I walked around, trying to get a sense of where we were when I saw a truck pull in. The guy got out and looked around before he got back in. I had to take my chance on him. I yelled, "Excuse me, sir," and he turned around. I briefed him on our journey and asked if he could give us a ride to the next town.

His wife was in the truck and asked for the whereabouts of my friend. I explained, I walked ahead to find a ride because she could barely walk. They had me put my pack in the truck, offered me water, then we went to pick Rosa up. Relief flooded Rosa's face when she looked up to see the cavalry. We had hiked almost 20 miles the day before.

I jumped out, grabbed her pack, then gave her a water bottle. Once we were settled, we told more of our adventure and how we wound up at that spot. They let me borrow a phone charger and after talking more, Rosa and I decided we weren't going back to the trail.

Independence was the closest town, but the guy said he didn't feel right about dropping us off in the middle of nowhere. They lived in San Bernardino and would take us to their house where we could shower and make travel plans to San Diego.

There was a bus we could take that night to San Diego if we wanted. They were our trail angels. We would never be able to repay their kindness.

I sent Branch a text and asked if he could pick me up from Rosa's house when he got off work the next day.

The couple took us to Target so we could get clean clothes, flip-flops, and underclothes because we only had our trail clothes and shoes. We got stuff, then stood in line. I bought a soda and she bought Cool Ranch Doritos. That was our first "real" food off the trail, but we were taking the couple to dinner at their favorite Italian restaurant before we went to the bus station.

We got to their house, and I showered while Rosa soaked her feet in a bucket of water. Rosa booked our seats on the bus that left at 8 P.M. to San Diego. I washed my hair four or 5 times before it felt clean. There was so much dirt after my shower, I had to clean the shower.

Rosa showered next then treated and bandaged her blisters before we went to eat. We had wine, pasta, bread, and dessert before we left for the bus station. I felt like I was going to pop from all the food. I was ready for a long nap.

We got to the station, said our goodbyes, then boarded the bus. There weren't many people on the bus, but we took the front seats, not wanting to walk further than we had to. We were scheduled to arrive in SD about midnight.

From the station, Rosa ordered an Uber while I got our bags. The Uber arrived then it was about 20 minutes before we got to Rosa's house. We walked in, set our bags down and went straight to our beds. She had set up an air mattress with a pillow top for support and comfort.

I laid down and went right to sleep. Branch sent me a message letting me know he was on his way to get me. I went to the bathroom, took my meds, and laid back down. I slept until Branch got there, about 2 P.M. I felt drugged because I was so tired.

Branch made us dinner that night. We had a couple beers then went to bed. I slept almost 12 hours before I woke up. We had breakfast before Branch and I left for home. Rosa didn't have to work for 2 weeks. She wasn't doing anything on her feet until then. I had almost 2 weeks off too because we had planned on being on the trail until September 4th or 5th. We had hiked over 111 miles and spent 12 days on the trail.

Branch took me home, we went to our local bar and grill for dinner then went home, showered, and back to bed. Branch had to work, and he was studying for his tests. I slept for most of 2 days. When I stood up to go to the bathroom, my knees were killing me.

The downhill hiking, the sliding on rocks, carrying the pack and the overall hike had taken a toll. Every joint and muscle hurt. Rosa and I checked in on each other every other day and her feet healed.

I worked for a couple days before I flew to D.C. for our ACS CAN summit. This was my first year as the State Lead Ambassador. While we were in our wrap-up session, I got a call from one of the Heroes of Hope that I met years prior.

When I answered, she told me I was selected as a Hero of Hope. She told me who nominated me, what she said about me and what my next steps would be as a Hero of Hope. I couldn't believe that I had been selected. It was such an honor to be nominated and humbling to hear the words written about me.

Everyone on my team asked what was going on when they saw the tears in my eyes. Everyone hugged me and said I was truly a Hero of Hope when I told them the news. I called Branch and told him before I left for the airport, still in disbelief.

KM invited us to dinner to celebrate her birthday and divorce. The following weekend, we had a wedding to go to with Branch's work crew. I was flying to St. Louis the next week to see LJ.

That weekend we went to Buffalo Wild Wings to watch the Broncos game with friends and KM. Meanwhile, I was training as much as I could for my upcoming triathlon.

Bab loaned me a wetsuit, then Branch and I were loaded up and heading back to SD. We stayed with Rosa again, went to get my packet and got ready for Sunday. I had tried the wetsuit on and joked that I was going to get eaten by a shark because I looked like a seal.

There were riptide warnings for the beaches, and we didn't know if we would swim Sunday morning until we got there. We arrived about 6 A.M., got my bike and gear set up, then I put my wetsuit on.

As I walked out of the staging area, I saw Branch and Rosa, then my eyes went directly to someone dressed in a shark costume. I stopped walking and looked at Branch with a deer in the headlights look.

I was holding my breath, then let it out and laughed. I was going to get my picture taken with the man dressed as a shark to overcome my fear. After we took the picture, Branch showed it to me, and the shark was holding a sign that said, "Swim Buddy."

I was part of the cancer survivor group that was going to start the triathlon off. After we started, another group would start every 3 minutes. I was nervous. They called the survivors into the water, which was cold, told us the layout and if we needed help there were swim buddies in the water and on paddle boards.

I looked at Branch, put my goggles on, took a deep breath and jumped in when the gun went off. We hadn't been swimming more than 30 seconds before the "elite" swimmers started.

As I turned my head for my breath, someone swam over top of me, splashing water in my mouth and pushing my head under as they kept going. I stopped swimming and began treading water. I was coughing and my chest felt heavy. I thought it was the wetsuit. I started to panic when one of the swim buddies saw me and asked how he could help. I asked if he would unzip my suit and when that didn't work, he helped me take the top off.

I tried swimming again, but every time I leaned forward, there was a heavy weight in my chest. I tried swimming the backstroke and that did the same thing. Frustrated, I did the bicycle, doggie paddle so I could finish.

My swim buddy stayed with me the entire time. He was the guy in the shark costume. When I could touch, I looked up and saw Branch looking at me with a pinched look on his face. He asked me what happened, and I said I swallowed water at the beginning.

I was walking out of the water, heading towards transition and he was walking beside me on the outside. He was asking if I threw up water and other questions that I wasn't computing. I had to get ready for the bike portion. I could make up time because the bike portion was my best event.

I got my suit off, put my helmet and shoes on then ran out to transition with my bike. I mounted and took off, but I was still having trouble breathing. I kept pedaling, passing people along the way, made it to the island we had to circle twice before riding back to transition.

I tried doing deep breathing, sitting up straighter on my bike and everything I could think of to help me breathe. The last lap of the circle, I pushed hard and as I came out of it, I could feel the pressure sitting on my chest.

I saw Branch and Rosa when I came in. I waved and quickly transitioned to my running shoes. I took off running and had run about ½-mile when I was gasping for air. When I saw Branch and Rosa, Branch knew something was seriously wrong. I told him I was finishing, even if I had to walk. He was mad at me and my stubbornness.

I would run, walk, run until I saw the finish line. I picked my feet up and mentally pushed myself to run the last portion. By the time I crossed, I could hear myself wheezing. Branch could too.

I got my medal, took a photo with the shark again, then got my stuff from transition. I was starving and knew places would be crowded because it was Sunday. We went to a pancake place, but I couldn't eat. It was getting harder to breathe. Branch said he was taking me to urgent care, but I said I just needed to shower and lie down a bit.

We went back to Rosa's, I showered and laid down. I couldn't lay on my back because it hurt to breathe so I laid on my side, but I was still wheezing. Branch asked me again if I got sick after I swallowed water and I angrily said, no, why does it matter. He told me if I didn't get sick then I probably got water in my lungs from the sea water.

I told him I just wanted to rest and if I wasn't better when we left the next day, I would go to urgent care. Branch didn't sleep well because he kept watching and listening to my breathing. He was afraid of me drowning from the water in my lungs.

The next morning, we headed home. I half reclined the front seat to try to get comfortable and I wasn't wheezing as bad, but it was still there. Tuesday, Branch had to go to work, and he asked me to please go to urgent care because there was no one at home if something happened to me. I told him I would go after work before I came home.

I went to work, went to our Relay meeting then after finishing, I took my normal route, running up the stairs. I made it up the first set but by the time I got to the turn of the second set, I had to grab the railing because I was light-headed. Some people were in the hall, coming from the elevator when they saw my face.

I told them I was okay, but I needed to go to urgent care. I sent Branch a text, letting him know I was leaving work early, going to urgent care.

They got me in right away and the doctor ordered chest x-rays so she could see my lungs. After all the tests and explaining what happened, the doctor told me that I asphyxiated saltwater into my lungs. The water caused a chemical reaction with my bronchi, causing a similar reaction as an asthma attack.

She told me I was lucky. She concurred with my hubby that I was pig-headed and stubborn. I asked her if I had any sea horses in my lungs and she rolled her eyes. She gave me an antibiotic in case there was any infection in my lungs and an inhaler.

She told me I needed to stop running, climbing, etc., for a couple weeks, to let my lungs heal. I had to use the inhaler before I ran or did any type of exercise and during if I felt heaviness. I had a marathon on December 11th, and she said I should be okay for it if I gave my lungs the chance to heal.

I was now 7 weeks out from my marathon and a 15k challenge in 3 weeks, the week before Thanksgiving. I needed to get a few long runs in before we flew to Hawaii, but my lungs needed a break.

We hosted our MISSter Relay pageant the first weekend of November at a local restaurant with a large covered outdoor venue. Branch and his crew built the wood pieces to form a stage with a runway. We lit the area with soft twinkling lights and our MC for the event was a local news anchor, as well as the Diamondbacks, fan host.

We had more guys than we expected signed up to participate. By the time the event started, the contestants had raised over $5000 to fight back against cancer. We had a great turnout. Each contestant had to model a casual/sporty outfit as well as the evening dress.

Not only did the event raise several thousand dollars for the American Cancer Society but it helped with morale in our office. All of us were nervous about the upcoming election for sheriff, knowing our worlds would change drastically if Sheriff Joe didn't win.

Election day brought changes. In January we would have a new sheriff and administration running our office. The community outreach team continued doing the events and work planned, until we were told differently. We had just over 3 months before our RFL event and didn't take our foot off the gas.

The next weekend was my 15k challenge run. Jewel flew in for it because she was attempting to get to Hawaii to run the marathon with me. She said I was her inspiration to start running and she was my hope, to keep running.

Jewel flew in Thursday and there was a survivor recognition event at CTCA that we went to together. I found out before she flew in that I was nominated and selected to be one of the veteran/cancer survivors to be honored at the Coyotes hockey game.

I told my chief about it, what had been written from the media about me and he made a post on our office social media page as a deputy spotlight. Reading the words he wrote brought me to tears. It was going to be tough to stay dry eyed at the game.

I had tickets from CTCA which I gave to Jewel and her granddaughter because Branch and I were given seats in the Salute to Service section. I would be on the ice when they sang the national anthem, for my tribute.

I was nervous until fans in the audience started saying hi to me while I was standing beside the ice. I saw "brother husband" and his son, one of my RTOs from the academy, and a few other people from work. I decided to enjoy the moment and stay present for it, allowing whatever emotions I felt to show.

The coyotes showed my photos from basic training, Desert Storm, with my son and with family. Hearing my story over the loudspeaker by the Coyotes announcer hit me differently. I awakened to the power of my story. The National Anthem was sung by "Jax" and very powerful.

After the opening ceremony, I had the Coyotes' cheerleaders surround my seat, hugging me and taking photos. It was an emotional night, and I was glad my hubby and Jewel were there to be part of it.

That Sunday, Jewel and I ran the 10k then ran a 5k right after, for our "Girls on the Run" challenge. I had been put on more meds for my kidneys and stones a couple weeks before. This was my first long run with the medication in my system. I finished, sucking air, my lungs on fire, but it was part of my training plan.

Branch and I were driving a truck to KJs house as soon as my run was done. After we got to KJs and slept, we dropped Branch off at the airport. My sister and I drove to NY. We stopped in IL to see LJ.

We made it to NY late Tuesday night after driving straight through for 30 hours. We slept that night then I was up early to run errands with my dad, see some of his old friends and getting stuff ready for Thanksgiving. I was scheduled to fly out Friday morning, so we had an early Thanksgiving dinner, Wednesday night at my aunts, with my mom and cousins.

The next morning it was rainy and chilly, but I knew I had to get a run in before dinner. I ran around the lake. It was quiet, with a slight drizzle as I ran. I saw deer in the meadows, some trees that hadn't lost all their leaves yet and the mist over the lake.

I kept my mouth covered to help protect my lungs during my run. After I flew home, I did my final long run, that Sunday. I was still frustrated about my lungs, but I would push through, even if I had to crawl over the finish line.

Branch and I flew to HI, which was a first for both of us. The day we flew in was the 75th anniversary of Pearl Harbor, so Honolulu was more packed than usual. Jewel and Mack made it in, after a crazy couple days of flying stand by. We went to the expo, got our race packets then Jewel and Mack stayed with us at my cousin's. His apartment was on the corner where the race started, and it was on the main route of our run.

We were up at 3:30 A.M. and at the start line by 4 A.M., for a 4:30 A.M. start. Jewel and I had matching run skirts that I had made for us, the same tank tops, and sparkly white run visors. As we stood in the crowd of runners, I went through my breathing exercises to help calm me.

The announcer said there were over 44,000 runners, with approximately 40,000 of them flying in from Japan. I knew it was crowded but hearing that number of people in one area sent my anxiety soaring.

We started the run with a great pace. Each mile I was running for someone I loved with cancer, praying for them, or remembering memories with them. We bypassed the first water station because it was busy, and we had our own hydration. At the 2nd water station, it was busy and there was water all over the ground. I stepped into a puddle which drenched my entire foot, shoe, and sock.

We were still running at a good pace and broke away from the crowd. The sun was up, and it was heating up. We made a quick pit stop at mile 19 to use the restroom. About mile 20, I could tell I didn't get my spandex back in the right spot and was starting to chafe from sweat and salt.

At mile 21, there were people cooling us off by spraying us with hoses and I could feel blisters starting on the foot that was drenched from the 2nd aid station. Now both of my feet were wet after being sprayed by hoses. We ran up a hill for mile 23/24 and I could feel the blister on the bottom of my foot, from my foot sliding backwards.

On the way down, mile 25, I could feel my foot sliding the other way and blisters building on top of blisters, on both feet. They were squishing in my shoe on every step. By now it was about 85°, and the humidity was ridiculous. I felt chafed everywhere and my feet hurt from blisters, I wanted to cry.

We were close, but it was going to take everything I had to finish. After the hill, we had 1.2 miles to finish. I could barely walk, let alone run. Thank God for Jewel, entertaining me with dancing, motivating me, telling me I inspired her to begin running, I was her hero. She never stopped, kept me going. She was 58 and running like a rockstar. I finally saw the park with the finish line, the 26-mile marker and started run/walking the last .2 miles.

Jewel stayed with me the entire time, even though she could have easily blown the time out of the water. We crossed the finish line together, holding hands in the air celebrating. It took everything I had to walk to Branch, my cousin, and his girlfriend.

Branch asked me what happened. He had tracked our pace and knew we did well most of the race. I told him about my feet. It was taking everything I had to stand. Based on Branch's app he used to track me, we would have had a great finish time had we maintained that pace.

I was just glad I finished. We called an Uber. I wouldn't make the walk back to my cousins. Jewel and I wanted showers and real food.

Branch helped me take my compression socks off when we made it back to my cousins. When he saw my feet and the blisters, he was shocked. "Holy shit, how did you run with these?" he asked. "I didn't, I walked/ran," trying to laugh it off.

Branch helped me shower after I crawled to the bathroom. I wanted to scream when the water hit my chafed skin. I showered quickly. The stinging from the chafing was unbearable and in places most inconvenient. Branch helped me dress, then I crawled to the couch where he dressed my blisters.

Branch learned a trick when he was younger where you take a needle with thread, pull it through the blister to let it drain slowly, with the thread left in and the area dries out. I laid on the loveseat, elevated my feet on a couple pillows, with towels under my feet for the draining.

I didn't do anything the rest of the day. On Monday, I could walk some. I kept the thread in while I walked to get my finishers certificate, then let my feet rest again.

My cousin and Branch got up each morning to go swimming in the ocean and by Tuesday morning, I could walk down the hill with them. I enjoyed the peacefulness of the ocean, right before the sun broke the horizon. Branch and I drove around the island that day, went snorkeling and relaxed before our flight home the next day.

I had a doctor's appointment that Friday and after testing my urine, they said I had another kidney infection. I was so done with the pain, meds and swelling. After we got home, it took my feet and legs several days before the swelling went down from flying. The urologist added more medication to my daily regimen, and I had to monitor the amount of calcium I took in daily.

My daily calcium intake had to be between a certain number. If I didn't get enough for the day, the stones would pull the calcium from my bones. If it was too high, the stones would take the extra calcium, increasing in size. My entire diet changed again.

12
Hope

2017 brought changes at work. We had a new sheriff, new administration, and new chiefs. Some command staff were being demoted, others put in their retirement paperwork, and some went to different agencies. I had no idea what was going to happen to my team after my chief was demoted and sent to a patrol district.

The new command for community outreach came in, most of them from Phoenix PD. They had zero clue or concept of how our office worked, how big our beat areas were, or our rural areas.

I continued with the Relay planning. We had a cornhole tournament fundraiser and DJ was home in time for it. He left Germany and was heading to Alaska for his new duty assignment. He would be home for 51 days, which included the RFL event.

Our event was the first weekend of March, and with all the command changes, staff movement and transfers, our teams were scrambling to make things work. The week of my event, we had a meeting with our enforcement support team, to see how we could work together with resources and people for events.

On our way back from the meeting, I was riding with our new commander, as I still didn't have an assigned vehicle. He overheard me talking to Marty, my "buddy ole pal," when we left the building, reminiscing on when we had our office there.

My commander started asking me about our story. Marty and I had been assigned to the Criminal Employment Squad as detectives, investigating companies that knowingly hired undocumented immigrants. There were some that were helping them use other people's social security numbers to pass the new E-Verify system.

I told him we investigated the companies and the employees for fraud, forgery, and identity theft, after someone called in a tip. Once we found the tip to be valid, we started our investigation.

His comment was, "Oh, I didn't know you were part of that unit." I didn't think anything of his comment at the time. We had our last Relay meeting when we got back to our office. All the event t-shirts had come in, which I separated by size and team. I had to finish the event program and the script before our bank night, which was Thursday.

We were setting up all day Friday for our event Saturday, which was starting at noon. I had my schedule and agenda packed for the week, but if I stayed on task, I would be fine.

Tuesday afternoon, I was told, I needed to go to a local Phoenix school to read for Dr. Seuss week. I told my supervisor I had no time to read, and I had my bank drop scheduled during that time. He didn't give me an option but told me to be there.

The commander set it up and the sheriff was supposed to go, but then couldn't make it. There was no way I could do it and I sent the principal an email, letting him know.

I sent the email early Wednesday morning, with a CC to my supervisor and commander. I was out of the office most of Wednesday, taking care of last-minute coordination with other divisions that were going to be at the event.

When I came in Thursday, my supervisor told me one of the deputies from enforcement support was taking care of the reading. I said, "Okay, thanks," and continued with the last-minute program changes before teams picked up their shirts and dropped their money off. I had to count the money and credit their team or individual for their fundraising on the back end of our website.

As the teams and money came in, I knew it was going to be a late night. I was trying to get home to see Branch. He had to leave early in the morning for Army, in Flagstaff. Before I left the office, I received an email from the principal, saying how unprofessional I was and other things.

At that point I didn't care. I told my supervisors that the rural schools were our priority.

When I got up Friday morning with Branch, I knew I had another kidney infection. He could feel me burning up. I got dressed and went to urgent care before going to the training center.

DJ came in later with the trailer, stage, and decorations. I had him pick up my prescription on his way in. We marked off the team sites, set the equipment up before we brought the stage, bleachers, and other heavy stuff in the middle of the track.

By the time DJ got to the track, I was running a fever with sweat pouring from me. I was supposed to stay out of direct sunlight when I took the meds but that wasn't going to happen. I took my pill, ibuprofen, drank gallons of water and went to work.

We finished setup, I finished my itinerary and provided a copy to the DJ to play certain songs during the ceremony.

The next morning, our committee arrived at 8 A.M., to set up our tents and fundraising areas, set up the tents for the survivor dinner, put the luminaria bags around the track, with sand and candles.

As the teams arrived, we finished decorating the stage with butterflies. We decided the butterfly represented the new changes at the office, growth, and new beginnings. We made the stage look like a garden, with painted wood flowers and a butterfly curtain hanging as the backdrop.

We were ready to go at 11:30 A.M. I had asked the sheriff to say a few words during the opening ceremony, to show he supported his employees and the event. The sheriff arrived right before noon. After a quick briefing with him, we started.

The event was a huge success. The new chiefs, command staff and sheriff all said how much they enjoyed the event. By the end of the night, when we finished and started tear down, I was drained.

Thankfully, DJ was there to help with the heavy stuff. Him and one of the girls on the committee did all the stage disassembly, then they loaded the trailer and took the bleachers back by the volleyball court.

The event ended at 10 P.M. We were done with tear down and ready to go by 11:30 P.M. On Monday, DJ, Branch, and I took the trailer to work HQ, to unload everything in our storage area.

We finished unloading everything, then I went upstairs to my office cubicle. I saw several of the participants and command staff when I walked in, all thanking me for a great event and telling me how much they enjoyed it.

After sitting down and booting up my computer, my supervisor said the commander wanted to see me in his office. I walked in, with my supervisor, who shut the door behind us. I knew with a closed door; things weren't going to go well.

The commander said I did a great job with the Relay event but effective the following Monday, I was being transferred to District 2 patrol. "It's nothing you did; the office is just going in a new direction," he said. Nothing was said about my not reading at the school or that I used to be part of the human smuggling unit, but I suspected both were part of the reason behind the transfer.

I went back to my cubicle with tears of frustration glimmering in my eyes and Marty asked what was wrong. I told him I was being transferred. His eyes went wide with shock, "What?" I went to the restroom to get my emotions under control then decided if I was being transferred, I wasn't staying at work.

I called Branch and asked him and DJ to come back to get me. I told them to bring the dolly up with them, for my boxes. I didn't tell them what happened. I just said I was being transferred and didn't want to stay.

I packed up my cubicle, used every extra box I had, then hubby and DJ helped me carry stuff to the truck. While I was packing, several people came by and asked what was going on. I told them I was being transferred because "the office is going in a new direction."

While I was packing up, the supervisor stopped by and said my transfer wasn't until the next week. I told him I understood, but I had doctor appointments and scans the next 2 days. I was going to take Thursday and Friday off, so I was packing everything before I reported to the district. I explained everything to Branch and DJ after we left the office. Had I tried to explain at the office, I was going to cry from frustration and anger, with the possibility of cussing someone out.

I stopped to talk to the captain I would be working for, Cpt. Brand, and he asked me if I would be his administrative deputy. He said I was organized and "got shit done," in addition to the community outreach experience. I started looking at the pros of not working downtown once I calmed down. I wouldn't sit in traffic for 3 hours each day. I wouldn't be driving 63 miles, one way and I was still able to do community outreach, but specifically in our district, working with the rural communities.

I got a call from one of the deputies I had worked with in the HSU. He asked me about my transfer because him and another guy were just transferred out of their specialty units, to the districts. After that, we knew it was because we had all been part of the HSU.

DJ left the weekend before I started my new job. He was excited to get to Alaska because he had ordered his Dodge truck directly from the manufacturer and they shipped it to Alaska. We said our tearful goodbyes at the airport, then watched this "grown-ass man" begin his new chapter.

The next day my hubby and I went to the dealership to get a car with better gas mileage. I would be driving fewer miles but wanted something small and fun. We found a 5-speed turbo, red Chevy Spark. It was a small 4-door, and it was great for me. Not a family car.

The frustrations caused by being transferred significantly lessened. I got 32-34 mpg and my drive time was drastically reduced! I was saving time and fuel, while having fun in my little "Hot Tamale" car. Even with the "coaching" note the commander and my previous supervisor had written about my "unprofessionalism," I felt lighter.

After seeing the urologist again, they referred me to the kidney specialist at the Mayo clinic. I was still having kidney infections. Now I was on a medicine to help with uric acid and a daily low-dose antibiotic, but still had no answers. The medicine caused my potassium to drop significantly. The doctor told me to stop all physical activity, stay out of direct sunlight and heat, so I didn't cause damage to my heart. Any damage would be irreversible.

It was a major roadblock for me. A roadblock built with depression, frustration, anger, and suffering from chronic pain. For years, it was the activity that motivated me and kept me going when depression and anger would take root. Limiting my activity while continuing to have infections, medicine messing with my body, hormones, and weight gain, was limiting my lifeline. Running and hiking also served as a stress management tool and now that was taken from me.

The district lieutenant was my direct supervisor. She shouldn't have overseen anyone, let alone wear a badge. She had a clique of people that tattled on everyone and started gossip. My stress increased. No matter how much I did, how well I did, there was always something she found to nitpick.

One of our detectives committed suicide, after arguing with his wife. They were in the backyard, and she called the cops. I don't know what was going through his mind, but as the cops were coming to the house, they heard a gunshot from the backyard. Our entire district was hit hard after hearing the news.

Several of the guys had gone through the academy with him and had known him for years. I talked to him daily as he passed my office and we spent that Friday, laughing and joking before we all went home.

A group of us became our own support team, talking to each other when we needed, crying, or just sitting in silence with our thoughts.

I started thinking of all the people I had known over the years that committed suicide and somehow understood how they couldn't find another way out. It started with my uncle when I was young, then a girl I went to high school with. We had just finished the soccer season and I was training her for goalie.

I thought of Clay. He hung himself. Then I thought about all the calls I responded to of suicides and suicide attempts. The images were like a slide show in my head. A girl who tried hanging herself while waiting in a cell for trial. I found her hanging from the cell door. She used her inmate's pants to wrap around the bar then around her throat.

Another deputy was with me. He lifted her torso and I cut the pants away from her neck. After fire responded and took her to the hospital, I learned she was in her early 20s. A guy I arrested for DUI got out of the hospital, went home, drank, got into an argument with someone at the house, then shot and killed himself.

I only knew bits and pieces of their stories and their lives. I used to believe suicide was selfish, but I started to realize it wasn't selfishness. They had lost hope in that moment. Maybe they lost it for a longer period, but it was a feeling of hopelessness, unable to see any light or way out. None of us ever truly knows what another is going through or what they're capable of, until it's too late.

We got a new district captain, Cooper. While he learned the ropes at the district, he saw all the work I was doing and assigned another deputy to help me with the admin duties so I could do more community outreach. We had an inspection with the monitors and chiefs, so we had to make sure all our property and evidence was in order, as well as our equipment.

I made new inventory sheets, set up a new system for property and evidence as it came and went to the property room. I was keeping track of the district's equipment, from voice recorders to weapons and vehicles.

One of the Lt.'s doing the inspection was impressed with our P&E system and asked if he could set it up to be used district wide, so everyone was on the same page. Captain Cooper thanked me for helping us pass the inspection and wrote up a commendation for me. It became a joke to see the coaching notes with the commendations.

In June, Branch found out that his mom's cancer had come back, and she wasn't doing well. Branch flew to MN. He was able to convince her to go to the hospital where they got her rehydrated and replenished with the minerals she was lacking. He set her up on a diet that was easy for her to eat and digest, while keeping her nutrition up.

After he came home, he didn't know how long she was going to last. She didn't look good when he was there. The kids told Branch they weren't coming down that summer because they had jobs or summer practices for sports. I knew Branch was bothered by it.

At the end of June, my Berryhead's boyfriend, Mike, called. She needed me. She was having a hard time with her divorce because her ex-husband kept trying to screw her over with money, taxes, and bills. The drama and stress, on top of her fighting PTSD from the Army and continued medical issues with herself and kids was taking its toll.

I had to surprise her. I got to work on a quilt for her birthday, put in my leave time and bought my tickets. I would be there for our "basic training" anniversary, July 19th.

She loved the quilt, and we were able to chat via FaceTime for her birthday. A couple days after her birthday, I flew into Baltimore, where Mike and the 2 younger kids picked me up. Her friend from work, Velma, was going to make sure Berryhead got to the restaurant where we were surprising her.

Mike text Berryhead saying he wanted to eat at this place, because he was craving it and didn't feel like making dinner. He told her to meet him and the kids there after work. She said okay and we headed there, before going to the house.

Her daughter and I hid in the restroom when Velma said they were on their way. We let her sit down and say hi to Mike then her daughter walked out of the restroom to sit across from her, and I came the other way. I recorded her as I sat down in the seat next to her.

We couldn't have planned a better surprise or the way we carried it out. It was perfect. After we laughed, cried, and snorted, we ran to the restroom to avoid wetting ourselves. Velma arranged for her to have the next few days off from work, so we could spend more time together.

On our anniversary, we got matching soul sister tattoos, with our anniversary date, the infinity symbol with an arrow. The 1 and 9 are both semicolons, showing this is not the end of our story. Cancer, PTSD, depression, and nonstop physical battles were obstacles, but not our end.

The colors, teal and purple, represent our survivorship and us. They were placed on our left shoulder, on the front of our collarbone. Our friendship will never end, and our lives will continue, no matter which way life goes. She is my "alma gemela," soul twin.

After I got home, I caught up on all my work, and set up a back-to-school donation drive for one of the bigger rural schools. We wanted to get a new backpack to each kid from K-6th grade, with some miscellaneous school supplies. We wrote letters to corporate Target, got the posse involved, received donations and cash donations to buy backpacks.

The event was scheduled for the second week of September, to collect more backpacks. I set up the helicopter, K9 and SWAT teams to do a demo after the kids got their backpacks, showcasing the different divisions in our office.

In August, on a Wednesday night, we got a call from Branch's aunt. She said Caryn wasn't doing well, they had just started her in home hospice and Caryn was asking for Branch. Branch had Army that weekend, but his unit let him have Sunday off.

We left AZ Saturday night. We packed the dogs in the truck and took off. I sent a message to my supervisor, letting her know what was going on. I told her that everyone had the information for the backpack drive, there were still donations coming in, otherwise, we were set for the drive in September.

We drove straight through to MN, arriving Sunday night. When we got there, Branch went directly into her room. I let the dogs out to use the bathroom so Branch could have some one-on-one time with his mom.

I was in the backyard when someone called for me to come in. Branch was asking for me. I left the dogs in the backyard while preparing myself to see Caryn.

I walked in her room, taking in her almost bald head, yellowing skin, frail body, and glassy-looking eyes. My heart broke for the strong, healthy woman she had always been, and that Branch had always known as a mom.

I grabbed her hand, kissed her on the cheek and sat next to Branch, by her bed. She wasn't fully with us because she was repeating herself and mixing memories together. The nurse came in to give her the nighttime meds, then she fell asleep.

Branch's brother hadn't told us how bad she was and if his aunt hadn't called, I don't know if we would have made it in time. The nurse said Caryn called for Branch several times before we arrived. Now that she knew he was there, she may go quickly. We talked about her meds, when to call and how to keep her comfortable until she passed.

I told Branch to get some sleep and I would sit with her that night. He went to lie down. Branch's brother and wife went home and said they would be back the next day.

I settled in with my iPad playing soft worship music Caryn liked. I did some typing on my computer, sent some work emails tying up loose ends. I read, prayed, did an online puzzle, journaled, and colored, in between talking to Caryn, when she woke up.

She had been getting up to use the restroom, but the nurse said we needed to use the adult diapers because she had fallen and hit her head. I gave her more meds and she ate some applesauce before going back to sleep.

The next morning Branch and the nurse were in the room while I took a nap. I only slept a couple hours before getting up for a shower. Caryn was somewhat awake and tried eating lunch but couldn't swallow. We had to be careful of her choking.

The nurse said it was going to be hard to get meds in her and if she couldn't take them, not to push. Friends and family stopped by that afternoon and evening, but Caryn never responded to them. As the night went on, Branch and I looked at each other knowing she was close to passing. Every hour she seemed to slip further away.

Branch and I spent most of the night in the room with his mom. We took turns napping and by Tuesday morning, she didn't open her eyes at all. We kept her mouth from drying out with the little sponge sticks and the nurse was able to get some medicine in her, but she didn't wake up to eat anything.

We cleaned her up, changed her nightgown, sheets and bedding and I washed her hair with dry shampoo. She still didn't wake but she moaned every now and then. Wednesday, we met with the pastor from her church and asked her to pray over her.

I was spending every night in her room because I couldn't sleep. I read scripture to her, read stories, and thanked her for giving me such a great man as my husband. I cried during the night, to stay strong during the day. I cherished every moment I sat with her.

Thursday was a quiet day. Branch's kids came over and stayed until late that night. We sat in her room sharing stories, memories and laughing together. I knew she was still with us, and I wanted to make sure she heard the joy and laughter of her grandkids and sons.

By Thursday night, none of us were sleeping much. I stayed in the room and the others would come in and out, between getting a couple hours of sleep. Friday morning the nurse came back. We cleaned and changed her again, then the nurse said it wasn't going to be long. There was no urine output and her breathing had changed.

Friday night we all stayed in the room, talking quietly, reading, and praying. I told Branch that him and his brother needed to let Caryn know it was okay to leave, that they'd be okay. They grabbed her hands, leaned over her, kissed her cheek, and told her they were going to be okay; she could rest peacefully.

A couple hours later, Saturday morning, she took her last breath, with all of us sitting around her. Even though we were prepared for it, knowing the final breath was taken, brought all the tears again. She wasn't in pain any longer, but it didn't ease our pain of loss, knowing we'd never talk to her, laugh with her or cry with her again.

I kissed her forehead and gave Branch and his brother time with her. I called hospice to let them know and things started moving quickly. Branch hung up the phone with the pastor when his kids called. He told them she passed.

The kids started yelling at Branch, asking why he didn't call them first. As the call went on, I could see how upset Branch was with the kids. He was trying to take care of the details for his mom. I couldn't believe how selfish the kids were, thinking only about themselves, not considering their dad had just lost his last parent.

The morgue picked up Caryn's body, while Branch finished all the hospice paperwork. The pastor called and told us when the church was available for the service. Caryn wanted to be cremated so we weren't doing an open casket. I helped write the obituary that would run in Monday's paper, and we picked out the pictures we wanted to use for the service.

Monday, we went to the funeral home, picked out the urn for his mom and took care of the payment for cremation. Branch called the insurance company and the other people he needed to notify. We set the service up for Thursday, giving people time to make plans when they saw the obituary in the paper.

Branch and his brother spent the rest of the day going through their mom's paperwork, figuring out who needed a copy of her death certificate. We knew the house was to be split between the boys, with his brother taking care of it when they moved in. If they sold it, the profits were to be split. His brother was responsible for any repairs and upkeep because he didn't have to pay rent or mortgage.

On Tuesday, Branch and I decided to go to the state fair after talking to some of his mom's friends. We needed to take time to ourselves after the prior week. We got there right after the gates opened and set out to explore.

I had to be careful with the heat and humidity, but we both needed a change of scenery. We checked out all the old tractors and went on the tallest ride so we could see over the entire fairgrounds. We explored several of the vendors, sat in a ridiculously comfortable porch swing and bought one to be shipped to our house.

We bought a large wooden plaque sign with our last name and a moose carved into it. The guy told us to come back so he could paint it and it would have time to dry. We found a shaded place to eat. A band started playing so we drank cold beer and put our feet up.

We ate, drank, played, laughed, and left the fair smiling and exhausted. We went shopping Wednesday, then spent some downtime at home. Thursday, we took everything to the church for the service. We had made several photo boards and set the pictures we had enlarged, all around the lobby and 2 at the front of the church, by the urn.

The kids asked to speak then ignored me and their dad while at the service. The front row was saved for family, but Branch chose to sit in the 2nd row, giving the kids the front row since they didn't want to sit with him.

I already knew most of the family and her close friends, which helped with the awkwardness of the kids and their mom. When the oldest gave her speech, she talked about some of her memories. Not one word was mentioned about Branch or the memories with him and his mom. It was a slap in the face but as we were used to doing, we rose above the petty behavior and moved on.

We left Friday so we could stop in Colorado to see Hazel and Liam. We spent Friday and Saturday there, relaxing with Hazel because she'd just had major surgery. We went to the brewery Friday night, had several beers, danced, and sang, then went back to their place for cigars. I ended up getting sick, then went to bed and slept like a log.

We stopped to see KJ before we headed home so we could both go to work that Tuesday, after Labor Day. Our event was set for that Thursday, at the school. We finished all the last-minute preparations, sorted the backpacks, picked up the donated books and realized we had enough packs for K-7th and the 8th graders would get extra school supplies.

The event was amazing. The kids loved the backpacks, books, and the demos. There were several teachers and community members that came out and Cpt. Cooper said he was impressed with the event.

After testing for captain, Branch found out he was getting promoted in October. He was going to C shift at the same station he'd been at. I went to D.C. again for the ACS CAN lobby day summit in September, then started preparing to go to Texas for the regional training.

We found out DJ's unit was deploying to Afghanistan. As a soldier, I understood the underlying excitement of a deployment, especially as a single soldier. As a mom, I was scared to death because my baby boy was going to war.

Sgt. Glen called me one day. We always joked around and were both smart asses, so I answered with a smart ass greeting. When I heard his voice, I knew something was wrong.

He told me he was leaving the doctor's office to go to the emergency room to prep for surgery. He said the pain he'd had in his eye and the headaches was from brain tumors. I felt sick and sat down. He had melanoma years before, which they removed but the doctor said sometimes it comes back and goes to the brain.

I got the information of where he was going, told the Cpt and Lt then grabbed my stuff to head to the hospital. I met his wife and kids, waited for the doctor to come in. They were getting a room ready for him, but they had to do more MRIs and scans before surgery.

The doctor said surgery would be the next morning then we could see him in his room. I left when they started all the tests, after giving my cell number to his wife and family. I told them I would make sure all the paperwork was started for his FMLA.

Sgt. Painter, who we had both worked with, contacted me, and asked what was going on. I told him about the surgery, and I was going to the hospital again. He told me one of his deputies would pick me up, so I wasn't driving. I thanked him and waited for Deputy GQ.

Sgt. Glen was awake when we got to his room. He was talking, laughing, and doing better than I expected. I talked with him and the family for a couple hours before heading home. I knew the next couple days would give us more answers to treatment and prognosis.

I was voluntold to put together a presentation for Red Ribbon Week, working with a retired DEA guy. He was part of the new community outreach team, so I knew him, but I thought it was funny they still needed my help in the community.

We did a day-long presentation with demos on the field from other units and speakers from Border Patrol, DEA, and MCSO. Cpt. Cooper wrote me another commendation for a well-organized and informative event. That weekend I was going to be back in the little town for a Halloween event.

Some of the girls I met at the red ribbon event asked if I was going to be a princess and I told them that I might wear my tiara. Branch came with me for the event. We handed out candy, let the kids sit in the patrol car, talked to parents and other community members, all while I was wearing a tiara with my uniform.

The girls loved it and we took several pictures together. The next weekend we were doing a public safety event at the new fire station with MCSO and Buckeye Valley Fire.

November 1st, I was scheduled to see the kidney specialist. He did more x-rays, a CT scan, bloodwork and another urine collection, prior to the appointment. Branch picked me up from work for my appointment. The specialist told me I had good kidney function but the only way to get to the stones in my kidneys was to cut into my kidney and remove them. He didn't want to do that because it would mess up my kidney function which could lead to dialysis in the future.

I listened, with tears in my eyes, and asked, "What now?" He said there wasn't anything else they could do for me. I had to learn to live with the stones, trying to manage with a low-dose antibiotic, medicine to lower my uric acid and pain management.

I asked him what pain management entailed and reminded him that I couldn't use narcotics while I was a deputy, carrying a gun and driving cars fast. I had to figure out what worked for me, then he told me I had to quit drinking coffee because of the acidity.

I gasped and said, "You mean to tell me that I may possibly have to give up my job AND coffee? What's the point of living?" I tried making light of it, but I could see the sadness in his eyes, and I felt the heaviness in my soul. He set up my appointment for the 30th to see pain management before we left the office.

As we walked outside, I didn't say anything but squeezed Branch's hand as if it were my lifeline. I let the tears fall as we got to the truck. I didn't know which emotion I was feeling the most. I was frustrated because there was nothing they could do; I was angry because I had to give up coffee and I may have to give up a job I had done for almost 17 years.

Branch took me back to work and dropped me off, right after lunch. I walked in the back door, trying to get to my office before anyone saw me. One of the guys that had been an undercover detective for years, Pollock, was at the station. His team was getting ready to pick up a dangerous guy on a warrant.

He called my name and I waved as I kept walking to my office. Just as I started to shut the door, I heard him say, "Hey, are you okay?" I shook my head no and he closed the door. He asked what was going on and I told him. My hands were shaking, and I was trying not to lose it. He told me to investigate medical retirement and gave me a contact person. I thanked him before he left, sent an email to the person then tried to compose myself with busy work.

I was flying to Texas the next day for Relay training for the regional leads. I was the new regional survivor lead.

The rest of the weekend passed in a blur of training and meeting people. We were able to tour the building that housed the 24/7 communication center for ACS. To see the building where people answering the phones and chatlines, all hours of the day and night brought me to tears.

I thanked them for always being there, especially when I needed someone to talk to at 3:30 in the morning during my isolation and going out of my mind. I told them they had also just helped a friend of mine with direction for a patient navigator and other programs available to him and his family.

The following weekend, Branch and I drove to Denver to go to the Salute to Service game between the Broncos and Patriots. We spent Friday night at KJ's then Saturday, explored downtown, did some shopping, and went to the game Sunday night.

This was my first time in the Broncos stadium, watching them. I had seen them in AZ and Buffalo but never at home. We sat in the extreme nosebleed section, but I loved it. It's an outdoor stadium and the energy from the fans can be felt throughout the entire stadium. It didn't matter that we got our butts kicked, we had a great time.

Branch bought me a t-shirt after we left that said "Von Fucking Miller" then we went to wait for a ride with the rest of the crazies. There was so much weed being smoked I told Branch we were going to get a secondhand high. By the time the uber picked us up, I had a raging headache from the smoke.

Branch and I stopped at KJ's again then drove home Tuesday. Branch had to work the next 2 days, then he left for Army training right after.

I went to work Wednesday when Branch left for work, but I wasn't feeling it. I had to reschedule my range day because I had to go to my pain management appointment the 30th. They told me to come in the 29th to get my yearly qualification and training done.

I left work early Wednesday. I couldn't be around anyone. I had gotten an email back reference the medical retirement, breaking down the process and timeline. I didn't know if I had it in me to fight for 9 months. I had a Relay event that Friday night and I decided to put a purple rinse in my hair.

When I went to work Monday, there was a hint of the purple left but I was wearing a hat with my polo, running vehicles to the shop all day. Tuesday, one of the guys came in and made comments about my hair. He joked he was going to do his pink. Later, I was called into the captain's office because someone complained about my hair color.

I found out it was one of the sergeants I didn't get along with. I had taken his spot as admin deputy. I told Cpt. Cooper it would wash out in a couple days, but in the meantime, I was going home instead of dealing with bullshit from cowardly snakes.

I went home, crawled into bed, and slept several hours. I let the dogs out and back in, fed them and crawled back into bed. I called in sick Wednesday. When I woke up Thursday, I called in sick, again. I told them I was taking Friday off also and went back to bed.

I had been so busy that I pushed all my emotions and feelings to the back, going from one thing to the next without really being able to process everything. I was on autopilot for so long, I didn't know how to feel anymore.

I didn't eat, shower, brush my teeth or anything for 5 days. I got up to use the restroom, took care of the dogs then back to bed. I only answered the phone when Branch called and tried to sound upbeat, knowing I was drowning in darkness.

It's hard to describe what I was experiencing. I had no up, no down, I didn't care about anything and didn't want to do anything. For the first time in my life, I couldn't see a light at the end of the tunnel. I couldn't see hope, a new beginning or even a fork in the road to take a different path. I was just there. A blob of a body, swollen to the point that I looked like I was 18 months pregnant, filled with nonstop pain.

I couldn't wear anything that pressed on my back or abdomen, I couldn't wear anything but my ortho flip-flops because my feet were so swollen, and I felt like the Pillsbury Doughboy. While I laid in bed, I didn't care if I got back up again. The more I laid there, the darker my world got. I was swirling in a dark vortex with nothing to hold on to.

Branch came home late Sunday night, falling into bed after a shower. I went to work Monday, but I was in a fog. I didn't smile at anyone, didn't talk to anyone, took care of the cars then went home. I listened to Branch tell me about his weekend when I got home Monday, but I didn't add anything. Tuesday, I was out of the office, doing some community events and Wednesday I worked half a day, knowing most of the admin staff would be out of the office.

We were doing thanksgiving at Branch's station. It was his first official holiday shift as a captain, so we planned for all the family members to come for dinner. The crew was making the turkeys, ham, and some of the sides. I thought I would try to give myself a boost by doing my makeup and wearing a dress with my knee-high boots.

I needed to try for Branch's sake, he was the captain. I made my dishes to bring, showered, did my hair and makeup. I wore my dress with flip-flops until I got to the station because it was hot. I took my dishes in, talked to the crew then brought the rest of my stuff in.

The guys had a call, so I laid down in Branch's room to read until they got back, after checking the food. I was early, but I felt like I hadn't seen Branch in forever. When the guys got back, some of the family started showing up so I went to put my boots on. I was sitting on Branch's bed and couldn't get my foot into the boot.

Branch heard me cursing and heard a bang when I threw my boot against the wall. He came in, to me lying on the bed, curled up, crying. He asked me what happened. I told him I was so fat I couldn't even wear my boots to look cute for him. He told me I wasn't fat and sat down trying to help me.

He grabbed my boot, then put my foot on his knee. I could see when he realized my feet were too swollen to even get in the boot. I started crying again and he held me, telling me it was okay. He was just happy I was able to be there for dinner. I told him I was sorry for being a baby and I didn't want to ruin the holiday.

I cleaned my face, put my flip-flops back on, then went out to talk with the families. We played cards after dinner and enjoyed the evening without the guys leaving for a call.

The next morning, Branch was going to the dealership, for black Friday, before he came home. He joked about a new truck with his captain's raise and I told him to do what made him happy. He came home a few hours later, with a brand-new Chevy Duramax so he could haul things with a diesel now.

We went for a ride to show it off to me. He told me all the things he wanted to upgrade on it, and I just shook my head, but I was happy for him. He had been wanting a diesel for years and he finally had a new one.

That weekend I had to buy a new duty belt and under belt, as well as a new pair of pants that wouldn't sit right on my back or abdomen. I could get my other belt around me, it pressed on everything and brought me to my knees with pain.

I told the guys at the range I was only qualifying with my handgun for my annual qual, before I saw the doctor the next day. The guys knew I was battling kidney issues for years and told not to worry about my rifle, just get my qual out of the way and be done.

I finished my qual and went through the shoot/no shoot scenarios before I left. While I was packing my gear, waiting for my duty ammo, I overheard a deputy talking about healthy coffee. They were a couple tables from me, but I set my stuff down and hurried to where they were talking.

I said, "Excuse me, I don't want to be rude, but I overheard something about healthy coffee." Both guys started laughing and I told them I hadn't been able to drink coffee in almost a month because of the acidity.

The deputy told me the coffee was brewed differently, with Ganoderma added into it, to help the acidity level. I asked how I could get some because my pH was less than 4.

He gave me his card with the website. When I got home, I looked at the website, looked at the affiliate marketing side from a small business standpoint and knew I found the light. This was my hope, my lighthouse calling me safely in.

November 29th, 2017, I made the decision to take a chance on me, for my health. I became a founder with the company, which not only gave me healthy coffee, but several nutritional products to help my overall health.

When I tasted the coffee, I loved the smoothness of the black and the latte. I started my days with a cup of hot coffee, loving the way it soothed my soul.

I had called and left a message with my doctor, asking about the coffee and he said I should try and see if it helped. I drank the coffee for 3 weeks, while I ran from event to event for work. LJ came home right before her birthday, and I told her she should sell coffee on campus.

I saw the new breast cancer surgeon the beginning of December. She wanted to do genetic testing to rule out any genetics for cancer. I was sick of having the "when" hanging over my head so we set up an appointment for surgery consult and I met with the plastic surgeon who would do the reconstruction.

I told him that I wanted to do the reconstruction using the fat from my body, instead of putting any implants in me. I knew the recovery time would be longer, but there was less chance of rejection. We talked about size and Branch told him he wanted a handful, which was about a C-cup.

I didn't care, the smaller the better. After reconstruction, I could get tattoos on my breasts, of rifles, AKA machine guns, then I could point my nipples at people and act like I was shooting them. The doctor looked shocked, but Branch laughed and shook his head.

We set up the genetic testing then the surgery would be in February or March. I came home from work one day and found a bill from CTCA for $26,000. I called CTCA and they called my insurance company. We were on the phone for an hour, trying to figure it out, when a supervisor from my insurance company found a clause from Maricopa County. The clause said CTCA, and other specialty hospitals had been excluded from coverage.

I contacted the benefits section and asked about the exclusion. The supervisor told me that everyone had been sent a letter in July 2017, reference the exclusions. I told her I never received a letter and asked why we were notified after open enrollment.

After 3 hours of back and forth, it came down that the county wasn't going to cover the insurance mishap and I could no longer receive care at CTCA unless I paid for it out of my own pocket. I went outside and fell into Branch's arms, bawling. He knew I had been on the phone about the bill, but he couldn't understand what I was saying.

After I had cried for several minutes and I was thoroughly exhausted, I explained everything. I contacted the VA because I had full coverage through them with my disability. They outsourced me to a new breast cancer surgeon, and I began my new journey with them. My first appointment was in January, for bloodwork and consult.

I had no idea how I was going to pay the $26,000 in medical bills. Branch got a check from his mom's insurance, which we used to pay off his back child support and alimony. We were going to go from his credit being messed up to mine being messed up from the medical bills. I sucked it up and moved on.

LJ had to go back to college and Branch was in the kitchen while I got dressed to take LJ to the airport. I didn't think about it but grabbed my knee-high boots, which I always wore with the outfit. I put them on, zipped them up and walked into the kitchen.

Suddenly, it dawned on me I could fit my feet into my boots again. And they weren't tight in the calf area, either. I grabbed Branch's arms and was tearing up, so he had no idea what was going on. Finally, he understood that I was wearing the boots from Thanksgiving. He pulled me in for a hug and for the first time in 3 years, I didn't flinch from the pain.

I looked into his eyes and saw the emotions flicker across his face before he whispered, "This is the first time in 3 years that I've been able to hug you without you wincing in pain." I nodded my head, with tears and emotions stuck in my throat. When LJ came out and I told her, she hugged us both, knowing how much pain I had been in for so long.

13
Hope Blooms

Work was busy, with several community events, right before Christmas. I was out of the office a lot, meeting with the community, planning more events and reading with kids.

I put all my events, meetings, and whereabouts in my calendar which the Lt. and Cpt. could see. I sent a reminder email and text when I was out of the office, and I logged onto the radio when I was in the community. When I came back from an event with Cpt. Cooper, my Lt. told me I needed to start filling out a Daily Activity Log.

Other people questioned where I was during the day, so she wanted a daily log of how much time I spent in the community, on emails, phone calls and admin stuff. I asked her why it mattered to others where I was when she was my direct supervisor, but she didn't give me an answer.

I was working on painting the hallway wall, which had the photos and plaques of deputies killed in the line of duty. I asked my captain if I could paint a blue line, representing the thin blue line, with the words "All gave some, some gave all" above the pictures.

I bought the paint and supplies then worked on the wall, between other projects. I also started a community bulletin board, filled with letters and cards from kids in the community. Some of the guys liked to stop and read them, reminding them of why they wore the uniform.

2018 began quietly, then Branch and I spent our anniversary in Alpine, again, at our favorite lodge. I was starting to feel like a new person. Branch had been under a lot of stress, with his career, losing his parents, and my medical issues. We were celebrating 12 years of marriage and I wanted to enjoy the health part of in sickness and in health.

I drifted so far away from who I was that I didn't know how to keep our relationship strong. I was being called to do something completely different but didn't know how to explain it to Branch.

The end of January, we went to a SBH training in Tennessee after stopping to pick LJ up from college. I hit some big goals and earned a seat in the front, but I sat with Branch, LJ and my friend from the academy, Stephen, instead. The more I sat and listened, the more confused I became about what to do with my life.

By the end of the training, I was antsy. I wasn't ready to go up to the hotel room, so I stayed in the lobby, talking to Stephen.

After Branch and I got home, I found out there was going to be another training, in KY. Branch told me to go and I found a cheap ticket into Chicago, then I would drive to KY for the training. After the training, the plan was to drive to see LJ, then drive back to Chicago, to fly home.

Tuesday, I had been at an event with my captain, all day. By the time I got back to the district, it was after 10 P.M., and I had been up since 4am. I had to be at the doctors for lab work at 7:30 A.M., Wednesday. I was out of the office Wednesday and Thursday for doctor appointments, for upcoming surgery.

When I came into the office Friday, I had an email from my Lt., telling me she hadn't received my Daily Activity Log for Tuesday. She then went on to say the reason it's called a Daily activity log is because it's due daily. I rolled my eyes when I read it, then saw she had also added a coaching note to my blue team, the system that kept track of complaints, commendations, coaching and disciplinary actions.

I took care of all my work, cleared my desk, turned in my daily activity log, then changed for my flight. I left work at 4 P.M., to catch my flight and landed in Chicago just after midnight.

I began my 6-hour drive, after getting snacks for the trip. I had been up for almost 24 hours but didn't want to overdo the caffeine.

I was able to check into my hotel room early and after a shower, I crawled into bed and slept for 90 minutes before I had to leave for the training. There were about 70 of us at the training, which was a more intimate setting. After lunch, the CEO was talking about working your life away and not owning our time.

The more he talked, the more my vision cleared. I could see the email from my Lt., knowing I couldn't continue working for her. I knew that it was time for me to own MY time and my life. I was like a hamster running on a wheel inside of a cage for years and it was time for me to get off the wheel and out of the cage. When I got home, I would figure out how much sick time I had so I could use it before I resigned.

Branch and I would discuss it more after I got home, but I was resigning from MCSO. I loved my job, working with the community and the kids, but I was tired of the backstabbing, my supervisor, and her cronies, as well as the new administration and sheriff. The physical pain had caught up to me, affecting me emotionally and mentally.

I had a few events planned with my captain, so I figured out my sick leave, then figured out my resignation date. I would work until the 9th of February, then start my sick time. When I went into Cpt. Cooper's office to turn in my resignation, I asked if he was busy, and he told me to come in.

I started to shut the door behind me, and he asked me if it was my Lt. I laughed and told him no, not entirely. I told him I was turning in my resignation and February 9th would be my last day in the office. My official DONE date was set for March 3rd.

He had been typing when I came in. When I told him why I was there, he stopped typing, sat back in his chair, grabbed the chair arms, and looked at me with a shocked expression. He asked me if I was serious, and I nodded yes. He told me this was the last thing he expected from me. I told him I needed to take care of myself, my health, and my family.

He asked me if I was going to another agency. I wasn't, I was going to do my coffee business, on my time, get back into my writing and travel. He said I was one of the hardest-working deputies he'd ever known, and he didn't know how he was going to replace me. He said I did the work of at least 4 deputies and was making a difference.

I appreciated his words and had enjoyed working for him, but I was mentally, emotionally, and physically done with being a cop. I would finish the blue line on the wall and the display, before I left, and I would be with him for the last event on Thursday.

I felt so much lighter, knowing I only had a couple more days before I was done. I went to work on the wall and started boxing up my office. I don't know who found out first, but the deputies started coming to my office, asking if what they heard was true.

I laughed, "Oh, now you want to know the truth from the source instead of listening to gossip?" One of the guys told me I was stupid because I was only 3 years from being able to retire. I didn't know if I would make it the 3 years if I stayed. I told him that 50% of nothing was still nothing and my time was worth more than a retirement check.

When I came in Friday, I finished boxing my last-minute items, cleared all my hard drives, then hung the pictures, badges, and memorials on the wall I finished. A couple sergeants, deputies, the Lt. Cpt. and a couple others had cake for me in the breakroom. One of the sergeants said he would never forget some of the lessons he learned from me in the academy and thanked me for everything I had done.

The sergeant that had surgery for the brain cancer, Sgt. Glen, came in to say goodbye. He was still on medical leave and had started treatment, but he had his son bring him to the district. Some of the guys made me teary eyed with their stories and others I didn't care if I ever saw again.

I left the office on time, for the first time, right at 4 P.M. When I drove home, I felt a weight was lifted from me. I didn't know how things were going to go, but I had choices now. I put my work stuff in the home office, knowing I needed to go through files, equipment, office supplies and misc. items.

I was going to make a purge pile and a keep pile. I took my duty belts and uniforms to the training center for new recruits that couldn't afford everything and gave equipment and supplies to others who could use them as I would never use it again.

I went to Patrick's wedding on Wednesday, February 14th, and saw several people from the office. Cpt. Cooper was there. He said he almost didn't recognize me because I was glowing and dressed up. He asked me how it felt. I told him my coffee tasted better, the air felt lighter, and the sky was bluer. He laughed and said he couldn't wait.

Over the next couple weeks, I went to more doctor appointments while my surgeon was trying to find a plastic surgeon that would perform the reconstruction, using the fat tissue from my body. We set up surgery for the end of June, which gave me time to lose some weight before surgery.

After the trouble I got into for my purple hair, I decided to have fun with other colors. I put purple, blue, lavender, teal, and pink highlights in my hair.

On my last official day of work, I took my duty ammo, taser, radio and ID card to training, making sure everything was checked in. I had to officially be on the clock for an hour before I was done. I was done at 10 A.M. and I wasn't upset about leaving. There were no emotional ties to the job. I had made the right decision.

The next morning Branch got up early to do a hike, then we spent the day together. Sunday, I went through some of my office stuff and Monday morning, I woke up smiling. I felt renewed and got ready for a coffee meeting. Branch was still in bed but said if he'd known how much happier I would be, he would have told me to quit years ago.

That evening I was at a training when I found out some of the SBH leaders were expanding in Vegas. I had nothing holding me in Phoenix and after I talked to Branch about it, I decided I was going to Vegas. We had a training in April, so I would grow my business until training.

The leaders rented a house, there were people from KY, TN, VA, OH and 2 of us from AZ. One of the other ladies from AZ came with me. She was staying for a week before she had to go back to work. I loaded my Hot Tamale with product, clothes and hit the road.

The CEO had a challenge for those of us in Vegas. Anyone that met the challenge would get to have dinner with him at Maestro's. I've had lots of steaks, but this steak was unlike any other. They added truffle butter to it, and it melted in my mouth. I felt like a kid, getting to sit at the adult table for dinner for the first time. It was such a laid-back evening, but there were lots of pearls of wisdom I walked away with. He told me I was ready to step into my destiny. 3 years later, I have done just that.

I got a call from DJ one night. He was leaving Afghanistan soon so he could go to Advanced Leadership Course. After we talked for a while, he asked if his Bible was still in his closet. I thought it was and asked him why, concerned something had happened. He said that sometimes you just need Jesus.

He was off work, so we talked for several hours, which made me feel better. A few days later I found out one of the guys in his company had been killed, making 3 total since he'd been there. I was grateful he was on his way back to the States.

The end of March, I drove home so Branch and I could drive to San Diego to see Nicole perform on the Midway with her high school band. We spent 3 nights in San Diego. We spent a couple hours at the beach with Nicole, saw Rosa, and relaxed.

I drove back to Vegas after we got home and decided to go to a resort once we left the Airbnb. Some people were flying home for Easter, before training, but I had Branch drive to Vegas. I was staying until Friday morning, then I had to pick LJ up from the airport. I got my nose pierced the first part of April and LJ wanted hers done again which we did that night.

The intensity of the training was a new experience. Once we sat down and got into the training, LJ leaned over and wrote on my notebook that she was dropping out of college to pursue the business full time. I said okay and we finished the training.

The next morning, we were asked what we thought about the training and LJ said she was quitting college so her and I could travel and build our business. The CEO hugged her and said she made a great choice.

After I dropped LJ at the airport, I drove home. I was ready for my bed and to snuggle with Branch. I got home about midnight and crawled right into bed. The next morning, I told Branch about LJ's decision and we planned for me to fly into St. Louis where she would pick me up, after her last class of the semester.

Branch said it was a good plan and he was excited for us. KJ was driving from NM to D.C., and it worked out for us to meet outside St. Louis to follow each other. LJ and I were driving to KY, where we were unloading her car of all her college stuff.

We dropped LJ's stuff off then drove to KJ's friend's house. They'd stayed in touch after the Army. We met his wife and after talking for a while, we showered and went to bed.

The next morning LJ and I left for Nashville, while my sister left for D.C. We went back to the house in KY to go through LJ's things and decide what we needed for the trip to NC.

We sorted things we were going to mail home, then repacked the car to drive to NC. While we were driving, I got a call from the VA telling me I no longer qualified for the community care program because the VA just opened a center, 39.5 miles from our house. The distance was 40 miles or more from the VA to qualify for community care.

I told the lady I had surgery set up already and she said I would have to see a primary care at the VA, then be referred out. I told her that I wasn't going to be back in AZ until the end of June so that wasn't going to work either.

Branch said we could use his Tricare insurance, but we would be paying more out of pocket. I called the doctor, explained what was going on and moved the surgery out until after I got home.

LJ and I stayed with my Army friend, Q. It was great to spend time with her. We went by the house I had built. The trees now dwarfed the neighborhood, 18 years later.

We drove by the house and decided to knock to ask if we could look around outside. I explained to the owner that we used to live there, and I had chosen everything before it was built. After we walked around, she told us we could come inside to look around. It was crazy how much LJ remembered of the house because we left when she was 3.

We drove to see Kiki, then had a BBQ at Chip's, our Army friend. He had moved to NC from NYC, and I hadn't seen him since 92. Another guy that had been part of our unit was visiting from Atlanta. We had fun catching up and LJ loved hearing the stories of us in Germany, especially when I got Q drunk at Berchtesgaden.

After leaving NC, we drove to the outskirts of TN before driving back to KY. We mailed LJ's stuff, then drove to pick Branch up in Chicago, before we continued to MN. We watched the Nicole and Eric at their track meet, then took everyone to dinner. Nicole wanted to sell product to make extra money while she was in school. I gave her some bags and told her to keep what she made then if she wanted to reorder more, she could use some of her profit to order online.

The next morning, we left for Colorado. LJ and I were staying with Hazel and Liam, while we expanded in the area. We stayed in a hotel near the airport after we got to Colorado for Branch's flight home.

LJ and I explored the area, spent time with Hazel and Liam, and stayed in a hotel for a few days. While I talked to Liam, I could tell he was struggling with depression and PTSD. Hazel told me he woke up from nightmares and she would find him trembling. I told Liam he needed to get help and to apply for disability with the VA. I gave Hazel the info to get started and let them work on it from there.

LJ and I explored different parts of CO, visiting friends, and building our business. We stayed a couple days with another affiliate at her sister's house, hung out at the pool, did yoga, and some goal setting.

LJ and I then went to Colorado Springs to spend some time with Brad and his wife. They had bought a new house and invited us down.

Branch flew in for training and after we picked him up, I dropped LJ off at Brad's, then Branch and I got a room next to his training site. LJ helped Brad start putting up a gazebo then Branch and I helped once he was done with training.

After dropping Branch at the airport in Denver, LJ and I went back to Hazel's house. There was a parade for one of the soldiers that was killed in Afghanistan, and we found out it was the guy in DJ's company that was killed in March.

LJ flew to St. Louis to see her boyfriend from college. I was picking her up on the way to KY. I took a couple days for myself and stayed at a local inn down the road from my friends. Each room had a different theme, and I chose the downstairs one with a huge jacuzzi bathtub, king-sized bed and a Cleopatra theme. I loved the quiet time to reenergize.

Hazel decided to go to KY with LJ and I for training. We picked LJ up in St. Louis then drove to KY. We stayed outside of Lexington the first night, shopped, swam, and caught up on sleep. We arrived in Lexington the day before training, walked around, got our nails done and window shopped.

The first day of training was intense and extremely rewarding. After training was over, some of us were invited to one of the leaders houses for an after-training wind down. We decided to leave for CO after we left the leader's house.

We got to CO about 11 A.M., unloaded the car and repacked it for our trip home. DJ and Branch were driving from Alaska, and it worked out for us to meet in Moab, UT, then follow each other home.

The next couple days we all relaxed, unpacked, and caught up. That weekend, DJ and Branch were taking their motorcycle class to get their license. We got a hotel room so we could go to the brewery then TopGolf when they were done.

After dinner at the brewery, we took an Uber to TopGolf. We drank more at TopGolf, and everyone was having a blast, laughing, and spending time together. Somehow it came up that Jack wanted to see DJ and to golf with him. DJ asked me if Jack was really his dad. I told him the truth. Jack was not his biological father.

I explained Tom had threatened to kill me while I was pregnant, how I hid from him; and Jack wanted to help raise DJ. I had promised Jack I wouldn't tell DJ any different unless I was asked outright. DJ took it in stride, and I felt a weight lift off my chest from carrying the lie for 20-plus years.

I went through all my stuff from MCSO, separating anything I wanted from the rest. It was time to purge. We had a bonfire as we all watched 17 years of my life turn to ashes. As I watched it burn, I knew I made the right decision. It felt like the last lock had been opened in my soul.

As we sat around the bonfire, DJ and I stayed out later, talking about deployments, war, and things we'd seen/heard. We were able to relate on a new level, as mom/son and soldier/soldier. I began to understand why he asked about his Bible.

DJ's Army buddy flew in to help DJ drive the truck and trailer back to Alaska. The day after they left, Branch was leaving for his Army training, so LJ and I decided to paint. She was painting her bedroom, now that DJ had his stuff out of it, and I was painting my bathroom.

We both wanted peaceful, relaxing colors. I chose a pale green color, ordered a new shower curtain with bamboo, rocks, water and lotus on it, along with bamboo organizers. It felt good to redo the bathroom and soon I found myself crying randomly.

I would be painting, then sitting on the floor or counter with tears running down my face. It took me a few days to finish painting because I couldn't stop crying. The more I cried, I realized that all the trauma was escaping from the locked places of my mind and soul.

I had submitted my information to a new show about first responders and PTSD after we got home from our travels. I got a call to set up a video interview from the casting company. I set it up for the first part of August and didn't think much about it.

The day of the interview, Branch was outside with the dogs and LJ was in the office working. I can't remember the questions, but I remember sharing the story about taking the call when the stepdad killed his wife and 2 daughters.

I was lost in the story, not realizing the details or the pain was coming out. When I finished, I could tell the lady was at a loss for words. She was also crying and then I thanked her for listening because it was the first time, I shared the entire story from my perspective.

I heard the door open, and Branch came in the house, as I was finishing up. He took one look at me, my face, walked straight to me, wrapping me in a fierce hug. He told me he had finished the last items in the airstream, and it was ready for a test run. He said he was taking us to Alpine for my birthday weekend, knowing the pines would help heal my soul.

I sat in the pines, listening to the breeze blow through the trees, the birds calling to each other and soaked up the peacefulness of nature surrounding me.

We explored with the dogs, adventured on back roads, ate ice cream, and enjoyed each other's company as we sat around the campfires. Our CEO announced a training he was holding in October, called MVP, Unlimited. He described the training, gave the cost and where it would be.

I didn't think about the training. LJ looked at me and told me that we needed the training so she was going to call KJ to ask for the money and we would pay her back in a couple weeks.

After LJ talked to KJ, had the money wired to my account, she bought the tickets while I talked to KJ. She told me that she had written a letter to our dad about us being sexually abused when we were younger and asked if I would read it before she sent it. After reading it, I called her back and we talked more about it.

LJ overheard me talking and when I hung up the phone, she hugged me, told me she understood now why I was so protective of who they spent time with when they were younger. She told me that I needed the training to start breaking some of the binds. I thanked Branch for the hard work of restoring the airstream and for knowing just what I needed for my birthday.

LJ and I drove to Kansas the first part of September for a training event. We got to know some of the other affiliates better during the training, and at lunch. A few of the affiliates told me how my story inspired them.

LJ told me the more I shared, the more people I inspired and gave hope to. I knew I had started this book in 2014 but I still wasn't ready to sit and continue it. After the KS training, LJ and I got ready for our MVP training, in CA. We stayed at Rosa's house, because it was only a couple miles from the training event.

During the training, we were given workbooks with the material being covered. Some of that material was scenarios dealing with our past. We were broken into groups to discuss the scenarios before we shared our thoughts.

I was okay until our CEO looked directly at me and asked me what was going on in my head. He could tell by the look on my face, something needed to come out. I told him about how my mom told me I ruined her life because she was so young when she had me.

The words had felt heavy rolling out of my mouth, but as the sobs tore through my body, I started feeling lighter.

That night we were given an assignment, to write down everything we felt was holding us back from going after our goals and dreams. We had to write them down then bring them to training the next morning.

The next morning after showering, I looked in the mirror and was able to fully look myself in the eyes, the windows to my soul. I saw the broken pieces, the scars, and everything that made me, me. I was able to smile at myself, knowing that I was taking steps to heal the brokenness.

Right before class ended, we had to take our list out, crumple it up, then as we threw it in the fire, we said, "It is done." As I watched the flames catch my list, I began to believe I was done carrying the baggage of my childhood.

LJ and I decided to drive to the beach before we went to the party that evening. A group of our friends came with us, and I told them I wanted to cleanse myself. We spent an hour at the beach, playing in the water, taking photos, watching the sunset, and letting go of the baggage.

After the party, LJ and I showered, went to bed, then got up, packed the car after breakfast and I wrote a long letter to Rosa, explaining some of my thoughts/feelings from the training. I had shared so much with her during phone calls, visits, and our hike, that I wanted to share me coming out of the cocoon.

LJ and I drove home that afternoon and Branch surprised us, telling us we were going camping in Flagstaff, the next weekend. I loved the hidden area we had been camping at for years and gathered all my winter clothing for the trip.

After we got back from Flagstaff, Branch and I went to Parker, AZ, along the Colorado river for 3 days, while LJ flew to see friends from college. She had broken up with her boyfriend so they could each grow and knew she needed to close that chapter, in person.

My friend Sgt. Glen passed away after fighting the brain tumor for over a year. Another friend lost at a young age.

The beginning of December, Branch found out Eric needed to have another heart surgery, to replace the valve. I paid for Branch's flight, and he planned to stay at the hospital. A few days before Branch left, Eric sent him a message saying he didn't want me there. Branch told him that I wasn't coming but Eric kept reiterating he didn't want me there.

After a few messages, I got mad at Branch because I felt like he was letting his kids tell him what he could and couldn't do. We got into a fight and after I sat for a while thinking about it, I realized every time Branch dealt with the kids or Devlin, he immediately fell back into being the weak, low-self-esteem guy he was when he was married to her.

I told Branch he needed to figure out who he was, as a man, husband, and father while he was gone because I knew him as a strong, confident, and determined man, not a weak punching bag. I told him that as much as I loved him, I couldn't live with him if he was going to revert to someone I didn't know or like. I was calm, with tears running down my face when I said if he didn't stand up for himself when he was in MN, not to bother coming back home.

I dropped him off at the airport, told him I loved him, would always love him, but he had to decide who he was going to be. I told him that I got a hotel room for him, not far from the hospital so he could get some sleep before the surgery. I had crocheted him a scarf, knowing how cold it was going to be and to wrap in love, strength, and prayers.

We talked several times while he was gone. He told Eric that he didn't get to tell Branch what to do when it came to me. Branch told him that he loved me, I was his wife, and nothing was going to change that. Eric apologized and Branch felt good standing up for himself.

Branch, LJ, and I spent the new year in Alpine, playing in the snow with the dogs. We stayed at the lodge enjoying family time together.

We welcomed 2019 in with new adventures, fun and laughs. 2019 was going to be busy. I was part of the Power in Purple event in Las Vegas. The event was all women and leaders of the community, with the goal of raising money for the American Cancer Society, while educating the community about cancer awareness, treatments, programs, and research.

I was asked to participate after raising money for the Las Vegas Relay event the prior April. There was a kick-off in Vegas the first part of January that I was asked to be the survivor speaker at.

Branch said we should look at a new vehicle, trading in mine and LJ's for one car, instead of 2 car payments because LJ and I went everywhere together. We were planning to drive to Orlando, FL, for our company launch event, the end of January and it made sense to have something new and a little bigger.

We found a 2019 Chevy Equinox, and within the first couple weeks, LJ and I had put over 3000 miles on it. We drove to Vegas for the PIP event, left for Orlando the next day, stopping in Dallas for a few days.

Branch flew into Orlando Friday, then flew out Monday. It was a great weekend, with family and friends. After LJ and I left we decided to drive to the Alamo as we went through San Antonio. It was 3 A.M. when we arrived so we were able to drive around, take photos and admire the Alamo, with no one else around.

One of my friends, Mary, I knew from MCSO, said she wanted to quit the post office and do the business full time. I told her I was going to an event by my house and asked if she wanted to come out.

We talked further about what she wanted to do, how the products were helping her and her family and what she needed to make to leave the post office. While we were talking, she said her husband's family in Mexico, liked the products and wanted to know more. I told her I would go with her, and she could interpret.

About 4 hours later, we were in Mexico, meeting her husband and his family. He looked at us like we were crazy but introduced us to his racehorses and acted like us showing up was normal. We left by 9 P.M., to make sure we got back across the border before they closed it at midnight.

On the way home we talked about the training in Dallas, in March, then Vegas, in April. She said she could get the time off in April but would have to see about March. One of her daughters started going to events and joining us, also. We decided to go to Mexico again, to talk to more of their family.

After we finished with business, we drove to Rocky Point. We ate and enjoyed margaritas with the sunset over the water. She taught us how to haggle in Spanish at the little markets and vendor booths.

The following week she was flown to a local hospital with stroke symptoms. She'd had something similar a few years prior. After Branch and I arrived at the hospital, I gave her a bag of products she didn't have, had written down when to take, how much and when. We stayed and met the rest of her family before we left. I knew her oldest daughter, Kristi, from MCSO, because they had both participated in the Relay events.

The next week, Mary thanked me for the products, said she felt much better and asked if the offer to go to Dallas for training was still open. We made plans for the drive and how long we would be gone.

Stephen, my friend from the academy, was going with us, too. We met at 6 A.M., loaded everyone up and headed to Dallas. After the weekend of training, we decided to drive back to AZ Sunday night. We had a concert in the car, singing to Prince, old-school rock, R&B, and country until our voices were hoarse.

Mary sent me a message. She'd resigned from the post office and was ready to grow her business. We drove to Mexico again, to California, up north and around the valley, getting her going. In April, we drove to Vegas for training, where Hazel met us.

We got 2 suites that connected, with 4 beds and 2 pull-out sofas. LJ's friend from college and another girl came with us. We had 8 people in the 2 rooms. We had a blast. We swam, drank, ate, and explored the day before training started.

I got a gym membership, with plans to work out before trainings, presentations, and meetings. I started noticing less motivation, more procrastination and lack of focus. I was barely sleeping and when I did sleep, I was having awful nightmares.

I faked my way through the socializing. I started pulling away from others, didn't leave the house unless we had a team meeting or training and became more reserved. I didn't notice the pattern until months later.

The end of May, our CEO announced a training he was doing in September. LJ bought a ticket and I started making more quilts to help purchase my ticket. We had plans to fly to Alaska the end of June to see DJ so I started sewing what I could beforehand.

I noticed I had no excitement or joy about anything. I was faking smiles I didn't feel, I stopped working out, had no interest in trainings or leadership and although I was sewing quilts to help pay for training, I felt nothing. I was barely taking care of myself.

When we got to Alaska, we hiked, camped, explored, worked out at the gym with DJ and I played with his puppy, Sniper. Branch left to go home for work, and I decided to stay longer. LJ left after a couple weeks, and I decided to stay until the end of July. I was worried about DJ, realizing we were both struggling with PTSD.

DJ and I talked daily about him being in Afghanistan, being shot at, losing soldiers he knew, always on guard, not sleeping and what he endured during special forces selection the previous October.

I didn't want to leave, but I felt better after we'd talked and knowing he had Sniper. I flew to NV, where Branch picked me up and we drove to Lake Tahoe for his Union event.

We drove to Area 51 on the way home, because so many people were talking on social media about storming Area 51.

Our coffee team was hosting a huge training event the weekend I got home. We had a naturopath flying in from CO and one of the corporate leaders. I was busy getting things ready, making sure we stayed on schedule and that food was delivered for lunch and the after-training get-together.

There were several people that stayed for a more in-depth product training before we had to go to the airport. After the weekend was over, I withdrew more into myself.

Branch took LJ and I to a local resort for my birthday before Branch left to fly to SC for the Drill Sergeant academy. We swam, played mini-golf, floated the lazy river, and had a great dinner before we left in the morning.

LJ and I dropped Branch off at the airport at 5 A.M., then headed home. I didn't want to do anything for my birthday, except stay home and relax. The week before the ICON event, I made the decision to go.

LJ and I became certified CPR instructors before we headed to CA for training and told Mary we would help her teach classes when we got back. LJ and I arrived in CA, checked in and I told her I wanted to stay in the room. She agreed and we got pizza, then hung out in the room until the next morning for training.

The energy at the ICON training was high, seeing people we hadn't seen since April, catching up with hugs and settling in for training. The training was intense, but I had a hard time staying focused or sitting still. I felt antsy and couldn't settle in, which was unusual for me. The more the training went on, the more I knew something was wrong with me, deep down.

My cousin had moved to San Diego after Hawaii. He asked us to stay with him after the training, before we went back to AZ.

The last day of training, I felt completely disconnected from my body. I didn't socialize and I didn't feel anything emotionally. LJ could tell I wasn't myself.

We drove to my cousins, hung out at the beach, played with his dog, went for a long walk, and the next morning before we left, LJ and I went to the beach again. I sat in the sand, feeling tears running down my face, but couldn't explain why.

After talking to Branch, I told him I would drive his truck to SC, spend the weekend with him, then fly home and he would have a vehicle. He didn't finish until the end of October, and I wanted to see him. It was the middle of September; he'd been gone a month.

Once in SC, I took a nap at the hotel, showered, then went to meet Branch on post. We had dinner and hung out in the room until I had to take him back.

He had the weekend off, so we were going to drive to Myrtle Beach. The next morning, I had everything ready when I checked out, picked him up and we headed to the beach. We enjoyed the drive on the back country roads, getting to our hotel about 7 P.M.

After dinner, we walked on the beach before going to the room. Branch had to study for his modules so after breakfast, laundry, and a walk on the beach, he studied for a couple hours, then we went to play in the ocean. After lunch, he studied some more, while I sat on the balcony watching the ocean.

It was time for me to start working on this book. Something was telling me to stop putting it off. I told Branch and he agreed it was time.

I was flying out Tuesday morning so I arranged to meet Q. Q drove me to her place in Charlotte so she could take me to the airport the next morning.

We spent time catching up on the drive. It was late when we went to bed because we surprised Chip and his wife. They had just bought a new house 10 minutes from Q.

When I got home, I was feeling edgy, but I kept sewing quilts to keep my hands busy. It was harder and harder to get out of bed. LJ and I were helping teach CPR, but it took everything I had, to get up and do it. The extra money was nice but even while teaching the students, I wasn't in my zone.

LJ and I flew to SC for Branch's graduation. Afterwards, we drove to my aunt and uncles, to spend a few nights before we drove to AZ. My dad and stepmom met us at the graduation, and we were going to all drive to AZ together, the next week.

We had a party for Branch, played games and had plans to drive to the beach the next morning. My parents decided to go with us, and I booked a suite with 3 beds. We watched the sunset and the next morning got up to watch the sunrise.

I was becoming extremely moody, snapping at Branch, going to our room instead of playing games and pulling more into myself.

Branch and I hadn't been intimate since my arrival for his graduation and I was angry and irritated at everything. The drive home was awful. I was so ugly, short tempered and moody, but I couldn't control it.

We got home Tuesday, and I contacted the VA because I ran out of my thyroid medication. They were able to get me in on Thursday. I went in for labs, then waited for the initial intake. The VA does a PTSD screening during vitals, and all my answers were "Meh" on how I felt, energy, etc. My PCP told me that my thyroid levels were very high. I should be suppressed at almost zero because of my cancer but I was at 240.

After talking to the doctor, getting my prescription started again, we talked about my screening. He told me he would like me to see the mental health clinic before I left. He said some of my feelings were possibly due to my thyroid levels and/or PTSD.

I stopped at mental health before going home and after talking to the therapist, she told me I had Major Depressive Disorder, MDD. We talked about meds and therapy, and I told her I didn't want to start meds until my thyroid levels were evened out. She set me up with a therapist for the following week and gave me emergency numbers if I needed to see someone before then.

My prescription wouldn't be ready until the next morning, so we planned a family outing the next day, getting my meds, having breakfast, going to the shooting range, and shopping.

My eyes had been bothering me for a couple weeks. It was hard to read because everything seemed blurry. I stopped at the eye clinic after getting my prescription to see if I could get in. They didn't have anything open, but the lady said she would have a triage nurse call me.

We had breakfast and drove to the range. I told Branch I wasn't shooting because I couldn't get anything into focus. While I waited in the lounge, my phone rang. It was the nurse and she started asking me a bunch of questions about my eyes, vision, etc.

After talking to her, she referred me to urgent care or the ER within 24 hours. I just said okay and hung up. When Branch and LJ finished shooting, I told him what the nurse said. He gave me a look, like "Are you kidding me, it's that serious" and said we would stop at urgent care on the way home.

Branch seemed irritated and I told him to drop me off, go home and LJ could come back. He didn't. I had no idea what was going on in his head. I felt he was so frustrated with me for being sick all the time, but he went into the room with me. The urgent care doctor asked me several questions while examining me, then told me I needed to go to the ER.

There was a possibility of Thyroid Eye Disease which affects the optic nerve and could cause my eye to come out of the socket, as well as vision loss. We went to the ER, across the street and they did a CT scan. After looking at the scans, the doctor ordered CT scans with contrast.

They took more blood and vitals. My blood pressure was high, and my thyroid levels were still in the 200s after taking my pill. After the second CT scan, the doctor said she wanted an MRI of my brain to make sure there was nothing else going on with my history of cancer.

I had to go to another hospital for the MRI because they didn't have the equipment and she referred me for an overnight stay. I could tell Branch wasn't happy. He had Army the next day.

Branch said he wasn't leaving me and gave the nurse the names of the hospitals we were comfortable with. It was 8ish when they said there weren't any open beds but would let us know when there was. Branch took LJ home and brought a change of clothes for me.

At 11:30 P.M., a bed opened, and Branch told the staff he would drive me instead of having the rescue do an inter-facility transport. The doctor agreed to it and gave us the packet to give to the hospital.

We got checked in, they drew more blood, checked vitals, and made sure my IV needle was still in place. Branch and I tried sleeping but couldn't get comfortable. At 4 A.M., Branch sent his sergeant a message that he wasn't going to make it in for drill. The sergeant told him to take care of me and they would see him Sunday.

In the morning, Branch talked to LJ and my parents. About 10 A.M. they took me in for the MRI. About 11, just as the doctor showed up, my parents, LJ, Mary, and her husband showed up.

My thyroid levels were still high but were now down to 173, my bloodwork looked good, and my MRI was clear. I was discharged and went home to sleep.

I saw the eye doctor, he gave me glasses, checked my peripheral vision for thyroid eye disease, saw a little degeneration and set an appointment for a follow-up.

I started mental health therapy and it was hard to find the words to describe what I was feeling/not feeling.

Branch wanted to look at a couple RVs with black Friday specials. We looked at 2 and I fell in love with the second one. We talked about payments, financing, etc., then told the guy we would think about it and let him know the next morning. It was about 3 P.M. and both of us said we should do it. We picked it up the middle of December.

Before New Year's Eve, LJ flew to Alaska to help DJ because he was having knee surgery. Before he went to the special forces Q course, they found his knee, lower back, shoulder, and some other things were messed up.

Branch and I spent a couple days in Flagstaff, getting used to the new camper. We hiked, played in the snow, and enjoyed some down time.

We went to the dog park, walked to the liquor store, and ate. We watched movies, read, and played games before we left the snow and Branch started as a Recruit Training Officer at the fire academy.

I told him that it was going to be hard getting used to a new schedule, with him home every night. Since we had been married, one or both of us worked overnights, with him working for 2 days/nights a week for his shift.

I talked to my therapist about the new schedule because I was having trouble sleeping. We started doing cognitive behavioral therapy and I was practicing what I'd learned.

Branch left the end of February for his 2 weeks annual training for the Army, coming back in March. The day before he was supposed to come home, I had a therapy appointment. I told her I should be excited to see him, but I just didn't feel anything. I told her it wasn't just him, I had that feeling about everything. She told me that I had anhedonia, a disconnect from the depression.

It was the first time in therapy I broke down. I was naturally a positive person, but I felt meh all the time. We talked more about medication, and I told her I would think about it.

On my drive home, Branch called me. He had finished everything and was waiting to leave for the airport to fly back the next morning. I told him about my therapy appointment, was honest about how I felt so he knew what he was dealing with and that I was thinking about trying the medication. My thyroid levels were more stable.

After he got home, we talked about the medication. He asked me why I took thyroid medication daily and I said because I need it. He then asked, "Then what is different about trying medication to help with depression?" I had never thought about it that way.

The next appointment was via video because everything was closing due to the COVID-19, coronavirus pandemic. I told her that I would be willing to try meds now that my thyroid seemed to be stable. She set me up with the psychiatrist. We talked about which ones did what and how they may affect me.

Branch and I went to the pub we had first met at for St. Patrick's Day. While we were hanging out, the bartender told everyone that the city issued a mandate to close all bars and restaurants at 5 P.M.

The governor ordered a shutdown mandate that week, for all bars, restaurants, and other nonessential places. There was also a statewide mask mandate issued for all public places. All schools were closed, and students went to online learning and all nonessential jobs were closed.

Many people found themselves with no job, no money, and kids at home all day, to feed and entertain with no socializing. We were lucky because we lived in the country, with acreage, could still go outside and do things we enjoyed.

I started sewing masks because I had so much extra fabric and donated them to first responders, nurses, and essential workers. Soon I had so many orders for masks, I was sewing all day. I asked Branch what it would take for us to expand my sewing shed.

He prepared a list of everything we would need. He said I could keep sewing, while him and LJ started working on the outside. As they worked, I sewed. I helped when needed and soon we had the exterior up. The roof was one of the hardest because the shed was so far off the ground.

We decided to redo our house floors with tile and used the wood floor in my shed. We had gotten most items from my dad's treasure island which helped the project move quick.

Soon I was able to paint and get the inside set up. I had gone from an 8X12 space to an 12x20 space. I made wood crates out of pallets for yarn storage, and I went to work sewing.

I decided to name my sewing business, Purple Angel Productions. I continued to organize, rearrange, and decorate until I had it exactly how I wanted.

During this time, I was doing an online prayer study group, moved from CBT, cognitive behavioral therapy, to nightmare therapy and was getting used to my new medication. Branch had finished the academy and was back to his normal schedule until a new academy started in July.

The beginning of June, we had to put RockSea down. She woke up one morning and couldn't stand up or stay standing. We knew it was coming because she was 15 but it didn't make it easier to make the call. LJ, Branch, and I sat with RockSea in the vet's office while they put her to sleep. She knew she was well loved as she crossed the rainbow bridge.

DJ was getting out of the Army due to his medical issues, so LJ and I flew to Alaska to help him drive home. His last day was June 22nd, a Monday and we left as soon as he was done.

We got to the Canadian border about midnight, and they weren't going to let LJ and I through because we weren't on military orders. After telling him we were driving straight through, had been quarantined and had no symptoms, he finally let us through. He told us we had 24 hours to be out of the Yukon territory.

After we crossed the border, we drove for another few miles before we found a rest stop area with a restroom. I couldn't sleep because it was warm, and we couldn't put the windows down due to mosquitos. At 3 or 4 A.M., I told DJ I was going to use the bathroom and start driving.

I drove until we needed fuel, while DJ and LJ slept as much as they could. I loved the scenery as we drove and there was almost no traffic. After fuel, we hit the road again. After a few more hours we were out of the Yukon territory and I told DJ I would get us a hotel room for the night, so we could shower, sleep, and let Sniper stretch his legs.

We were back on the road the next morning. That night we were close to the US border, so we stopped to sleep in a truck stop parking lot for a few hours. We hit the border the next morning, coming into Montana. We talked about driving until the border of Utah/Nevada before we stopped, then I told DJ if he got us to Henderson, Nevada, I would drive the rest of the way home.

We stopped to use the restroom, get some food, let Sniper run for a bit then headed home. We crossed the AZ border at the Hoover Dam about midnight.

We listened to a podcast LJ had talked about and it kept us all entertained and awake. LJ fell asleep the last 30 minutes before we got home but DJ and I were hooked.

I had a video appointment scheduled with my new therapist and she officially diagnosed me with complex PTSD. She said I didn't have one trauma, I had several traumas, beginning in childhood, building on top of each other. She said we would start slow.

The therapy was intense and as the layers started getting peeled, the longer the recovery. There were times I felt like I was drowning but Sniper sensed it and would sit with me.

Branch started the 2nd fire academy as an RTO, and they had training in Lake Pleasant. We decided to take the camper again and stay there. I ended up staying for 1 ½ weeks and DJ came up the day he finished his EMT certification. We stayed a few more days then went home and repacked so I could go to Flagstaff.

LJ and I stayed in Flagstaff for a week, then the guys came up for my birthday weekend and I continued therapy. I had started typing this book again, the end of October 2019, but found myself having to stop due to therapy and working through trauma.

I had a breakthrough in Flagstaff, during therapy and took Sniper for a hike after. As we climbed the hill, I felt the sobs tearing through my body. I found a log and sat down, letting the tears, pain, and memories come. Sniper knew I was hurting and laid his head in my lap. I sat there for at least 45 minutes before I could walk again.

We walked for 6 miles with random tears running down my face that I didn't stop. I told LJ I felt like I released so much that day, but the door to a tsunami was opened.

We headed home the end of August and I continued hiking in the early mornings with DJ, LJ, and Sniper. One day we were coming down our normal trail, when the ground under my right foot gave way and I rolled my ankle. It was bad, but we had a mile left.

I kept going, limp hopping then the tears of frustration and pain came. I was frustrated because every time I got my stamina and endurance back up, something physical seemed to stop me or slow me down. I also knew that it was more than just a sprain because of the pain.

I had LJ drive me to urgent care. It was a break. They said when I rolled it the tendon pulled so hard that it snapped the ankle bone.

Sniper sat with me every morning when I got up, after Branch left. He sat on my ottoman with his head on my good leg, while I typed.

We celebrated his 2-year birthday that weekend with new toys. On Monday afternoon, I was in the house, Branch and DJ were outside with Sniper.

Soon I heard yelling and screaming, opened the door to DJ carrying Sniper in the house.

DJ tried giving him CPR, but Sniper was gone. We called the vet and they told us to bring him in. The vet thinks he had a heart attack because he had been playing, then started seizing. We all went home in shock and disbelief.

A year later, my heart still hurts, and tears still fall for Sniper. He helped me when I needed it the most and he was there for DJ when he needed it. I can't imagine a world without the love of dogs.

Branch had a few days off and we drove to the Big Lake area, near Alpine, AZ to camp. LJ and I were still a mess about Sniper and DJ was working. I started working on my book again, while Branch and LJ explored.

I finished my therapy the end of September and was referred to the PTSD clinic at the VA. We set up the intake, but it wasn't until the beginning of November, so my therapist checked in with me every other week.

LJ and I drove to Gatlinburg the first part of October to celebrate my cousin's 10th anniversary. Thursday, we met everyone at the cabins and Friday there was a huge breakfast at our cabin.

My cousin had rented 3 cabins to fit everyone. LJ and I took the rooms next to each other on the top floor, while KJ was in the basement. I told her that our floor was the escape floor because we had a balcony we could go out to.

Friday morning, I needed to elevate my ankle so LJ and KJ sat on the balcony with me, drinking coffee and reading while I typed.

Later, LJ, KJ and I went for a walk. We walked to the other cabin where we were all meeting for dinner. After a couple hours, I couldn't be around people any longer and we got a ride to our cabin.

LJ and I helped make sure the cabin was clean before we left Monday and drove through the rain. There was a hurricane drenching parts of Tennessee and we wanted to be out before any flooding happened.

In November, I started physical therapy for my neck and shoulder, LJ started working and DJ was working at the fire station.

I went back to sewing, typing and started my PTSD therapy. In December we went to Flagstaff again so the kids and Branch could snowboard.

Everybody but me worked New Year's Eve and after LJ came home, we were in bed early. Branch had felt sick at work and did a covid test. LJ and I drove to Sedona. The test came back negative, but he had all the symptoms. One of the guys he worked with came back positive so Branch retested Sunday.

On Monday the results were positive, so LJ, DJ and I drove to a testing site. All of us tested positive for COVID. We weren't even a week into the new year of 2021 and all of us were sick. Thankfully none of us had major issues. Our symptoms ranged from muscle pain and soreness, a cough and runny nose, and losing our taste and smell, but none of us ran a fever longer than 12 hours.

My parents brought us groceries and lots of orange juice. They left everything in the driveway, and we stayed by the porch. Everyone had to be off work for 2 weeks, so we watched movies, played games, cleaned, and decided another trip to Flagstaff was needed for snowboarding.

I told Branch in December that I felt like I needed a place for inpatient treatment. I found myself distracted all the time and felt like a hamster on a wheel, again, just spinning, going nowhere. I investigated treatment facilities specializing in PTSD for military and first responders. Branch checked to see which ones his insurance covered.

Branch and I met Kurt and Goldie for our 15-year anniversary. After catching up on kids, jobs, and family, we talked about therapy, the trauma we pushed to the back of our minds to finish the job and the effects it had on us now.

I made plans to go to the Colorado River, by myself. Branch was going to be gone for 2 weeks for Army, so we went to the river the first part of March. I had to see an eye specialist because I was still having vision problems. I had to see orthopedics for a shot in my shoulder to see if it helped with pain, from tendonitis, bursitis, arthritis, and impingement.

I took care of all my other VA appointments, finished a sleep study, and was placed on 2 more medications, one to help me sleep, to relieve anxiety and one to help boost my mood. I officially started menopause which didn't help.

Branch spent a night with me at the river before he had to go back to work. We had just bought a baby pygmy goat, along with a couple chickens so it was busy at home. I didn't take any of the dogs with me and it was the first time that I was completely by myself, without anyone else to worry about, in years.

I continued my therapy, started writing again, went kayaking, rode my bike and slept. Some nights I would go to bed at 9 P.M. and sleep until 8am. Of course, I had to go pee 2 or 3 times during the night, but I slept.

Branch stayed with me the 16th of March and we picked LJ up to spend the night in a hotel near the airport on the 17th. Branch had to leave early the 18th for Army so we had early dinner for St. Patrick's Day. After I dropped Branch off the 18th, I took LJ home then drove back to the river for 2 weeks by myself.

I continued writing, kayaking, biking and my therapy. The sleep apnea specialist called to let me know I had mild sleep apnea and I would need to use the CPAP machine. I wasn't excited about it but if it helped me, then it was worth it.

Branch came home the last day of March then he and LJ came to visit at the river. I ended up staying until April 10th and came home feeling better. I got my CPAP and started using it, got my new contacts to help with my "ghosting" vision, had my mammogram, and Branch said he booked us almost 2 weeks at Big Lake, in May.

Before we left, my dad was leaving for NY for the maiden voyage of his Kenworth RV. He couldn't fit the jeep onto the trailer with his other truck so I told him I could drive the Jeep, with their dog, because he was healing from surgery.

We left a couple days before Mother's Day and I coordinated with KJ, to do a Mother's Day train ride, with our mom, her sister, and our stepdad. We surprised everyone when we showed up because they thought I had just bought tickets for them to go. We rode the train to a small town, sampling wines along the way.

We were given little snack boxes with cheese, grapes, crackers, and chocolate. It was the first time there were no arguments, snide comments, or awkwardness. KJ said I did a great job of controlling the conversation and keeping everything smooth.

KJ and I left Monday morning to drive to her house. On the way, we stopped to surprise Berryhead. I had text her husband to see where she would be, and he said they were having dinner at her parents and invited us there.

KJ and I arrived before Berryhead, and her parents were happy to see me. We were sitting in the living room, having a drink when Berryhead showed up. She came in all flustered, looked around then came back to me. The smile and look on her face were well worth the little detour. Berryhead and I talked about us both doing therapy, fighting through the PTSD, trying to find joy again.

We had dinner with the family, enjoyed some dessert then hit the road again. We had a couple more hours of driving and I had to catch a flight the next day.

I spent the next couple days doing laundry and making sure I was ready for camping. Branch and I left Sunday morning because they finished everything a day early. We got to the campground and asked for a full hook up site. They had one left and we took it.

While talking to the campground host, I said I would love to be able to spend the entire summer in the mountains. She asked me if I had ever thought of being a host and I asked what it entailed. She gave me an application and said the managers would love to have me.

Branch and I set up our campsite, sat around the fire that night and spent Monday relaxing, playing with the dogs and bike riding. Tuesday morning, I was enjoying my coffee and still in my fleece pullover robe when I heard someone pull up. I heard someone talking to Branch then he said, "Yeah, my wife."

He called me outside and the woman Branch was talking to said she heard I was interested in being a camp host. They had an opening at a campground, about 10 miles away. She said it was primitive and told us to take a look, then she would find us later.

Branch and I drove to the campground, initially thinking there was nothing special. Once we crossed the cattle guard a mile in, we came around a curve and there was nothing but trees. Aspens, birch, and pine trees, all over. I loved it and Branch did too.

Branch and I returned to our camper. About 10:30 A.M., the managers came back and asked what we thought. I handed her my application. She said that was great and asked when we could start. I laughed and said we could be packed up and out of here in less than an hour. She blinked with surprise and said okay.

She said she could meet us there about 11:30 to do some quick training before she had to leave for a meeting. Branch and I were packed and at the new campground within 45 minutes.

By noon, Branch and I were officially on the job. I couldn't believe I was going to get paid to camp. Yeah, there would be some work involved, but nothing traumatizing or stressful.

I did my rounds in the morning, checking and cleaning bathrooms, restocking toilet paper, and checking anyone in that came in overnight. I got the next few hours to myself then reservations would start coming in. Branch spent the week with me, and we made a list of things we would need for being here all summer.

My mom and stepdad stopped on Sunday night, as they were driving to Phoenix, from NY, for my niece's graduation. They left Tuesday morning, following Branch. Branch got what we needed, grabbed the things I ordered from Amazon then drove up the next morning.

Branch stayed until Friday morning then had to go home to work. I thoroughly enjoyed being a host. As the weeks went on, I found my rhythm. My therapist and I were still meeting every Wednesday.

As we moved into June, there were wildfires popping up all over AZ. The forest service moved us to Stage 2 fire restrictions, which meant no fires of any kind.

Branch had gone home when I got the news the forest service was closing our forest, effective that Thursday. I let the campers know they had to be out no later than 4 P.M. on Wednesday, so I could clean lock everything, and get my camper out.

They allowed all the hosts to stay at one campground, with restrictions on travel. We were at the campground with full hook ups and none of us had to drive far. Branch came up Wednesday afternoon with a friend from work, got the trailer hooked up and moved.

I was done by 2:30 P.M. on Wednesday, locked my gate and went to my new home. We had no idea how long the closure would be, but we stayed ready to evacuate within 30 minutes.

Branch had the trailer set up and ready by the time I arrived. We drove into town for some supplies then went back for dinner. Branch had to leave the next morning, but he left me the truck and they drove the equinox home.

We had a mandatory meeting on Friday, to see what was going on. We were in an area with zero cell reception and limited information. The corporate manager explained the closure, why we closed, and the length of the closure was unknown. If we got a lot of rain, and some of the fire resources opened, we would reopen.

He told us every forest in AZ had closed due to the fires. It was less than 2 weeks before the 4th of July. I started writing diligently, knowing I was close to the end of this book, while also trying to do some bike riding.

That Sunday it started raining but not enough to reopen. I made friends with other hosts but most of us stayed inside. It started raining the end of June and rained every day.

I tried a marijuana edible to help with sleep. Soon I felt sleepy, climbed into bed, and slept all night long, without having to get up to pee. I was shocked. I never liked the smell of marijuana, but the edible was a little gummy without the THC taste.

I told my husband they worked and asked if he would get me more when he came back up. I continued typing up until this last chapter before we were told we were opening back up and could go to our campgrounds on Tuesday, July 6th.

Branch was scheduled to arrive that afternoon, but I got everything hooked up and hauled the trailer to my campground. I backed it in, got it all leveled and hooked up, then started opening the campground.

As the month of July continued, it continued to rain, every, single, day. Granted we needed it, but I couldn't hike, bike and my restrooms were a muddy mess. Some of the campsites were flooded with standing water. We got hail, wind, thunder, lightning, and rain. There were several lightning strikes in the campgrounds, hitting trees, causing them to explode.

Our managers were out dropping off our daily reports when lightning struck a tree next to their trailer. When they got home, they found a tree impaled their RV, in the master bedroom. The insurance company salvaged the trailer and they had to find another.

Every time I saw lightning, I watched the trees. There were times I would be sitting on the couch and could feel the thunder rumbling the ground. We lost power multiple times. It became the norm. My muck boots, raincoat, and umbrella became my standard apparel. I was caught in hailstorms while doing rounds and made sure to get back before thunder started.

The end of July, my friend Mary, who followed me into the coffee business and taught CPR, got COVID. A few days later, she started having symptoms. Soon she was admitted into the hospital because she was having trouble breathing. I spoke to her a couple times and sent messages. She was fighting and seemed to be going in the right direction.

By the first weekend of August, they moved her to the ICU, then intubated her and by August 10th, she passed away. I cried for hours; full-body sobs tore through me. It felt like someone crushed my heart. I couldn't believe my strong and beautiful friend was gone, that I would never hear her voice again, would never hug her or let our hearts talk to each other.

Some of the other hosts, Grace and Dylan, invited me to their place Saturday so I wasn't by myself. They knew how hard I was taking her death and Branch wouldn't be up until Tuesday. Mary's oldest daughter asked me to speak at the service, held August 19th. I cried again, but wanted to share how truly special Mary was, not just as a wife, mom, sister, aunt, but as a dear and special friend that was like a sister.

I was able to get through my speech, sharing how amazing she was. After the service, the family hugged me and thanked me for sharing my heart about her.

After we left, I was drained. I had driven down that morning, so Branch was driving us back. I tried holding a conversation, but I had nothing. We stopped in a small town for burgers on the way back, had a beer to toast Mary, then finished driving to the campground.

It was the pine trees, the mountains and nature my soul needed. Branch stayed 2 weeks. We celebrated my 49th birthday, the first DJ was able to spend with me in 10 years. LJ came up the next weekend with DJ and his girlfriend and it felt wonderful to be surrounded by family.

LJ was having a tough time with Mary's death, too. She had been like a second mom to LJ. We talked on the phone daily, sometimes multiple times a day, even when we were getting ready to see each other. We traveled together, ran our businesses together, taught CPR, did Relay and vendor events together. Mary was a daily integral part of our lives for 2 years.

I sat in the mountains at 9300-feet elevation, listening to the birds chirp, the elk bugle, the wolves cry, the chipmunks squeak, the frogs singing and the wind blowing through the trees. Surrounded by living things, in what felt like my own magical forest was the balm I needed for my sore heart. My destiny led me to the mountains, to finish this book and continue writing more, as I spend my summers surrounded by God's beauty.

I am continuing my PTSD therapy, although I will never be able to leave the trauma or the damage done to my brain and body behind me, I am stronger for the many mountains I climbed and survived. This book was a slow climb, sometimes with stumbles and backward tumbles, but there is the light of hope aglow inside of me.

During the years, I have seen and felt the darkness, and at one point I didn't know if I would see the light of hope again, but I did, and it was like a lighthouse safely guiding me in the direction I needed to go. The tattoo on my arm says, "Hope grows in a garden of Faith." Even when hope seemed out of reach, my faith kept me tethered and hope bloomed again.

There are seasons of darkness, with loss and sadness. With patience, the tide turns, and you find happiness. Experience is what you get when you don't get what you wanted.

Change is supposed to be good for the soul and turmoil helps create patience, but it's hard to accept either. The harder emotions are what make life happen. I keep showing up because it's important. Live in the moment, we only get today. Yesterday is gone, tomorrow is a day a way and the present is a gift.

There have been times I struggled to see the hope, but it was always there. It takes time before the seeds of hope bloom. Never lose hope, even when everything is gone or you feel empty, because life without hope is a living death. Hope is the magic that heals hearts and souls, and seeds of hope will always bloom. It's time for my next chapter, and books.